ON THE SCREEN
ON THE AIR
ON MY MIND

ON THE SCREEN
ON THE AIR
ON MY MIND

BY CLAIR SCHULZ

BearManor Media
2011

On the Screen On the Air On My Mind

© 2011 Clair Schulz

All rights reserved.

For information, address:

BearManor Media
P. O. Box 71426
Albany, GA 31708

bearmanormedia.com

Typesetting and layout by John Teehan

Published in the USA by BearManor Media

ISBN—1-59393-626-5
978-1-59393-626-6

TABLE OF CONTENTS

Introduction 1

The Entertainers
    The Jolson Story 7
    A Great Nose, a Great Man [Jimmy Durante] 15
    Doing What Comes Naturally [Betty Hutton] 23
    Wonder Man [Danny Kaye] 31

The Funnymen
    Slip, of the Tongue [Leo Gorcey] 39
    A Twosome and Then Some [Abbott and Costello] 45
    And Now, A Word from Our Prankster [Stan Freberg] 53
    A Skelton Scrapbook 59
    Here's Morgan 67
    The Road to Laughter [Bob Hope] 75
    The Really Nutty Professor [Jerry Colonna] 83
    The Importance of Being Ernie 89
    Small Wonder [Arnold Stang] 97
    The One, the Only…Groucho! 103
    The Best Second Banana in the Bunch [Gale Gordon] 113

Ladies, Take a Bow
    All About Eve 119
    She Was More Than a Dream [Gene Tierney] 127
    What a Girl, What a Life! [Joan Davis] 135
    Legendary Lady [Tallulah Bankhead] 143
    Life with Lucy 153
    A Touch of Sass [Iris Adrian/Sandra Gould] 165

The Frightmeisters
    The Man of Our Dreams [Bela Lugosi] 173
    Prince of Players [Vincent Price] 181
    The Face of Fear [Boris Karloff] 189
    Far As the Curse Is Found [Lon Chaney Jr.] 197
    A Little Terror [Peter Lorre] 205
    The Phantom (Yikes!) Again [Lon Chaney] 213

The Reliables
How the West Was Fun [Gabby Hayes] 219
Never the Groom, Always the Best Man [Frank Lovejoy] 225
A Prisoner of Doubt [Alan Ladd] 233
Mr. Reliable [Jack Carson] 241
The Lovable Lug [William Bendix] 249
A Man of Many Parts [J. Carrol Naish] 257
King of Spades [Howard Duff] 265
A Well-Graced Actor [Basil Rathbone] 273

The Movies
Fascinating Rhythms 281
The Case of the Overlooked Series 289
2 Wits, 2 Pics, 0 Hits 305
B's, Please 321

The Radio Shows
Fibber McGee and Molly: Always Good for a Laugh 329
Watchman, Tell Us of the Night [*Night Beat*] 333
The Best Zings in Life Are Freberg's 339
A Joker and a Queen [*The Phil Harris-Alice Faye Show*] 343
The Human Comedy [*The Great Gildersleeve*] 351
In a Class by Herself [*Our Miss Brooks*] 357
For He's a Jolly Bad Fellow [*The Henry Morgan Show*] 365
We Interrupt This Program to Bring You a Blooper 371
Brush Up Your Gildersleeve 377
The Sweetest Music This Side of Waukegan
  [*The Jack Benny Program*] 383
The Thing on the Radio Dial [*Quiet, Please*] 393
The Wizardry of Oz 403
The Best of Benny 411
From Gags to Snitches 415
He Walked by Night [*Pat Novak for Hire*] 421
The Master's Voice [*The New Edgar Bergen Hour*] 429
Forgotten Shows to Remember 437
The Best Years of Our Lives 445

The Collectibles
Tom Mix, a Premium Star 457
Those Wonderful Big Little Books 463
Booking Films: Movie Tie-Ins 469

The Stories
The Man Who Knew Too Many 477
One Principal Too Many, One Principal Too Meanie 483
The Dummy Up Caper 497

Extra Added Attractions
The Passing Parade: Past Times, Passed Signs 503
Johnson Smith Specialties: Magic Moments 513
A Travelogue Down Memory Lane 521

Selected Short Subjects
Pleasure Palaces 527
The Song Is Ended (But the Malady Lingers On) 531
Sweet Mystery of Life, At Last We've Lost You 535
Sign Here (and There), Please 539
Casting Calls 543
The Best Is Not Yet to Come 547
Double Your Pleasure 551
A Classic Dilemma 555
When You're Called to Play That, Mumble 559
To Have and Have Lots 563

Index 567

In 1947, long before the USPS issued a Legends of Hollywood series, Hollywood Star Stamps could be purchased for ten cents a sheet.

Ten of the stars on these two sheets are profiled in this book.

Let's vamoose to a time when everyone knew the score.

INTRODUCTION

LIKE MOST PEOPLE BORN IN THE 1940S, I fell under the spell of motion pictures and radio programs. (That spell might have been cast even at birth when my father, who favored the laconic style of a certain Ladd, selected Alan as my middle name.) Some of the earliest recollections I have are of listening to *Fibber McGee and Molly* while perched on a stool with elbows on knees and jaws cupped in my hands in front of a console set in our living room and of trying to hold down a cushioned, fold-down seat in our cavernous downtown theater long enough for me to get a knee up so I could crawl aboard the magic movie express that was showcasing the antics of Abbott and Costello and the Bowery Boys.

My interest in those frolicking fun makers continued right into my high school years. Even as I began to appreciate the writings of James Thurber, Robert Benchley, and Ogden Nash, part of me continued to laugh at Leo and Huntz's horseplay and Bud and Lou's routines that ran in an endless loop in my brain. (Somehow that combination of printed and visual humor saturating my existence contributed to being voted wittiest in my senior class.) By the time I graduated from college I absolutely *knew* that someday I would write something, be it book, article, elegy, graffiti, or classified ad, about those comedy teams.

That urge festered for twenty years while I renewed my interest in old-time radio by collecting and listening to shows and by stocking my nostalgia room devoted to the 1940s with movie posters, radio premiums, advertising signs, WWII items, vintage radios, and autographed photographs of those stars of screen and airwaves who meant so much to me. I had the message but I didn't have the medium until I discovered Chuck Schaden's *Nostalgia Digest* in 1988. My submission describing Leo Gorcey's malapropisms was accepted the following year, my overview of Abbott and Costello's career appeared in 1991, and since then I have been a regular contributor to that quarterly (formerly a bimonthly).

The profiles of performers in this book were published in *Nostalgia Digest* in slightly different form except for the new pieces "A Well-Graced Actor" and "Legendary Lady."

Most of the articles about radio programs and the survey of Gale Gordon's career were featured in *Old Time Radio Digest* except for "From Gags to Stitches" which appeared in *Radiogram,* and the overviews of *Pat Novak for Hire, The New Edgar Bergen Hour,* and forgotten shows which were printed in *Nostalgia Digest.*

The articles about collecting as well as "The Case of the Overlooked Series" and "The Best of Benny" appeared in defunct periodicals. The three articles grouped with the study of the Perry Mason films and the three "Extra Added Attractions" were featured in *Nostalgia Digest.* The story "One Principal Too Many, One Principal Too Meanie" and the essay "The Sweetest Music This Side of Waukegan" were published in the Bear-Manor collections *It's That Time Again! The New Stories of Old-Time Radio* and *Well! Reflections on the Life and Career of Jack Benny,* respectively. The other works of fiction appear here for the first time as do all the essays in the "Selected Short Subjects" section at the end of this volume.

As readers move through the subjects selected for this book some questions that might be raised are "Why Al Jolson and not Eddie Cantor? Why Danny Kaye instead of Bing Crosby? Why Arnold Stang rather than Alan Reed?" The answer is "Because I was asked to write about the formers and not solicited to research the latters." Nine of the profiles were written "by popular request" of Chuck Schaden.

Others grew in a natural progression. A piece on Eve Arden led me toward those other funny ladies, Joan Davis and Lucille Ball. After an article I wrote about Bela Lugosi appeared in the October/November 1992 *Nostalgia Digest,* it seemed only fitting to keep right on covering those actors associated with horror films for the next five Halloween issues. And, as I describe in "She Was More Than a Dream," passing a photo of Gene Tierney set off a siren that had to be answered.

But most of the profiles came about because, like the Gorcey and A&C articles, the personalities got under my skin more intensely than the famous Cole Porter melody and almost compelled me to get the lead out by writing their stories. Being a nonconformist myself, I had followed the lives and careers of Henry Morgan, Stan Freberg, and Ernie Kovacs not just as a fan but as a kindred spirit. (The lone stranger among the personal mementoes in my old scrapbook is a newspaper clipping from January 13, 1962 reporting the circumstances of Ernie's fatal accident.)

Those three men were unique both in talent and temperament and I think that is what drew me to write about a number of the other stars as well. Meaning no disrespect to their individual abilities, there will always be somewhere in our minds a link between some similar celebrities of recent decades because we picture them in the same frame: between Newman and Redford, De Niro and Pacino, Leno and Letterman. Not so with the inimitable ones: the dervish known as Betty Hutton; unpredictable Tallulah; gleeful Skelton; cantankerous Gabby; irrepressible Groucho; winsome Durante.

Notice how many of the men and women portrayed in these pages routinely made stops all along the wondrous carnival midway that was show business then, knocking 'em dead in vaudeville or on Broadway as well as ringing the gong on radio, in motion pictures, and on television. Sadly, the race of versatile actors who can deliver both credible dramatic *and* comedic performances on a movie set *and* in front of audiences like Jack Carson, William Bendix, and J. Carrol Naish did effortlessly for years is almost extinct.

Bringing out "the best of the rest" like Naish, Iris Adrian, Frank Lovejoy, and others who never reached the heights but who still deserve honorable mention for their achievements has been one of the significant pleasures of writing these profiles. After my two articles about Lovejoy were published, I sent copies of the periodicals to his widow, Joan Banks, with a request for an autographed photo. She responded with a letter of gratitude for the magazines but also with an expression of regret that because she had been away from the "show biz scene" she did not have any glossies for fans, just personal family photographs. I sent studio shots of her and Frank which she graciously inscribed ("Thanks for remembering our radio days" and "I really appreciate the articles on Frank very much") that I placed in a hinged frame so Frank and Joan are close to each other on one of my tables just as they are now in Holy Cross Cemetery in Culver City.

Being remembered meant a lot to Joan and, as I have shown in several pieces in this collection, recollecting our entertainment history correctly is also important. Colorful as they were, we need to see the flaws of Bankhead, Jolson, and Morgan which took some of the luster off their stardom. "The Wizardry of Oz" demonstrates that, contrary to the popular misconception that has been passed on for decades, the radio world inhabited by the Nelson family was not that different from the one in which we lived. The fallacy that radio reached its zenith in the 1930s and during World War II is disproved in "The Best Years of Our Lives," a detailed analysis of the medium which delineates the superiority of programming after 1945.

My editors continue to kindly allow me freedom to experiment with form such as writing Bob Hope's life story as a Hope monologue ("The Road to Laughter") and presenting *Quiet, Please* in the same first-person narrative style of the program ("The Thing on the Radio Dial"). My goal for most articles was to cover the subjects in 1,500-2,500 words which made for bite-sized reading of four to six pages in the magazines.

In those few pages I tried to convey the essence of a program or to capture the distinctiveness of the notable person profiled. My intention was to whet the appetite of readers, to make them want to see that performer on video, to listen to that show on tape or CD, or to read more about the subject of the article. The goal of this book is very much the same with the added hope that readers will appreciate more what has gone on before and thank our lucky stars.

THE ENTERTAINERS

Al Jolson and wife Ruby Keeler in 1935.

The Jolson Story

AFTER A MEMORABLE WAR OF WORDS between those perennial squabblers, W.C. Fields and Charlie McCarthy, Edgar Bergen tried to excuse his little chum's behavior by saying, "Charlie is his own worst enemy" to which Fields snarled, "Not while I'm around." Al Jolson probably would have delivered the same retort if someone had told him "I'm your greatest fan."

That Jolson had a high opinion of himself was obvious to those in show business who knew him. He let the meek inherit a part of the chorus while he stepped boldly into his natural place in the spotlight. His strutting carriage said it before he did: "Here I am, folks. Prepare to be entertained." Even the detractors who considered him an unctuous peacock had to acknowledge that he made good on his promise. No one dared approach the box office for a refund after one of his performances because the name Al Jolson out front guaranteed that everyone would get their money's worth.

That name was merely a slight alteration of Asa Yoelson, the one given him after his birth on May 26, 1886 in a small Russian village. Four years later Rabbi Moshe Yoelson, fearing that pogroms would soon claim his family, fled with them to America where he found a position in a Washington, D.C. synagogue. After Asa's mother died in 1895, the conflict that had been growing between his stringent father who wanted him to become a cantor and the son's desire to use his voice to entertain was exacerbated when the boy belted out ballads on the street for coins or ran away from home to sing in saloons. If this sounds like the plot of *The Jazz Singer*, it is, for Jolson was actually living the part he would play some thirty years later.

After getting a taste on the stage as one of the *Children of the Ghetto*, he hit the vaudeville circuit with brother Hirsch in a new act with a new identity as Harry and Al Jolson. During Al's rise to fame he appeared often in burnt cork as end man in minstrel shows and also as a single. It was in those early days on his own when, billed as "The Blackface with the Grand Opera Voice," that he first rattled the rafters with songs and quieted an applauding throng with "You ain't heard nothin' yet."

Jolson eventually made noise along Tin Pan Alley by putting his mark on tunes such as "Hello, My Baby" and "Alexander's Ragtime Band." Starting in 1911 he rapped out three straight hits on Broadway: *La Belle Paree, Vera Violette,* and *The Whirl of Society.* Al, his chief supporter even back then, took out an ad in *Variety* that read "Everybody loves me. Those that don't are jealous."

Not even the envious could deny that he carried the shows and sometimes stopped them. During *The Honeymoon Express* Jolson interrupted the proceedings and asked, "Do you want the rest of the story—or do you want me?" and then unleashed every song in his repertoire to the glee of enthusiastic audiences and the chagrin of the cast who had to spend the rest of those nights backstage. Jolie had a way of tapping into the emotions of those who heard him so that when he performed a number like "You Made Me Love You" down on one knee with his arms outstretched he made it seem like a love letter addressed directly to them. Jolson didn't just sell a song; he also wrapped, embellished, and delivered it right into the laps of his listeners.

By 1914 he was earning $70,000 a year and taking his act on the road in extended tours of his musical comedies which allowed people all across the country to see why he had become the toast of New York. In *Sinbad* he sang "My Mammy," "Swanee," and "Rockabye Your Baby with a Dixie Melody," three tunes that will probably be associated with his name forever. As his reputation grew, Jolson lived up to his legend by engaging in one-upsmanship. On September 15, 1918 he followed a performance by Enrico Caruso by dashing onstage and stealing the celebrated tenor's thunder with his already famous assurance of "Folks, you ain't heard nothin' yet."

In *Bombo* he introduced over twenty new songs including "April Showers," "Toot, Toot Tootsie," and "California, Here I Come." *Big Boy*, a hit in 1925 and 1926, is best-remembered for the one that got away. Jolie regretted his decision to give a number he pulled from the show to Eddie Cantor every time he heard someone sing "If You Knew Susie."

But he made a wise career move in 1926 when he sang "Rockabye," "April Showers," and "When the Red, Red Robin Comes Bob, Bob, Bobbin' Along" in front of the cameras for a one-reeler. The following year Warner Brothers wanted George Jessel, star of *The Jazz Singer* on Broadway, to be in their talking version of that play, but when he asked for too much money they turned to Jolson, someone they had already seen singing on the screen.

The Jazz Singer is only partially a talkie, but the revolution had to start somewhere. Although the maudlin story may seem crude when viewed today, audiences who had never seen Jolson in person got a taste of how he could wrap a song around the heart when Al, as Jack Robin, sang "Kol Nidre" to his dying father and "My Mammy" to his mother.

The Jazz Singer proved to be a sound sensation from the night of its premiere on October 6, 1927 so Warner Brothers wasted no time in putting Jolson in another weepie, *The Singing Fool*, about a father's affection for his doomed son. The bouncy strains of "I'm Sitting on Top of the World" helped to lighten the gloom, but nothing could prevent the parade of hankies when Al sang "Sonny Boy" to sweet Davy Lee. The picture, which earned a whopping $5.5 million, no doubt helped sell over a million copies of "Sonny Boy."

Jolson's third film, *Say It with Songs,* said the same hokum with the same Davy Lee. Both of his 1930 releases, *Mammy* with songs by Irving Berlin and *Big Boy*, an adaptation of the Broadway smash, featured featherweight stories. Jolson himself must have felt audiences deserved more because at the premieres he jumped up on the stage after the movies ended to go into his act.

In 1933 he starred in *Hallelujah, I'm a Bum* which featured the novel use of dialogue delivered in rhyming couplets. In this singsongy tale the life of the hobo king of Central Park (Jolson) was juxtaposed with that of New York's mayor (Frank Morgan) to the accompaniment of a Rodgers and Hart score. The film failed miserably because it was too innovative or because the plight of the poor struck too close to home during the Depression or because moviegoers wanted escapism rather than strained whimsy. After the movie lost a million dollars, United Artists shelved plans for three more Jolson pictures.

Although screen magazines began asking the question "Is Jolson Through?" Warner Brothers still thought enough of the singer to team him with his third wife, Ruby Keeler, in *Go Into Your Dance*. Al viewed the success of this picture with a jaundiced eye for he suspected that people wanted to see the dancing star of *42nd Street* instead of him. In 1936 *The Singing Kid* gave him an opportunity to reprise his most popular numbers, yet he thought co-star Beverly Roberts stole some of his luster. Jolson did not like to share the limelight even when off the set. One night at a party when George Burns tried to join him in a refrain of "Rockabye Your Baby," Al grabbed Ruby and left in a huff.

After his dyspeptic reaction to how *The Singing Kid* had hurt his chances for future projects with Warner Brothers, Jolie accepted offers from Twentieth Century-Fox to appear in two musicals, *Rose of Washing-*

Jolson in *Go Into Your Dance*.

ton Square* and *Swanee River*. The four numbers he sang in *Rose* resonated with his old verve and so outdistanced the efforts of Alice Faye and Tyrone Power that one reviewer claimed Jolson was "the only member of the starring trio whose performance has warmth and vitality." Similarly, he rose above the vapid cast of *Swanee River* when he presented his stirring rendition of "Old Folks at Home." Despite the fact that he had to settle for third-billing in both pictures, these handsomely-mounted productions have worn much better and showcase his talents in a brighter way than those early helpings of schmaltz in which he was the main attraction.

To Jolson's credit he didn't let the vicissitudes of his career or his divorce from Ruby prevent him from giving his all for the troops during World War II. After the bombing of Pearl Harbor, Al was among the first entertainers to offer his services. He also put his money where his heart was by purchasing war bonds in quantities few stars could match. When illness kept him from making more trips overseas, Jolson visited military hospitals in the states to lift the spirits of the wounded with cheerful music.

In 1945 after a bout with malaria cost him part of a lung and his first record in a decade flopped, it seemed like Al was going down for the last time. The next year Columbia Pictures threw him a lifesaver. When the concept of filming his life was first pitched to him, Jolson naturally wanted to play himself, but eventually he resigned himself to just recording the songs and demonstrating that even with less than two lungs he could still be a powerhouse.

The Jolson Story followed the motto of most screen biographies: don't let the facts get in the way of telling a good story. Jolie's philandering, early troubled marriages, profligate gambling, and the wounds caused by his sharp-edged demeanor had no place in this exaltation of a man whose life was absorbed by show business. It didn't seem that important that Larry Parks lacked the dynamism of the man he portrayed. What mattered was that through the lip-synching the real Jolson emerged in all his show-stopping glory.

The newspapers that had been reserving space for printing obituaries and tributes were now carrying stories of how the popularity of the movie had rescued him from the ashcan. But any journalists expecting a new and improved Jolie would have been disillusioned had they seen his present to Stephen Longstreet, author of the *Jolson* screenplay, given "to show how much I appreciate what you did." The gift? A signed photograph of himself.

Jolson became a singing sensation all over again by going into the studio for Decca and releasing similar versions of the songs he had recorded for Brunswick and Columbia over twenty years before. The Jolson sound seemed to be coming out of every phonograph and emanating from every spot on the radio dial.

His track record on radio had been spotty at best. *Presenting Al Jolson* and his first turn as host of the *Kraft Music Hall* fizzled as incompletes in the early twenties. His stay at the *Shell Chateau* lasted just thirty-nine weeks. *Café Trocadero* had a better run from 1936 to 1939, partially because Martha Raye and Harry "Parkyakarkus" Einstein provided some much-needed humor. When he tried once more during the 1942-1943 season on the *Al Jolson Show* for Colgate, neither the star nor the sponsor was pleased with the result.

But four years later as the hottest property in Hollywood he was popping up on all the networks to sing and joke with Amos and Andy, Burns and Allen, Jack Benny, Eddie Cantor, Bing Crosby, Jimmy Durante, Bergen and McCarthy, and Bob Hope, who asked Al on his April 8, 1947 show why he didn't have his own radio program and was told "What? And be on the air only once a week?"

Due to the positive response following his appearance with Bing on *Philco Radio Time*, Kraft invited him back to be in charge of the *Music Hall* again. Because no one could play a Gershwin melody like Oscar Levant and no one could sing a Gershwin lyric like Jolson, the neurotic pianist joined the show to perform at the keyboard and to trade quips with the star, although the mating of two abrasive personalities with oversized egos made it seem that some of the zingers directed toward one another were delivered with more relish than necessary. Jolie made certain everyone knew it was his show and undoubtedly caused some imprecations to be muttered in the control booth when he regularly deviated from the script or insisted on singing his favorite standards over and over. After two seasons Kraft, noting the cooling of the Jolson mania and the slipping ratings, closed the *Music Hall* for good on May 26, 1949.

Three months later *Jolson Sings Again* had people lining up at ticket booths to see the next segment of the Jolson saga. Parks assumed the lead role again as an older Jolson who struggled through the valley of loneliness caused by his stagnant period and the loss of his wife to the peak of his finding love again with a nurse and experiencing a revitalized career.

Al may have been too gray-haired and paunchy for audiences to accept him on the screen as himself, but radio presented no such barrier so he did get his chance to play the man he most admired on *Lux Radio Theatre*. On February 16, 1948 he appeared in the *Lux* production of *The Jolson Story* and on May 22, 1950 he starred in the *Lux* version of *Jolson Sings Again*.

Jolson listened seriously to offers trying to lure him into television, but he had doubts whether people would want to see the same faces week after week. Instead he headed for Korea to pour his energies into performing for soldiers in camps and hospitals. Throughout the tour he battled a cold that sapped his strength. When he returned home in September 1950 after doing forty-two shows (which, in typical hyperbole, he inflated to 160 for reporters), his face and body showed all of his sixty-four years. A month later he died of a heart attack in a San Francisco hotel but not before reportedly telling the two doctors who came to his bedside to "Pull up some chairs. I've got some stories to tell."

That was Jolson being Jolson right up to the end, the master showman who knew how to work an audience regardless of whether he was flat on his back in a bedroom or on the tips of his toes in a nightclub. Jolson the man may have been little in more ways than one, but Jolson the performer reigned as a giant who towered over his contemporaries. Only Jolson would have the gall to wear a badge bearing the initials AJTWGE (Al Jolson, The World's Greatest Entertainer); only Jolson had the talent to prove that claim every time he opened his mouth to sing.

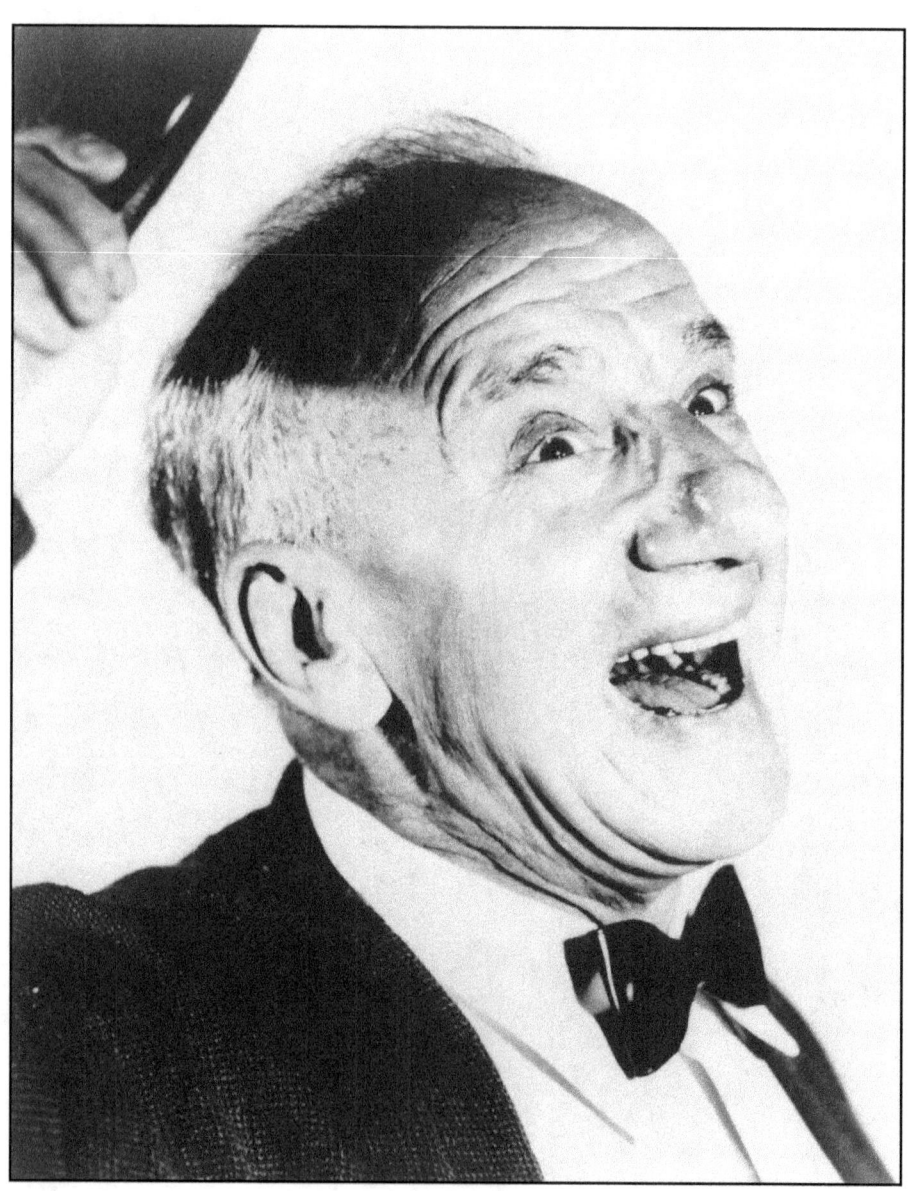

A tip of the hat to Jimmy Durante.

A Great Nose, a Great Man

IT STANDS TO REASON that anyone constructing an entertainer for the ages would hardly bring together elements resulting in a balding, big-nosed joker whose face bore more creases than a hobo's pants, who frequently said rather than sang lyrics in a gravelly voice, and who had trouble reading speeches of longer than two lines or words of more than three syllables without tripping over his tongue. Yet logic had little to do with the life and lasting appeal of Jimmy Durante.

Durante couldn't even make a conventional first entrance. Unlike the dancer in the Beatles' song who came in through the bathroom window, James Francis Durante came in on the kitchen table on Manhattan's Lower East Side February 10, 1893. Photographs of Jimmy suggest that what he called his probositor was already blooming at birth, which he used later in jests of the "folks took one look at me in the crib and wondered if the stork had come to stay" variety.

But the teasing he encountered in the classroom was not a laughing matter. James endured the ridicule until the seventh grade, then left school to concentrate on playing the piano for a living.

Although his father wanted him to develop into a pianist specializing in classical music, Jimmy aimed at more practical venues such as playing accompaniment for silent films at local theaters. He developed an affinity for ragtime tunes and by the age of seventeen could be found tickling the ivories in what might charitably be called honkytonks at Coney Island or in Chinatown.

During those early years Durante became friends with waiter Izzy Iskowitz, who later changed his name to Eddie Cantor. In the 1940s and 1950s when the pair reminisced about the good old days, they weren't just whistling "Dixie"; they were singing, making whoopee, and wondering how they were going to keep 'em down on the farm.

Although Cantor is sometimes acknowledged as the first person to encourage Durante to employ humor as part of his act, the quaint characters Jimmy met while pounding the keys in dives sharpened his wit by necessity. Close shaves at nightclubs with hoods bearing the Runyonesque names Hurry-Up Harry, Pretty Boy Moran, and Razor Riley taught Durante that he better have a pleasing quip on hand to convince mobsters not to shoot the piano player.

While working at the Alamo nightclub in 1918 he met a singer named Maud Jeanne Olson who became his wife three years later. Jim had another reason to remember the Alamo: there he met song-and-dance man Eddie Jackson who was his partner and most loyal friend for the rest of his life.

Jimmy insisted that nightspot also figured in another important slice of the Durante legend. After hours one evening when some of Al Capone's triggermen were taunting Jimmy about his nose, vaudevillian Jack Duffy lightened the mood by addressing him as Schnozzola. So Schnozzola he became, first to the show business crowd and then forevermore to the rest of the world.

Durante continued to land jobs in joints like Club Pizzazz that had very little of it and Club Paradisio whose smoky atmosphere made it seem like the other place. When prohibition rolled in, Jim opened Club Durant, a speakeasy that did standing room only business until it closed in 1925.

By that time the team Clayton, Jackson, and Durante had become a hot ticket. Lou Clayton, a hoofer with a pliable face not unlike Frank Fontaine's, encouraged Durante to emphasize his most prominent feature by making that nose the starting point of their routines. Lou got the ball rolling with a comment on Jimmy's small feet, Jim came back with "That's because nothing grows in the shade." Clayton moved on to "And what about your fingernails? Do you file your nails?" which Durante countered with "No, I just throw them away," and they were off, marching in a parade of hoary gags.

For a while during the Roaring Twenties the trio became the rage of New York. Having an editor of *Variety* affectionately laud them as the Three Sawdust Bums in print helped business as did Damon Runyon's assertion that "I doubt if a greater café combination ever lived."

By 1927 "dem Bums" were commanding $3,000 a week at clubs and even garnered $5,500 weekly when they reached vaudeville's Valhalla, The Palace. There they showcased the highlight of their act, a burlesque routine called "Wood" which, like the bit immortalized by Abbott and Costello as "Mustard," involved snowballing. While Jimmy described lumber's importance to our way of life, his partners filled the stage with wooden items from canoes to a privy. When they brought on *that* house, it brought down the house.

By the time the trio took their show on the road their fame had preceded them. Audiences expected, and Jimmy delivered, novelty songs that he wrote and that only he could put over: "I Can Do Without Broadway, But Can Broadway Do Without Me?," "I Ups to Him and He Ups to Me," "Who Will Be With You When I'm Far Away?," and "A Dissa and a Datta."

Flo Ziegfeld, knowing a good thing when he saw one, hired the team for *Show Girl*, a show that was fail-safe with music by George Gershwin and with Ruby Keeler playing the lead. Jimmy's recitation of the repetitious poem, "I Got a One-Room House," delighted both theatergoers and critics alike. Durante mined that concept for decades: years later on radio and television he regaled audiences with tales of travails in stores going between floors for merchandise or trips at home up and down ladders to go to the phone or the door.

Following a successful appearance in *The New Yorkers*, a Cole Porter musical, an offer of a movie contract was extended by Metro-Goldwyn-Mayer—but only to Durante. By the early 1930s the act clearly became one of a star and two sidekicks. Though reluctant to split up the group, Jimmy left for Hollywood, but in a typical gesture that marked his innate generous nature, he took his pals along and pledged to give them part of his earnings.

The pictures *New Adventures of Get Rich Wallingford* and *The Cuban Love Song* made little impression and did nothing for his career except to get his face before a national audience. MGM capitalized on Jim's most recognizable feature by churning out publicity that the studio had insured his nose with Lloyd's of London for a million dollars.

Durante fared better in three Buster Keaton films, perhaps the best being *Speak Easy* (1932) in which Durante's outfit of striped suit, checked vest, and polka dot tie spoke louder than he did.

The Phantom President (1932) is now regarded as a curiosity because it marked one of George M. Cohan's rare screen appearances. Jimmy's most notable contribution in his role of political advisor is the quotable aphorism, "A Depression is a hole, a hole is nothin', and why should I waste my time talking about nothin'?"

Fame of a more lasting nature came in *Palooka* (1934). Ostensibly the lyrics he warbled as Jolting Joe's manager Knobby Walsh served as a warning to the boxer regarding signing his name to anything, but in most renditions of what became his theme song Jimmy rarely got far beyond the "Ink-a-dink-a-dink-a-dinka doo" stage.

Durante continued to enjoy his greatest triumphs before a live audience. As the star of the Broadway hit *Strike Me Pink* in 1933, he wowed the critics with his boundless energy and infectious way of belting out a song.

The writer who suggested that "a herd of elephants could not crash through a show more passionately" turned out to be prophetic for Durante's next (and biggest) stage success came as Brainy Bowers in Billy Rose's *Jumbo*. In addition to the obvious proboscis humor, the show focused on the interplay between Bowers and the titular animal, climaxed by a scene in which the elephant held a hoof over Durante, a feat even virile Frank Buck confessed he would not do even once, much less 233 times as Jimmy did.

In the fall of 1936 Jim joined Ethel Merman and Bob Hope as the stars of the Porter musical *Red, Hot and Blue*. During the third act he stole the scene from his co-stars (no mean feat, considering their ebullient personalities) when, acting as his own lawyer, he did an "ups to him and he ups to me" routine by jumping in and out of the witness stand to cross-examine himself.

Two other musical comedies, *Stars in Your Eyes* and *Keep off the Grass*, failed to produce long runs and Durante's screen career had regressed to the point where he accepted work at Republic to provide feeble comic relief in Gene Autry's *Melody Ranch*. When Jeanne died in early 1943, it seemed just another in a series of "catastostrokes" designed to break his spirit.

But within weeks of his wife's death the Cyrano of clowns was back on top, packing them in at the Copacabana with an act that is still mentioned in the same reverential terms reserved for the legendary nightclub engagements of Frank Sinatra and Joe E. Lewis. A two-week booking grew into a three-month smash which in turn blossomed into a new contract with MGM and, more importantly, an offer to bring his act to radio.

And that is exactly what Durante did: he brought his cabaret act to the airwaves. When announcer Howard Petrie said, "And here he is, ladies and gentlemen, the one and only…Jimmy Durante! In person!," he was like a Las Vegas emcee beckoning to the star in the wings. Amid applause Jimmy approached the mike singing "Chitabee," "You've Got to Start Off Each Day with a Song," or one of his other ditties before being interrupted or halting the proceedings himself with a gruff order to "Stop the music!"

After some chitchat with Petrie or Garry Moore and a commercial, Durante brought on a guest star who sometimes joined Jimmy in parodies of songs or numbers specially written for the occasion. Frequently there was an opportunity for the guest, be it Dorothy Lamour or Van Johnson, to punch home a joke with an impersonation of the Schnoz and appropriating his famous "I got a million of 'em" line, which would provoke the expected "Everyone wants to get into the act" or "I'm surrounded by assassins" response from the host.

On *The Jimmy Durante Show* music served not only as a bridge linking the sections of the program but it also acted as a magic carpet that carried Jimmy and friends on journeys to different parts of the country, voyages to exotic islands, or just on a tuneful quest to find the lady from Twentynine Palms.

Jimmy surrounded by his radio regulars: partner Garry Moore, announcer Howard Petrie, singer Georgia Gibbs, maestro Roy Bargy, producer Phil Cohan.

People "loved that kind of carrying on" because "it gets around, it gets around" that, even if *The Jimmy Durante Show* may not have been the funniest program around, it was a great deal of fun because of its unpredictability. No one, Durante included, knew what would come out of his mouth.

The sesquipedalian writers purposely placed polysyllables into the script straight because they knew Jimmy would wring them out of shape without any help from them. And twist them he did in declarations like "You are equivocly and indubiably kisserken and your precocious ratio in non compos mentis dentis" or "The exubiance of this unxious occasion and the quintessence of your celestrial radiance premediates my bountiful soul with palipition of grandicious jocanunitity." Durante even struggled gamely with shorter words that were not surrounded by jawbreakers; after four attempts of trying to ask valet Arthur Treacher for a certain kind of pipe, the closest he could get to it was "mashearscham."

Some of the most amusing lines on the show turned out to be the speeches following the malapropisms. If Lucille Ball suggested that "I'm sure you'll take that back," Durante countered with "Take it back, nothing! I had a hard enough time getting rid of it!" After Treacher reminded Jimmy that "Those are the words of Patrick Henry," the reply was apt: "I hope he had them insured. I mangled them up quite badly."

The good-natured spirit with which Durante joined in the jokes about his nose and his fracturing of the language endeared him to audiences and his peers. When frequent guest Victor Moore tossed out the groaner "With your voice, you could put Perry in a coma," Jim counteracted possible criticism about punny humor with the self-deprecating comeback "Dialogue like this could bring back silent radio" that immediately made us laugh along with the old troupers who were giving it their all with a wink and a sly grin.

Just a few months after *The Jimmy Durante Show* left the air in 1950, Durante turned his attention to television as he became one of the rotating hosts of *The Four Star Revue*. In 1953 he received an Emmy as TV's best comedian and by 1954 he had earned his own program.

The Jimmy Durante Show took viewers into the Club Durant. On these live and lively shows Durante performed his "hot cha" numbers with Eddie Jackson and a chorus line of cuties called (what else?) the Durante Girls. At the end of the program when he walked through a series of spotlights after bidding Mrs. Calabash goodnight, he was strolling into video immortality for few images in television history are as heartwarming and enduring as that one.

By the late 1950s Durante had reduced his schedule somewhat to just doing guest appearances and working in clubs. In 1960, as if to prove there was still plenty of life in him, he married a thirty-nine-year-old woman he had dated for sixteen years and became a father not long afterwards when the couple adopted a baby girl.

With renewed vigor he returned to the movie sets to take a featured role in the film version of *Jumbo* (1962). His bit as Smiler Grogan in *It's a Mad, Mad, Mad, Mad World* (1963) triggered the action in the comedian-laden funfest when he literally kicked the bucket.

When hosting *The Hollywood Palace* or appearing with veteran comediennes Eve Arden and Kaye Ballard on *The Mothers-in-Law*, the Schnoz still radiated that old sparkle, but when teamed with the Lennon Sisters in a 1969 ABC series and placed in skits as a wigged and bejeweled Elvis look-alike, the effect was, as Jim might say, "mortifrying."

Durante fans have a chance to erase the memory of that embarrassment when *Frosty the Snowman*, the animated program Jimmy narrated and which first aired in 1969, returns to recreate its magic every December. Durante imbued a song with more fervor and sincerity than perhaps any other performer in show business. Scoffers may doubt whether Jimmy Durante was a singer at all, but when he promised that Frosty would be back again some day or when he told the young at heart that fairy tales can come true or that as time goes by the world will always welcome lovers, we believed.

A stroke in 1972 turned Jimmy's rasp into a whisper and forced him to spend the remaining years of his life in a wheelchair. Although he appeared in public a number of times (most notably at a fete for his eighty-third birthday at which he valiantly tried to utter the words of "Inka Dinka Doo"), Jim's friends knew that his condition would continue to worsen. He tipped his fedora in life's spotlight one final time on January 29, 1980.

Durante was, in the words of one of his songs, a little bit this and little bit that: ragtime pianist, comedian, performer on radio, television, stage, and screen, and one of the most beloved people in the entertainment industry. Often imitated, never duplicated, for when they made him, that nose broke the mold. He may have had a million of 'em, but the world has had only one Jimmy Durante.

Betty Hutton getting what she aimed for: the lead in *Annie Get Your Gun*.

Doing What Comes Naturally

SHE WAS THE BLONDE BOMBSHELL who rose from poverty to reach stardom, changing her name along the way. When she moved across the screen, audiences found it hard to notice anyone else. Yet just a few years after her best movies were released her career lay in ruins and her personal life had become a shambles due to poor decisions and character flaws.

Her name could have been Marilyn, but it wasn't. Elizabeth June Thornburg, born February 26, 1921 in Battle Creek, Michigan, barely had time to learn how to walk and talk before she was singing and dancing with her sister Marion in a speakeasy owned by their mother, Mabel, who also tried to support the family by working in an automobile factory after her husband deserted them in 1923. Mabel later admitted that even as a youngster the tyro who would grow up to be known as Betty Hutton loved to attract attention to herself by shouting or standing on her head.

Mrs. Thornburg believed that the only ways for her children to emerge from a hand-to-mouth existence were to go to college or to exploit their talents so she took the route she could afford by encouraging them to sing at beer gardens and on street corners for small change in the hope that a break would come their way.

A year of touring the Midwest with a small band gave Betty some experience but little exposure. One evening after Vincent Lopez saw her singing in a Detroit nightclub he signed her to a contract for $65 a week, a sizable salary for a teenager during the Depression. Betty, who had never tasted steak before, celebrated the good news in her typical exuberant fashion by eating that tasty meat every chance she could.

Billed initially as Betty Darling with the Lopez orchestra, her manner of delivering numbers differed little from that of other singers until the night she heard rumors that Lopez might fire her. When she pulled out all the stops on a rousing version of "The Dipsy Doodle," Betty's "whoop and holler" style of throwing herself into a song saved her job and gave her an identity. Ironically, while this change secured her position with Lopez it may have cost Betty a chance to join the Glenn Miller Orchestra. Miller selected tamer sibling Marion as band vocalist instead.

Betty's delivery included everything in the book: grimaces, double takes, popping of the eyes, cartwheels, arm swings, leg kicks, finger-pointing to punctuate lyrics sung in tones designed to raise the rafters; anything and everything to sell the song. Singing may have been her occupation, but showstopping became her trademark.

In 1939, her earnings having risen to $175 a week, the entertainer called Betty Hutton who had been seen on tour and heard on Lopez's radio program joined Eve Arden, Alfred Drake, and Keenan Wynn in the Broadway musical *Two for the Show*. Hutton's renditions of "Little Miss Muffet," "Calypso Joe," and "A House with a Red Barn" earned her the Blonde Bombshell moniker.

Everything seemed to be rolling her way. She didn't have to audition for *Two for the Show* and, based upon her success in that revue, she was hired to aid Ethel Merman in *Panama Hattie*, receiving almost as much praise in the press as the star. *Panama Hattie* ran for over 500 performances, but neither Merman nor Hutton appeared in the MGM version of the musical.

Betty's opportunity to step before the cameras came when producer B.G. DeSylva, who had hired her for *Panama Hattie*, signed the singer to a contract for Paramount Studios. In her first film, *The Fleet's In* (1942), Hutton's job was ostensibly to support the love story involving Dorothy Lamour and William Holden, but after she explained "How to Build a Better Mousetrap" and confessed that "Arthur Murray Taught Me Dancing in a Hurry" in song and dance, all attention shifted from the sappy romance of the co-stars to the 5'4" ball of fire who repeatedly astounded her boyfriend played by Eddie Bracken.

For better or worse Hutton was paired with Bracken in several of her early films. In *Star Spangled Rhythm* she played a telephone operator at Paramount who introduced Eddie and his sailor friends to the stars on the lot. *Happy Go Lucky*, a 1943 vehicle starring Mary Martin and Dick Powell, contained at least one shining moment: "Murder, He Says," a number in which Hutton described Bracken's responses to her kisses.

That same year Betty moved up in billing when she played opposite Bob Hope in *Let's Face It*, a farce of false and mistaken identities with spies thrown in for good measure. Most of the songs from Cole Porter's musical had been scuttled before production began, but Hutton did get to solo on "Let's Not Talk about Love" and joined Hope for "Who Did? I Did." Betty seemed at ease with Hope (perhaps in part because she had appeared on his radio show) and demonstrated that she could handle a leading role in a comedy. That experience proved indispensable for her next feature demanded that its lead actress assume one of the most delicate roles of the 1940s.

The scenario of an adventuresome young woman becoming inebriated, having a wild time on the town, and discovering she is pregnant after the escapade but not being able to recall the identity of the man responsible for her predicament is not unusual for a movie produced today; for a film released in 1944 it was tantamount to audaciously declaring that year that rationing and buying war bonds were un-American activities.

The Miracle of Morgan's Creek really was a miracle. It succeeded both with the Breen Office and the public because of Preston Sturges's witty screenplay and deft direction and superior performances by Diana Lynn as wise-beyond-her-years Emmy, William Demarest as the blustery father, Bracken as a love-struck schnook, and Betty as the wide-eyed, erring but lovable heroine Trudy Kockenlocker, who gave the film its name when she gave birth to sextuplets.

The Miracle of Morgan's Creek proved that Hutton didn't need frenetic songs and dances to validate her presence in a motion picture. Sturges himself called her a "full-fledged actress with every talent that noun implies" and suggested that her abilities might be better utilized if producers cast her in movies other than musicals.

Hutton gained another positive reference from critic James Agee who claimed that "Betty Hutton is almost beyond good and evil, as far as I'm concerned" in commenting on her performance in *And the Angels Sing*.

In *And the Angels Sing* her versions of "His Rocking Horse Ran Away" and "Bluebird in My Belfry" prompted another critic to call her the "human approximation of a buzz bomb." She appeared slightly more subdued in *Here Come the Waves* with Bing Crosby only when playing the more dignified of identical twins; when hopping around singing "There's a Fella Waiting in Poughkeepsie" as the hyperactive sister, Betty the Bombshell was in full bloom.

Hutton stretched her acting muscles in *Incendiary Blonde* (1945), the first of several pictures she made based on the lives of real women. Betty had the ideal personality to portray Texas Guinan, one of the people who put the roar in the Roaring Twenties. Her "knock 'em dead" renditions of "It Had to Be You," "Ragtime Cowboy Joe," and "Row Row Row" captured perfectly the "anything goes" spirit of that reckless decade.

Incendiary Blonde succeeded because a fabled character was played by a larger-than-life actress who had memorable compositions to sing and an interesting story to tell. But *The Stork Club* emerged principally

Betty seems to be thinking "Sonny Tufts?" in this tongue-in-cheek pose from *Cross My Heart*.

as a commercial for the famous night spot with its only saving grace being Betty's toe-tapping "Doctor, Lawyer, Indian Chief" number, and *Cross My Heart* suffered from the improbable story of a woman confessing to a murder just to help the career of her boyfriend who happened to be a lawyer which must have caused viewers to agree with the title of one of the movie's songs: "Love is the Darndest Thing."

In 1947 Hutton returned to form in *The Perils of Pauline*. She seemed right at home as Pearl White, the star of silent serials whose roles found her perpetually knocking on death's door. No one should mistake *Perils* for an accurate portrayal of the early days of moviemaking and at times the sentiment was troweled on with a heavy hand, but the picture is tolerable because of a few notable songs ("Poppa, Don't Preach to Me" and "I Wish I Didn't Love You So") and Betty's performance which prompted one reviewer for the *New York Sun* to state that "Miss Hutton grabs hold of the picture and squeezes all possible entertainment out of it."

Plans for more biopics, including those about Mabel Normand, Clara Bow, Theda Bara, and Sophie Tucker, died on the vine while Betty labored in the forgettable *Dream Girl* and the lackluster *Red, Hot and Blue*, which is worth watching if only to see Betty sing "Hamlet" and to catch a glimpse of composer Frank Loesser playing a crook with the Runyonesque name of Hair-Do Lempke. But the part that Hutton coveted most did not need inventing or developing. Ever since she saw Ethel Merman in buckskin on Broadway, Betty set her sights on playing Annie Oakley as surely as the legendary sharpshooter eyed her targets.

Judy Garland won the lead in MGM's *Annie Get Your Gun,* but when it became apparent she couldn't continue Hutton moved into the role of headstrong hoyden she was born to play. When Betty sang "Doin' What Comes Natur'lly," she appeared to be doing just that. Her challenges to Frank Butler (Howard Keel) in "Anything You Can Do" came from a woman whose feisty demeanor suggested she could back up every boast. "I'm an Indian, Too" is a number right out of her "Doctor, Lawyer, Indian Chief" repertoire of boisterous belters. And yet in "They Say That Falling in Love" she hinted at some vulnerability in Annie's character. A writer for *Time* noted that "along with her unbridled vitality, she gives the role something Merman never attempted: she kindles the love story into poignancy."

Hutton's triumph in *Annie Get Your Gun* marked the zenith of her career. In 1950 she appeared on the cover of *Time,* received *Photoplay*'s most popular actress award, and earned over $350,000. However, her other 1950 release, *Let's Dance,* in which she got top billing over Fred Astaire, proved to be tepid entertainment.

Two years later she headed the cast of *The Greatest Show on Earth.* Whether swinging above the crowd on the trapeze or springing into action to save the circus in times of crisis, Betty's character Holly sparkled as the most lively two-legged creature in the Oscar-winning film.

Betty's final film biography, *Somebody Loves Me,* based on the life of Blossom Seeley, was replete with songs including the standards "Way Down Yonder in New Orleans," "I Cried for You," and the title tune. Little did Hutton know that *Somebody Loves Me* would be her last movie for Paramount and virtually her swan song.

Hutton wanted her husband, choreographer Charles O'Curran, to direct her next project, a film about the Duncan Sisters. When Paramount balked, Betty walked. She soon discovered the doors of the studios closed quickly on those who had earned a reputation for being "difficult."

For a number of years Hutton had been supplementing income derived from films with personal appearances at important music venues like The Palladium in London and The Palace in New York, sometimes earning as much as $17,500 a week, so when her movie career stalled she returned to the stage. Unfortunately, Hutton the earner couldn't keep up with Hutton the spender. A 1950 article reported that she had saved very little of the $1.5 million in salaries paid her since 1936.

In 1954 an attempt to capitalize on her popularity in *Annie Get Your Gun* by bringing Hutton to television in a ninety-minute extravaganza called *Satin and Spurs* in which she played the star of a rodeo landed flat on its chaps. A one-hour special fared little better the following year. After her only series limped through the 1959-1960 season, she adamantly claimed that it was her decision and not the mediocre ratings that ended *The Betty Hutton Show*.

During the 1960s Hutton tried comebacks on tours of *Gypsy, Gentlemen Prefer Blondes,* and *Annie Get Your Gun* without much success. In 1967 she couldn't fulfill her contractual agreement with Paramount to make two westerns and was fired. That same year she filed for bankruptcy. Problems with drugs and alcohol as well as regrets over her four failed marriages and estrangement from her children hampered Betty's progress as well.

A humbled Hutton worked as a housekeeper at a rectory in Rhode Island and later taught some acting classes after earning a college degree. She took over the role of Miss Hannigan in *Annie* for a few weeks in 1980 on Broadway and granted a few interviews, but was not often in the public eye during her last years. She died March 11, 2007.

The actress who, in the words of film historian Ken Wlaschin, "was probably the most energetic personality ever to explode on the screen" deserves a champion to rescue a number of her films from the dusty archives. Some of them have not aged well because of the blandness of her leading men: Don DeFore in *The Stork Club*, Sonny Tufts in *Cross My Heart*, John Lund in *The Perils of Pauline*, Macdonald Carey in *Dream Girl*, Victor Mature in *Red, Hot and Blue*, and Ralph Meeker in *Somebody Loves Me*.

Too often Betty stood alone as the only power hitter in the lineup. For example, in *Somebody Loves Me* (1952) the support Paramount mustered for her consisted of Meeker, Billie Bird, Robert Keith, Adele Jergens, and Sid Tomack. That same year at MGM Gene Kelly had Donald O'Connor, Debbie Reynolds, Jean Hagen, Rita Moreno, and Cyd Charisse to help him sing in the rain.

Regardless of who stood around her, the status of the star should not be diminished. The players were torchbearers who just lit the fuse. When Hutton exploded, that's when the fireworks began.

Monroe and Hutton made their screen debuts in the 1940s while in their early twenties and both hit audiences with a powerful impact. One became a screen legend, the other languishes on the verge of obscurity in the minds of many Americans today. But to a certain group of film aficionados who fondly remember an irrepressible singing and dancing dynamo, their clarion call remains "Goodbye, Norma Jean. Hello, Betty."

Danny Kaye hit his stride in *Wonder Man* (1945).

Wonder Man

BOB HOPE TOLD JOKES BETTER, Fred Astaire was his superior on the dance floor, Bing Crosby crooned songs more pleasantly, and Red Skelton demonstrated a greater gift for pantomime, but Danny Kaye did so many things well it didn't matter if he wasn't the best at any of them. Most show business figures can be labeled in a word: actor, comedian, dancer, musician, director, singer, etc. Danny Kaye is best described simply as an entertainer.

He started entertaining early in life by singing and making faces at P.S. 149 in Brooklyn. After a few years of secretly practicing vaudeville routines and songs with a friend, the pair literally took their show on the road by performing on the sidewalks of New York. One night a man who worked for a resort in the Catskills saw their act and hired them to be tummlers for the hotel.

This job proved to be an excellent training ground for the young redhead because tummlers did everything they could to amuse guests from telling jokes and acting in plays to conjuring up impromptu escapades and scavenger hunts. It was during that summer of 1929 that the young man born David Daniel Kaminski sixteen years earlier was reborn as Danny Kaye. A quick learner, Danny began putting his own stamp on musical numbers by adding bits of business to take advantage of a natural gift for inflection and his limber body. The phrase "throwing yourself into a song" aptly described the lengths to which Kaye would go to captivate an audience.

During the early thirties he also developed his ability to improvise nonsensical lyrics like "Git gat gittle" and to affect foreign dialects. All of these little extras took the rough edges off his inexperience and began to give him the aura of a polished performer.

However, he was still going nowhere until he met a composer named Sylvia Fine who adapted her songs to fit Danny's talents. The team raised a few eyebrows in a Broadway revue and soon their act at the Martinique nightclub became the hottest ticket in town. Sylvia and Danny worked so well together that it surprised none of their friends when they married in 1940.

Before long Kaye was wowing them on Broadway in Moss Hart's *Lady in the Dark* with an electrifying number called "Tschaikowski" which demanded that he rattle off the names of fifty Russian composers without missing a syllable. More than one critic expressed the belief that no one could have improved upon his performance. It would not be the last time his contribution to a production would be considered unique.

After six months in *Lady in the Dark*, Danny accepted an offer to star in Cole Porter's musical *Let's Face It*. This time he stopped the show twice with numbers that featured what had become his trademarks: double talk and peculiar body movements. On the strength of the Porter music and the Kaye pyrotechnics *Let's Face It* ran for sixteen months until Danny left the show to accept a contract from Samuel Goldwyn to make motion pictures.

It became clear even in his first film, *Up in Arms* (1944), that showstopping numbers written by Sylvia and expertly executed by Danny were going to be a Kaye staple regardless of whether he appeared on stage or the screen. "The Lobby Number," in which Kaye ran all around a theater lobby, bubbled over with so much vivacity that audiences could hardly be blamed if they left their seats and joined in when Danny invited everyone to "Conga!"

His next movie the following year, *Wonder Man*, featured the plot device that almost became the standard for his films: Danny impersonating someone else. He left audiences marveling over the way he moved his head as if it was disembodied during the "Bali" sequence and laughing at his gibberish during the mock operetta which closed the film.

During 1945 he starred on his own radio program while simultaneously working for Sam Goldwyn. *The Danny Kaye Show* certainly had much going for it: Kaye, Eve Arden, and Lionel Stander in front of the microphone, Goodman Ace, Abe Burrows, and Sylvia Fine handing the star funny lines to say and sing, and the swinging sounds of Harry James in the background. Even though it was a popular program for its short run, the writers, rather than developing a radio personality for the star, relied on extended musical parodies in the second half of the episodes which played like soundtracks from his pictures. Kaye's manic antics had to be seen to be believed.

1946 marked the apex of Danny's career. At times during that year his earnings surpassed $40,000 a week. As a meek milkman turned boxer in *The Kid from Brooklyn* he was still fast on his feet, even if the "Pavlova" number he wobbled through looked like it belonged in a different movie. The face seen often on posters and in theaters also peered out from every newsstand as *Time* and other magazines put that wavy-haired, puckish head on their covers.

The Secret Life of Walter Mitty, released over a year after the premiere of *The Kid from Brooklyn*, demonstrated that Kaye had not lost a step in the interim. Danny had a knack for being funny both as milquetoast and bon vivant, and Mitty's split personality provided the actor with a chance to show this ability gloriously.

No matter how successful Kaye's pictures were, he couldn't wait for production to end so he could return to the stage. He loved the intimacy of appearing before an audience and the immediacy of their response to his singing, dancing, and clowning.

Danny Kaye left them rollicking in the aisles everywhere from Broadway to London.

Kaye also enjoyed conducting the New York Philharmonic and other orchestras which allowed him an opportunity to entertain both the musicians in front of him and music lovers behind him. Danny didn't miss one piece of shtick when he reached into his bag of tricks: stumbling on the way to the podium, pretending the score was upside down, sitting on the lap of a surprised violinist, becoming so caught up in the act that the baton sailed out of his hand, acting like an umpire trying to eject a clarinetist for allegedly hitting a clinker, and leading his charges through a rousing rendition of "The Flight of the Bumble Bee" with a fly swatter for a baton. During these concerts he readily admitted that he was "having the time of my life" and those watching him undoubtedly experienced the same feeling of exhilaration.

He continued to deliver music and merriment in his movies as well. He performed masterfully in *The Inspector General* as Farfel, a poor schnook who was mistaken for a high-ranking government official. With his boundless energy he appeared to be all over the screen and, in fact, he was just that in one sequence in which four Danny Kayes (Farfel, an Englishman, Russian, and German) sing the "Soliloquy for Three Heads."

In *Hans Christian Andersen* (1952) he revealed his wonderful rapport with children and his distinctive way with a song that could produce both giggles and tears. As Andersen, Kaye appealed to the child in all of us.

Officials of the United Nations hoped to transfer some of the Kaye charisma into real life when they appointed him ambassador-at-large for UNICEF in 1954. Over the next twenty years Kaye gave generously of his time to travel all over the world raising millions of dollars for needy children.

In *The Court Jester* Kaye got the laughs and Basil Rathbone the hisses.

Also in 1954 he again rolled out his dialects as a ventriloquist on the run from spies in *Knock on Wood*, a picture culminating in a rollicking climax that takes place on a stage in the middle of a ballet. Danny displayed his versatility in the yuletide favorite *White Christmas* by dancing smoothly with Vera-Ellen and camping it up with der Bingle as the silly "Sisters."

Although Kaye considered *Knock on Wood* his best picture, some of his fans would probably vote *The Court Jester* as their top choice. This is the film that required Danny as the hypnotized jester to change from timid to bold and back again at the snap of a finger. Whether dueling with villainous Basil Rathbone or trying to sort out the "vessel with the pestle, chalice from the palace, flagon with a dragon" dialogue, Kaye bedazzled viewers as a wizard of sight and sound.

Surprisingly, *The Court Jester* did not regain its production costs and his next film, *Merry Andrew* (1958), brought in even less money. Danny took on more serious roles as a Jewish businessman trying to escape the Germans during World War II in *Me and the Colonel* and as jazz cornetist Red Nichols in *The Five Pennies*, but nothing could stop his slide in popularity at the box office.

For years Kaye had rejected offers to work on television, but with his movie career in decline he tried his hand at a few specials. After a very amusing show with Lucille Ball in late 1962, he accepted an offer from CBS to do a weekly series. *The Danny Kaye Show*, although never near the top of the ratings, lasted four full seasons and featured Harvey Korman, Danny, and assorted guest stars in some of the more memorable sketches of the decade.

In 1970 Kaye returned to Broadway to star as Noah in the musical *Two by Two*. After tearing ligaments in a leg, he continued on as master of the ark with his foot in a cast. Danny's well-documented ad-libbing and upstaging may have hurt as much it helped the production, yet *Two by Two* ran for a respectable 343 performances.

Kaye then became more interested in the hobbies of cooking and flying his own planes than in performing, although he did step out of retirement in 1981 to play a concentration camp survivor in the television movie *Skokie*. The fine reviews he received foreshadowed the honors that followed: the Jean Hersholt Humanitarian Award at the 1982 Academy Awards ceremonies, the Knight's Cross of the First Class of the Order of Dannebrog in 1983, and a Kennedy Center award presented by President Reagan in 1984.

Throughout his career Kaye played gentle souls who through quirks of fate had their destinies altered. By just one chance occurrence his own life was cut short. During quadruple bypass heart surgery Danny received an infected blood transfusion that saddled him with hepatitis C from which he never fully recovered. Death got the last laugh on March 3, 1987.

Or could it be that we get the last laugh as we watch the kid from Brooklyn bewitch us with his feet, face, and tongue? His exuberant, boyish charm and manifold talents continue to fascinate both adults and children.

Drama critic Clive Barnes once wrote that "Mr. Kaye is so warm and lovable an entertainer, such a totally ingratiating actor, that, for me at least, he can do no wrong." To which the best response is "Git gat gittle da gat gat gittle," which in this case means, "You can say that again."

THE FUNNYMEN

A familiar sight in the Bowery: Louie (Bernard Gorcey) trying to collect from Whitey (Billy Benedict), Slip (Leo Gorcey), Sach (Huntz Hall), Bobby (Bobby Jordan), and Chuck (David Gorcey).

Slip, of the Tongue

IN 1775 RICHARD SHERIDAN IN HIS PLAY *The Rivals* introduced to the world a character named Mrs. Malaprop whose misuse of similar words created not only laughs but also employment for generations of writers and comedians. The easiest visual laugh is the pratfall; to get the same effect with words the comic merely falls over the tongue instead of the feet. In radio an abuser of the language seemed to be *de rigueur* on most comedy programs. Among the chief offenders were Phil Harris, Jane Ace, Fibber McGee, Jimmy Durante, Irma Peterson, Chester Riley, George "Kingfish" Stevens and Andrew H. Brown, Gracie Allen, Stretch Snodgrass, and Archie, the manager of Duffy's Tavern. Another Archie (surname Bunker) did considerable damage to the King's English on television. But of all the people in show business who trampled words before our ears, the one who did it most exquisitely was probably Leo Gorcey.

It wasn't always so with the characters he played. In the seven Dead End Kids films released from 1937 to 1939 Leo played it straight. It was not until the fifth entry in the East Side series, *Flying Wild* (1941), that he unleashed his first malapropism. Seventeen more movies followed before Muggs of the East Side gang became Terence Aloysius "Slip" Mahoney, the brains of the Bowery Boys.

From 1946 to 1956 Monogram (later Allied Artists) churned out forty-one films in the Bowery Boys series. It was as the Boys that the fellows grew into buffoons and acted less like the young toughs they were as Kids. Crime melodrama began to be replaced by horseplay, slapstick, raillery, and Gorceyisms. Criminals were still very much in evidence, but now the Boys triumphed as the good guys. They outwitted crooks in every plot known to writers who had studied at Hope University and Abbott and Costello College and therefore they tried their hand at boxing, chasing ghosts, running from monsters, playing detectives, shooting outlaws, mixing up photographs, wrecking the armed services, returning a foundling, trailing spies, destroying a college, feuding with hillbillies, racing cars and horses, hobnobbing with the upper crust, and stumbling through jungles. The bottom half of double features rarely offered originality; the pleasure of watching these films came from seeing how much could be done with so little.

Edward Bernds and William "One Shot" Beaudine, who directed many of the movies in the series, knew how to turn base metal into gold with a budget of $100,000 or less per film and a shooting schedule of seven to ten days. It was no coincidence that action in a fair number of the pictures took place in Louie's Sweet Shop; that meant one less set to find or build. No film in the series received a nomination for an Academy Award for costume design or musical score. Some of the villains and molls are so obscure they look like they were hired from laundry lists. Yet every one of the films made money because fans didn't come to theaters to appraise production values; they wanted to watch the Boys clown around for sixty minutes.

The Boys they really wanted to see were Slip and Sach. Gabe had a little to do in the early films, but Butch, Chuck, and Whitey existed primarily so the principals would have someone to react to their comments

Huntz and Leo in *Smugglers' Cove* (1948).

or actions. Huntz Hall milked laughs out of Sach by giving him a mincing walk, effeminate gestures, facile lips, and a liberal dose of lunacy. Gorcey also had a rubber face and he could do a double take worthy of a second look, but it was when he opened his mouth that the real fun began.

Never at a loss for words, Slip possessed an admirable vocabulary. But when we heard *what* words he used we were tempted to echo Goodman Ace's catch phrase: "Isn't that awful?"

It didn't bother Slip at all to announce to a roomful of people that "somebody has captured a friend of mine and is keeping him as a hostess" or to give instructions regarding "what sign of the cardiac you were born under." The heat never bothered him; "it was the humility." Once he became so enraptured with Sach's powers of prediction that he proclaimed that "it's astounding, it's condescending, it's gregarian" and promised that Sach would "divine the movement of the stars and their stalagtites."

Even in moments of stress his powers did not fail him. Holding his friends back from danger he warned, "We're out on the edge of a terrific precipineappple." About to engage in a duel he shouted, "Toupee!" He scolded a friend in *Bowery Buckaroos*: "Don't you know I'm in disguise? I'm inmagneto."

Many of the malapropisms had more truth in them than Slip realized: "I don't know how to show my ineptitude" and "It's just a little idiotcyncracy of mine" (*Bowery Buckeroos*); "We'll not only be glad to return your money, but we'll also be highly mortified" (*Master Minds*); "We did some fancy defective work" (*Trouble Makers*); "Mr. Jones only executes one number a show" and "It's my intermediate pleasure to introduce…" (*Blues Busters*); "When you talk like that about our childhood, I get very neuralgic" (*Jalopy*); "Call Mr. Bowman and he'll vilify everything we've said" (*Jail Busters*); and "Maybe we should get into a business a little more ludicrous" (*Private Eyes*).

In *any* business Slip would have been ludicrous. Mahoney always dreamed of the Boys becoming financial cocoons, lizards of the bank business, or malted millionaires so that debutrants everywhere would put them up on a pedestrian. When dictating a letter he began with "We regret to deform you," stopped at the end of a sentence to add, "Put catastrophes around that," and then ordered a carbonized copy of it.

When Slip defended himself, he truly had a fool for a client. He knew his rights: "What's the charge? Flagrancy? I'm not flagrant. I know my institutional rights. I'll take this to the Extreme Court of the United States." He could stop a potential arrest by charging that "You can't take him. You don't have expedition papers." Once in court he proved to be an unimpeachable witness: "I'm fully prepared to detest that I saw the crime." The dead body was the uncorpus delicious. After digesting the testimony of his deponents, he cast off the evidence as a case of mistaken indemnity.

Mahoney felt at home in other disciplines as well. He knew mathematics. Sort of. In *Spook Busters* he calmly asked, "If I'm not being too perpendicular, what do you plan to do?" He stated emphatically in *Hold That Line* that there would no more fractions of the rule. In *Hold That Baby* he used an excuse that many high school sophomores could sympathize with: "We was the victim of circumferences."

What he knew about the human body will not be found in any edition of *Gray's Anatomy*. For people with very close veins or infinitesimal latitude he prescribed blood confusions. Loss of memory? Simply a case of magnesia. He would cremate things over in his mind and come to a contusion. To him maladies like larengetis could be cured with the correct anecdote.

Most of the time we knew what word Slip was approximating, but sometimes he became so obtuse that nobody, Mahoney included, knew what he meant. In *Paris Playboys* when he said, "I don't like to sound incandescent, but what is this all about?," we are tempted to ask the same question. "If I may be indigenous, I'd like to pardon all three of you," he said in *No Holds Barred*, malapropos of nothing. And in *Private Eyes* he told the Boys to "sit down and we'll masticate the escape plans." Now that's *really* food for thought.

Mahoney remained absolutely convinced that he was using impeccable English and therefore placed himself above criticism. In *Spy Chasers* he told a little girl that he was a numerologist. She corrected him by saying, "You mean a numismatist." He patiently explained to her that "You collect the kind of coins you want to and I'll collect the ones I want." In *Live Wires* he made the accusation that "You're nothing but a pacifist." Told that the word he wanted was *pessimist*, he announced pleasantly that "I was using the past tense." In his mind ignorance *was* an excuse.

Slip Mahoney may have had his problems, but so did the man who played him. It is surprising that there has not been a film about Gorcey because his life had all the ingredients necessary for a show biz biography: rebellious youth, the big break, domestic spats, multiple divorces, a battle with the bottle, and then decline and fall.

He was born June 3, 1917 in New York City, the middle of three sons of Bernard Gorcey, who played Louie Dumbrowski in most of the Bowery Boys films. Bernard, an actor in *Abie's Irish Rose* and other plays, encouraged his son to try out for a part in the Broadway production of *Dead End*. Leo started out with a bit part before eventually replacing Charles Duncan as Spit and he was soon on his way to Hollywood.

Once out West the screen image of tough guy seemed to creep into his personal life. Leo became Spit when he got behind the wheel of a car. Although other members of the gang were also reckless on the road, only Gorcey garnered traffic tickets by the handful.

He also saw the inside of courtrooms in actions regarding his wives. Gorcey's first marriage ended in 1944 after five strained years. In 1948 he took a few shots at his estranged second wife who was snooping for evidence against him. Her illegal entry was judged the greater offense, but she still got her divorce. The third marriage phfffted in 1956 and wife number four hung around until 1962. Gorcey's final marriage in early 1968 did not have much time to either develop or explode, for he died at fifty-one on June 2, 1969.

That his liver eventually failed him did not come as a shock to anyone who had observed his drinking habits in the fifties. He sometimes appeared on the set more fit to work on *The Lost Weekend* than knockabout comedies like *Bowery to Bagdad*. After Bernard died on September 11, 1955 from injuries incurred in an automobile accident, Leo's drinking got worse and so did his performances. In 1956 Gorcey cited grief over the death of his father as the reason for quitting the series which sounded better than confessing that he had become too unreliable and had been told that the Boys would go on without him.

They didn't go far and they didn't go very well. With Huntz Hall as headliner and Stanley Clements brought in to be the second lead, the last seven films were repetitive and humorless. The final Bowery Boys picture, *In the Money*, was released in 1958, but the series effectively ended with Leo's bleary-eyed effort in *Crashing Las Vegas*. The name above the title was Leo Gorcey *and* the Bowery Boys; it could have been Leo Gorcey *is* the Bowery Boys.

Watching Leo Gorcey mug shamelessly in all directions is still better than chicken soup for the soul, but listening to what comes out of his mouth is just what the doctor ordered. As many as twenty times an hour we can be treated to some of the most delightful mangling of the language that has "ever been secreted by the human mind." When he comes into view we should feel like the man in *Angels in Disguise* who said, "Glad to know you," to which Slip replied, "The feeling is pari-mutuel, I'm insured." So until we meet him again let us bid goodbye to Slip Mahoney. "Not goodbye," said Slip in *Spy Chasers*. "Leave us just say, 'Hasta banana.'"

There were many big paydays for Lou Costello and Bud Abbott in the 1940s and 1950s.

A Twosome and Then Some

For math teachers who are fond of creating theoretical situations that occur when two geometric forms intersect here's one that won't be found in any textbook: In 1936 straight line A met rotund curve C. This union produced hundreds of laughs for twenty years. By what names do we know these two figures?

Nobody has to look in the back of any book to find the answer. During the 1940s the dapper dude and the bumbling Rumpledstiltskin were as ubiquitous as Kilroy. Even those born in the days of disco fever who love to recite "Who's on first?" know who put those words in their mouths. Abbott and Costello remain one of the most famous duos in history.

William Abbott wasn't actually born in a trunk in 1895, but he easily could have been for his parents belonged to the circus family. It was most propitious for Bud that his father later switched to a part of show business that was just taking off: burlesque. Bud worked for a time as treasurer of a theater in Brooklyn and as a producer of one in Detroit, but these jobs merely served as an apprenticeship for his days as an entertainer because he observed the performers closely and memorized the standard routines. After he learned the trade out front and in the wings, he moved onstage and became the best straight man in the business.

Lou Costello did not have show business in his blood when he was born in 1906 as Louis Cristillo, but he quickly developed a love for the movies, particularly those featuring Charlie Chaplin. In his youth Lou excelled at basketball and boxing. His agility proved useful when called upon to act as a stuntman during his first stay in Hollywood in 1927, but he gave it up when he began to acquire more bruises than dollars. On the way back to his native New Jersey he heard of a theater in St. Joseph, Missouri that needed a Dutch comedian. At that point Lou was not very funny and certainly not Dutch, but he applied anyway and was hired. He learned on the job and quickly moved up the burlesque ladder to the Orpheum and other top-of-the-line houses in New York. While performing at the Eltinge Theatre Lou saw Bud and Bud studied Lou and before long they realized that their styles complemented each other well.

Once they formed a team the dominos began falling. Success in burlesque was followed by a ten-week run at the Steel Pier in Atlantic City which resulted in nightclub bookings and an engagement at Loew's State Theatre which led to *The Kate Smith Show* on radio and an appearance on Broadway in *The Streets of Paris* which punched their tickets into the movies.

Although their first film, *One Night in the Tropics* (1940), is the only one in which they are not the main players, it is significant because it demonstrates a basic tenet of their motion pictures: don't ever let the action get so involved that it cannot be interrupted by a patter routine. The only purpose in having the pair in *Tropics* was so they could deliver a handful of their best bits between musical numbers and love spats.

Cinema scholars are fond of claiming that the first picture in which Abbott and Costello got top billing, *Buck Privates*, is one of their best movies. It is certainly one of their better offerings, but it is not *their* movie. They had to share screen time with the Andrews Sisters, a sub-plot involving a love triangle, and military maneuvers. But the episodic nature of the film made it easy for the team's writer, John Grant, to slip in old standbys like the dice game, the drill bit, "Go ahead and sing," and "Lend me fifty bucks."

The success of *Buck Privates* indicated that Americans in 1941 were in the mood for service comedies so before the year was over the team served up *In the Navy* and *Keep 'Em Flying*. But their most significant film of that year, *Hold That Ghost*, set the table as the first of their "giggle and gasp" films.

Lou Costello could do more with practically nothing than any comic actor in the talkie era except perhaps W.C. Fields. The highlight of *Hold That Ghost* is a scene with Lou and a pair of candles. When one candle begins to move horizontally and the other vertically, the expressions on Costello's face and his fear-choked cries for help demonstrate clearly why he was one of filmdom's great clowns. But he is just as funny when shakily trying to drink from a glass that may contain poisoned water or when doing a double take after seeing a frightening sight. In most of their movies of the forties Abbott and Costello earned the audience response through expert timing and precise execution.

They were also earning top dollar at the peak of the popularity charts in 1942 as *Ride 'Em Cowboy, Rio Rita, Pardon My Sarong,* and *Who Done It?* kept them rolling merrily along. In the seven films that followed during the war years the pair continued to please audiences with a mixture

Lou, Bud, and Joan Davis try to *Hold That Ghost*.

of fast-moving stories, surefire routines, and frantic chases. In 1946 they tried a change of pace with a straight, lackluster story, *Little Giant*, and a charming fantasy, *The Time of Their Lives*. With the lukewarm reception to these two films their popularity declined and it wasn't until 1948 that they made a comeback with what very well might be their best movie.

Abbott and Costello Meet Frankenstein holds one advantage over *Young Frankenstein, Transylvania 6-5000*, and other parodies of horror films: it had the original cast. Bela Lugosi *was* Dracula and Lon Chaney Jr. *was* the wolf man; anybody else playing those roles is wearing borrowed robes. Karloff had long since stopped being Frankenstein's creation, but Glenn Strange had played the part in two films, proving himself to be sufficiently terrifying in the Universal-copyrighted monster makeup. The frightening presence of the Big Three juxtaposed with Lou's antics created a unique blend of laughs and chills that even Abbott and Costello themselves could not duplicate when they met the killer, the invisible man, Dr. Jekyll and Mr. Hyde, and the mummy. The scene with Lou and the wolf man in an apartment and the one in which Costello unwittingly sits on the monster's lap in an underground chamber are two gems that outshine anything produced by battalions of ghost busters.

It wasn't all downhill after 1948, but the quality of their films which, up until this time had been relatively consistent, began to be erratic. The pair would put together a couple decent films, then do a turkey like *Comin' Round the Mountain*, follow that with a vehicle clearly geared toward the juvenile market (*Jack and the Beanstalk*), take a small step forward by meeting Captain Kidd, and then slide back again with a brace of sorry efforts, *Lost in Alaska* and *Abbott and Costello Go to Mars*. Their last film together, *Dance with Me, Henry* (1956), is painful to watch, not because the movie is so bad but because the special chemistry between the two men and the animation that marked their most spirited performances had vanished. By the summer of 1957 so had their partnership.

Lou starred in one film without Bud, *The Thirty Foot Bride of Candy Rock*, and dabbled with some solo television work on *The Steve Allen Show, General Electric Theatre,* and *Wagon Train,* but a 1943 bout with rheumatic fever had taken its toll on Costello's heart and he was not a well man when he returned to the world of burlesque for an engagement at the Dunes in Las Vegas in 1958. He suffered a heart attack on February 28, 1959 and died on March 3.

Bud encountered both financial and physical problems. The IRS disallowed many deductions he had claimed, and repaying the taxes plus penalties cost him a home in Encino and his ranch in Ojai. He found some work doing the old bits in nightclubs with Candy Candido in 1961 and by providing the voice for his character in the Hanna-Barbera series of Abbott and Costello cartoons in 1967, although neither activity did much to relieve his monetary woes. An epileptic who had leaned on the bottle for solace for years, Bud soon was confronted with a succession of maladies: strokes, prostate operation, broken hip and leg, and, finally, cancer. He spent his last two years in a wheelchair and died at his small house in Woodland Hills, California on April 24, 1974.

When people look at the careers of the two men, they tend to think of Abbott and Costello the movie stars and overlook the fact that they were very much at home on radio. In fact, most Americans heard them before they saw them. After their stint with Kate Smith, they made regular appearances on *The Chase and Sanborn Hour* before acting as a summer replacement for Fred Allen in 1940. Two years later they could be heard on their own show.

Their radio programs do not wear as well as their motion pictures. Bud remained the same fast-talking, take-charge slicker, but Lou often was not the well-meaning "little fellow" we had seen on the screen. Instead, the writers transformed him into a loud-mouthed wise guy hurling insults at everyone from the wife of the announcer to Mrs. Abbott. On radio the team served up routines like "Mustard" and "Down is up" with the usual relish, but the exchanges that usually opened the program were helpings of corn of the purest sort which are not easy to digest today. However, audiences ate it up and the show lasted until 1951 when the team moved to television.

After appearing a number of times on *The Colgate Comedy Hour,* they filmed fifty-two episodes of *The Abbott and Costello Show* which premiered on December 5, 1952. If some of the TV shows look familiar, it is because they are condensed versions of plots used in their feature films. The people who like the lemon bit from *In the Navy* can see it again in a segment of "Charity Bazaar." Never seen "Slowly I turned" in *Lost in a Harem*? Tune in the "Jail" episode and follow the moves step by step, inch by inch. Despite the uneven quality of these episodes, at least Lou is playing the sympathetic klutz we recognize and Bud is in his familiar position as glib prime mover. Though the program does not contain their best work, the early fifties remains the best of times for those who remember the ecstasy of enjoying a double dose of fun (at home and at local theaters) dished up during the same week by their favorite laugh makers.

Abbott and Costello are clearly not the favorites of film historians. Many critics place Abbott and Costello in the middle of the totem pole of comedy teams: below the Marx Brothers and Laurel and Hardy and above Martin and Lewis and Wheeler and Woolsey. It probably would be useless to remind them that Bud and Lou were the leading players in thirty-five feature films released over sixteen years by major studios like Universal, MGM, and Warner Brothers, that no other team matched that feat, and that only the Three Stooges (basically a two-reel team with several changes in personnel) produced a continuous stream of movies for a longer period of time. The pundits might even concede another point: among team players, only Abbott and Costello succeeded in pictures, on television and radio, and on the Broadway stage. Having admitted that, the learned ones will sigh and say, "Yes, yes, but they were so lowbrow, so plebeian."

True, but the same accusation could be tossed at some of the humor employed by Chaucer and Shakespeare. No matter how far they roamed from their early haunts Bud and Lou always had their feet firmly planted in the earthy roots of burlesque, a forum that will never be mistaken for drawing room comedy. Slapstick, pratfalls, double takes, snappy patter, and those venerable routines were what they offered whether they performed at the Steel Pier in 1937 or in Hollywood in 1955. Their armor creaked badly near the end and it might have been all they had to wear, but it sure proved to be a perfect fit.

Frank Capra crowed about having his name above the title. Through all the years motion pictures have been flickering before the eyes of the public, only two of Hollywood's headliners had their names *in* the titles of *ten* films, a testament to the drawing power of that popular pair who made the annual list of top ten box office stars eight times in the 1940s and 1950s. It is comforting to know that as long as film and video exist what will always be playing is Abbott and Costello Meet the Fans Who Love Them.

A novelty song in 1955, a parental threat to naughty children ever since.

And Now, a Word from Our Prankster

THERE ARE SOME CREATIVE PEOPLE we should thank daily: Edison when we flip a switch, Bell when we call someone, Goodyear when we go for a ride, and Freberg when we see or hear a commercial that makes us laugh. Freberg? How did he get in there? With his wit and hard work, some luck, and more than a little chutzpah.

Stan Freberg's life story reads like it was written by Stan Freberg. (In fact, Stan did write his life story—at least up to 1963—in a 1988 memoir entitled *It Only Hurts When I Laugh*.) As the saying goes, they couldn't even get the name right. His grandfather's name was Paul Andrew Johnson, but because so many Swedes had been coming into Ellis Island with that surname an impatient immigration officer badgered him into selecting another name. He added the last name of his mother before she was married and became Paul Johnson Friberg, which one officer wrote as Paul pronounced it: Freberg. As Stan might say, "It's a good thing her maiden name wasn't Hammerschlauger!"

Stan's maternal grandparents were ordained ministers and so was his father. Rev. Victor Freberg had aspirations of becoming a missionary, but the closest he got to darkest Africa was naming his son born August 7, 1926 after the man who found Dr. Livingstone.

Stanley Freberg credits his father for having a moral influence on his life, though he also taught Stan by example how to be versatile. To make ends meet during the Depression Victor not only served as pastor of a church fifty miles away from their home but also sold vacuum cleaners and insurance policies. One day officials of the insurance company were pleased to hear that he had sold hefty accident policies to one family until they learned their occupation: high-wire aerialists in a circus.

Among Stan's fondest memories of childhood are the days after his Uncle Raymond (aka Conray the Magician) came to live with his family in South Pasadena. It must have seemed like a road company production of *You Can't Take It With You* to see a prestidigitator following a Baptist minister around the house, imploring him to "pick a card, any card" as they sidestepped the cages of doves and other paraphernalia, but it all served as grist for Stan's mill. Stan even contributed his rabbit to his uncle's act and thereby got his first taste of show business. To attract audiences Raymond used the ploy of promising that some lucky boy or girl would be given a rabbit during the performance. Guess which boy was picked to come up on stage to assist with the silk hat trick time after time?

During the thirties Stan kept his ear tuned to another form of magic. While other boys his age were out playing baseball, he was being carried away on the wings of imagination to Hollywood and beyond. He acknowledges that the time spent listening to Fred Allen and *Vic and Sade* strongly influenced his sense of humor, and it is hard to argue with that belief. From Allen he inherited that keen blade of satire that he has swung so adroitly for decades and from the quarter-hour offerings of Paul Rhymer he acquired the talent of deftly mingling the mundane with the absurd.

Other youngsters his age loved their Louisville Sluggers; Freberg cherished the discarded scripts that Raymond brought home from his job as a security guard at CBS in Hollywood. Stan played all the parts and even sang the songs to a truly captive audience: his rabbits and guinea pigs. A defining moment in his life occurred when, after eventually getting up the nerve to perform an original script complete with sound effects at a high school assembly, he stood basking in the glow of a standing ovation, knowing that he belonged in the world of entertainment.

Thousands of people have headed for Hollywood on a bus with hopes of making the big time. Freberg was one of the few who cashed in right away. Talent agents in the building right where he got off the bus arranged for him to try out his repertoire of voices for Warner Brothers and before he could say, "Wilhelmina Klapenscott" he was providing voices for cartoons alongside the man of a thousand voices, Mel Blanc.

Maybe Stan didn't have a thousand personalities in his arsenal, but he did develop a regular menagerie in his throat while working on *Tell It Again*. When a show called for a particular animal sound, Freberg took off for the Griffith Park Zoo to hear it from the horse's mouth. At least if someone claimed that the impersonation did not sound authentic Stan could say, "Can I help it if the leopard had a cold today?"

Uncle Sam called Freberg in 1945 so for two years his career was on hold except for some entertaining of injured soldiers in Special Services and an infrequent pass that allowed him to record some *Loony Tunes*. After his discharge, he joined a novelty band called Red Fox and his Musical Hounds who at times out-Spiked Jones. Stan acted as the group's comedian and presumably played the guitar, although he faked it convincingly until one night in South Bend when called upon to perform a solo. As Stan might have said, "Which way's the bus to Pasadena?"

Actually he left the band of his own volition to take part in a televised children's show called *Time for Beany*. Freberg and another master of voices, Daws Butler, not only operated all the puppets and played all the characters but they also wrote the show. The scripts proved to be the hardest part for Freberg, not because of *what* they were writing but *where* they were asked to come up with ideas. In the early days the producer led Butler and Freberg on a merry chase, having them typing the scripts in restaurant booths, back seats of strangers' cars, and a condemned building. As Stan might have said, "Are you sure George S. Kaufman started like this?"

But living on the edge must have appealed to Stan in the early fifties. In addition to doing *Beany* five days a week and a weekly show called *Musical Chairs*, he also was writing and recording the musical parodies that would bring him national attention. His tongue-in-cheek versions of "Cry," "Sh-Boom," "Heartbreak Hotel," "The Yellow Rose of Texas," "The World is Waiting for the Sunshine," and "The Banana Boat Song" are still funny today because Freberg lampooned both the singers and the songs. Stan is also responsible for that granddaddy of all recorded satires on television, "St. George and the Dragonet," which, in the words of the bandleader who was another of his targets, remains to this day "wunnerful, wunnerful."

Such a gifted performer deserved his own show and in 1957 when CBS finally gave him his chance to shine, Stan passed out an eccentric mix to his listeners. Interviews with the abominable snowman and extraterrestrial visitors, musical acts of a tuned sheep chorus and a man who played the Hawaiian nose flute, and panel discussions with puerile experts on comic characters like Little Orphan Annie and Tarzan were served up alongside his record parodies and spoofs of westerns, detective shows, and *Lux Radio Theatre*. The two longest sketches, "Incident at Las Voraces" and "Gray Flannel Hatful of Teenage Werewolves," cut deeply to get right to the heart of advertising sham. More than a few listeners were probably confused by the proceedings, but the radio critics loved the inventive audacity of the program. Unfortunately, *The Stan Freberg Show* attracted no acceptable sponsor and it appeared after the battle with television had been lost so it was taken off the air after fifteen weeks.

One character who appeared on the program was the network censor who found so many things objectionable with Freberg's version of "Old Man River" that Stan threw in the towel before finishing the song. That conflict is indicative of the battle he has fought with legal departments, ad agencies, network officials, and company executives over the years. These differences of opinion rarely concerned off-color material for Freberg has a reputation of moral integrity that is exemplary. In fact, he has turned down lucrative offers to handle campaigns for manufacturers of tobacco products and even rejected the dollars of two cigarette companies who wanted to sponsor his radio show.

Over the years Fighter Freberg recorded some wins, some losses, and a few draws. "Incident at Las Voraces" was considered too provocative because it made fun of crass Las Vegas and played the hydrogen bomb as a trump card. Shortly after the demise of his radio program, he walked away from the possibility of doing a television series in the same vein when network bigwigs turned down his pilot script because he took potshots at inane commercials and because they wanted him to conform more to a sitcom formula.

Freberg stood his ground on the record "Green Chritma," a satire on the materialism of the holiday that cut too close for comfort to the world of business. Capitol Records caved in and released it, but with so little publicity that Stan took out an ad to promote it himself.

It may have been a Pyrrhic victory for Freberg when he walked out on David Merrick, who wanted to produce a version of "Stan Freberg Presents the United States of America" on Broadway because of Merrick's capricious decisions and his tampering with the production. But some of Stan's most satisfying triumphs occurred not in the arena of show business but rather behind the closed doors of corporate boardrooms.

After his rejection by CBS Television in 1958, Stan decided to form a production company called Freberg, Ltd. to inject some truth (and humor) into advertising. Stan persuaded reluctant sponsors that weaknesses could be turned into strengths by using a light touch instead of a heavy hammer. If only five percent of the population have tried a certain food product, use that statistic in a singing commercial that sticks in the ear. If the package is small, tell the folks how many tomatoes are in that "little bitty can." Don't gripe about the stores that won't stock a certain brand of aluminum foil; instead, make fun of it in a cartoon showing a persistent salesman and a tough-sell grocer. Face the fact that prunes aren't very pretty, but emphasize that at least they are pitless and that the problem of wrinkles may soon be ironed out. Freberg kept reminding advertisers that if they could get people to smile and think they could get them to buy. Today the type of witty ads he pioneered is so ubiquitous that it may be difficult for many consumers to remember a time when they were not on the air.

It would certainly be a mistake to dismiss Freberg as merely a prankster for surely his humor cuts deeper to the bone than that, but on one level he has been just that: a playful conjurer who, without being deceitful, has played amusing tricks on us for over thirty years. The carrots he has tantalized us with on radio and television and in print have led us to purchase what his clients have been selling and we do so willingly, laughing all the way to the store.

With Stan Freberg it appears there's always more where that came from. Since the time this article was first published, he released a second volume of his take on the United States of America and served as host of *When Radio Was*. Perhaps now he takes time to reflect on his many accomplishments and awards, including a Grammy, Emmys, prizes from film festivals, and so many Clios for advertising excellence that there doesn't seem to be any honor left to present to an iconoclastic wit. As Stan might say, "I'm still hoping for the Ignatius J. Reilly Trophy in the shape of Spade Cooley that plays 'Rag Mop' when you twist the head."

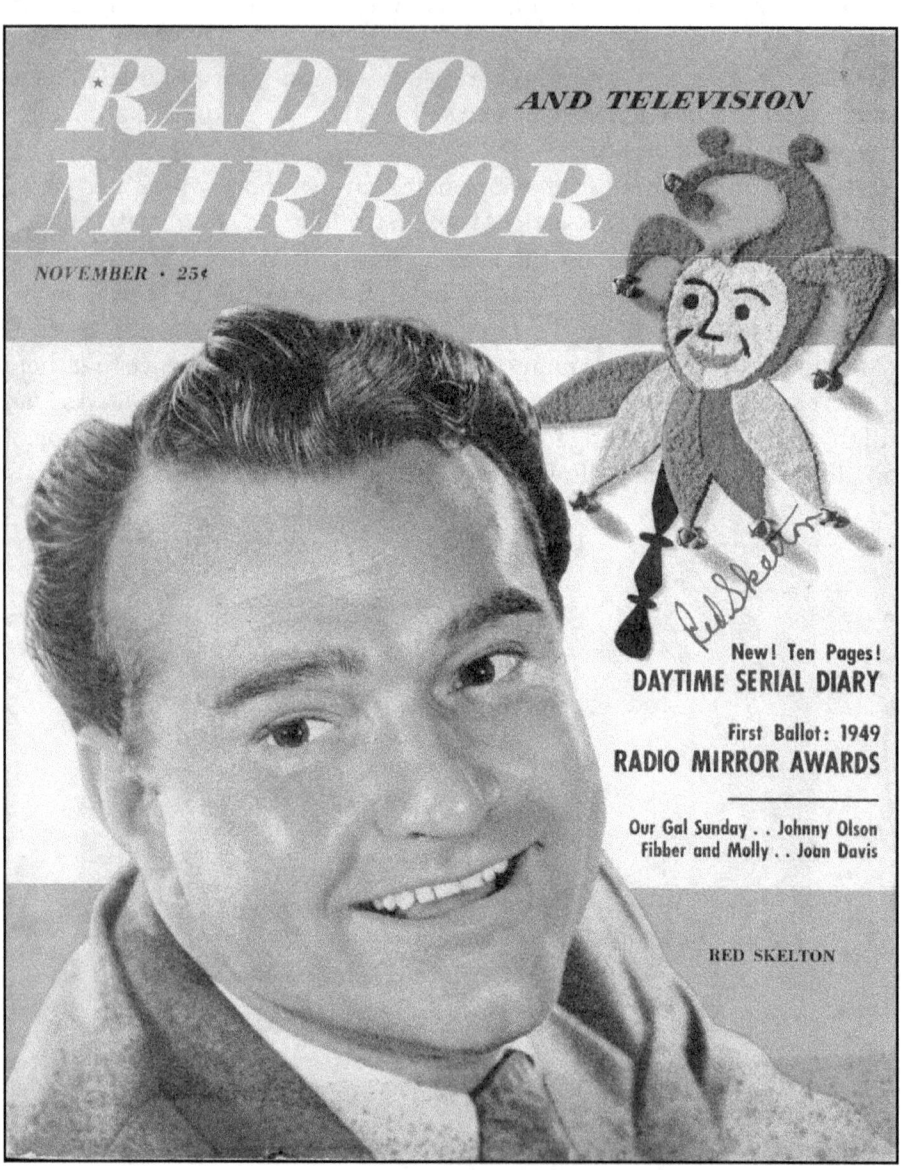

America's jolly jester in November 1949.

A Skelton Scrapbook

IT DOESN'T TAKE MUCH IMAGINATION to picture an adult scolding a boy with the words "You're acting like some kind of clown" and the child replying with a quivering lip "I can't help it." If that youngster happened to be Red Skelton, both parties were right on the money for he certainly was some kind of clown and he could not have been anything less than a born laugh-maker.

Richard Bernard Skelton, although not actually born under the big top in Vincennes, Indiana on July 18, 1913, came mighty close for his father was a clown with the Hagenbeck and Wallace Circus. It didn't take long for redheaded Richard to acquire the nickname that would one day be seen on marquees around the world.

Because his father died two months before Red was born, four Skelton brothers had to go to work as soon as they could to support the family. At the age of seven while selling papers as a newsboy Red found that by sassing people on the street they made a purchase just to get rid of him. Seeds planted then in his brain sprouted later in the form of Junior, the Mean Widdle Kid.

Perhaps Skelton's first big laugh came the day in 1923 when he accidentally fell off a stage while trying out for a medicine show. For a couple of summers he traveled with the Doc Lewis Show and later with a stock company of actors before spending some months walking in his father's big-shoed footsteps as a clown for the same Hagenbeck-Wallace Circus. For a short time he considered becoming a lion tamer—until the day he saw Clyde Beatty being clawed in a cage.

By 1928 Red had joined the burlesque circuit doing live versions of comic strips such as Mutt and Jeff as well as acting in parodies of popular Broadway plays. Two years later while at the Gaiety Theater in Kansas City he met an usherette named Edna Stillwell who became his bride in 1931. Meeting Edna could be considered the turning point in Skelton's career because she not only encouraged him to get ahead in show business and arranged for tutoring so he could earn his high school diploma via a correspondence course but she also had a flair for knowing what tickled funny bones and for writing amusing dialogue.

The Skeltons performed for a few years as a vaudeville team without much success until they clicked with Canadian audiences for half of 1936 at a Montreal theater. The highlight of the act became Red's extended pantomime of a man dunking doughnuts. Eating four doughnuts a show three times a day brought down the house, but it also brought Red's weight up thirty-five pounds.

Skelton found an alternative which was kinder to his waistline in the form of the "Guzzler's Gin" routine. This bit, which he performed countless times over the years, involved a liquor salesman freely sampling his own product until he became so inebriated he could hardly stand up. Red, who had always been a keen observer of human behavior, credited his ability to mimic drunkards from watching the unbalanced steps children take when they are learning to walk.

His new act at the Paramount Theater in New York proved to be such a hit that it led to a guest shot on Rudy Vallee's radio program in 1937 and a small role the following year in a Ginger Rogers film, *Having Wonderful Time*.

In 1939 Skelton became a regular on *Avalon Time*, a radio show that mixed songs by Red Foley and band numbers with tidbits of comedy. The playful character that captivated millions later was already very much in evidence as he broke up cast members with ad-libs like "I think I'll look on the next page to see if there are more laughs" and "We get more fun out of this than the audience."

However, the program was laden with wheezes that were old even then (e.g., Man: You want to see Big Chief Running Bear? Woman: Certainly not. Tell him to put some clothes on.) and Skelton did not have much opportunity to stretch out in his other strength besides pantomime, sketch comedy.

Red earned small parts in two Dr. Kildare pictures as an orderly, then hit the jackpot in *Whistling in the Dark* as Wally Benton, a radio detective known as the Fox, who has to solve a real case. Suddenly, after just one starring role, Skelton became "the comedy find of 1941" and "the comic who will give all other comics a first-class run for their money."

Just as Universal had been cashing in on the demand for Abbott and Costello movies so Metro-Goldwyn-Mayer quickly turned out two more Wally Benton films, *Whistling in Dixie* and *Whistling in Brooklyn*. Unfortunately for Skelton, MGM's strong suit was musicals, not madcap silliness, so throughout the duration of his contract with the studio he bounced back and forth between ninety-minute frolics in which he dominated the action and syrupy songfests like *Ship Ahoy* that restricted him to providing comedy relief. *Du Barry Was a Lady* (1943) is a period comedy that might today be regarded in the same favorable light as Bob Hope's *Monsieur Beaucaire* if it had been strictly a farce spotlighting his talent instead of an intermittently amusing revue equally memorable for Gene Kelly's graceful moves and Cole Porter's music. Likewise the plot of the picture that bears one of his trademark expressions as the title, *I Dood It*, took frequent detours while Jimmy Dorsey's Orchestra, Lena Horne, and Eleanor Powell played, sang, or danced.

At times Skelton must have considered himself water boy for Esther Williams. He helped Esther get her feet wet in *Bathing Beauty* (1944) and had a few sparkling moments of his own, especially when he impersonates a ballerina. In *Neptune's Daughter* Red and Betty Garrett played second fiddle to the romance between Esther and Ricardo Montalban, although they did have a chance to sing their version of the Oscar-winning song "Baby, It's Cold Outside." After sticking his head in for a cameo in *The Duchess of Idaho*, he managed to inject some chuckles into *Texas Carnival* to balance the Williams-Howard Keel songs by pretending to be a swaggering oil tycoon.

When left on his own and given a solid story, Skelton demonstrated that he could make a picture without the singing and dancing and still leave audiences saying, "That's entertainment." Red, like Buster Keaton, was adept at playing, with or without words, ordinary men like clerks and ushers who stumble up or down life's ladder in comical ways as he did in two post-war comedies, *The Show-Off* and *Merton of the Movies*.

But Skelton had to go to Columbia on loan-out from MGM to get one of his best roles, that of *The Fuller Brush Man*, an inept salesman trying with Janet Blair's assistance to extricate himself from a sticky web of circumstances that implicated him in a murder. Two years later in 1950 MGM fed off the success of that film by putting Red in the similarly-titled *The Yellow Cab Man* and repeating the man-on-the-run story line.

By this time Keaton, recognizing that Skelton's talents were akin to his, had asked Louis B. Mayer for a chance to work with Red to produce comedies in his distinctive style and had been turned down. However, Keaton's influence appeared on screen in the scene of *A Southern Yankee* in which, following Buster's suggestion, Red wore the "half and half" uniform of blue and gray which allowed him to walk across the battlefield unscathed, and in *Watch the Birdie,* a remake of Keaton's *The Cameraman*, that featured Skelton in three different roles.

Betty Garrett and Red helped themselves to some tasty bits in *Neptune's Daughter*.

Although Skelton the movie actor may have vacillated between hit and miss, comedy and musical, and starring and supporting role, Skelton the radio comedian hit the bull's eye from the time his own program debuted in 1941. The show shot into the top ten almost immediately and stayed there for a decade, sometimes even challenging *The Bob Hope Show* and *Fibber McGee and Molly* for the number one spot.

During the war years Ozzie Nelson and his orchestra provided the music while wife Harriet Hilliard sang and played foil to Red's readymade cast of puckish Junior, bumpkin Clem Kadiddlehopper, gravelly-voiced Deadeye, punchy Willie Lump-Lump, and impetuous Bolivar Snagnasty (spelled, as Bolivar always insisted, with "one shag and two nasties") in sketches introduced as pages taken from the Skelton Scrapbook of Satire. The program went off the air soon after Skelton received his draft notice in early 1944. (Red claimed to be the only film celebrity to go in a private and come out a private. At least he wasn't demoted.)

By the time Skelton returned to radio late in 1945 Ozzie and Harriet had their own show so he carried on with the able support of Verna Felton and Lurene Tuttle who did all they could as Junior's grandma and mother to raise the brat who was quite aptly described by one of his victims as "a hotfoot with legs." Lurene and GeGe Pearson acted as girlfriends to Kadiddlehopper, the inane rustic who took pride in his stupidity and openly resented it when Mortimer Snerd threatened his claim to being America's foremost moron.

Despite the fact that Red and Edna had divorced in 1943, their relationship remained amicable as she assumed the roles of his business manager and chief gag writer. From time to time Skelton acknowledged her contribution as he did on the October 27, 1947 broadcast when he said, after delivering a mild joke, "I wrote it myself. It gives you an idea of what kind of material you'd hear if Edna didn't have anything to do with this."

Red's asides often provoked bigger laughs than the gags. When he saw a plum coming up he would say, "Prepare yourself, folks. Here it comes." In the middle of an involved story, he would interrupt himself and tell listeners "Don't go. It's gotta get better."

Skelton handled muffs brilliantly like the night Verna said "poodle" instead of "puddle" when he quickly added, "That's OK. It's been raining cats and dogs" or cover one of his own by explaining that "I fell in my mother's washtub and got a little bluing in my gray matter."

But if *The Red Skelton Show* had attempted to get by on bloopers and improvised lines, it would have been leveled by a low-swinging Hooper and buried by its competitors. The writers gave the Skelton crew a steady stream of decent jokes that were funny to the eyes and the ears such as the image formed when Clem said he used a mackerel on the roof of the barn as a weathervane because "that way you can tell which way the wind's blowing without looking up."

Most comedy programs that were not sitcoms regularly featured guest stars, but Red didn't need a big name to generate laughs or to raise ratings because he had his own stock company locked up in his larynx.

At one time a laugh-meter registered his program drawing guffaws every eleven seconds, a record probably only "Rapid Robert" Hope could have matched.

Of all the radio comedians who took the giant step over to television, none of them made a smoother transition than Red Skelton did. Whether the script called for jesting in a monologue, acting out a scene in pantomime, or cavorting in a sketch, Skelton was the right man for the job for twenty years from September 1951 to August 1971.

On TV Red showcased his repertoire of zany characters and over the years modified them a bit. The gallery still included Deadeye, although some of the larceny running through his veins had been transfused into San Fernando Red, a con man who probably could have out-fleeced Sgt. Bilko, and canvas-backed boxer Cauliflower McPugg, who borrowed some of Willie's grogginess. Junior, Clem, and Bolivar also came along for the ride. Hobo Freddie the Freeloader gave Red a chance to speak volumes without words. Anyone who has seen Skelton's version of O. Henry's "The Cop and the Anthem," detailing Freddie's efforts to get arrested so he could spend the holidays in a warm jail cell, knows why we remember the best Christmas presents with both a smile and a tear.

Just as "I dood it" was a catch phrase in the early 1940s so another generation of children found pleasure in emulating Deadeye's "Whoa. Oh, c'mon horse. I said, 'Whoa,'" McPugg's "There goes another flock of them," and the playful hops Red made to the accompaniment of tinkling bells.

Few if any programs on television conveyed a greater sense of unbridled joy than *The Red Skelton Show* did. Skelton reveled in breaking up guest stars after they had delivered a punch line with "You're proud of that one, aren't you?" Celebrities from Vincent Price to Carol Channing to Mickey Rooney gleefully accepted a chance to romp with the small screen's finest clown. No doubt many TV viewers today who wonder where the fun has gone would eagerly welcome an opportunity to see once again that redhead with the waggish grin cutting capers in their living rooms.

After Red Skelton was called off life's stage on September 17, 1997 at the age of 84, his legion of fans echoed the words he often spoke with a twinkle in his eye after someone fluffed a line on one of his shows: "We're going to miss you around here."

Henry Morgan in 1962 with *I've Got a Secret* colleagues Betsy Palmer, Bill Cullen, Bess Myerson, and Garry Moore.

Here's Morgan

THE ONE MOVIE HE STARRED IN was a flop. He bounced from one radio station to another as if he had a ricochet romance with that medium. His contribution to the history of television is inconsequential. So why does Henry Morgan have a small but loyal coterie of admirers?

Henry Morgan spoke the words that most of us wanted to say but lacked the gumption or temerity to enunciate. To Morgan it didn't matter if the other party happened to be a sponsor, executive, influential columnist, superior officer, or audience; he said what he felt regardless of the consequences.

Morgan's straightforward approach to life even extended to his own shortcomings. About his first job, for instance, given to him in 1931 at WCAU in Philadelphia when he was sixteen he later said, "I was one lousy page boy." Dismissed after three weeks, he was hired as an announcer at the station because, according to Henry, he had a loud mouth and worked cheaper than anyone else. Because announcers needed to have zippy names and Henry Lerner von Ost Jr. tied up the tongue rather than slid off it, the fledgling adopted the surname of Niles Morgan, a ballroom bouncer.

Either due to his incompetence or the vagaries of the Depression, Henry didn't last very long at stations in Brooklyn, Philadelphia, Duluth, and Boston before heading back to New York. At WOR, more to amuse himself than his audience, he began tossing in humorous remarks on remote broadcasts and between recorded songs in the studio. The station manager gave Morgan his own fifteen minutes on Saturdays, hoping that would get the playfulness out of his system, but when the show caught on with listeners it became a part of the daily schedule at 6:45 leading into the evening programming.

Morgan freely admitted that the program was "kind of weird." After the theme of "For He's a Jolly Good Fellow" faded, he followed with the saucy "Hello, anybody. Here's Morgan." Then he improvised monologues about items in the news that struck his fancy and played "oddball records" from the Spike Jones school of discord.

But when Morgan broke a taboo by ridiculing the sponsor's products he brought about a broadcasting rarity: people were actually tuning in to his programs to hear the commercials (or, more precisely, what Henry *did* to the commercials).

He referred to the president of Adler Elevator Shoes as Old Man Adler and vowed that he "wouldn't wear those shoes to a dog fight." When taken to task for his brash statement, he later told listeners, "I apologize. I would wear them to a dog fight. But no place else."

Henry accused makers of Life Savers of gypping customers because they had drilled out the centers of their candy and promised that he would keep quiet about their "mulcting the public" if they would give him the centers which he planned to sell as Morgan's Mint Middles.

Manufacturers of Oh! Henry candy bars screamed "Oh, brother!" when Morgan followed "Oh! Henry is a meal in itself" with "But you eat three meals of Oh! Henry and your teeth will fall out" and claimed that if people consumed enough of the candy bars they would "get sick and die."

Even his weather forecasts which concluded the program bore his unconventional stamp. "For New York and vicinity, snow followed by little boys with sleds" might be followed by "Falling barometer, followed by a loud crash" might be followed by the station manager waving a pink slip.

Advertisers and meteorologists probably sighed with relief when Morgan enlisted in the Army Air Corps in 1943. His general distrust of authority figures carried over in the shows he emceed in which he satirized the brass sitting up front for the amusement of the GIs in the back, "the hired help who win the wars."

After the war ended, Morgan resumed his daily program which reached a national audience on ABC. But quarter-hour shows were a dying breed and one-man bands have a tendency to play the same tunes over and over so network bigwigs convinced Henry to try his hand at the typical thirty-minute format with orchestra, singers, and a regular cast in the fall of 1946. They should have known better.

When the announcer asked rather than shouted "*The Henry Morgan Show*?" at the start of the program, listeners knew the ride was going to be a bit bumpy and they prepared themselves for frequent lurches away from conformity.

Perhaps more than another program *The Henry Morgan Show* resembled a revue: a series of skits, mock interviews, and parodies often joined together by absolutely nothing. It was that freewheeling air of "What's going to happen next?" that made the show a fresh departure from traditional radio fare. Henry and Arnold Stang chatting in Brooklynese might be followed by a version of *Hamlet* done à la Sam Spade or a bit of psychobabble spoken by daffy Heinrich Von Morgan or a British quiz show called *Take It or Leave It or If You'd Rather Not You Needn't* or the Question Man whose answers were farther out in left field than Andy Pafko.

Listeners at home scratching their heads after hearing these bits and peculiar musical interludes like a tuba player singing "Jingle Bells" in Greek and Stan Freberg rendering "The Flight of the Bumble Bee" on his lips might have been hoping the commercials coming along shortly would signal a return to normality. They should have known better.

When Eversharp Schick razors came on board during his first season, Henry treated his new sponsor like a voodoo doll: he needled the "push-pull, click-click" slogan by using inappropriately loud sound effects, cited instances of men who bloodied their fingers handling the razor blades, and, in the unkindest cut of all, cast doubts about the shave-a-thon ("the world's worst commercial") by intimating that the winner using the Schick razor was an eight-year-old boy.

It didn't matter to Morgan whose toes he stepped on. One evening, after telling parents to leave the room, he encouraged all the children listening to run away and adopt smuggling as a career. "It's a wonderful life," he said in a way that must have sent shivers up the back of Frank Capra. "Get out now before it's too late."

Here's Morgan in a familiar pose: taking a stand behind a microphone.

After Schick bailed out in 1947, Rayve Cream Shampoo became Morgan's next victim. Not content to poke fun on his own turf, he visited *The Fred Allen Show* in May of 1948 to "Rayve" about the product with the man he admired more than anybody else in show business. Henry told Fred that, according to the small print in his contract, he not only had to make the shampoo and hawk it but he also was required to throw dirt in men's hair to increase sales. He assured Allen that if Fred didn't like his first shampoo "we give you twenty-four tubes of the same stuff to teach you a lesson."

Another link connecting the two men is that each made a film which somehow missed the mark and left both comedians and their ardent fans feeling that more should have been made of the material and the talent on both sides of the camera. Although Allen never feasted on *It's in the Bag* in the same way friendly foe Jack Benny gobbled on his fabled turkey, *The Horn Blows at Midnight*, Fred thought the penny-pinching methods of the producer hampered the hide-and-seek plot and left some of the best footage on the cutting-room floor. Morgan's opus, *So This Is New York*, could have been the sleeper of 1948, but the shortcuts to save money were all too obvious. Henry never had much to say about *So This Is New York*, but if he had been asked about this rarely-seen picture he might have commented sardonically, "It isn't a lost film. It's just hiding." [Both films are discussed in greater detail in the article "2 wits, 2Pics, 0 Hits."]

Morgan liked to close his shows with the promise that he would "be on this same corner in front of the cigar store next week." In the spring of 1948 he stepped in front of the cameras of WPIL in Philadelphia for a program called *On the Corner* which is believed to be the first televised network series for the American Broadcasting Company. As the man on the street Henry flipped through the pages of *Variety*, came across the name of a puppeteer, dancer, singer, or impressionist who then performed his or her specialty, and tossed in an array of gibes between acts. As usual, he saved some mordant remarks for the commercials of Admiral Corporation, who tolerated his scoffing remarks about their appliances for just five weeks before pulling the plug.

In 1949 Morgan appeared on the final episode of *The Fred Allen Show* and the following year he followed Allen off what Fred called the treadmill to oblivion of network radio. But producers didn't forget the efforts of cast members Stang and Art Carney who soon found work in television. Meanwhile other influential figures remembered the curmudgeon with a caustic wit and an affinity for baiting sponsors and presumed that he must be a jolly bad fellow with a radical tinge.

After Henry's name appeared in *Red Channels*, a book citing people in the entertainment industry supposedly sympathetic to communism, he found himself blacklisted. This came as quite a surprise to Morgan who, as an equal-opportunity basher, had taken frequent potshots at Russia and had openly confessed that, as a free-spirited iconoclast who called no man master, he could not have endured communism's restrictions on personal freedom for even one minute.

Despite his protests of innocence he found himself out in the Cold War looking for work. Finally WMGM let Henry broadcast from Hutton's, a Manhattan restaurant, from midnight to three a.m. The temptation to pull pranks in the middle of the night just to see if anybody was listening, as he did in 1933 at WCAU in Philadelphia when he inserted names of studio executives into missing persons reports, may have been hard for him to resist, but with personalities like Jackie Gleason and James Stewart regularly stopping by, Morgan found no shortage of lively subjects to interview.

Producer Mark Goodson, a regular diner at Hutton's who had been hatching an idea for a game show, decided that Morgan might be the right person to function as resident wit on the new program just as Fred Allen had been doing on *What's My Line?* For the next fifteen years, from 1952 to 1967, Henry sat between the likes of Jayne Meadows, Bess Myerson, and Betsy Palmer on *I've Got a Secret* and asked questions with a sly smile that seemed to say, "I've got a secret of my own: for the first time in my life I've got a steady job!"

Morgan, an adventurer at heart, had to be ready for anything the Mark Goodson-Bill Todman team cooked up. If Ann Sheridan's secret was "I'm going to the Belgian Congo. With Henry Morgan" and other celebrities had plans for him that involved trips to the Far East or Greenland, he went along for the ride as a good sport because he loved traveling and meeting real characters like a raggedy old man in France who might have been the only privately-owned hermit in the world.

After *Secret* ended its season each spring, Henry either satisfied his wanderlust in Asia or Europe or played in summer stock. It may seem hard to picture the natural improviser in roles requiring him to stick to the scripts, but he acquitted himself well as pompous Sheridan Whiteside in *The Man Who Came to Dinner*, clever Sakini in *Teahouse of the August Moon*, and fussy Felix Unger in *The Odd Couple*.

Nor is it easy to imagine this humorist playing a straight-as-an arrow district attorney in *Murder, Inc.*, a 1960 crime movie. Morgan never appeared in another film, wisely heeding the advice of the critic who summarized his performance by stating that "Mr. Morgan does better when he is telling jokes."

Even less likely is the prospect of the man who derided the products of countless advertisers doing voice-overs for TV commercials, but that is what happened after *Secret* left the air. Morgan continued working with agencies taping thirty-second spots until just a few months before his death at the age of seventy-nine on May 19, 1994.

But at heart he remained a nonconformist who fought convention all along the line. His wife Karen, whom he married in 1978 at Sealand with only dolphins and a magistrate in attendance, carried out his deathbed request that, instead of a funeral, his friends should remember him with a memorial party at Sardi's, his favorite restaurant.

Even his own obituary, written in early 1994 as a preface to his autobiography, steered away from the usual path and, instead of describing his accomplishments, listed all of his liabilities from childhood illnesses to adult maladies like gout, lumbago, and heart ailments. Also contributing to his demise: "500 pastrami sandwiches, 3,000 quarts of beer, 7,000 quarts of liquor, 17,250 bacon and egg breakfasts, 21,000 steaks and hamburgers, and 1,296,000 cigarettes." Ever the comedian, he saved the zinger for last: "2 wives."

There is no evidence that Henry Morgan ever wrote his own epitaph, but if he had quite likely the wording on the headstone would have been "Here's Morgan—This Space for Rent."

There's a reason Dottie agreed to poses like this with me.
It's also the reason she fired her agent.

The Road to Laughter

[Author's note: When I was seeking inspiration for this article, I received a visit from the muse of comedy. I always thought that muse was Thalia, a female who carried a shepherd's crook, but my visitor was definitely a male with a distinctive nose who held a microphone in his hand. He said, "Let me tell the story. You'll just confuse people with little things like the truth."]

I'D LIKE TO START AT THE VERY BEGINNING when only God and Al Jolson were around, but let's go back to 1907 when I was little four-year-old Leslie Hope getting settled in Cleveland after leaving my native England with my family. When the kids at school switched my name around and called me Hopeless, I got my revenge by fighting them and leaving my blood all over their fists.

I had a gift for being a mimic in those days and won a contest in 1915 with my imitation of Charlie Chaplin. I've had a flair for that sort thing all my life because I often heard people who saw me passing by say, "There goes that little tramp."

I left school as soon as I turned sixteen and boxed under the name Packy East. I knew my days in the ring were over when I couldn't remember anything between "Come out fighting" and "Give him some air."

I had always been fast on my feet so I did a little hoofing in the twenties with a guy named George Byrne and before long we mixed in a few jokes. We called ourselves "Dancemedians." (I can't repeat what the audience called us.)

After we were given a bit part in *The Sidewalks of New York* on Broadway in 1927, I did a solo one night and decided that since none of the tomatoes thrown my way made a direct hit I should try it on my own as an emcee and monologist. Byrne was so upset when we split up that he couldn't stop giggling all the time he was packing my suitcase for me.

It was when I went out on my own that I changed my name to Bob Hope. I was soon moving up the ladder of vaudeville and playing the better houses, but I still had a rough time of it. At the Coliseum Theater in New York I had to come on after the sad end of *All Quiet on the Western Front* and make people feel happy. That was like trying to cheer up Dewey on the day after the 1948 elections with a singing telegram delivered by Margaret Truman.

But there was no stopping me then except empty seats and the reviewers so while I was playing the Palace, Broadway called in the form of *Ballyhoo of 1932*. That led to a part in *Roberta* with Sydney Greenstreet (you remember Greenstreet: a duffel bag with jowls) and a role in the *Ziegfeld Follies of 1935* with Fanny Brice, Eve Arden, and Edgar Bergen, three bit players who just vanished after the show closed and were never heard from again. In 1936 I carried Ethel Merman and Jimmy Durante through *Red, Hot and Blue*. What I didn't have to go through in those days!

But I wanna tell ya that it was during that time when I started to develop the character that people would soon be seeing on the screen: the glib braggart with a yellow streak a foot wide down my back. In reality I've always been a sweet, well-adjusted person with no hang-ups. If you don't believe me, just ask my analysts.

That conceit just oozed out of Buzz Fielding, the ham I played in my first feature, *The Big Broadcast of 1938*. (The shorts I made from 1934 to 1936 were shown to traitors in closed rooms after the Chinese water torture failed.) I didn't have much to do in that film except introduce acts and sing "Thanks for the Memory" with Shirley Ross. I wonder what happened to that song?

I had dabbled a bit with radio on the *Rippling Rhythm Revue* so when Pepsodent came calling in 1938 I signed on the dotted line (with a tube of toothpaste, of course). I brought along a zany character named Jerry Colonna who I met while filming *College Swing*. You've heard of the cat that swallowed the canary? Colonna looked like he swallowed the cat and the tail got caught on his upper lip. Elvia Allman and Blanche Stewart played dimwits Brenda and Cobina and later Barbara Jo Allen took the part of the man-hungry Vera Vague. And we'd have lots of guest stars like Judy Garland, Jack Benny, and, yes, even an old groaner named Crosby who we felt sorry for when one of his sway-backed plugs finished fifth in a four-horse race.

My program was really different. Other comedy shows had lulls between the jokes. We came out with a thirty-minute lull.

But I wanna tell ya...It really was different in that before the guests were brought on I opened with a monologue about the economy or politics or what actress just got married or other current topics. Fred Allen tossed jokes around with his wife or Kenny Delmar, but I was out there dying by myself. Just think: the path that Johnny Carson followed to stardom was paved with the eggs I laid way back then.

During World War II we were broadcasting out before the troops more than we were before a studio audience because I felt that was the least we could do for our boys who were giving their most for us. But radio was just one medium. Everyone seemed to want me then (including those guys who take the photos that go up on post office walls). In 1940 I made the first of my frequent appearances as Master of Ceremonies for the Academy of Motion Picture Arts and Sciences annual giveaway. I always hoped that I would get an award for one of my pictures, but the closest my acting ever got me to an Oscar was the night they said I could take Homolka home with me.

I knew the odds against winning that prize were against me each time I went on the road with ol' Dad. Bing and I were actually rather subdued in the first one, *The Road to Singapore*, but by the time we traveled to Zanzibar in 1941 and Morocco the next year we were batting our dialogue all over the place. When Dorothy Lamour got frustrated trying to squeeze her lines in while we improvised, we'd tell her "When you find an opening, toss something in."

What made those movies so much fun was that all of us went along for the ride when Bing and I talked directly to the audience or set up our patty-cake routine or kept looking left and right when talking about "the papers" in *The Road to Rio*. Everyone was in on the joke.

I was really clicking movies out there for a few years: *The Cat and the Canary, The Ghost Breakers,* and *Nothing But the Truth* with Paulette Goddard, *Caught in the Draft* and *They Got Me Covered* with Dottie, *My Favorite Blonde* with Madeleine Carroll, *The Princess and the Pirate* with Virginia Mayo. Notice the pattern? Put a pretty face in to go along with the gags. The women they got for those pictures were cute, too.

Woody Allen once said that I was a "woman's man, a coward's coward, and always brilliant." (And I didn't even have to pay him!) But that was the character I played many times: a would-be Don Juan who wilted at the first sign of danger. I'd say, "It takes courage, brains, and a gun to be a detective," then follow it with "I've got the gun." One minute I was making fun of the Errol Flynn/Tyrone Power hero, the next I was saying outrageous things that could get my neck in a noose. I think it was that split personality of fraidy cat/wise guy that brought people to theaters to see those pictures. That and Crosby's radio show.

There are those who say I reached my peak after the war years. (There are also those who say that everything I did after I left England has been downhill, but who listens to Henny Youngman's relatives?) *The Bob Hope*

Show rode high in the ratings, my syndicated column called "It Says Here" appeared in newspapers across the country, I was among the top ten box office stars right through 1953, and the WACs voted me the man they'd most like to eat Spam with in a Quonset hut.

Monsieur Beaucaire is one of the better costume pictures I did with a great cast of Joan Caulfield, Marjorie Reynolds, Cecil Kellaway, and Joseph Schildkraut. Joan actually had to pretend she didn't like me throughout most of the movie. What an actress! I did my own dueling with Schildkraut. I also did my own love scenes with Joan. What an actor!

In 1947 Dottie joined me as *My Favorite Brunette* on the run from a group of villains which included Peter Lorre and Lon Chaney Jr. Lorre and Chaney. That's Lum and Abner with fangs. It's true that because I was involved with the production of this picture I paid Crosby $25,000 for the cameo at the end as the disappointed executioner who is denied the chance to kill my character, Ronnie Jackson. Bing said he'd return the money for a chance to strap me in that chair and turn on the gas. So that's what he meant by "Going—my way."

Critics keep saying that *The Paleface* is my best film and they may be right. It certainly made a lot of noise at the box office and that was music

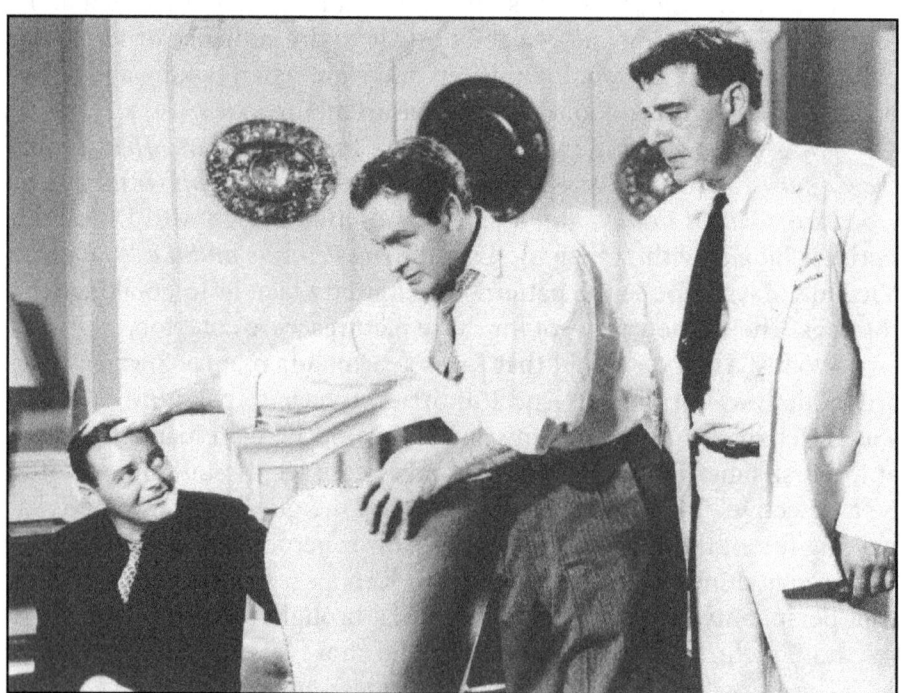

Here in *My Favorite Brunette* I'm asking Lorre what witchdoctor did his skull while Chaney wants to take to the infirmary—one limb at a time.

to my ears. Now that I've had time to see the movie a number of times and review the high points like the dentist chair scene, the laughing gas bit in the cabin, "Buttons and Bows," Potter's reaction to a jolt of potent whiskey, the confusion over the directions Painless is given before the gunfight, and the scare takes, I have come to two conclusions: 1) it's not too bad; 2) I'm glad theaters had a policy of no refunds after the picture had started.

Four years later in 1952 Jane Russell and I did a sequel with Roy Rogers called *The Son of Paleface*. It wasn't bad either. Even Trigger gave it 3½ spurs.

It's nice that television stations blow the dust off *The Lemon Drop Kid* every December. That Damon Runyon story is good for a few chuckles and "Silver Bells" is now a yuletide standard, but before Marilyn Maxwell and I could get in the studio to cut a record of the song that croaker who did "White Christmas" beat us to it. I got even with Bing when I made his toupee stand on end after I told him that instead of going to Bali our next film would be called *The Road to Baldy*.

By 1954 my program had gone the way of most radio shows, and I must say that I miss those days. Part of the fun of doing my own show and guest shots came from the lines I tossed in to liven up the script. The versions of *Fancy Pants*, *The Lemon Drop Kid*, *My Favorite Blonde*, *Monsieur Beaucaire*, *The Paleface*, and *The Great Lover* I did on *Lux Radio Theatre* or *Screen Director's Playhouse* sometimes took unexpected detours from what was written. I was always quick with an ad-lib—and I had the writers to prove it.

I think I also proved that I could do a bit of serious acting when the part called for it. My scenes with little Mary Jane Saunders in *Sorrowful Jones* didn't scare Spencer Tracy into turning in his union card, but I earned a few good words in the papers for showing that I didn't need a raft of quips to keep me afloat on the screen. Ditto for the speech I gave to get custody of my children in *The Seven Little Foys*. In *Beau James* I took on a tragic role as New York Mayor Jimmy Walker and went the distance to show his rise and fall from power. I must have been a good actor in order to play with such conviction men like Eddie Foy and Walker who sometimes behaved like downright heels. No comments, please.

Of course, while I was making pictures I was also doing TV specials for NBC. (I signed my long-term contract with them because I thought the initials stood for Nothing But Corn.) Doing just a handful of shows a year gave me the freedom to make personal appearances at nightclubs and benefits, do tours promoting my books *I Owe Russia $1200* and *Five Women I Love*, entertain the boys in Korea and Vietnam, turn out a film a year through 1969, and still have time to golf and hobnob with some fellows in Washington named Ike, Jack, and Gerry. My wife Dolores must have felt that the only way she could have gotten my attention during those years was to become a director, enlist, or get elected.

I can honestly say that I received the clippings about my last films more warmly than they were reviewed—I burned them! But Lucy shone through in *The Facts of Life* and *Critic's Choice*, and *The Road to Hong Kong* had its moments (three, to be precise). But by that time the people who had grown up seeing my films were watching my movies on TV while waiting for their children to come home from dates. I might have been more successful during those years by breaking into pictures then playing in theaters like *Easy Rider* and *M*A*S*H* with the announcement "Children! Do you know where your parents are? Go home and watch *My Favorite Brunette* with them."

And I think they would have enjoyed it because my humor appeals to all ages regardless of whether they like slapstick, satire, double takes, or one-liners. That's one test this dropout can still pass: my movies and shows make people laugh out loud.

When all is said and done that is what made my life worth living. All the honorary doctorates and medals and plaques and speeches about humanitarianism and other accolades touched me deeply, but you do me the greatest honor when you remember me with a smile.

Jerry Colonna, always in wide-eyed pursuit of the elusive Yehudi.

The Really Nutty Professor

IMAGINE A PROFESSOR WHO, during an evaluation by his employers, exclaimed "I don't ask questions—I just have fun!" Then picture the bosses saying, "Fine. That's just what we want you to do."

Such a scene wouldn't happen on a college campus, but in the wacky world of radio anything was possible when "Professor" Jerry Colonna came on the air.

People sitting in a classroom or in a studio could not be blamed for having fun as soon as they saw that head that might have been stolen from a carnival poster with those pop-eyes that made Eddie Cantor look like a sleepwalker, a mouth that, when opened, resembled the entrance to a tunnel of love, and a walrus mustache that seemed to have a life of its own when Colonna bellowed notes of such volume and duration he could have made boilermakers think the noon whistle had just blown.

Gerardo Luigi Colonna first opened those peepers and that mouth on September 17, 1904 in Boston. He got a chance to exercise his muscles and lungs as a longshoreman but saved most of his wind for after hours when he practiced on the trombone, the perfect musical instrument for the extrovert.

During the 1930s when Colonna played with bands no one ever labeled him an awful trombonist, but it became clear when he began hamming it up with eye-rolling and flamboyant manipulation of the slide to amuse his colleagues and friends that he belonged closer to the spotlight in front of the bandstand. Those not enamored with his mugging might have commented disdainfully, "As a musician, Colonna was a great comedian."

Bing Crosby brought Jerry out from the brass section for a few laughs on his radio program and Fred Allen used him to put over some gags on his show. But it wasn't until Bob Hope began his ten-year run with Pepsodent on NBC in the fall of 1938 that Americans realized that Jerry

Colonna wasn't something to be purchased at the cosmetics counter of a department store.

Colonna quickly became Hope's sidekick in an odd sort of way: the star became the straight man and the second banana got all the good lines. Bert Gordon's Mad Russian assumed a similar role on Cantor's program, but he was reasonably sedate compared to the "Wild Italian" who, apropos of nothing, burst into ear-popping song, interrupted the proceedings just to say one or two words, or engaged in other manic behavior that must have made listening audiences wonder if he was wrecking havoc with a seltzer bottle.

Although the exchanges between Hope and Colonna gave Jerry the punch lines (e.g., Hope: You're an idiot's idiot. Colonna: I didn't know you cared.), much of the humor he brought to the show derived strictly from this "character" Jerry Colonna who did madcap things like calling Hope from a pay telephone and talking backwards because "I put the nickel in upside down."

Given his relatively small contribution to the show (frequently a bit with Hope before the first commercial and perhaps a part in a sketch), Colonna's influence on the colloquial language of the era is significant. The hip crowd began saluting each other with "Greetings, Gate" after Jerry used the phrase as his own sign-on weekly. "Whatsa matter? You crazy or something?" became a sure laugh-getter in just about any situation. Nearly everyone who heard the name of violinist Yehudi Menuhin could not help posing the question that Jerry and the entire country kept asking for months: "Who's Yehudi?" At that time he could then do a switch on his notable catch phrase by saying, "I *do* ask questions—and I still have fun!"

It is no wonder that one of his routines in which he said, "Hello," paused a beat, added "Goodbye" and topped it off with "Short day, wasn't it?" became playground fodder for hordes of schoolchildren. His humor was simple (cynics called it simple-minded) and that appealed to the child in everyone hearing his voice.

It was perhaps best that he appeared in bits and pieces on the Hope program because his zany act could grow tiresome if doled out in larger portions. The failure of his own television show, which did not even last six months in 1951, demonstrated that he could not carry a program as a headliner. With Jerry Colonna, a little went a long way.

And, as part of Bob Hope's traveling show during World War II and after, Colonna *did* go a long way. In 1946 he recounted some of his escapades while entertaining troops in the South Pacific in his book *Who Threw That Coconut?*

Colonna and Don Wilson test the microphone before a *Command Performance* broadcast.

By the time Hope opened his 1948-1949 season Colonna had been dropped from the cast. He had become Jerry One-Note and no matter how loud he sang it or how long he strung it out it was a monotone that had truly become monotonous.

He kept busy by doing personal appearances both in the states and in Great Britain, where he met with some success, perhaps because he was viewed as another gap-toothed eccentric like Terry-Thomas. During the 1950s Colonna could be seen occasionally on television comedy and variety shows as well as the syndicated *Super Circus* series.

Over the years he recorded his peculiar versions of songs such as "Down by the Old Mill Stream," "You're My Everything," "The Yogi Who Lost His Will Power," "Where is my Wandering Boy Tonight?," "Hector the Garbage Collector," and a rendition of "Sweet Adeline" that might have driven people *away* from drink. Some of his best (or worst) warbling was gathered together in a Decca album aptly titled *Music for Screaming*.

Producers and directors followed the dictum of *The Bob Hope Show*: a little dab of Colonna will do ya. Therefore moviegoers got little more than cameos as Colonna acted quirky as a psychiatrist in Fred Allen's *It's in the Bag*, rode by periodically in Hope and Crosby's *Road to Rio*, or rose out of a bubble bath for a sight gag in *Sis Hopkins*. Even if he generated a laugh, his contribution to the narrative was minimal and his performance likely forgotten by the time audiences hit the streets.

But Bob Hope never forgot the man he called a "very dear friend" and included him on his trips to entertain the troops until Colonna suffered a stroke in 1966 which virtually ended his career as a performer. His few appearances with Hope thereafter showed that the spirit was willing but his flesh was very weak. The once-booming voice of Jerry Colonna was silenced on November 21, 1986.

What lasting lesson Colonna had to teach is hard to fathom, but, who knows, perhaps his spirit is passing from land to land as the Ancient Professor confounding students with his strange power of speech: "Greetings, mates." Pause. "Class dismissed." Pause. "Short semester, wasn't it?"

Ingenious Ernie Kovacs with cigar.

The Importance of Being Ernie

A MAN SAWING THE LIMB OF A TREE he is sitting on watches placidly as the final stroke sends the trunk falling to the ground while he remains suspended in mid-air. That sight gag from the early years of television is symbolic of the life of Ernie Kovacs, one of the medium's most creative personalities whose profligate spending and disregard for financial matters kept him in a precarious position until a rainy January evening in 1962 when he came tumbling down from that perch on a slick street in California.

Almost forty-three years before that fateful night Ernest Edward Kovacs began life on the other side of the country in Trenton, New Jersey and at the opposite end of the socioeconomic structure as the son of Hungarian immigrants. His father vacillated from job to job, finding some success as a bootlegger but exhibiting the spendthrift tendencies which Ernie inherited and that kept the Kovacs family fortunes always in jeopardy.

Even then Ernie didn't concern himself with money matters. To him life was a bowl of cherry bombs. He loved playing pranks like putting Feen-a-Mint laxative tablets in Chiclet boxes and passing them out to classmates on April Fool's Day or telling everyone in the house that the family feline had crawled in the hot oven after he had placed a cutout of a cat inside the range with a sign reading "Whew, that was a close one" or shooting the ornaments off the Christmas tree with a BB gun.

In his younger years Ernie demonstrated some eagerness to learn and to succeed in school, but by the time he entered Trenton Central High School he had become an indifferent scholar who only applied himself to English and the few other subjects that interested him. That he failed to graduate with his class in 1936 didn't upset Kovacs much because it gave him an opportunity to work one more year with a drama teacher named Harold Van Kirk who helped him with his part in *HMS Pinafore* and awarded him the role of the Pirate King in the 1937 TCHS production of *The Pirates of Penzance*.

Kovacs found performing very much to his liking and therefore needed no encouragement when Van Kirk invited him to join the Rollins School of Acting. While constructing and painting sets Ernie gained experience behind the scenes as he observed how productions were put together and eventually earned a chance to act in *Liliom* and *Arms and the Man*.

In 1939 while at the New York School of the Theater he contracted tuberculosis which put his aspirations for a career in show business on hold for eighteen months. After Ernie recovered, his experiences as a clerk in a drugstore running back and forth trying to please capricious customers must have seemed to him like the trials W.C. Fields endured in *The Pharmacist*, and his next job behind the tobacco counter at another pharmacy did little for him except to introduce him to cigars and gambling. Playing poker in smoky back rooms hardly seems an ideal regimen for someone just a few months out of a TB sanitarium, but Kovacs already was living up to his motto: "Nothing in moderation."

Because the condition of his lungs had kept him out of the armed forces, Kovacs was Ernie on the spot when Trenton station WTTM, short on manpower because of the war, needed a staff announcer. Soon Ernie assumed other duties such as playing records, reading comics on the air, inventing quiz programs, taking parts in locally-produced dramatic shows, and hosting a chat show called *Coffee with Kovacs*, all done while holding down his job at the drugstore. This hectic schedule of trying to burn the cigar at both ends accelerated the development of another habit, that of speeding in his automobile as he raced between store and studio.

Although much of Ernie's work for WTTM consisted of straight reporting, his playful nature sometimes won out when he concocted stunts like broadcasting nonstop at the 1949 New Jersey State Fair and such antics as scaring singers with rubber spiders or setting fire to the scripts of his colleagues while they were still on the air.

After Kovacs married in 1945, he took on yet another job, that of writing a column for the *Trentonian* which gave him a soapbox from which to vent his feelings about everything from commercials to pulp heroes. The roots of numerous skits that later flourished in full bloom on the television screen can be found in those ink-stained pages.

Ernie's first taste of television came at WPTZ in Philadelphia, initially as an announcer, then as host of a cooking show called *Deadline for Dinner*. Late in 1950 Kovacs stepped in front of the cameras five mornings each week from 7:30 to 9:00 on *3 to Get Ready*, considered to be TV's first "up and at 'em" show. At last he had the chance to stretch his wings: ninety minutes to fill and the only limits were the boundaries of his imagination.

The same level of enthusiasm and spontaneity that existed between the characters in movie musicals who exclaimed "Let's put on a show!" must have existed on the set of *3 to Get Ready* because there were no scripts and improvisation was encouraged.

"Rehearsal" consisted of nothing more than "You wear this. You hold this. I'll walk by and then you do this." Crudely-printed cards, held up to the camera at intervals, often had more dialogue than the actors did.

Kovacs used such self-imposed limitations of speech to his advantage because he realized full well that television is a visual medium, that it is what audiences see that matters, not what they hear. In those early years he was perfecting the art of the blackout, short skits, often in pantomime, that ended with a bang: a pie in the face or an unexpected twist that capped the scene as surely as a punch line clinched a joke.

Unlike other hosts of programs aired in those early years, Kovacs did not appear stiff or tied to pieces of the set like desks or chairs. He frequently walked past the cameras into the wings or even into the control room, all the time carrying on a conversation with the audience as if to say, "C'mon, let's take a look behind the scenes."

If someone had dared to ask, "Is this any way to run a television show?" the answer coming from appreciative Pennsylvanians would have been a resounding "Yes!" In 1951 Kovacs received some national exposure on NBC in *Ernie in Kovacsland*, a summer replacement for *Kukla, Fran, and Ollie*. A blonde singer named Edie Adams, best known at that time as Miss U.S. Television of 1950, soon became a fixture on both of his programs and in his life. Edie and Ernie married on September 12, 1954, eight months after his divorce from Bette, his first wife.

Kovacs continued to use his morning show as a testing ground for experiments like inverting images by affixing mirrors to cameras and inserting comic-strip style balloons above heads of actors or blotting out portions of bodies by employing matting techniques. He also brought along a staple of radio, sound effects, into television, often mixing incongruous elements like the flicking of a pen with gunshots.

In early 1952 Kovacs, appearing locally on an expanded version of *3 to Get Ready* and several times a week on *Deadline for Dinner*, also served as host of *Kovacs on the Corner*, a late morning variety series on NBC. Creating material to fill over thirteen hours of programming a week became almost as much a challenge for Kovacs as finding time to sleep. Fortunately for his health, that hectic schedule lasted only a couple months until he accepted an offer from CBS to take on a daytime show called *Kovacs Unlimited*.

For a national audience he carried over some of the characters from his early shows such as fanged Uncle Gruesome who told "kiddie stories" in a macabre fashion. Although Kovacs didn't have to produce as much material in New York as he did when based in Philadelphia, the scripts needed to be more structured and the humor more appealing to a larger audience so Ernie began mining his own medium for satiric humor which resulted in parodies of *Mr. and Mrs. North*, *What's My Line?*, and *The Stork Club* called *Mr. and Mrs. South*, *Where D'ya Work, John?*, and *The Crow Club*.

His work on *Kovacs Unlimited* convinced the decision-makers at CBS that they should give Ernie a chance at a prime-time show. However, the slot they selected for him was on Tuesdays opposite Milton Berle, a spot that could be described as Video Death Valley. Berle had plenty of brass, but at least that brass showed some polish. Live television requires fluidity and planning if skits and sight gags are going to succeed. The A's for audacity that

Poet Percy Dovetonsils with mascot.

Kovacs had earned did not overcome the feeling that the prevailing mood backstage was "What'll we do next?" What CBS did next was mercifully pull the pull on *The Ernie Kovacs Show* after the April 14, 1953 broadcast.

A new but not necessarily improved version of *The Ernie Kovacs Show* surfaced a year later on the DuMont Network. This spot, late in the evening, not only provided Kovacs with little competition but also allowed him to employ some improvisational comedy that was ideally suited to his talents and temperament.

In addition to cast members Edie Adams and Barbara Loden, other characters from the Kovacs gallery of weirdoes joined Uncle Gruesome as regulars on *The Ernie Kovacs Show* including German disc jockey Wolfgang Sauerbraten, Chinese lyricist Irving Wong, and Frenchman Pierre Ragout, who put a grim twist on fairy tales. Percy Dovetonsils, an effeminate creature who wore glasses that looked like the X-ray specs sold in novelty stores and who, when sipping periodically from a martini glass, resembled a debauched John Barrymore, read doggerel in lisping tones and accented certain lines with a tremulous shake of his head as if to say, "Mmmm, that was good one!"

Perhaps the most famous musical group to appear on any of his programs was The Nairobi Trio. Ernie assumed the role of the "he who gets slapped" conductor with the cigar, the seated figure who took the beating from the standing gorilla, who accented appropriate moments in the song "Solfeggio" with the rat-tat-tat of his wooden hammers. Edie frequently sat in as the piano player who diverted Ernie's attention the only time he caught his attacker in the act so he could take one more beating on the bowler hat before rising to enact his revenge with a handy vase. The Nairobi Trio might have been called The Mute Three Stooges because the musical routine played out as pure slapstick and audiences loved it even though they knew how the bit would end.

On the DuMont show Kovacs continued to hone his satiric skills with amusing spoofs titled *Son of Seven Year Itch, Martin Krutch, Private Eye, Arsenic and Crumpled Tweed,* and *Little Orphan Amy,* but in 1955 the network was wobbling on its last financial legs and within a few months both DuMont and Kovacs had been knocked out of TV's ring.

"Scrapper" Kovacs, often down but never out, rebounded again with not one but two programs called *The Ernie Kovacs Show*, the first a daily daytime show opposite Arthur Godfrey and the second a summer replacement in 1956 for *Caesar's Hour* on Monday nights. The evening show exemplified glorious lunacy from the garbled introductions of the announcer, double-talk wizard Al Kelly, to special effects that split dancers in half to wild parodies that left both actors and audiences gasping for breath. The program earned an Emmy nomination as best new series of 1956 and landed Ernie a spot the following year filling in for Steve Allen on the *Tonight Show*.

It was on *Tonight* that another famous character in the Kovacs repertoire made his debut. Eugene, a likable schlemiel akin to Jackie Gleason's Poor Soul, stumbled through life without saying a word, yet everything he touched set off a cacophony of noise. Ernie's stoic reactions to the litany of raucous sound effects that accompanied the simplest of actions like opening a book or peeling a banana brought out the inevitable comparisons to the artistry of Buster Keaton. Early in 1957 the misadventures of Eugene served as the centerpiece of a half-hour NBC special done without any dialogue that is widely regarded as one of the most ingenious programs of television's growing years.

When "The Silent Show" generated much critical praise but no offers from networks, Kovacs hit the road to Hollywood where he hoped a career in film might allow him more opportunity to unleash his anarchic style of comedy. Although he displayed some ability as a character actor in *Operation Mad Ball, Wake Me When It's Over, Our Man in Havana,* and *It Happened to Jane,* more often than not he played "by the book" martinets or corrupt authority figures, the very people Ernie held in contempt. By the time he appeared in his final picture, *Sail a Crooked Ship* (released late in 1961), he had fallen to being billed fifth, below Frankie Avalon.

Kovacs returned to television in October 1959 to host *Take a Good Look*, a quiz program for ABC that offered him creative license and a steady paycheck. As might be expected, a Kovacsian panel show bore no resemblance to any other for the skits Ernie and his cohorts acted out before celebrity panelists Hans Conreid, Cesar Romero, Edie Adams, and Carl Reiner which should have contained simple clues to the identity of the contestants instead appeared open to more interpretations than a painting by Salvador Dali. *Take a Good Look* gave Kovacs his longest prime-time stint on national television (1959-1961) and, even if it doesn't represent his most inventive work, the show provided him with $5,000 a week at a time in his life when he desperately needed money.

Because Kovacs had virtually ignored paying any income taxes since his days at DuMont, by 1960 his debt to the IRS had reached staggering proportions, yet he continued to hedonistically spend what little the government did not attach. Ernie seemed determined that if he was going to the poorhouse he would drive there in his Rolls-Royce.

Commenting on shortened versions of silent films as host of *Silents Please* took little of his time, but the monthly specials he taped in 1960 for ABC titled (what else?) *The Ernie Kovacs Show* drained him financially and physically. Rather than split the taping of these half-hour shows over two weekends, Ernie pushed cast and crew through thirty-hour sessions that he deemed necessary to capture the effects he wanted. As producer of the programs, the money for the overtime came from his already impoverished pockets which became even emptier after the lavish parties he threw for everyone involved with the program for which he picked up tabs as high as $5,000. "Nothing in moderation" really had become his credo by this time for his situation seemed hopeless. In one of the blackout sketches he painted himself into a corner and then used the brush to create a ladder on the wall that allowed him to escape from his predicament. In real life the only escape for Ernie was to immerse himself in the surrealistic world of his art.

By the end of 1961 the fabric of that artistry started to show signs of wear due to overwork, a mountain of debt, and all-night poker games. Even though Ernie only needed to fill thirty minutes every month, he started repeating gags and giving indications that exhaustion had begun to sap his creative powers.

As his money woes mounted, Kovacs became less fussy, courting publishers with inchoate ideas for quickie books and even filming an uninspired pilot for a proposed series called *Medicine Man*, a show that might have made *F Troop* a model of subtle western comedy by comparison.

The evening he finished work on the pilot Ernie Kovacs was killed when his car crashed into a utility pole on Santa Monica Boulevard. Kovacs remained true to form right to the end: he had attended a party, was speeding, had a blood alcohol count of 0.11, and was found with one hand extended toward his cigar. At one time he told friends he would die with diamonds on his vest and owe over a million dollars; at least he lived up to the second half of that prophecy.

What the world owes Kovacs is a debt of gratitude for being a pioneer in expanding the dimensions of television outside the boundaries of conventional entertainment. As a freewheeling innovator who thrived on experimentation, his parodies, blackouts, pantomimes, and outlandish brand of humor stamp him as one of the most influential figures in television history.

On his shoulders have climbed the casts of *Rowan and Martin's Laugh-In*, *Saturday Night Live*, and *Monty Python's Flying Circus* as well as Benny Hill, David Letterman, and numerous other comedians. Some of his successors have learned their lessons well, but when one compares the work of his followers to that of the master…

Close, but no cigar.

Arnold Stang making merry with his unique voice.

Small Wonder

ONE OF THE PLEASURES OF LISTENING TO RECORDINGS of radio broadcasts is recognizing the actors and actresses, and it isn't just hearing the distinctive voices of William Conrad, Jack Webb, Orson Welles, Vincent Price and other major figures that flicks on the switch in our heads. Supporting players such as Walter Tetley, Elvia Allman, Howard McNear, and Bea Benaderet each possessed a timbre that made their lines particularly amusing. Arnold Stang stood apart from many of his contemporaries because his nasally voice often induced laughter regardless of what he had to say.

Arnold started whining on September 28, 1918 in New York City. Even as a youth Stang's bright eyes and alert expression stamped him as a willing and capable performer when he tried out for radio jobs. His glasses, which sometimes gave him the appearance of an owl, and the shape of his head with a weak chin, coupled with his small stature molded him into the prototype of what people would decades later call a nerd.

As a child actor Stang's schedule was quite hectic, performing on *Let's Pretend* on Saturdays and on *The Horn and Hardart Children's Hour* and *The American Pageant of Youth* on Sundays.

During the summer of 1942 on a replacement show for *The Jack Benny Program* he appeared as nephew to *The Remarkable Miss Tuttle* played by Edna May Oliver.

Stang's slight build and bookish appearance led to roles on Broadway and in films that typed him as "lead's best friend" such as the play *All in Favor* and the MGM musical *Seven Days' Leave*. In the latter production he leaned on the shoulder of Victor Mature, who befriended the teenager by protecting him from unsavory Hollywood personalities and offering the hospitality of his home.

Parts in *My Sister Eileen* (1942) and the Bob Hope picture *They Got Me Covered* (1943) unveiled glimpses of a flip side to the mild-mannered square his appearance suggested. Under the Clark Kent demeanor of this apparent pipsqueak beat the heart of a feisty gagster who might rip open his shirt at any time to reveal an S for Smart aleck.

Although Stang had appeared on the air with Fanny Brice and Al Jolson and had a featured role on *The Goldbergs* as kvetch Seymour Fingerhood, it was his bits with Milton Berle and Henry Morgan for which he is best known and which paved the way for his later work on television.

On *The Milton Berle Show* Stang, like actor Jack Albertson and announcer Frank Gallop, took turns excoriating the star. Arnold frequently appeared twice or three times per program with only a few lines to speak, but he milked every word for maximum laughage.

In the forum section during which Berle solicited questions about everything from literature to agriculture, Stang provoked chortles as soon as he gave his name as Andre Kostelanetz, Guy Lombardo, Jersey City, Oxydol Sparkle, or Lady Esther (which he had changed from a boy's name, Lady Mendel). All Berle had to do was ask a question and Stang would be off and running at the mouth, building a fortress of paranoia which wouldn't allow Milton to get a word in edgewise, usually culminating in Arnold skewering his interviewer with a putdown like "Shut up, you homewrecker!" or "Drop dead!" Stang really threw his body into these tirades, prompting Berle one night to say, "Young man, don't jump at me!"

During the burlesque of familiar songs like "Dixieland" and "Camptown Races" sung by Berle, Stang tickled the audience just by tossing in a dispassionate "away" or "hoo-hah" as a refrain.

In the domestic sketches Arnold played Berle's son Junior as an insult comic who regularly accused his father of stealing jokes and laying eggs. Told to go to bed, Junior prepared the way for his temper tantrum by asking a series of questions ("Are you ready? Are you set? Are you tuned in?") before launching into a screaming fit that made father cry uncle.

Stang's appearances on the Berle program, though brief, were significant when one compares those shows with the ones in which Billy Sands took his place. The spontaneous laughter Arnold generated is missing from the later shows as the emphasis shifted to the repartee between Miltie and either Gallop or Albertson.

Although Arnold proved himself to be surefire chucklebait with Berle, he usually sang the same note and a pretty shrill one at that. On *The Henry Morgan Show* the writers gave him a chance to loosen his ever-present bow tie now and then so he could slip out of the straitjacket of typecasting.

On one episode in the fall of 1946, for example, he played a youngster razzing Morgan, an angry husband complaining about his wife's spending habits, and a thug in a Jack Armstrong parody. On another night he fit the bill as a tired Frank Sinatra wheeze at the old jokes home. He also portrayed raspy Mr. Worcestershire, the leader of mutineers in "Blubber," a spoof of sea epics, then concluded the skit by providing the end credit "at the Henry Morgan Theater of Coming Attractions" in his milquetoast voice.

In semi-regular sketches Stang as Gerard conducted quasi-romantic telephone chatter with girlfriend Hortense (Florence Halop) in New Yorkese with mixed results. Whether anybody in or out of the Bronx talked like that is not important. There was a certain appeal to these two maladroit lovers, and their peculiar signature line, "I acquiesce," became, for a short time, the in way to end phone calls.

The writers soon recognized Stang's ability to load a phrase with maximum import and began handing him bigger parts. Sometimes he only had to repeat a line and slather it with sarcasm to produce guffaws. On a program in which Morgan planned to use characteristics borrowed from other comedians like Jack Benny, Arnold merely reiterated "From now on he's a tightwad" and "From now on we're going to pretend my mother hates him" and the point was driven home with his precise inflection.

Stang had few rivals in getting laughs out of a minimum number of words. In a satire of Swan commercials, after various actors had chimed in with the enthusiastic phrases of praise "Oh, yeah!," "Yes, Sir!," and "And how!," Stang's "Hoo-hah" capped the routine nicely. The buildup preceding a movie parody followed the same pattern: Announcer: You were horrified when you saw *The Spiral Staircase*. Your blood curdled when you saw *The Dark Mirror*. You'll get sick to your stomach when you see… Stang: *The Dirty Kitchen*.

By June of 1947 Arnold's small but integral contributions became such an eagerly-awaited part of *The Henry Morgan Show* that his first words one evening, "Say please," drew giggles and applause, causing Morgan to stop the proceedings and comment, "You know, that's probably the only time in radio a line like that ever got applause." Later that year, after dialogue between the Gerard character and Henry as Hank became a regular feature, just the mention of Gerard's name produced a big hand which Morgan greeted with "Please don't do that. I can't pay him a cent more."

During these conversations Gerard acted as laconic as a clam and as energized as a sloth. His favorite response to anything was a noncommittal "Eh." He certainly would have gone broke if paid by the word. A typical exchange: Hank: What's new? Gerard: Same old thing. Hank: How's the wife? Gerard: Same old thing. Hank: How do you like sunny California? Gerard: What's not to like? Hank: Like it, huh? Gerard: What's to like?

When Morgan encouraged him to loosen his starched collar and relax a bit, Gerard confessed that he did that once. Hank: So? Gerard: So I froze my neck.

However, impassive Gerard was not without sentiment. For Mother's Day in 1950 he offered these words on a greeting card: "Congratulations, dearest mother,/You're not my father,/You're the other."

Although Gerard became his most famous role on *The Henry Morgan Show*, Stang had ample opportunity to try on different hats and dialects with characters like pompous Senator Dribble, avaricious baseball player Abe Snake who endorsed products at the drop of a box top, wacky scientist Willie Von Morgan, and bellicose Britisher Harold Hotchkiss who, as a contestant on a quiz program, answered questions with a gruff "They got it, never you mind how."

By playing mild-mannered and assertive types on the same show Stang demonstrated a range that surprised some listeners and perhaps astonished others when he made the transition between characters almost in mid-sentence. One night after listening to Morgan's lecture about manners and responding in a nonchalant way, he flared up when Henry suggested that he would need to practice such refinements "if you go to formal dinner parties." "If…If," an indignant Gerard sputtered. "If my grandmother had tubes, she'd be a radio!"

Stang, who stayed with Henry until the show left the air in 1950, first appeared on television in 1949 in a juvenile *Hellzapoppin'* called *School House* before joining his friend on *Henry Morgan's Great Talent Hunt* in 1951. Arnold supported Eddie Mayehoff as millionaire Winfield Dill on *Doc Corkle*, a comedy series that ran for just three weeks on NBC in October 1952. He also appeared occasionally as a panelist on the game show *The Name is the Same*.

His chief television experience during the 1950s came as a stagehand on *The Milton Berle Show* who harassed both from the wings and from under Uncle Miltie's chin. Stang also performed capably as a screen actor during that decade, most notably as Sparrow, a dull-witted friend to *The Man with the Golden Arm*.

After spicing up the programs of Berle, Danny Thomas, Jackie Gleason, Red Skelton, Bob Hope, and Ed Sullivan with bits and pieces, he finally earned a starring role in *Top Cat* (1961-1962), an animated ABC series. The ungainly trio of Arnold Stang, Maurice Gosfield, and Marvin Kaplan may never have succeeded in a situation comedy, but their voices seemed just right as the funny felines perpetually complicating the life of Officer Dibble (Allen Jenkins).

During the 1964-1965 season Stang again made the most of a small role by infusing chef Stanley Stubbs with enough quirks to irritate Commander Roger Adrian (Edward Andrews) on *Broadside*.

In 1965 Arnold played *Second Fiddle to a Steel Guitar*, although he and ex-Bowery Boys Huntz Hall and Leo Gorcey received prominent spots on the poster art above the numerous country music stars who appeared in the film. Other film appearances included parts in *It's a Mad, Mad, Mad, Mad World* (1963), *Skidoo* (1968), and *Hello Down There* (1969). Later on television Stang could be seen in the syndicated series *Tales from the Darkside* and as pitchman for Chunky candy and for other products. He could still be heard on *The CBS Radio Mystery Theater* in the 1970s. His love for radio remained undiminished as he continued to participate in recreations of vintage shows into the 1990s. He died December 20, 2009.

Like the weakling in the Charles Atlas ads who built himself up into a powerhouse, Arnold Stang packed a wallop in his delivery that still is a knockout with listeners and viewers. Pound for pound, line for line, laugh for laugh, he proved to be a scrappy crowd-pleaser who never had to wonder why almost everybody down here likes him.

Until 1947 Groucho Marx had reason to eye radio suspiciously.

The One, the Only…Groucho!

GROUCHO MARX WILL ALWAYS BE REMEMBERED as the chief wisenheimer from the Marx Brothers movies, the gag-a-minute rascal who was in there swinging even as the quality of the films diminished. When he got his turn at bat on the air, he hit a few foul balls before finding a pitch that allowed him to touch all the bases.

Groucho and Chico Marx spent the 1932-1933 season bandying words in *Flywheel, Shyster and Flywheel* over the Blue Network. Few episodes from that program have survived, but extant scripts reveal that the series tried to capture the action and lunacy of the Marx Brothers pictures instead of developing character and witty situations through the skillful use of dialogue and sound effects.

From late March 1943 to mid-June 1944 Groucho appeared on *Blue Ribbon Town* as host, a role that fit him like a straitjacket. Hosts of variety shows need to be hail-fellow-well-met types and Groucho was, well, Groucho. He was called upon to stop his persiflage with a guest in mid-rib to introduce songs ("Let stop this wedding day palaver and listen to Bill Days sing a real song of romance") or deliver dreadful lines that might have been rejected from an Abbott and Costello script ("What eyes, what lips, what teeth. She's got the teeth and she's giving me the brush").

Everywhere he turned in *Blue Ribbon Town* he seemed to be playing out of position. When acting as straight man to Leo Gorcey (who called him Marxie), when placed in domestic skits unsuited to his demeanor, or when spouting baby talk to guests like cooing "Genie, my queenie" to Gene Tierney, Marx was handcuffed to situations better tailored to the temperaments of an Eddie Cantor or a Jimmy Durante. Worse yet, he had to sublimate his dominant personality in favor of the guests. When man-hungry Vera Vague approached one evening, the audience heard Groucho Marx, the man with the roving eye who had pursued women for lust or money on stage and screen, becoming a panic-stricken craven who shouted, "Lock all the windows! Shut the doors! Bar the entrances! I've got to keep that she-wolf from the door!"

Amid all this twaddle Marx occasionally departed from the printed page to put his distinctive twist on a joke. When singer Fay McKenzie asserted that "I always approved of a man getting married. That's something I endorse," he replied, "You do? Well, just sign on the back of my neck." After the laugh, Groucho added, "Or neck on the back of my sign."

Ad-libs, however, could not boast the ratings of *Blue Ribbon Town* or save Groucho's job, and he was replaced by Kenny Baker and later, in a different version of the program, by Danny Kaye. In 1959 Marx wrote that "I still think the show…was a pretty good one," which brings to mind James Thurber's response to the question "How's your wife?" The humorist shot back with "Compared to what?"

"A pretty good one" did come along for Marx after his talent for improvisation opened the door for him. During a 1946 show with Bob Hope the two comedians threw down their scripts and a gauntlet of spontaneous jests. After observing the battle of wits, John Guedel, producer of *People Are Funny* and *House Party*, approached Marx with a proposal for a different kind of audience participation show, one that would marry the quiz program with Groucho's keen sense of humor.

Although Marx was initially unreceptive to the idea, stating, "There are a hundred on the air," he agreed to participate in *You Bet Your Life* because he realized that his movie career was virtually over and because of Guedel's assurance that Groucho would not be forced into the mold of other quizmasters who just posed questions. The game would be secondary while the show's spotlight focused on the fun generated from the interviews between real people being themselves and Groucho being, well, Groucho.

It could not have worked out better for Guedel or Marx when the program found a sponsor in Elgin American who took the package to ABC, the same network that had allowed Bing Crosby to tape his shows. Freed from the strictures of an inflexible script or a fixed amount of time, Marx could allow his freewheeling wit to meander, knowing that the director would delete longueurs, jokes that misfired, bloopers, and risqué lines. (Although some television reruns bear the title *The Best of Groucho*, every show lives up to that billing because they all are a condensed version of an hour's worth of taping.)

During the early years of *You Bet Your Life* the premise of the game was firmly related to the title. Contestants started with a sum of money and wagered any or all of their funds on each question. If they answered all questions correctly, their earnings could reach $160. Winners advanced to the jackpot round near the end of the program that might earn them

$1,000 to $3,000. Usually participants wagered even sums such as ten dollars, but some bettors chose odd figures that kept George Fenneman, the show's announcer and scorekeeper, scrambling to keep the fractions proper and vice versa. One man, at Groucho's playful urging, upped his bid to $39.08½. Fenneman, always a good sport and a genial straight man for Marx's japes, kept a precise record of the man's earnings, even down to announcing his winnings in mills, which allowed Groucho a chance to quip glibly about the mills of the gods and the Mills Brothers.

One problem with the wagering format is what keeps Las Vegas and Atlantic City solvent: betting involves chance and chances are that, on a given night, everyone could lose. A primary function of quiz shows is to award prizes or cash and nothing, short of the answer-giving scandal of the mid-fifties, is more harmful to a giveaway show than to give nothing away. When the worst happened on a show in 1953, no amount of editing could alter the fact that all the players had struck out so Guedel changed the format to one that allowed contestants to select from questions weighted in difficulty from one to ten and in value from $10 to $100. To make certain there would be no losers, contestants started with $100 and could only lose half of their stake at any time.

Gradually the betting aspect became less important and was replaced by a format that Marx or Fenneman repeated succinctly each week: answer four questions in a row correctly to win $1,000; miss two consecutive questions and the game is over. Winners could return at the end of the program for a chance to win either $2,000 or $10,000, depending on whether a spinning carnival wheel landed on their selected number. Even if a pair of contestants missed the jackpot question, they still left the studio with $500.

Actually, Marx always had some "gimme" questions handy which allowed even losing couples to split twenty-five dollars. This consolation prize took the form of the queries Tom Howard presented to his panel of dunces on *It Pays to be Ignorant* in which the answer is apparent in questions like "In what state did the California Gold Rush occur?" and "What color is the little brown jug?" It hardly mattered if the participants even responded for Marx was eager to give them the money and also ready with a send-off jest like his "We take that for granite" after asking "Who is buried in Grant's tomb?"

Another method of earning money on *You Bet Your Life* came from saying the secret word which triggered the orchestra to play "Hooray for Captain Spaulding," a song associated with Groucho since his appearance in *Animal Crackers*. Shortly after the program appeared on television in 1950 a bespectacled, mustachioed duck that vaguely resembled

Marx descended on piano wire carrying $100 to reward those who had uttered the magic term. Marx usually reminded couples of the rules when he greeted them by offering clues such as "It's something you always have with you." By presenting a hint and by selecting common nouns like *face, chair, paper, shoe,* and *hand,* the show's staff gave contestants more than a fair chance of winning the extra cash.

On some episodes the production team increased those favorable odds to a virtual certainty by lobbing a word right into a particular guest's home court. Thus an author referred to *book,* the owner of a Mexican restaurant mentioned *food,* and the maitre d' of the Brown Derby uttered *table* in the natural course of the conversations. And it could not have been just coincidence that C.S. Forester appeared on a program when *name* was the secret word and Groucho led off with the loaded question "What does the C.S. stand for?"

The only player who turned the lame duck into a golden goose by bending the rules was Ernie Kovacs one evening in 1958 when he pinch-hit for bridge guru Charles Goren, who withdrew from the game portion after being interviewed and saying the right term (*name* was also the secret word that night). After Ernie and his partner won $1,000, Kovacs began yelling, "Name, name" and beckoning the duck to come down and pay off again. It was all in fun and, because Kovacs had announced that any money he won would be given to charity, the bird returned with more loot. Groucho played along, saying it didn't make any difference "since it's all counterfeit money," which was true as any close-up photograph of the duck reveals that it carried bogus bills.

Marx frequently gave money away during the quiz with the same offhand "We don't care" attitude and accepted questionable answers with a "That's close enough" because the game portion of *You Bet Your Life* interested him considerably less than the probing and diverting interviews. In the early days of the program members of the studio audience became the contestants, but gradually a willowing process developed in which people who had written letters or had done something newsworthy or who knew someone who worked on the show were selected for interviews from which scripts were written so that, although Marx usually had not met any of the non-celebrities before the taping began, he knew enough about them so that he could guide the direction of the dialogue his way. But, being Groucho, he took his customary detours down Ad-Lib Lane so frequently that almost as many improvised remarks made the final cut as did scripted yuks.

Attentive listeners to episodes of *You Bet Your Life* can separate the planned drolleries from the impromptu wisecracks. Jokes like "If it weren't for stealing hubcaps, kids today could barely make a living" and

"All my life women have been throwing themselves at my feet. And after they tackle me, they usually haul me to the police" could be dropped in whenever there was an opening. Other witticisms were specially prepared for a particular guest. He told a woman who worked for Lloyds of London

The 1954 issue that revealed Marx's secret weapon.

that "I have a policy with them now. If I'm torpedoed at Hollywood and Vine, I get eight dollars a week for the rest of my life." Often the exchanges with guests have a custom-tailored feel to them, e.g., Groucho: What does your father do for a living? Model: He delivers mail in Chicago. Groucho: Well, he delivered a good female, too.

Even the tunes in a category such as "Songs of the 1930s" were chosen to stack the deck in Marx's favor so that when comely contestants said, "You're Driving Me Crazy," "Everything I Have Is Yours," and "You Do Something to Me," those answers served as straight lines so Groucho could respond with the leering response "Wouldn't it be great if that were true?"

Despite having the safety nets of a filmed rather than a live show and of an arsenal of written one-liners that would not leave him speechless, Marx fought the jitters before every broadcast. To Groucho's credit, his nervousness is well-hidden on *You Bet Your Life*, the program a writer for *TV Guide* aptly described as producing "the finest manufactured spontaneity television has yet known."

Some famous personalities like Liberace, Joe Louis, and Ray Bradbury appeared as guests, but for the most part the contestants were ordinary folks who perhaps engaged in an offbeat occupation or came from a quirky family. Although the pairing did not occur on every show, teaming a male with a beautiful woman made for some built-in humor so Groucho could dismiss the man with a cursory remark and then state one of his Marxian questions that sounded more like complaints such as "Enough about you. Who's this gorgeous creature and why have you been hiding her from me?" Innocuous answers from newlyweds of all ages provided Marx with wide gaps through which he drove home wisecracks like "I'll never forget my last wedding. They threw vitamin pills instead of rice."

Mildly eccentric people, be they hobo, elevator operator who sang in Sanskrit, circus strongman, or president of the Society for the Domination of Women who wanted to rescind suffrage for females, were welcome on *You Bet Your Life*. At one point during the exchanges each person would cause Marx to raise a quizzical eyebrow or stare blankly at the audience before launching some of his characteristic retorts.

Several of the funniest interviews occurred when Groucho turned molehills of language barriers into mountains of hilarity. After a woman asked her sister her age in Italian and told the host, "Forty-seven," Marx came back with a scripted but still witty reply: "How much did she lose in the translation?" He later joined the pair in a strident version of "O Sole Mio" that could have forced a banshee to take a take a vow of silence. Only slightly more unconventional were a pair of Portuguese gentlemen, one of whom did not speak English but who could, by manipulating his cheeks and lips, replicate the sound of a variety of instruments. Marx's request of this musical marvel's companion lacked originality but could not be bettered for its wry delivery: "Ask him if he can imitate a drum and beat it."

Groucho's modus operandi on *You Bet Your Life* involved reacting rather than acting.

"I focus on the guests," he told an interviewer. "I let them talk until they get confused. Then, I move in…When some contestant puts his foot in his mouth, I just push it in a little further."

It was during Dr. Hackenbush's special remedy for this hoof-in-mouth malady that the natural ad-libs emerged. After a man admitted, "Yes, I'm married. I have a wife," Marx gently told the tittering audience, "You may laugh, but it's a very handy arrangement." The lass who said that her ideal man would be a combination of Swiss and American was asked, "Do you want that on rye bread or pumpernickel?" To the woman who boasted, "I've been married thirty-one years to the same man" Groucho said, "If he's been married thirty-one years, he's not the same man."

Groucho's favorite guests included Anna Badovinac from Badovinac, Yugoslavia, where everyone is named Badovinac and who was looking for another Badovinac after the death of her second husband named Badovinac; Zetta Wells, owner of a myna that refused to sing until the middle of the quiz portion when its version of "Stars and Stripes Forever" brought everyone in the audience to their feet; Mr. and Mrs. Storey, parents of twenty-three children; and Pedro Gonzalez Gonzalez who told the comedian that if they did a vaudeville act the team would be called Gonzalez, Gonzalez, and Marx, prompting Groucho to grumble, "That's good. Two people in the act and I get third billing."

Most episodes of *You Bet Your Life* contained a name that allowed Marx or writer Bernie Smith a chance to build a complete routine. Each time Groucho addressed a Fuller Brush salesman named Raoul he sounded like a baying coyote. He deliberately mispronounced or corrupted names such as Anna May Devereux into Anna May Wong, waited to be corrected, then came back with his kicker of "Well, in that case, I'm wong." Groucho couldn't be topped at this name game for, even if he didn't have a pun handy, he could always squeeze a small laugh out of the mild accusation "Well, if you're going to be shifty and change your name, it's all right with me."

Towns and cities gave Smith and Marx directions for other places to go for giggles. The Swiss miss who announced that her hometown was Gallen was asked, "Is that near Four Quarts?" and of the British gent from Highgate Marx inquired if that was anywhere near Low Bridge. He had some fun with a woman from Louisiana, Missouri and a gag man's holiday with an employee of the Owens Illinois Glass Company which was located not in Owens, Illinois but in Vernon, California. People answering the question "Where are you from?" with "Hawaii" should have expected the "I'm fine. How are you?" response they received.

Vocations also furnished Marx with plenty of material so he could go out on a limb by trying to open a branch office with a tree surgeon, present a sly invitation to be kept after school by a pretty teacher, and assault a jockey with an endless supply of nag gags. It was intimated by some people who worked on the show that the job-related lines preceded the selection of the contestant, meaning that researchers sought intriguing people who worked in professions that meshed with Groucho's material which might have caused the wit to look from the guest to a bad joke and ask, "Which came first, the pickin' or the egg?"

It didn't matter which came first because throughout his career Groucho tossed his darts indiscriminately at people, places, and things with little regard for people, places, and things. Just as Marx could have amused moviegoers watching *A Night at the Opera* if he had played opposite a mannequin instead of Margaret Dumont, he could have provoked laughter on *You Bet Your Life* if his guests had been a lamppost and a sofa with sallies like "I've come home lit myself sometimes" and "So fa, so good."

So far, so good might have described the course of *You Bet Your Life* which enjoyed a long run over ABC, CBS, or NBC from 1947 to 1960 on radio and from 1950 to 1961 on NBC television. Although the same contestants appeared on both versions, the programs were not identical because they were edited differently and the radio broadcast aired on different nights of the week while the television show remained on Thursday evenings throughout its run. Along the way the program received a Peabody Award in 1948 and Groucho garnered an Emmy in 1951 as television's "Most Outstanding Personality."

That outstanding personality, which had been inhibited by his roles on earlier radio productions by format or choice of material, was unleashed gloriously on *You Bet Your Life*. No matter how hoary some of the jokes might have been, Marx's lively exchanges with Fenneman and the guests distinguished it from all other audience participation/quiz shows whose emphasis centered on the contestants. From the moment Fenneman said, "Here he is…the one, the only…Groucho!" the cynosure of *You Bet Your Life* had been established.

Marx, who freely admitted during interviews and in print that he thoroughly enjoyed appearing on *You Bet Your Life*, thought he received the ultimate compliment when a woman he met on State Street in Chicago stopped him and pleaded, "Please don't die. Just keep on living."

The One, the Only…Groucho! • 111

George Fenneman and Marx relaxing backstage.

Groucho Marx, who passed away August 19, 1977, couldn't comply with the first request, but ask anyone who listens to his radio show or watches reruns of his television program, "Is Groucho Marx still with us?" and the answer is obvious: you bet your life!

Portrait of the character actor.

The Best Second Banana in the Bunch

Supporting actors were vitally important to the success of most comedy shows on radio. It is impossible to imagine *The Jack Benny Program* without Mary, Dennis, Phil, and Rochester. No doubt listeners regarded the residents of Allen's Alley with as much affection as they did the star of the show. Riley would have been lost if John Brown hadn't split his personality between Gillis and O'Dell. Bea Benaderet, Mel Blanc, Hans Conreid, Arthur Q. Bryan, Frank Nelson, and Verna Felton also played second fiddle most of the time, but they played it very well indeed. The person who perhaps played it sweetest of all was Gale Gordon.

Gale Gordon had more aliases during the forties and early fifties than those square-jawed felons who stared at us from the walls of post offices. We knew him as Mr. Judson, Homer LaTrivia, Foggy Williams, Osgood Conklin, Rumson Bullard, Clyde Scott, John Granby, Rudolph Atterbury, and Harry Graves. He also played pharmacists, doctors, clerks, conductors, and salesmen who had no names, just a voice. We knew that voice immediately and we waited for the laughs. We were rarely disappointed.

Casting comedy shows must have been easy with him around. "We need a sourpuss to be the principal for *Our Miss Brooks*. Get Gale Gordon." "We should have a running character that Fibber and Molly can provoke, somebody who can blow his top in a hurry. Get Gale Gordon." "Let's pick up a guy like Claghorn to joke around with George and Gracie. Get Gale Gordon." "I know who can play the sponsor and take the guff from Phil and Remley. Get Gale Gordon." It didn't happen that way, of course, but these three words could have helped any comedy program: Get Gale Gordon.

Much of the effectiveness of humor on radio depended on timing and delivery. During his monologue Bob Hope raced from one joke to another like a machine gun, taking aim at any target in sight. Jack Benny milked the pause to perfection, and his "Well!" and "Hmm" spoke volumes. Gale Gordon seemed at home with any style of comedy. When Mayor LaTrivia used an expression like "The council members felt they were on pretty thin ice" and when Fibber and Molly took it to mean that the members were actually skating, Homer got so confused and frustrated that he was practically blubbering. But Gordon, like Benny, knew that a little goes a long way. He would wait for the laughter to subside, pause a moment, then start it rolling again with just one word: "McGee." He could get a laugh as LaTrivia on *Fibber McGee and Molly* or as Scott on *The Phil Harris-Alice Faye Show* just by letting the stars rattle off some questionable statement, waiting two beats, and simply saying, "Yes."

Gordon's polished delivery on radio matched his unerring sense of timing. As Osgood Conklin on *Our Miss Brooks* his voice could be drier than saltines. If Walter Denton suggested something like "I think classes should be suspended this afternoon," just a sardonic "Oh, you do?" from Conklin caused the poor student to wilt before our ears. If Connie said something negative about her principal and he overheard it, "Good morning, Miss Brooks" delivered in his voice of doom struck fear in her heart and laughter in ours. Yet as Mr. Judson, the wealthy Texan who dropped in on Burns and Allen, Gordon became a completely different person, an ebullient braggart who roared heartily at Gracie's idiocies before drawling, "I like your sense of humor, ma'am."

Jackie Gleason did the best double take on television, Lou Costello and W.C. Fields had few peers in the movies, and Gale Gordon reigned as undisputed king on radio. How could a double take be done on radio? The character simply repeated what had been said moments before in an incredulous tone. The highlight of any *Our Miss Brooks* program was when Conklin raised his voice almost to a shriek because he could not believe what he had just seen or heard. Conklin would be looking for a receipt book in a drawer, discover a frog there, placidly say, "Hello, little frog," and then take three seconds before exploding: "Miss Brooks, it won't take a moment to get the … HELLO, LITTLE FROG!" The episode that best demonstrates that wonderful ability to go from absolute calm to total shock in an instant is "The Heat Wave" (August 7, 1949) in which he unleashes three double takes (Is that six takes?), one for each of the people he discovers in his closet. Edgar Kennedy may have had a slower burn, but it wasn't a funnier one.

Gordon's contribution to *Our Miss Brooks* cannot be overestimated because he lifted the level of hilarity immeasurably every time Connie confronted Conklin. In the taxidermy escapade (June 19, 1949), for example, when Miss Brooks tries to convince her principal to stuff the bass he recently caught on a rocky fishing trip that has left him with a queasy stomach, she does most of the talking but Gordon gets the biggest laughs of the episode in scarcely over a minute with just two groans and two pithy, precisely-accentuated replies ("I do not" and "Well, bully for him").

Gordon also had continuing roles on *The Judy Canova Show, My Favorite Husband, The Great Gildersleeve, The Penny Singleton Show,* and *Junior Miss.* He played the title character in *Granby's Green Acres, Flash Gordon, Jonathan Trimble,* and *The Casebook of Gregory Hood.* A most capable actor on radio, he performed in everything from serials like *Those*

Two comedy greats in character: Lucy flinching, Gale glowering.

We Love to crime drama to comedy. On one dramatic program he demonstrated his versatility by playing a villain, a policeman (he arrested himself), and the sound of a police siren!

Gale began his acting career in 1923 with a walk-on in a play for which he earned $15.00 a week. In the early thirties he appeared on his first radio program on KFWB in Hollywood. He played dramatic roles almost exclusively until assuming various identities in *Fibber McGee and Molly* episodes during the 1939-1940 season. By the late 1940s he had become one of radio's busiest actors, frequently appearing on three or more primetime comedy programs a week.

When I contacted Gordon in 1987 and asked him what it was like working with the Jordans, Phil and Alice, et al. he responded simply, "Wonderful!" Of all the shows he was involved with in radio he named *Fibber McGee and Molly* and *Our Miss Brooks* as his favorites. He still saw Jim Jordan and Eve Arden occasionally, and he had maintained his close friendship with Lucille Ball with whom he had worked on *My Favorite Husband, The Lucy Show, Here's Lucy,* and *Life with Lucy*. At that time he was still active, regularly performing in a variety of plays in Winnipeg, Toronto, and other Canadian cities. He died June 30, 1995 at the age of eighty-nine.

Gale Gordon has never received the recognition he deserves for over twenty years of yeoman's service in radio. In his time he played many parts and he played them very well indeed. We are fortunate that so many of his performances have been preserved so that when the urge to laugh hits us we can answer the old call and…Get Gale Gordon.

LADIES, TAKE A BOW

The result of placing inveterate scene-stealers Vincent Price and Eve Arden in front of a photographer shooting stills for *Curtain Call at Cactus Creek* (1950).

All About Eve

IN THIS AGE OF COMEDY CLUBS and rapid-fire jokespewers it is important to remember that there is a difference between women who merely recite gags and the gifted handful of true comediennes blessed with the ability to evoke laugher with intonation, a line from a song, or just a look. Offhand, it may not be easy to recall a single punch line spoken by Lucille Ball or Carol Burnett, yet they remain two of our favorite entertainers because of what they did that cannot be written into a script. We should never forget that Eve Arden also belongs in that select group of funny ladies.

The actress we know as Eve Arden started out as Eunice Quedens in Mill Valley, California. For years she claimed that her date of birth was April 30, 1912, but after her death on November 12, 1990 a spokesman for her family gave her age as 83 which would suggest that she was born in 1907. More trustworthy are her gravestone and obituaries which indicate her birth year was 1908 and her death certificate which lists her birth date as April 30th of that year. Whatever the date of her birth one thing is certain: here was a person who was probably "acting up" right from her romper days. While her divorced mother was working, Eunice engaged in make-believe games and entertaining neighborhood children by assuming all the parts in impromptu plays.

She remembered that her first real taste of show business came when she played a page in a pageant at a Dominican convent in San Rafael. In high school Eunice performed in song-and-dance skits and starred in the senior play. One night some friends of her mother who dropped her off in front of a San Francisco theater practically dared the fledgling to get an acting job. She left her name and address and within a few weeks was given a walk-on role that didn't pay much, but at least it got her foot in the stage door. It was with that theater troupe that Quedens had a memory lapse almost as embarrassing as forgetting her lines. One evening after the curtain came down she removed her makeup and headed for a streetcar only to be called back by the stage manager who reminded her that she would probably want to stick around for the second act of the play.

Like many performers young Eunice suffered through some lean times in the early thirties, but she did find work with the Bandbox Repertory Company that toured the resort and hotel circuit. She was acting in *Lo and Behold* at the Pasadena Playhouse when Lee Shubert spotted her while scouting singers and dancers for the *Ziegfeld Follies*. She was told to be in New York on August 15, 1934 if the salary of $100 a week interested her—and indeed it did.

Even more appealing to the young actress than the money was the chance to rub elbows with Fanny Brice, have her own musical number, and get her name on the marquee. But she would have to make one change. Shubert told her, in so many words, "We want you, but Eunice Quedens will have to go." So she plucked her new identity from two objects close at hand: *Eve* from a novel she had been reading and *Arden* from some Elizabeth Arden cosmetics.

Eve was pleased with her work in *Follies* and particularly proud of Robert Benchley's praise of her in *The New Yorker*. (Benchley later became a friend and appeared in two movies with her.) When the musical revue closed after two years in New York, she appeared in a Theater Guild production called *Parade* that contained material written especially for her comedic talents.

The trifle *Oh Doctor!* earned Eve her first movie credit and a screen test at Universal which caught the eye of the director working on *Stage Door* who then invited her for a reading. Her presence in the movie is more notable for what she wore than for what she said. She suggested to director Gregory La Cava that she could do some "business" with a cat and that idea grew into her appearance in the film with a living fur piece around her neck.

During the next few years she played everything from a saloon owner to a trapeze artist at RKO, Paramount, and Universal with the likes of the Marx Brothers, Clark Gable, Judy Garland, and Lana Turner. She teamed with Danny Kaye in the hit Cole Porter musical *Let's Face It* and repeated her role in the movie version opposite Bob Hope. She also appeared with Gene Kelly and Rita Hayworth in what may be the quintessential 1940s film, *Cover Girl*.

Because Eve felt that doing so many pictures in succession put a strain on her already shaky marriage and because she wanted more freedom to do plays and radio programs, she signed a seven-year contract with Warner Brothers that limited her work to two or three movies a year.

Her performance in one of those films, *Mildred Pierce*, earned her an Academy Award nomination for best supporting actress in 1945. In *One Touch of Venus* and *The Kid from Brooklyn* she was perfecting the kind of wisecracking characters she began playing in Lubitsch's *That Uncertain Feeling*. Arden, her own severest critic, claimed that one of the few pictures she made she actually could bear to watch in later years is *The Voice of the Turtle* which starred Ronald Reagan.

It may have been a turn on the dance floor in Chicago with CBS kingpin William Paley in 1948 that elevated Eve from the "Who's she?" level to the "I know her!" plateau. Although she had done some radio work on *The Danny Kaye Show* and *The Village Store*, Arden could not be considered a star in that medium. Shortly after that night at the Ambassador East she was asked to read for the part of an English teacher named Constance Brooks. Eve didn't like the script presented to her, and it wasn't until Al Lewis, the man responsible for developing the characters and for putting those very funny lines in their mouths, did a rewrite that she agreed to take the part.

Our Miss Brooks, simply intended to be a summer replacement series starting July 19, 1948, was promoted into the regular season schedule after it became a hit in the ratings.

Lewis had an ear for amusing dialogue, but the success of the program was due to its perfect cast: Gale Gordon, superb as the cranky principal Osgood Conklin; Jeff Chandler, who portrayed the frugal and shy Mr. Boynton with skill that belied his virile appearance; Richard Crenna as Walter Denton, the best snickering and adenoidal teenager north of *The Aldrich Family*; and Jane Morgan as the absent-minded landlady frequently meandering in a surrealistic world that Connie Brooks could only occasionally penetrate.

But Eve Arden gave the show not only its driving force but also its heart. Her Miss Brooks was a woman who, just after losing a battle in her unrequited romance with Boynton or receiving an unrealistic demand from dictatorial Conkin, turned a sympathetic ear to the problems brought to her by Denton, Conklin's daughter Harriet, or Stretch Snodgrass, the school dunce. It took a real actress to be convincing as both Mother Superior and Milton Berle, and it is difficult to think of anyone who could have brought it off as well as Eve Arden did.

Beginning in October 1952 *Our Miss Brooks* could be seen on CBS-TV as well as heard on CBS radio. Arden described that a typical week on the program consisted of a first reading on Friday morning, rehearsal from ten to five on Monday followed by an in-house dress rehearsal, an afternoon walkthrough on Tuesday afternoon, and then filming with three cameras at 7:30 that evening. That gave her four days to be with her family each week.

It may be surprising to learn that this woman who almost always appeared smartly dressed on television and in the movies felt very much at home in dungarees with her family on their farm in Hidden Valley. She had adopted two girls during the 1940s, but after her divorce she was beginning to think she would never find a good husband and father for the girls until Barry Sullivan suggested touring in a stage production with "a guy named Brooks West." It wasn't love at first sight. In fact, when Brooks asked her "Why don't we get married?" she responded not with a "Yes" or "No" but in typical Miss Brooks fashion: "Oh?" In 1951 the "Oh?" became a "Yes."

The newlyweds soon adopted another child and by the fall of 1954 Eve had brought home two more additions to the household: an Emmy as Best Female Star of a Regular Series and a baby boy named Douglas. In the delivery room Arden must have thought she was still playing a scene in a situation comedy for when one of the attendants mentioned that the patient happened to be the famous Miss Brooks, it started a parade of what Eve called "gremlins" lining up for autographs during her labor pains.

As Miss Brooks, Arden was earning $200,000 a year, receiving fan mail from teachers, and garnering honors from the National Education Association and the PTA. With the fame came a hectic schedule while working on the show on both TV and radio and trying to answer an avalanche of requests to teach or lecture. But she never regretted playing the role and fondly remembered the people who told her that the misadventures of the amusing Connie Brooks had helped them recover from life-threatening illnesses.

Our Miss Brooks rolled along smoothly for three seasons before the powers that be tinkered with a good thing. For the 1955-1956 season Madison High School vanished and Connie was sent to teach at an elementary school. Only Gale Gordon remained from the original supporting cast. On September 21, 1956 school was out for Miss Brooks.

The following season Eve starred in a program based upon the autobiography of Emily Kimbrough. She played novelist Liza Hammond who coped with the rigors of traveling on lecture tours and raising twin girls. *The Eve Arden Show* lasted just one year.

The break from television gave Arden a chance to work with husband Brooks in *Auntie Mame* on the West Coast. In 1959 both appeared in support of James Stewart and George C. Scott in Otto Preminger's *Anatomy of a Murder*.

In 1962 Eve's appearance in a Las Vegas revue demonstrated her versatility. Arden sang, she danced, she told stories, and during the course of her performances she impersonated everyone from Jackie Kennedy to

Whether Eve played Miss Brooks on radio or TV, the emphasis was on laughs.

Bette Davis. This successful run and her later work in *Hello, Dolly* and *Applause* indicated that, like Judy Holliday, she was very much at home in musical comedies.

After taking some time off to tour Europe with her family during 1963 and 1964, she returned to work in *Hello, Dolly* and make guest appearances on *The Man from U.N.C.L.E.* and *Run for Your Life* before being called by Desi Arnaz to co-star in a news series with Kaye Ballard. *The Mothers-in-Law* gave Eve and Kaye a chance to play distaff versions of Oscar and Felix who enjoyed meddling in the affairs of their children. Though the program only ran for two seasons, it produced a number of memorable episodes, perhaps most notably the satiric treatment of *The Valkyrie* that may have made Wagner turn over in his grave and scream for relief from the Marx Brothers.

Arden kept busy after many of her contemporaries had taken their final bows. She would appear in *Cactus Flower* in Miami around Easter, do a summer stock version of *Butterflies Are Free* in New Jersey, and be in Australia for *Applause* in September. In the movie version of *Grease* (1978) she went back to school with a promotion to principal and four years later reprised her role as Miss McGee in *Grease II*. It wasn't until the death of her husband in 1984 that she curtailed her performing schedule.

In 1985 she revealed that Brooks had been fighting alcoholism for most of the thirty-three years of their marriage. Whether this was caused by the insecurity of a career that was minor when compared to that of his wife's has not been ascertained, but it is patently clear that Eve supported Brooks by encouraging him to enter detox centers and by attending AA meetings with him. By raising four children, being a farm wife, and having a career, Eve was truly a modern woman who had it all, including the heartaches.

Eve Arden was surprised to learn in 1983 that Woody Allen considered her his favorite comedienne. She shouldn't have been for she has always had fans who love her even more than they love Lucy. For many of us, this Eve remains the apple of our eye.

Heaven Can Wait is the film being promoted.
The reason heaven can wait is obvious.

She Was More Than a Dream

ON A WALL IN MY NOSTALGIA ROOM there is a framed color photograph which was published as a supplement to *The Chicago Sun* on October 10, 1943. The glamour shot shows a ravishing brunette with shoulder-length curls, aquamarine eyes, and full red lips whose chin almost rests on a strap of the black-and-silver gown she is wearing. If the phrase "Hubba hubba" had not been coined before the *Sun* hit the newsstands that Sunday, this is the pose that would have done it.

In the 1940s Gene Tierney wasn't just getting double takes as a pinup; her breathtaking beauty was holding the attention of audiences in theaters across the country. Gradually people came to appreciate the actress behind that gorgeous face. It took even longer for the public to discover that under that pulchritude and talent was a mind deeply troubled by family problems.

Yet if Gene had not been born into the family she was on November 19, 1920 she might never have become a movie star. Her father, a prosperous New York insurance broker, provided her with a first-class education in Connecticut and Switzerland that gave her culture and poise. From her mother she inherited those "stop 'em dead in their tracks" good looks and in her mother she found the advisor she needed when she was a babe in Babylon.

Had it not been for her father's name that got her into the studios for a personalized tour in 1938 Gene almost certainly would never have met director Anatole Litvak who dusted off the "You ought to be in pictures" cliché for her. Within a few weeks she had a screen test, Warner Brothers had offered her a contract, and before she knew it …she was back in Connecticut.

Her father, who insisted that she finish school and have her coming out, hoped that she would marry a wealthy college boy and forget about a career. But when it became clear that Gene wanted an opening night before the footlights more than a debut into society, he gave in and agreed to help her make the rounds of agents and producers in New York. She landed a part in *Mrs. O'Brien Entertains* directed by the renowned George Abbott and, although the play lasted only a month on Broadway, she rang the bell with the critics. The most glorious words in Gene's ears from that experience came not from reviewers but from Abbott himself who told her during rehearsals "Today you are an actress." And an actress she would be from then on.

Her next play, *The Male Animal*, was a success and the critics were still in her corner. Soon her face appeared in the pages of *Life* and *Vogue* and before long Darryl Zanuck of Twentieth Century-Fox was knocking on her door with a contract. From the start Gene made it clear that Hollywood would have to take her as she was: her imperfect teeth, the color of her hair, and her name (she had been named for her uncle) were not to be altered.

The advantages of signing with a major studio like Fox soon became apparent to Gene. Fritz Lang directed her first movie, *The Return of Jesse James* (1940), which starred Henry Fonda. Being in the company of top-notch directors and leading men, she was learning from the best which in turn brought out the best in her. Even character actors like Nigel Bruce, who appeared with her in *Hudson's Bay*, were willing to take her aside and give some fatherly advice.

Some of the lessons proved to be more painful than others. In order to play the slatternly Ellie May in *Tobacco Road* Gene had to endure itchy skin after being covered with layers of dirt. During the filming of *Belle Starr* she developed an allergy to makeup completely so what audiences saw on the screen was truly natural beauty.

While her career was taking off in 1941, relations with her parents took a nosedive when she eloped with fashion designer Oleg Cassini, a decision so spontaneous that one of Gene's earrings served as the wedding ring. It became apparent as soon as 1942 that this was a rocky marriage when a writer for *Screen Album* casually commented that "Mr. and Mrs. Cassini have had their share of spats …even of couple of downright fights!" Their arguments, separations, and reconciliations were spicy grist for the gossip mill throughout the rest of the decade.

The rift between Gene and her father grew deeper when she felt he betrayed all the Tierneys by being unfaithful and by securing a divorce. His infidelity coupled with the discovery that he had been secretly using her money from the family corporation created when she signed her first contract opened a wound that never healed.

After the bombing of Pearl Harbor, Oleg enlisted and Gene also did her part by participating in bond rallies, entertaining the troops, and by joining her husband to live at Fort Riley. Unfortunately, during all this

Laura inflames the passions of the three men in her life played by Clifton Webb, Dana Andrews, and Vincent Price.

mingling with the public, she contracted German measles at a time that coincided with her first pregnancy. Gene came to regard her daughter Darla, born deaf and retarded, as her war effort.

In her only film of 1943, *Heaven Can Wait*, she demonstrated that she could handle a lighter role as the true love of a womanizer played by Don Ameche. During the filming when she found the Lubitsch touch a bit heavy-handed, she asked the famous director not to keep shouting at her. When he told her that he was being paid to shout at her she replied, "Yes, and I'm being paid to take it—but not enough." Her response so amused Lubitsch that for the rest of the production he directed her with more tact and less thunder.

Gene also starred in just one motion picture in 1944 and if it had been the only film she ever made her contribution to the history of cinema would have been assured. Over sixty years after its release *Laura* remains one of the best mysteries Hollywood ever produced. Otto Preminger deftly directed Dana Andrews, Vincent Price, and Clifton Webb as a perfectly-cast trio of men in love with the "late" Laura Hunt who turns up very much alive. The enchanting melody by David Raksin which lingers long after the case is solved contributed no small part to the mood of the film. *Laura* is the how-to-do-it of whodunits.

Gene actually got her best-known role by default because Jennifer Jones turned it down. Perhaps Jones rejected the part because the character was upstaged by a portrait. In essence Gene had to sit in the wings during the first act of the movie while the men rhapsodized about Laura. It was to be expected that some people were disappointed when she finally did appear. Venus coming down from her pedestal would lose some of her allure, too.

Laura was indicative of the pattern Tierney's career had taken. Despite being the leading lady in each of her films, Gene had made little lasting impression. Her function on the screen seemed to be to look pretty and fall in love with Ameche, Tyrone Power, George Montgomery, and other handsome stars. What she needed was a role she could sink her teeth into like those meaty parts offered to Bette Davis and Barbara Stanwyck.

In 1945 Zanuck finally gave her a chance to shine. In *Leave Her to Heaven* Gene played a jealous neurotic whose ultimate destination was assuredly in the other direction. As Ellen Berent she was so possessive of her husband (Cornel Wilde) that she allowed his crippled brother to drown and risked personal injury to cause a miscarriage so she could have his attentions all to herself. When these measures drove him into the arms of her sister Ruth, Ellen planned her own suicide so it would look like Ruth had murdered her.

Few actresses ever portrayed a monomaniac better than Gene did in that film. For her performance, which one film historian called "frighteningly credible," she was nominated for best actress and at another time she might have won the Oscar, but not in the same year Joan Crawford got her best part as Mildred Pierce.

In two of her next three pictures Tierney was back with Tyrone Power playing the role she did as well as anyone, that of the spoiled or self-centered socialite. Gene's characterization of worldly Isabel Bradley in *The Razor's Edge* (1946) contrasts nicely with Tyrone's performance as a man who searches for a deeper meaning in life beyond money and fame.

That Wonderful Urge (1948) is a romantic comedy in which a newspaperman with the ponderous name of Thomas Jefferson Tyler ridicules rich Sara Farley in print and lives to regret it when she arranges to have him fired, but everyone in the theater knew it wouldn't be long before Tyler and Sara would give in to that wonderful urge called love.

Tyrone Power never appeared with an actress (not even Linda Darnell) who complemented him better than Gene Tierney. They looked good by themselves, but they were great together. Certain pairings make cinema magic: Lake and Ladd, Powell and Loy, Astaire and Rogers, Bogart and Bacall, Hepburn and Tracy. More than one critic noted what a congenial team Tierney and Power made. Even the cynics who sometimes complained about her lack of range as an actress could not deny that Gene Tierney added something special to a film just by being in it.

After the war only rarely as in the romantic fantasy *The Ghost and Mrs. Muir* and *Close to My Heart*, the story of a woman adopting a baby, did Gene have a role to rival that of Ellen Berent. She appeared in a variety of films during this time: crime melodramas (*Night and the City, Where the Sidewalk Ends*); comedies (*The Mating Season, On the Riviera*); a western (*The Secret of Convict Lake*); and historical epics (*Plymouth Adventure, The Egyptian*).

By the time Tierney finished *The Left Hand of God* opposite Humphrey Bogart in 1955 her days as a star were over. She appeared noticeably older in her role as a nurse. Bogart, recognizing that she was visibly upset and had trouble remembering her lines, told executives at Fox about it, but by then Gene was beyond the point where anyone in the industry could help her.

The disputes with her father, her divorce from Cassini, guilt over Darla's retardation, the breakup of her romance with Aly Khan, stress from work, the fading of the bloom of youth from her cheeks, depression over a career in decline; any or all of these reasons might have caused her nervous breakdown. In the sanitariums to which she was committed she underwent electroshock therapy and cold pack treatments that failed to do anything except drive her deeper into a shell. Only after she found an understanding female psychologist at the Menninger Clinic did she start to climb out of the chasm into which she had fallen.

Help on the road back also came in the form of a Texas oilman named W. Howard Lee who supplied the patience and concern she needed. They became engaged while she was still at Menninger's and were married in 1960.

In 1962 Gene returned to the screen with a small role in *Advise and Consent*. She enjoyed renewing acquaintances with Preminger, Fonda, Walter Pidgeon, Charles Laughton, and other veterans from the old studio days. But two years later when cast in virtually a bit part in *The Pleasure Seekers* starring Ann-Margret, Carol Lynley, and Pamela Tiffin, it was obvious that there was little future for her among the new generation of moviemakers and moviegoers.

Except for a couple television appearances in 1969 and 1980, Gene Tierney retired from acting and settled into the role of a socially prominent Houstonian. She remained active in charitable work (especially with retarded children) right up to the time of her death on November 6, 1991.

Invariably whenever I walk past her photograph on the wall I am drawn to it just as detective Mark McPherson was hypnotized by her portrait in *Laura*. I cannot pass it without hearing the words Johnny Mercer wrote for the theme song months after the movie first appeared in theaters. I try to look beyond those lips that protected the most sensual overbite in Hollywood, through those familiar yet distant eyes that would one day see all the horrors of the snake pit, under those exquisite cheekbones that made her the fairest of the fair, but there is no clue there.

Laura/Gene Tierney is still a mystery. I guess she will always be the face in the misty light, footsteps that you hear down the hall…

Joan Davis gets her reward as Queen of Comedy in January 1946 after winning the title for the third time. Maurice Kann of *Motion Picture Daily* and five-time King Bob Hope make it official.

What a Girl, What a Life!

LATE IN LIFE WHEN FANNY BRICE surveyed the field for an actress to play her on the screen, she had an impressive list to choose from including Judy Canova, Lucille Ball, Martha Raye, Eve Arden, Cass Daley, and Betty Hutton, yet she skipped over all those qualified candidates to select Joan Davis, an entertainer who, like herself, had started early on the bumpy road of show business and who had the bruises to prove it.

For Joan, born Madonna Josephine Davis, life in the performing arts began in 1910 when, at the age of three, she played Cupid and similar angelic parts in tableaus and amateur shows in her home state of Minnesota. At the tender age of six she learned that audiences can be fickle when she dodged tomatoes tossed her way after a dramatic recitation bombed. The following week when she returned to the same stage with a comedy routine and a novelty song, she received praise instead of produce. Shortly afterward when offered a spot in a vaudeville tour, Joan decided that, for her, the path of comedy leads but to the gravy.

She became a spotlight act on the Pantages Circuit billed as The Toy Comedienne. During her fourteen-minute nonstop routine she acted like a singing-dancing-joking dynamo who wouldn't let up until she collapsed at the end of her act as if her mainspring had run down.

No one who knew her well ever doubted that, behind all that clowning, Joan Davis had brainpower to spare and possessed a shrewd head for business. She gave early evidence of her intelligence when she graduated at the top of her class at Saint Paul's Mechanics Arts High School, a remarkable feat considering that she had been on the road until the age of sixteen.

But a diploma, even with a valedictorian's medal thrown in, meant dollar-a-day jobs and Joan, having fallen victim to the show business bug, had been "once bitten, no longer shy." She would take any job, from one-nighters at local lodge halls to parodying the hoochy kootchy dancers on carnival stages for the chuckles she craved and the bucks she needed to pay the rent.

In 1931 she married Serenus Wills, a member of what might be called the Pinky Lee school of baggy pants comics, and toured the country billed as Wills and Davis. By 1934, with baby Beverly in tow, the team reached California and three conclusions at the same time: vaudeville belonged in the past; movies represented the future; Joan alone had the talent needed to succeed in the present.

Davis recruited a coterie of vaudevillians to react favorably to her "impromptu" act done at a party to impress Mack Sennett. When the producer-director invited her for an audition, Davis, apprehensive that she might appear to be too old for the part, showed up in a Shirley Temple outfit complete with a short dress and a bow in her hair. Perhaps her risible getup impressed Sennett for he cast her in *Way Up Thar*, a 1935 comedy short about a hillbilly family wanting to break into radio. Davis made the most of her debut, unveiling one of the staples of her stage act, the falling dishes gag in which she raced back and forth with a constantly-shifting stack of dishes.

Her appearance in *Way Up Thar* led to bit parts in two pictures and eventually a contract with Twentieth Century-Fox in 1936. In two of the Fox films, *The Holy Terror* and *Time Out for Romance*, she showcased her "anything for a laugh" style by punching herself in the jaw as routinely as other actresses might slap themselves on the forehead for forgetting some detail.

She earned more screen time as secretaries in two Alice Faye musicals, *On the Avenue* and *Wake Up and Live*. Whether running in and out of offices carrying messages or flailing her arms as a dancer seemingly infected with hives, her small parts, ostensibly thrown in for comic relief, increasingly became more of an object of lobby conversation than the syrupy romantic story line or the songs as moviegoers began to wonder, "Who is that funny woman? When are we going to see more of her?"

The answer to both questions came quickly as she moved up to fifth billing in *The Great Hospital Mystery*. Sliding down corridors as if on skates and juggling bedpans like bean bags, Joan lived down to her name of Flossie Duff by landing on her backside several times. In perhaps the most telling still from any of her pictures, Davis, who later claimed with only mild exaggeration that she had taken 20,000 pratfalls in her career, is seen on the floor in a nurse's uniform with one leg still in the air from her latest tumble looking quizzically into the glacial expression of her supervisor (Jane Darwell) as if she is about to ask, "Did you get the license number of that truck?"

That her parts in films were allowing her more lines to say indicated producers at Fox realized that Davis had a rare way of delivering lines with just the right touch of sarcasm or self-doubt that yielded the maximum humor out of the minimum number of words. Joan, like Eve Arden, could draw bigger guffaws from a question than many comics could squeeze out of punch line.

Though her pliable legs continued to be featured in films, she began to be given novelty numbers like "I'm Olga from the Volga" in *Thin Ice* and "Help Wanted—Male" in *Sally, Irene and Mary*. Fox kingpin Darryl Zanuck, hoping that a little hoopla might go nicely with Joan's fatter parts, boldly predicted in publicity releases that Joan Davis would be the top comedienne in the country by the end of 1938.

Perhaps her best chance to live up to Zanuck's boast came as an accomplished kicker in *Hold That Co-ed* who won the critical football game for State University not with her foot but with her supple body as she scored the winning touchdown after battling winds like those blowing around the Goldwyn set of *The Hurricane*. One critic aptly described her as taking off "into space in an array of limbs and arms resembling nothing other than an octopus taking a flying test and ends by falling on her caboose with a crash that… shakes the stadium."

Although each role allowed Davis to toss in snappy comebacks, physical comedy remained her bread and butter whether it involved disrupting office routine by fumbling with envelopes in *Day-Time Wife* or turning a house into a hovel in *Too Busy to Work*. Even when taking a break between films to perform in nightclubs, she continued to sock it to herself both on the chin and on her derriere to complement her singing and dancing because she believed audiences expected such antics and, as she often averred, "a good fall always gets a laugh."

After being used in only two pictures in 1941, Davis refused to renew her contract in hopes of finding better roles as a freelancer, and she rarely had a better one than her first part as radio screamer Camille Brewster who helped Abbott and Costello *Hold That Ghost*. Whether jesting with Costello by the car, dancing clumsily with him in the haunted house, or taking part in the moving candle routine by the window, Davis proved convincingly that she was the screen's top comedienne and that she deserved starring roles even if she had to step down to Columbia and Republic to get them.

Movies like *Two Latins from Manhattan*, *Two Señoritas from Chicago*, *Yokel Boy*, *Beautiful But Broke*, and *Kansas City Kitty* do not play revival houses, earn spots on the syllabuses of college film courses, or form the core of museum retrospectives, but these B pictures filled the bottom half of double bills nicely, provided a pleasant hour of jokes and songs at theaters, and added $50,000 per film to Joan's bank account.

In the 1943 comedy *Around the World* Davis played a man-chaser, a carryover from the character given to her on *The Rudy Vallee Show* and *The Sealtest Village Store*. She quickly proved wrong the doubters who wondered if a comedienne who relied heavily on slapstick could succeed on radio with routines such as taking the songs "Hey, Daddy" and "My Jim" and developing the lyrics into a monologue. In 1943 she was also voted radio's top comedienne in a poll conducted by the Scripps-Howard newspapers.

Davis had her own show on CBS which ran at various times from 1946 to 1950 under the titles *Joanie's Tea Room*, *Joan Davis Time*, and *Leave it to Joan*. The program's opening lyric played on the same theme often seen in her movies: "Joan ain't got nobody."

What Joan did have was top-flight announcers Harry Von Zell and Bob LeMond, a premier bandleader in Paul Weston, a popular singer in Andy Russell, and the able support of Shirley Mitchell, Verna Felton, and Willard Waterman. And, of course, she had mastered the art of delivering a line with just the right inflection, milking a gag down to the last drop. Joan possessed a distinctive voice, a sort of cross between a quiver and a squeal that sometimes left her lips as a squawk.

Unfortunately, her writers saddled her with jokes that might have been rejected as being too corny for *The National Barn Dance*. Upon being told she should admit the obvious Joan said, "Harry, open the door. Obvious wants to get in." When asked if she knew what a rift is she answered, "Oh, sure. When two rafts get married, they have a little rift." Listeners at home who had seen her on the screen knew that Davis spoke such wheezes with a straight face, which may have mirrored their expressions.

That Davis overcame weak dialogue and scripts which hung on tenuous premises by assuming various guises and bringing moribund lines to life by sheer will power should have surprised no one for in almost every movie she made after 1941 she rose above the level of her material. In 1942 and 1943 she topped *Motion Picture Daily*'s poll as top comedienne. In two comedies for Universal, *She Gets Her Man* (1945) and *She Wrote the Book* (1946), Davis punched some life into the threadbare whodunit and mistaken identity plots. Universal might have added one more picture to describe what these profitable quickies did for the studio: *She Brought Home the Bacon*.

Joan teamed with Eddie Cantor in a pair of musical comedies for RKO, *Show Business* and *If You Knew Susie*, that remain enjoyable for the banter between the stars, the familiar Cantor standards, the show business milieu, and casts brimming with wonderful supporting players like Fritz Feld, Ellen Corby, George Chandler, Isabel Randolph, and Sig Ruman.

Character actors comprised her only support in *Traveling Saleswoman* (1950) and *Harem Girl* (1952), Joan's final picture. At the age of forty-

Joan gets her man in this 1945 release featuring William Gargan.

six she seemed more than a trifle old to be masquerading as a harem girl, though she still had a knack for losing her balance on any shiny floor and for getting in more chase scenes than a Keystone Cop.

Realizing her opportunities in motion pictures would continue to diminish, Davis turned her attention to television. In *I Married Joan* (1952-1955), a series owned by Joan Davis Productions, she played Joan Stevens who, though married and in no need to run after men, found herself up to her elbows in crises no less involved or hilarious than the ones she confronted in films.

Jim Backus played her husband, Judge Bradley Stevens, whose respectable standing in the community was constantly jeopardized by the embarrassing predicaments Joan found herself in every week. In a unique bit of casting Joan's daughter played her younger sister, prompting Davis to tell the press, "I always promised Beverly a sister, but neither of us ever imagined it would be me."

During those early years of television it might have been difficult to determine if Joan was doing a Lucy or vice versa for what harebrained schemes Mrs. Stevens hatched on Wednesdays for NBC seemed no less misguided or amusing than the havoc wrecked by Señora Ricardo Mondays on CBS. If Lucy could disrupt the routine in a candy factory, Joan would adopt the philosophy of "anything you can louse up, I can mess up more" by filling her kitchen with popcorn.

Knowing how Joan threw her body into her work, the writers for the show frequently placed her in slapstick situations where she would be dashing back and forth serving dinners in different rooms or battling a dryer that seemed intent on sucking her inside or inadvertently dismantling a roomful of furniture more efficiently than a demolition crew.

If *I Married Joan* achieved some success (the program became the third most popular network comedy show during its second season), the credit belonged chiefly to Joan Davis. Claiming "I never worked as hard in my life," she outlined a frantic schedule that had her virtually living at the General Services Studio where, as executive producer and star, she found herself "working on three programs at the same time, making the first study of the script to be shot next week, looking at the rushes of the film shot yesterday, and sitting in on the final cutting of the show before that."

Although Davis claimed at the time that the breakneck pace and the demands of knockabout comedy relieved her of anxieties that might have led to ulcers, she didn't calculate the damage that vigorous lifestyle was doing to her heart and the rest of her body.

Perhaps what motivated Davis to keep going was the fear that her work in films would be forgotten and that her only claim to fame would be her work in television. She believed that the shows had to be good "because they are my legacy both as a comedienne and a businesswoman."

One legacy of *I Married Joan* is a theme song that remains one of the most infectious from the 1950s. All people who have not even seen the program in decades have to hear is the first four notes of the catchy music and they begin singing, "I married Joan, what a girl, what a whirl, what a life/Oh, I married Joan, what a mind, love is blind, what a wife."

After *I Married Joan* left the air in April 1955, Davis made a pilot for a proposed ABC series about a woman astronaut, but the show didn't get off the ground. She retired in 1958 after the pilot for *Joan of Arkansas* never made it to the air, confessing "I've been afraid all along that I just wouldn't be funny or pretty enough for the long-time big time. I've kept going on a mixture of gall, guts, and gumption." And, she might have added, a gift for making people laugh.

Joan Davis, who died on May 22, 1961 at the age of fifty-three after suffering a heart attack, never came close to playing Fanny Brice in a movie. No matter. Every time we see Joan Davis on big screen or small we know who the funny girl really is.

Bankhead at zenith in *The Little Foxes* with Charles Dingle.

Legendary Lady

JUST THE MENTION OF HER NAME is all it takes to start the memories rolling in. Of a voice that might be described as Dixie foghorn. Of a walk that was all shoulders and arms. Of an actress so flamboyant to the core of her soul that no one could tell where the performer left off and the person began. Of the woman whose plaque in the pantheon of show business needs only one word to distinguish her from all others: Tallulah.

As befits a legend, Tallulah Bankhead entered stage right in Huntsville, Alabama on January 31, 1902 as part of a family that had long been basking in the political limelight, including a grandfather and uncle who served in the Senate and a father who rose to prominence as Speaker of the House of Representatives. She shared the mark of distinction with her paternal grandmother, who had been named for Tallulah Falls, Georgia. By the time she was a teenager Tallulah had survived a number of childhood diseases that had settled in her throat and chest, giving her a unique husky voice to go along with her singular name.

There have been legions of starry-eyed girls who have looked through movie magazines, dreamt of a career in Hollywood, entered contests, and never got out of the batter's box; Tallulah was the one in a million who left home on her very first swing. Because her photograph appeared in *Picture Play* magazine, she won a small part in a movie and a trip to New York. Through the influence of her father she landed a walk-on in a Broadway play. Even at the tender age of sixteen she knew that acting was what she wanted to do for the rest of her life. Tallulah was more than stage-struck; she confessed to being "consumed by a fever to be famous, even infamous."

Bankhead had no formal training so she learned on the job and it didn't hurt to keep her ears open after hours either. Just by being around Alexander Woollcott, Dorothy Parker, Robert Benchley, and other wits of the Algonquin Round Table, she cultivated an air of sophistication beyond her years. One evening in a theater with Woollcott she amused her companion with a Parkeresque assessment of the play they were watching: "There's less here than meets the eye."

Before her twenty-first birthday she was already calling everyone "dahling" and using *mad* and *divine* to describe everything from hats to cats. To some people she came across as being artificial, to others Tallulah was just being Tallulah. She once said, "Nobody can be exactly like me. Sometimes I even have trouble doing it."

Charles Cochran, an English impresario who saw her doing stunts, miming, and being the life of the party one night in 1922, arranged to have her come to London to perform in *The Dancers*. During the play's run of ten months Tallulah became the toast of the town as she attracted a fan club of Gallery Girls who emulated her style of dress and manner of speaking. To many British working girls Tallulah symbolized insouciance and had more of the desirable "it" than Clara Bow.

Although there were more misses than hits among her early plays, Bankhead felt on top of the world and happier than she would be the rest of her life. She thrived on publicity, controversy, and scandal. People expected her to be outrageous so she obliged them by calling out to men across crowded rooms with provocative questions such as "Don't you recognize me with my clothes on?" The maxim that guided her actions appeared to be "I don't care what they say as long as they talk about me."

In 1927 an English magazine listed Bankhead among the ten most remarkable women in the country. By then the cheering of her fans started even before she appeared and she provoked more applause by turning cartwheels and dancing so frenetically it looked as if she was trying to throw her legs all the way into the balcony. Almost every play contained a scene of Tallulah in lingerie which brought more people to the theater and more réclame for the star.

A contract from Paramount lured her back to America in 1930. The studio bosses considered her exotic enough to turn into another Greta Garbo or Marlene Dietrich. They placed her in vehicles that played upon her notorious reputation and selected the racy titles *Tarnished Lady* and *My Sin*, but in these films she came across as too much Dietrich and not enough Bankhead.

In *The Devil and the Deep* (1932) she played wife to naval commander Charles Laughton and lover to crew member Gary Cooper. She wasn't awed by her co-stars; in fact, before shooting began her greeting to Laughton was "Dahling, I hear you're going to be in *my* picture."

Bankhead headed for Broadway after her contract expired with the hope that the stage successes in England would transfer across the Atlantic, but circumstances conspired against her. *Forsaking All Others*, a production in which Tallulah had invested some of her own money, had the misfortune to open the same day the banks closed in 1933. During rehearsals for *Jezebel* she became ill and underwent a hysterectomy. She had to leave *Dark Victory* when she developed an infected lip. When a producer, hoping to stop her downhill slide, confidently promised that he would let her open in a theater that had never had a flop, Bankhead tartly replied, "Don't worry. I'll fix that."

Her luck didn't improve when she was bypassed for the plum role in *Gone with the Wind*. She wanted the part of Scarlett O'Hara more than any other in her career, but she didn't have the fresh-faced, coquettish look of a Vivien Leigh. That grim disappointment coupled with the acrimonious reviews for a Broadway version of *Antony and Cleopatra* which starred Tallulah and her new husband, John Emery, brought her fortunes to a low ebb and her carousing to a high tide.

Her unseemly behavior at parties often became the chief topic of breakfast-table conversations in New York and Hollywood. As she was being shown the door at one of Dorothy Parker's social gatherings the hostess asked, "Has Whistler's mother left yet?" The next day Bankhead, after looking at herself in a mirror, told Parker, "The less I look like Whistler's mother the night before, the more I look like her the morning after."

For years Tallulah and even her critics complained that she had not been given a play worthy of her talents. In 1939 just when it seemed like she had touched bottom she landed her best role in Lillian Hellman's *The Little Foxes*. Rapacious, merciless, and calculating as Regina Giddens, she was the talk of Broadway for over a year.

The influential critics who had torpedoed her previous work rolled out a litany of superlatives to describe her performance. "A superb example of mature acting that is fully under control" rhapsodized Brooks Atkinson of the *New York Times* before averring that her Regina "is not only the finest thing she has done in this country but brilliant acting according to any standards."

But even during this triumph Tallulah found a way to toss in a bitter apple of discord. After her suggestion to do a benefit performance on behalf of Finnish refugees had been rejected by both producer and playwright, she took the rebuff personally, gave them the silent treatment, and did not mend fences with Hellman until they met at Truman Capote's black-and-white ball in 1966. Tallulah jested at her scars but felt the wounds deeply.

In *Pentimento*, her "book of portraits," Hellman recounted how the feisty Bankhead argued issues to the point of absurdity such as the night Dashiell Hammett told her that he disliked people who use drugs. Tallulah's response: "You don't know what you're talking about. I tell you cocaine isn't habit-forming and I know because I've been taking it for years."

Bankhead's reputation for being temperamental was enhanced by her behavior in her next play, *Clash by Night*. She clashed by day with Lee J. Cobb who received better reviews than she did and with producer Billy Rose who dared to put "Billy Rose Presents" ahead of her name on the marquee. It didn't matter if the setting happened to be a party, a play, or a movie set; Tallulah had to be center stage or she started clawing. Emery could hardly be blamed for retreating to a neutral corner and then climbing out of the ring in 1941 after just four years of marriage.

Bankhead came out with her head high for the next round which was *The Skin of Our Teeth*. In Thornton Wilder's drama of time and space she assumed four different parts expertly and won the New York Critics Circle Award. As usual, she exercised her prerogative to be contrary by ignoring director Elia Kazan's instructions, throwing tantrums regularly, and literally taking matters into her own hands when, after her request for more room near the orchestra pit where one scene took place was denied, she began removing the seats herself. Bickering with the cast onstage and backstage vituperations regarding costumes, dressing rooms, and sets led her to drop out of the production before it left New York. Tallulah gloated when the tour of the play flopped dismally or, in her words, "was an epic of disaster."

For Bankhead the stage always represented a love-hate relationship. She welcomed the thrill of applause but dreaded the drudgery of repeating the same lines night after night. To her the movies didn't even offer the attraction of a live audience, just the ennui of sitting around sets and doing retakes. But the studios paid well so when she needed money in 1943 she returned to Hollywood.

For $75,000 she agreed to be one of the nine people adrift in Alfred Hitchcock's *Lifeboat* (released in 1944). As Connie Porter, a cagey journalist complete with mink and typewriter, Bankhead matched wits with a Nazi and helped the other survivors of a sinking through their crisis. During the filming repeated dousing of the cast to simulate conditions in a rocky lifeboat made Tallulah madder than a wet hen and also helped bring on a first-class case of pneumonia. For her efforts she was honored by the New York Screen Critics as best actress of the year, but it galled her to be completely overlooked for the Academy Award, a slight she blamed on her status as a renegade, one who didn't play by the studio rules.

The following year in *A Royal Scandal* she was Catherine the Great before the cameras and Tallulah the Terrible when the filming stopped. She did not get along with Anne Baxter and turned bellicose when Ernst Lubitsch accused her of stealing a scene from the younger actress. She

Bankhead temporarily at rest with John Hodiak in *Lifeboat*.

sulked in her tent like a foul-mouthed Achilles, threatened to quit, and gave the impression that Lubitsch had bullied her, although Billy Rose's response to the same accusation years before stated her position in disagreements more accurately: "How can you bully Niagara Falls?" It took an avalanche of conciliatory words from another director, Otto Preminger, to convince Bankhead to return to the set and complete the picture.

It is a wonder she listened to anyone's advice. After an interview with her, magician Fred Keating said, "I've just spent an hour talking with Tallulah for a few minutes." Lyricist and MGM publicist Howard Dietz felt that "a day away from Tallulah is like a month in the country." Those who swore that "Tallulah is her own best friend; no one else would want to be" were more perspicacious than spiteful.

Soured by the experience of *A Royal Scandal*, Bankhead virtually turned her back on the movies and returned to the stage in Jean Cocteau's *The Eagle Has Two Heads*, stunning audiences with her opening speech, a seventeen-minute soliloquy. Behind the curtain she was still exerting influence to get her way by making certain that a young Marlon Brando, whose method acting grated against her affected style, was dismissed before opening night.

In 1947 and 1948 she appeared in Noel Coward's *Private Lives* both in New York and on tour. She meshed well with co-star Donald Cook with whom she was romantically involved at the time but browbeat understudy Barbara Baxley with petulant demands to the point where at a party, after being rudely bumped several times by a tipsy Tallulah, Baxley retaliated by pushing her tormentor, who landed indecorously to the accompaniment of breaking bottles and glasses. If that scene played out as if it had been scripted, it should have surprised no one who witnessed it because wherever Tallulah happened to be *that* was her stage.

Topping Tallulah was an art not many people mastered, although long-time colleague Estelle Winwood emerged from any number of skirmishes with at least a draw. Once during a performance of *Here Today* when the phone rang at the wrong time, Bankhead quickly batted the boo-boo toward her friend by ordering her to "Answer the phone." Estelle tossed the hot potato back by picking up the receiver, pausing a moment, and then saying, "It's for you."

But the Huntsville Hurricane won more bouts than she lost, including a TKO over Procter & Gamble, their advertising agency, and the radio networks in 1949 over a jingle with the line "I'm Tallulah, the tube of Prell." Bankhead, who had zealously avoided testimonials, sought damages for what she considered unauthorized use of her name. The defendants claimed the song could have referred to any Tallulah. The plaintiff argued that there was only one Tallulah. The case was settled out of court with Bankhead pocketing less than the million dollars she wanted but deriving satisfaction from having sent the offensive lyrics to the showers, down the drain, and off the air.

While starring in *Private Lives* she told a reporter "I'm Tallulah in the play and I'm not ashamed of it. Just Tallulah and that's all." That she had been playing herself for a long time was obvious, although her flair for comedy came as surprise to many. Fans of *Duffy's Tavern* and *The Fred Allen Show* had heard a sampling of her wit, but it wasn't until 1950 that she was unleashed in full force on radio.

The Big Show, a ninety-minute extravaganza of drama, music, and comedy that promised more if not better entertainment than could be found on upstart television, featured Bankhead as mistress of ceremonies. She introduced various acts and joked with Groucho Marx, Jimmy Durante, Ethel Merman, Fred Allen, and other guests about everything about that other medium "where nothing is well-done" to her habits and foibles. Veteran writers Goodman Ace and Selma Diamond often fed visiting jesters lines that took aim at the easy targets of Tallulah's bass growl and formidable presence. On one show after she barked at Bob Hope to

"Leave the stage until I call for you," the comedian shot back with "Don't you lower your voice to me. I knew you when you were Louis Calhern."

For "breathing new life into radio" the New York Newspaper Guild presented their Page One Award to the woman who loved her new billing as Queen of the Kilocycles. To the loyal listeners laughing with her and the readers enjoying her lively, best-selling autobiography it was Tallulah and not Cecil B. DeMille's Oscar-winning film that was the greatest show on earth in 1952.

When *The Big Show* closed up after two years, she went back home—to the theater. Bankhead believed that Tennessee Williams wrote all of his plays with her in mind so she eagerly accepted the roles of Blanche DuBois in *A Streetcar Named Desire* and Flora Goforth in *The Milk Train Doesn't Stop Here Anymore*. A critic for the *New York Telegraph* considered her Blanche "one of the most extraordinary shattering performances of our time" while others thought she was posing more than emoting. Parading before the public as faded or drugged actresses was not difficult for by that time Tallulah was truly playing Tallulah.

And, as Tallulah, she still had a knack for being quotable. After viewing *The Fugitive Kind*, the screen adaptation of *Orpheus Descending*, she reportedly told Williams, "Dahling, they've absolutely ruined your perfectly dreadful play." Even if some of the anecdotes told about her are apocryphal, they live on because they fit her character. "Yes," those who knew her would say, "that sounds like Tallulah."

Other stories, those involving exhibitionism, inebriation, and scurrilous tirades, ceased to be amusing with the increasing frequency of such antics. Efforts to be as shocking in her fifties as she was in her twenties seemed merely pathetic attempts to get her name in the papers. Her standard response to the question "Are you Tallulah Bankhead?" asked by people she met on the street, "I'm what's left of her, dahling," contained more truth than she realized.

Seekers of curiosities from the 1960s will find two entries for Bankhead. One is a British film called *Fanatic* (1965) which became *Die! Die! My Darling!* in America to capitalize on one of her pet names. Playing a religious zealot who terrorized her dead son's fiancée, she needed little makeup to look like a harridan. Though becoming hard of hearing, her eyesight and wit were still sharp enough to observe that "They used to shoot Shirley Temple through gauze. Now they should shoot me through linoleum."

As the Dragon Lady on *Batman* in 1967 her exaggerated mannerisms seemed perfect for the one show that encouraged overacting with dialogue ending in exclamation marks. One can easily imagine her, in or out of character, telling Adam West/Batman, "Your cape is absolutely divine, but that ghastly leotard will have to go. Mauve just isn't your color, dahling." A friend who had urged her to be on the program told her it would camp. "Don't tell me about camp," she snapped. "I invented it."

She probably did. She certainly invented herself and made it hard for us to tell the inventor from the invention. Bankhead was a show by herself and the motto "the show must go on" kept her seeking the footlights even when her body was giving her the hook from the wings. She needed lungfuls of oxygen to keep emphysema at bay so she could appear on *The Merv Griffin Show* during her last year but seemed determined to make herself visible "so everyone won't think I'm dead."

She continued to burn the candle at both ends until the lights were snuffed out December 12, 1968 after years of self-indulgence with cigarettes, drugs, and alcohol along with peculiar eating habits like devouring ice cream sodas for breakfast. Not long before the end came she said, "The only thing I regret about my past is the length of it. If I had my life to live over, I'd make the same mistakes—only sooner."

Along the way impetuous Tallulah never stopped to consider whether it might be a mistake to kiss President Truman's hand at Madison Square Garden before predicting victory over Thomas Dewey or to drink champagne from a slipper in front of reporters in London or to pull Garbo's eyelashes to see if they were real or to scream "I told you so!" to the crowd after Joe Louis knocked out Max Schmeling in the first round or to publicly call Joe McCarthy "a disgrace to the nation" at a time when the powerful senator could still wreck lives with a slur. Life couldn't pass her by; it had to go full speed just to keep up with her.

The wag who called Tallulah Bankhead "more of an act than an actress" was right, and she has been a tough act to follow ever since she first raised eyebrows by cartwheeling down the streets of Montgomery back in 1910. Through all of the ups and downs of her tempestuous life she was never anything less than the incomparable Tallulah.

The best tonic for laughs: Lucille Ball.

Life with Lucy

IF A PSYCHIATRIST CONDUCTING A WORD-ASSOCIATION TEST with a patient used the terms *tonic, grapes, footprints, chocolate, starch,* and *loving cup* and received the same four-letter response each time, the doctor might mutter, "This patient seems to have a fixation with someone named Lucy."

If having images of Lucille Ball entangled in ludicrous situations on the brain is symptomatic of neurosis, most Americans are candidates for the couch because it is difficult to imagine a time when she has not been part of the national consciousness.

Lucille Désirée Ball, who first appeared on life's stage on August 6, 1911 in Jamestown, New York, gave one of her first acting performances as a toddler tied to a metal clothesline by her busy mother, who found the tot trying to con a milkman into releasing her. As Lucy grew older, she enjoyed playing fantasy games with an imaginary pal she called Sassafrassa, engaging in dress-up skits with friends, and watching Buster Keaton and Charlie Chaplin cavort on the screen.

Lucille became involved in theater at school where she organized the Dramatics Club. Regarding her work on *Charley's Aunt* she recalled that "I played the lead, directed it, sold the tickets, printed the posters, and hauled furniture to the school for scenery and props." Ball might have added that she also supplied the audience because her mother, DeDe, always a strong supporter of her daughter's career, sat out front laughing louder than anyone else as she would do years later from her choice seat during the filming of *I Love Lucy*.

A sure sign of having acting fever settled upon Lucille every time she watched vaudeville performers and said to herself, "I want to be up there." At the tender age of fifteen, with the financial backing of DeDe, Lucy entered a dramatics school in New York City and, although it was a case of "too much, too soon" and she had to return home a few weeks later, she already had the spunk of the title character in *Wildcat* which she would play many years later who, in her signature song, "Hey, Look Me Over," could have been singing Ball's credo: "Whenever you're down and out, the only way is up."

The "Look out, world, here I come" part followed shortly thereafter when Lucille forsook Jamestown and returned to the big city, determined to do any kind of work, be it dispensing sodas at a drugstore or modeling clothes, until her big break came along. Because Lucy bore a resemblance to Constance Bennett, she consented to have her hair peroxided, as if to adopt another motto: "Dye, if you must this young brown head if one day cameras will shoot this fresh white face."

Working as a model for Hattie Carnegie, it was not long before that face, seen in an ad as a Chesterfield cigarette girl, led to an offer to go to Hollywood. She can be spotted serving as some of the pulchritude supporting Eddie Cantor in *Roman Scandals* (1933), one of a series of uncredited roles that had Lucy adapting the lyric the Ricardos and Mertzes would sing when they headed West by taking it one step further: "California, Here I Stay."

Lucille, never a talented dancer or singer, grew tired of strutting in showgirl parts and doubling for Constance Bennett at United Artists, found little improvement at Columbia, and finally settled upon a contract near the end of 1934 with RKO where she learned more from watching Irene Dunne and Katharine Hepburn act than she did playing background scenery for Fred Astaire and Ginger Rogers in *Roberta* and *Top Hat*. By the time she appeared in *I Dream Too Much* in 1935 Ball had earned enough stripes to merit a name in the credits and a spoken line worth remembering: "Culture is making my feet hurt."

The first film that foreshadowed the manic Lucy Ricardo, *That Girl from Paris*, found her skidding across a slick dance floor on soapy shoes. The painful pratfalls she took probably caused her to wonder, "Where is Constance Bennett when I need her to double for me?" The reviews called her "a find" and, for the first time, used the term that later became her occupational title: comedienne.

As Judy in *Stage Door*, the young lady with the ready quip who chose marriage over a career, Lucille could not be overlooked, but even a boarding house reach left little to grab after noted scene-stealers Katharine Hepburn, Ginger Rogers, and Eve Arden were through feasting.

She moved up to second billing in *Go Chase Yourself* (1938) as the wife of Joe Penner and in two related films starring Jack Oakie, *The Affairs of Annabel* and *Annabel Takes a Tour*. The publicity stunts that Oakie, as a zealous press agent, forced plucky Annabel Allison into included assuming the diverse roles of maid, aristocrat, and jailbird.

After appearing in seven films in 1938 including *Room Service*, a movie that wasted the talents of both the Marx Brothers and Lucille, Ball began to wonder if the groove she was in had become a rut. Her suspicion that she had become a tool of the studio deepened when called upon to read for the part of Scarlett O'Hara before producer David Selznick. Knowing that she stood little chance of landing the coveted role in *Gone with the Wind*, Ball arrived wet from a rainstorm and, bolstered by a glass of brandy, delivered her test before Selznick in fine Lucy Ricardo style: from her knees.

Lucille got back on her feet and continued to grind them out for RKO. In *Dance, Girl, Dance* (1940) she added some bumping to the grinding by performing an animated but limited striptease while singing, "Mother, What Do I Do Now?" During the filming of this movie she met Desi Arnaz, a young Cuban who would be in her next picture, *Too Many Girls*, which, given his wandering eye, might have been an appropriate title for his autobiography.

It was not exactly love at first sight because Desi's first glimpse of Lucy came after her catfight on a set with Maureen O'Hara in which she looked beaten and bedraggled, but within weeks the couple became fodder for Hollywood's gossip columnists and by November 1940 they were married.

While Desi struggled to find an identity so he would not be known as Mr. Ball, Lucille battled for better parts in RKO features. *Look Who's Laughing* (1941) served as a showcase for radio's stellar comedy stars Edgar Bergen, Fibber McGee and Molly, and the Great Gildersleeve, but did not advance Ball's career a whit and *Valley of the Sun*, a dull western, almost sank it.

In *The Big Street* (1942), a Damon Runyon tale, she flourished in the emotional role of Gloria Lyons, a canny manipulator who selfishly used her paralysis to suit her own purposes. Ball considered this film, in which she received better reviews than co-star Henry Fonda, one of her favorites, perhaps because it validated her status as an actress.

The size of Lucille's contract with RKO and her dissatisfaction with parts she had been given made a switch to another studio inevitable so she welcomed an offer from Metro-Goldwyn-Mayer. For her first MGM feature, *Du Barry Was a Lady*, she became a Technicolor redhead and stayed a technical redhead for the rest of her life. With salary in her pocket, she put some celery in her mouth and wrestled with a headdress (not unlike the getup she donned in the "Lucy Gets in Pictures" episode of *I Love Lucy*) as she romped with Red Skelton, providing the comic highlight of the film.

But *Best Foot Forward*, a revision of the *Annabel* stories, showed anything but Lucille's best and in *Meet the People* audiences met the same Lucy playing another version of another actress whose career needed a boost. By this time Ball began to suspect that she was indeed playing herself.

Even though Lucy was seemingly ignored by the MGM brass who continued to place her in routine fare like *Two Smart People* and *Easy to Wed*, the critics were taking notice, calling her "a superb farceuse" and hailing the byplay of Ball and Keenan Wynn in the latter film as proof "that they are the funniest comic team on screen just now—and by a wide margin."

By 1946 Lucille realized that MGM would continue to parade her flaming red hair in color musicals while dubbing her singing voice or else pair her in B+ comedies with supporting actors like Wynn and William Gaxton so she decided to freelance. But lackluster pictures for Universal (*Lover Come Back*), United Artists (*Lured*), and Columbia (*Her Husband's Affairs*) should have convinced Ball that in that medium she was likely going to be just that, medium: never abominable but never a star of the first magnitude.

A welcome change of pace came in the form of an offer from producer Herbert Kenwith to star in the Edgar Rice play *Dream Girl*. In the title role of a daydreaming bookstore operator whose vivid imagination carried her from one fictitious crisis to another, Lucille blossomed, earning praise for her ability to mix pathos and sharp-edged repartee. The supreme accolade came from Rice himself who declared that, of all the productions he had seen of *Dream Girl*, "the only actress whose performance really delighted me was Lucille Ball."

Although *Dream Girl* played for just a few months on the West Coast, the spontaneity of live performances triggered a special gear in Lucille's mechanism that raised her to another level. In the summer of 1948 a vehicle came rolling up her driveway that provided the very ingredients she thrived on and which motion pictures had not offered: an audience and a role in which all the action centered on her.

Ball, who had appeared on radio back in 1938 on Jack Haley's program and had also been heard on *Lux Radio Theatre* and *The Abbott and Costello Show* among others, accepted an offer to star in a comedy series tentatively titled *Mr. and Mrs. Cugat*, based on a book of the same name by Isabel Scott Rorick. During the growing pains of this situation comedy, three changes occurred: Richard Denning replaced Lee Bowman as the male lead, the Cugats became Liz and George Cooper, and the title of the series became *My Favorite Husband*.

A young writing team of Madelyn Pugh and Bob Carroll Jr., mentored by radio veteran Jess Oppenheimer, developed a winning game plan that proved to be successful both on *My Favorite Husband* and later when they followed Lucy to television: give the ball to Ball and let her run her with it. By putting Lucille in situations that built toward absurdity and by letting the gifted actress grow along with kooky Liz and later into loony Lucy, the writers mined a lode of talent that had been untapped.

Liz Cooper, one half of the couple "who live together and like it," had her heart in the right place, usually on her sleeve, as she meddled in her husband's affairs. Her attempts to convince Rudolph Atterbury (Gale Gordon) to raise George's salary through a series of ruses portended the guises Lucy Ricardo would adopt to further her interests on *I Love Lucy*, just as her hilarious efforts to teach Iris Atterbury (Bea Benaderet) how to drive and corral a runaway car that started out behind them, passed them, and then backed into their front bumper is a delectable slice of audio slapstick that works best on radio but which would not have been beyond the machinations of Lucy and Ethel.

Ball's skill at milking a situation for every possible laugh was apparent even when she could not be seen by the audience at home. On televi-

Richard Denning between his radio wife (Lucy) and real spouse (Evelyn Ankers).

sion Lucy could puff out her cheeks and widen her eyes to indicate she had squeezed herself into an old dress that no longer fit her, but on radio to get the same effect she forced the words past her larynx in gasps while holding her breath lest the zipper give way.

In *My Favorite Husband* Ball also was mastering the art of varying her delivery to match her character's mood. If Liz felt upbeat, her tone glided toward giddy such as when she said to Iris upon being passed by the Atterbury's automobile, "You drive much better when you're not in the car." When on the defensive, however, after Iris accused her of putting on weight in the hips, Ball's voice assumed a note of icy sarcasm in a retort delivered with an air of finality: "I prefer to think of it as a little avoirdupois in the back of my lap."

Besides slamming the punch lines home, Lucy was developing her own defensive bag of tricks. The cry, alligator tears of the first water, which sometimes flowed out with a "You don't love me anymore" feeler, disappeared as soon as Liz/Lucy got her way or saw that the gambit had failed.

The "spider voice," a term employed to describe Ball's reaction as Little Miss Muffet after seeing a spider during a commercial, became Lucy's double take. The sound, which emerged from her lips as a "Yeeeooough," generally followed the extraction of her foot from her mouth, as in the scene at a posh restaurant when a waiter informed Liz that she had just selected from the French menu an order of "Closed on Monday."

Ball was already working on her curve ball, a change of direction in mid-sentence executed frequently in the Ricardo apartment, while warming up in the bullpen of the Cooper's living room. After George suspected that a stogie found in an ashtray had been planted there to make him jealous Liz declared, "It was not a phony cigar. It was a real one and a real man was here and how did you find out it was a fake?"

Despite the moderate success of *My Favorite Husband*, Lucy's escapades in films made during this period, including *Miss Grant Takes Richmond* in which she mishandled everything from typewriters to jackhammers, and *The Fuller Brush Girl* who got down and dirty in a smokestack and then came clean while stretched across some clotheslines, indicated clearly that she had to be seen to be fully appreciated.

Desi and Lucy, who had toured the country doing an act featuring antics with a cello and interruptions of his musical performances, decided to use their Desilu Productions to package a comedy series based upon the concept of Arnaz playing a Cuban singer and Lucy being Lucy. William Frawley and Vivian Vance were brought in as neighbors Fred and Ethel Mertz to help stir the plots concocted by Pugh and Carroll.

Regardless of what direction the story flowed, Lucy had to have her ham-handed fingers in it. Even if the title of the episode was "Ricky Loses His Temper" and Ricardo released one of his Spanish imprecations like "*Miraquetienecosalamujeresta!*," the cause of his outburst had to be one of Lucy's ill-conceived notions.

I Love Lucy was not an immediate success, but within a month of its debut on October 15, 1951 most Americans who owned televisions were tuning in their fuzzy sets to CBS on Mondays to find out what Lucy would do next.

Lucille Ball adapted quickly to her new playground by either refining her old shtick or by adding new tricks to her bag of sight gags. She turned her plaintive cry into a laughable wail by crinkling up her face like a sponge and pushed across her spider voice by extruding her lips like a horse that had just eaten a sour apple. Her skills as a pantomimist, lauded most notably in the mirror routine with Harpo Marx performed in 1955, were actually on display almost from the beginning of the series in bits such as her open-mouthed reactions to overheard tidbits and struggles with inanimate objects that seemed to have a life of their own like the yeasty loaf of bread which emerged from her oven with as much force as a battering ram.

By the end of the first season *I Love Lucy* had become the most popular program on TV. Lucy's pregnancy during the following year, far from hampering the show, was turned into the focal point of a number of amusing episodes.

One of the attributes of early television comedies also became its chief disadvantage: long seasons of thirty or more episodes provided loads of chuckles but devoured lots of ideas. If Lucy became locked in a freezer in the spring, seeing her entrapped in handcuffs in the fall was still funny because of Ball's affinity for physical comedy but it may also have seemed a bit like déjà Lu. Watching Lucy dismantle Fred and Ethel's flat in 1953 might have prompted viewers to ask, "Didn't she do something like that to the Ricardos' apartment last year?" (She did.)

After 100+ episodes of plopping Lucy in fine messes around New York, the writers put the show on the road to Hollywood and Europe during the fourth and fifth seasons. The change of place opened the show up, though the focus of the humor was often misdirected away from the real star to the guest celebrity of the week such as an unexpected witticism coming from John Wayne or the sight of William Holden being splattered with pastries. *I Love Lucy* still rode high atop the ratings, but the plots had shifted the emphasis from "What will Lucy do next?" to "Who will Lucy do it to next?"

It was not until the 1956-1957 season, when the Ricardos moved to the country, that domestic dilemmas became the center of attention again. One sequence alone in "Lucy Does the Tango," in which Ricky crushes Lucy and the eggs she had concealed on her person at the same time, clearly demonstrated that Ball had few rivals on television in taking physical comedy to its ultimate limit.

The arduous routine of doing a weekly television show took its toll on Lucy and Desi both physically and on their always-fragile marriage. From 1957 to 1960 they cut back to producing three to five one-hour specials per season that usually took them to places like Alaska where they met Red Skelton or to Sun Valley to complicate the life of Fernando Lamas.

By the time the final special aired on March 8, 1960 Lucy, who had tolerated Desi's private and public drunken displays and repetitive philandering for years and had first filed for divorce back in 1944 before reconciling, had been granted a degree ending two decades of rancorous sparring.

Never one to remain inactive long, Ball quickly entered into projects such as movies with Bob Hope (*The Facts of Life*, *Critic's Choice*) and the stage production *Wildcat*. If hard work and enthusiasm assured success, *Wildcat* would have been a smash because Lucy rehearsed exhaustively and threw her body into each performance, but musicals live and die on singing and dancing and no amount of mugging or gyrating could hide her deficiencies in both areas. When she virtually passed out one night on stage due to weight loss and overexertion, the decision to close the Broadway show after 171 performances proved to be a graceful and merciful end to an embarrassing misuse of her abilities.

In 1962, after a short period of recuperation and a marriage to comedian Gary Morton who later became her producer, Lucy returned to the medium that was her lifeblood on *The Lucy Show*. Vivian Vance and Gale Gordon added to the merriment of this series whose episode titles alone (e.g., "Lucy and Viv Put in a Shower," "Lucy and Viv Learn Judo," "Lucy is Kangaroo for a Day") bring back memories of riotous clowning by a woman in her fifties frolicking like a frisky teen. Reward for her antics came in the form of her second and third Emmys presented in 1967 and 1968.

By the fall of 1968 the program became *Here's Lucy*, Gordon changed from scowling Theodore Moody to glowering Harrison Carter, and Desi Arnaz Jr. and Lucie Arnaz joined the cast as children of their mother. Guest stars appeared with greater frequency in this version of *Lucy Faces Life*, but the funniest episodes continued to be those showing the havoc created by the red tornado at airports, drive-in movies, hospitals, laundries, ski lodges, etc.

When the end of the run came in March of 1974, *The Lucy Show* and *Here's Lucy*, with the same two main performers and minor changes in names and locales, had left a ratings legacy to be envied: nine consecutive years in the top ten followed by two more in the top fifteen. But when *Here's Lucy* dropped out of the top twenty-five during the twelfth season, the show was not renewed in what may have been a completion of the housecleaning CBS had begun several years before with the cancellation

This 1956 issue puts Lucy in her rightful place: on top of the TV world.

of *The Beverly Hillbillies*, *Green Acres*, and *Petticoat Junction*. Even though Lucy dwelt (or stumbled) in marble urban halls rather than tilled homespun soil, there was the perception in some circles that she belonged to the "By cracky" school of humor that the network was trying to shed.

Whether Lucy dished out the corn is debatable, but she certainly became the one to coax the blues out of the horn when she tackled the role of *Mame* for the screen in 1974 without managing to get her arms around the character and bring her down to earth. Ball's attempts to climb into Mame's eccentricity seemed as out of focus as the camerawork employed to mask the imprints of time upon her face. That a performer so innately endowed with charisma could flounder in a flop devoid of that quality and which virtually sounded the death knell of movie musicals should have told Lucy that the old magic was gone and what was left was just old.

Ball ruefully accepted the semi-retirement that the public's rejection seemed to have forced her into, emerging occasionally for a special. She gave TV another shot as a homeless woman in the dramatic telefilm *Stone Pillow* (1985) which disappointed her fans and yet another series with Gale Gordon called *Life with Lucy* that expired in less than two months in 1986. The grim reality facing her at the age of seventy-five was that the only television in her future would be sitting before a set watching herself in reruns.

Her last hurrah came at the Academy Awards ceremony in March of 1989 when Ball and Bob Hope received a standing ovation. A month later she underwent an open-heart operation and on April 26 died from complications resulting from that surgery.

Although Ball began to wonder during her last years if her public had abandoned her and if she might be forgotten, the obituaries which followed her death and the tributes that continue to this day indicate that her legacy is certain. A dominant force in popular culture and a ratings leader in three different decades, she was a Monday evening tradition in millions of homes. Milton Berle was called Mr. Television; there is little doubt who bears the distaff version of that title.

For those patients suffering from Lucyitis, the remedy is to take a dose of the tonic that has been bracing viewers for over fifty years, the cure-all known as Lucylaughaminuteregimen. The best dispenser of that prescription is Lucille Ball herself for, thankfully, that doctor is always in and, somewhere in televisionland, she is always on.

A saucy Iris Adrian pose that seems to say, "Whatcha lookin' at, Mac? Gams ain't on the menu."

A Touch of Sass

ANYONE STOPPING IN A NEARBY DRUGSTORE for coffee or in the neighborhood bar for a drink has a right to expect good service and, after being presented with a cup or a glass, will lap it up. But if we happened to visit the corner drugstore on *The Jack Benny Program* where Iris Adrian played the waitress or Duffy's Tavern where Sandra Gould held forth as Miss Duffy, what we might get is a big helping of sass, after which we laugh it up.

Although they never became stars on radio, television, or in the movies, Adrian and Gould enjoyed long careers as sharp-tongued minxes who pumped vivacity into productions by dispensing wisecracks in voices crackling with sarcasm. Their business cards could have read, "If you need a brassy dame, remember my name."

The name Iris Adrian Hostetter was born with on May 29, 1912 served her until she entered show business after the Crash of 1929 when she shortened it by a third to land a bit part in *The New Yorkers* which starred the team of Clayton, Jackson, and Durante. In 1931 she found her way into the chorus line of the Ziegfeld Follies. Iris readily admitted that she was not a great dancer and claimed to be more adept at just standing still with her large eyes and expressive face gaining the attention of the audience, a holdover from her work as a target in a knife-throwing act.

She did, however, possess enough nimbleness afoot to land roles in two 1935 George Raft movies, *Rumba* and *Stolen Harmony*. Called Goldie in the first film and Sunny in the latter, a pattern of namecasting preceded the typecasting. Never would she wear the mantle of Gloria, Vivian, Florence, or even a Susan. Instead, she was forever known as a party girl right from the credits that labeled her as Gertie, Myrtle, Jinx, Kitty, Wilma, Dolly, Lola, Peggy, Gee Gee, Lulu, Rita, or Maizie.

Iris occasionally stuck her dancing toes into musicals such as *Gold Diggers of 1937*, but producers usually cast her in comedies. More frequently than not, she had small parts in features supporting funnymen like Laurel and Hardy (*Our Relations*), the Marx Brothers (*Go West*), Bob Hope (*The Road to Zanzibar, The Paleface, My Favorite Spy*), or Abbott and Costello (*The Wistful Widow of Wagon Gap*), although she sometimes earned a fair-sized role in B pictures, most notably in 1941 as one of the *Too Many Blondes*.

Because Adrian had performed a mild but well-publicized striptease on Broadway in George S. Kaufman's *The Fabulous Invalid* in 1938, she became a leading candidate whenever a part called for a dance hall or saloon hostess, ecdysiast, or streetwise chorus girl. Ginger Rogers as *Roxie Hart* was forced to take desperate measures after Iris's Two-Gun Gertie came on the scene. In *Lady of Burlesque* her mordant comments as Gee Gee Graham provided some backstage comedy relief while Barbara Stanwyck attempted to solve a murder. She supplied a comic highlight in *The Trouble with Women* (1947) when, playing stripper Rita LaMay, she taught a staid professor (Ray Milland) some lessons in life. As fiery Pepper in *The Paleface* she tried to put a little spice in the life of Painless Potter (Hope) and all she got for her efforts was a sock in the jaw from Calamity Jane (Jane Russell).

But Adrian knew how to roll with the punches even when some of her best work ended up on the cutting room floor. A comedy sequence in *The Wistful Widow of Wagon Gap* (1947), somewhat reminiscent of the glass-switching scene in Abbott and Costello's earlier film *The Naughty Nineties*, in which Iris broke glasses, acted shrewish, and engaged in the escalating slapstick never made it to the final print. It was not until 1961 in *The Errand Boy* that she again had such a choice part and in that Jerry Lewis movie she was on the receiving end of the mayhem.

One of the ironies of Adrian's life is that, after earning her reputation by playing impudent tarts and other women on the fast and loose side, she found a home in the 1960s and 1970s in a string of pictures for Walt Disney which included *That Darn Cat!*, *The Love Bug*, *The Barefoot Executive*, *The Apple Dumpling Gang*, *Gus*, *The Shaggy D.A.*, and *Freaky Friday*. Although the long eyelashes were patently false, the hair garishly peroxided, and the figure somewhat flabby by this time, the bite remained in her voice whether acting as a carhop impatiently waiting for an order in *The Love Bug* or a wily landlady in *That Darn Cat!* loudly declaiming "Do you think I got off the bus from Stupidsville last night?"

During that time she also appeared on a number of television shows, slinging her caustic retorts at the stars. As a short-tempered neighbor to Agent 86 on *Get Smart*, she left Maxwell (Don Adams) blank-faced and speechless with rejoinders to his asinine remarks. *The Ted Knight Show*, a program about an escort service, lasted only slightly longer than a date with an escort, but during its short stay Iris as Dottie passed out an assortment of putdowns to one and all.

Dottie came out of the same mold as Lena Genster, the abrasive girlfriend of Lou Costello she played on radio. Lena, a jealous harpy, seemed to be the only person on *The Abbott and Costello Show* feared by Costello.

Although she had appeared on the air with Rudy Vallee as early as 1932, Adrian (who confessed to suffer from nervousness before a microphone) concentrated more on her movie career until invited to play the semi-regular role of acid-tongued waitress on *The Jack Benny Program* in the fall of 1952.

As soon as Iris spit out her first words on that September evening, "What d'ya want, Mac?," Benny and producer Hilliard Marks knew they had another character to go along with Mr. Kitzel, telephone operators Mabel Flapsaddle and Gertrude Gearshift, and the nameless tout. Every exchange seemed constructed so she could bat home a zinger. When Jack admitted that he could not see very far she replied, "With those glasses I thought you could see Catalina." When Don Wilson (whom she called Fatso) placed an order and asked, "Do you think you can remember all that?," we anticipated the snappy comeback: "I'll be lucky if I can carry it." Unlike other waitresses who might stop unobtrusively by the table to ask diners if everything is all right, Iris marched right up to the Benny crew and snarled, "Are you clowns through stuffing yourselves yet?"

Thereafter the Benny writers wrote visits to the drugstore into the scripts just so Adrian could stop the show with her strident retorts. She also appeared with Jack on his television program and traveled with him to entertain during his stage act.

Iris, who called Jack a divine man and "the greatest thing to hit the planet," made personal appearances with Benny after his television show ended and emitted one of her raucous guffaws when reminded how Jack would say with a merry twinkle in his eye that she had been driving him nuts for twenty years. But "driving Benny nuts" was part of the reason for Jack's enduring popularity, and Adrian was grateful that the noted "cheapskate" was generous enough to spread some of the laughter her way.

Sandra Gould, also the recipient of some of the Benny munificence when she subbed for Bea Benaderet or Sara Berner as Gertrude or Mabel on his radio show and when she appeared four times on his TV program, wanted to be in show business as a child growing up in New York so fervently that she ran away from home, crossing the Brooklyn Bridge to get to Broadway.

After attending the American Academy of Dramatic Arts, she finally did make it to the Great White Way in the 1930s when she assumed small parts in forgettable plays. Gould regarded her contributions to the soap opera *Bright Horizon* and the children's show, *Let's Pretend*, as more important to her development as an actress than her work onstage because it prepared her for employment during the busiest decade of her life, the 1940s.

After Shirley Booth and Florence Halop had vacated the part of Miss Duffy, Sandra stepped into the role from 1944 to 1947, thus qualifying her as the actress to not only play the role for the most number of years but also to tolerate the somewhat belligerent Ed Gardner for the longest period of time. Gardner insisted that she dress the part of a husband-hunting, less-than-bright daughter of a saloon owner in a peculiar hat complete with feather, a fuzzy jacket, and a tight skirt, looking more like a B girl in a C movie than an actress on a comedy program.

A democratic pursuer of men who freely admitted, "I'll run after anybody," Miss Duffy stood toe to toe with Archie in sarcastic exchanges in which she told the tavern's manager, "Why, Papa made you what you are today, you worthless good-for-nothing" or "It's men like you that make it a pleasure for a girl to be an old maid" or else baffling him with accounts of her many romances including this breakup of an engagement: "He said he was through with me and I agreed not to bother him anymore and I kept my part of the mutual agreement because every time I call him on the phone and he answers I hang up and on the other hand when he calls me which he doesn't and it's a fellow who sounds like him I hang up immediately because I'm not one to break a mutual agreement."

Of all the actresses to sing as Miss Duffy, Gould's caterwauling seemed to strike just the right (or wrong) discordant note, particularly when paired with the doltish outbursts of Clifton Finnegan (Charlie Cantor). Their versions of "Indian Love Call" and "Winter Wonderland" sounded, as aptly described by Archie, like "Jeanette MacDonald with a half-nelson on Eddy."

While acting daffy as Duffy, Sandra was also being ditzy as Mitzi, Judy's confidante and fellow intriguer on *A Date with Judy*. She served a similar function on *The Life of Riley* as a gushing girlfriend of Babs. During the short run of *The Sad Sack* in the summer of 1946 she tried, as adenoidal Lucy Twitchell, to buoy the spirits of the woeful Sad Sack (Herb Vigran).

Gould also took parts on *Lux Radio Theatre, Richard Diamond, Private Detective*, and other dramatic shows. Sandra once estimated that she worked on fifteen different programs a week during her peak post-WWII years, a reasonable figure because producers and directors counted on her as one of their reliables. Just as Gould filled in when needed on *The Jack Benny Program*, she picked up the dictation pad left behind when Lurene Tuttle took a vacation from her duties as secretary to Sam Spade

George Tobias and Sandra Gould, often bewildered on *Bewitched*.

in the summer of 1948, capably matching Howard Duff's wisecracks with a blithe barrage of malapropisms that kept the detective off-balance for three weeks.

Certainly Sandra's marriage to producer Larry Berns did her career no harm. Berns, actively involved with the production of *Our Miss Brooks*, was instrumental in finding spots for Sandra on both the radio and television versions of that series. Often cast as a coquette, she enticed every male from Mr. Conklin to the slowest student with her sexy cooing.

Gould's first role on television came in 1953 as Mildred Webster, neighbor to Joan Davis on *I Married Joan*. She appeared twice in episodes of *I Love Lucy* and *The Twilight Zone* and could also been seen in a variety of shows including comedies (*McHale's Navy, I Dream of Jeannie, Mister*

Ed), dramas (*Adam 12, Marcus Welby, M.D.*), and westerns (*Maverick, Wagon Train*). Her claim to fame on TV came on *Bewitched* from 1966 to 1972 as inquisitive Gladys Kravitz who wondered about what she saw or didn't see happening at the Stephens home. Gould found it humorous that she would grow up to "marry" George Tobias (Abner Kravitz) who was already an adult when she first met him while working as a child actress on *Let's Pretend*.

Sandra was not so amused by the typecasting that may have limited her potential as an actress. Although she appeared in over two dozen films from 1947 to 1992, most of the roles were uncredited bits in which she spoke just a few lines as receptionists, telephone operators, or other role players. Yet she could look back fondly upon largely-forgotten movies *The Story of Molly X* and *The Clown* because they gave her a chance to work with experienced radio performers Wally Maher, Cathy and Elliott Lewis, Red Skelton, Lou Lubin, Jess Kirkpatrick, and Frank Nelson.

In interviews given near the end of her life, Gould expressed no bitterness about the stereotyping because she recognized that the Brooklyn intonations in her delivery hampered her advancement so she took the roles tailored to her voice even if they went against the grain of her own personality. Cast with some frequency as a barfly, flirt, or bimbo, Gould professed never to have smoked or tasted alcoholic beverages in her life and could speak eloquently about many aspects of show business, including the contributions of her idol in radio, Fred Allen, although she did have kind words for Jack Benny as well.

Fans of comedy also have some phrases of praise for Iris Adrian who died September 17, 1994 and Sandra Gould who passed away on July 20, 1999. Because their brays or bellows still amuse us, let one man write their epitaph (taken from the title of Adrian's 1949 film): always leave them laughing.

THE FRIGHTMEISTERS

Bela Lugosi as Dracula.

The Man of Our Dreams

THERE PROBABLY WAS NO OTHER ACTOR whose film career showed more promise at the beginning and ended more ignominiously than Bela Lugosi. Possessor of one of the most distinctive voices in the history of cinema, he found that accent to be a stumbling block in the way of better parts. Even when a choice role presented itself he sometimes rejected it or bypassed it for inferior work. His Hollywood career was one of missed opportunities, poor decisions, and uneven performances. Yet he remains a charismatic figure who is still capturing new admirers decades after his death. Surely this was a man who may be scorned but not ignored.

The person most associated with Transylvania was indeed born near the Transylvanian Alps in Lugos, Hungary (now Romania) on October 20, 1882. He retained his real name of Bela Blasko until shortly after the turn of the century when he changed the last name to Lugosy and then finally about ten years later he converted the *y* to an *i*. His name is still one of the most commonly mispronounced. It is Bay-la Luh-gauche-she, not Bel-a La-go-see.

After his father died in 1894, Bela tried his hand at odd jobs involving manual labor, but nothing appealed to him until he saw some traveling acting troupes perform and he seemed to sense instinctively that he belonged with them on the stage. He began with small parts in plays and operettas, earned his way into leading roles in Shakespearean productions, and finally became a member of the National Theatre of Hungary at the dawn of World War I. After serving in the army for two years, he returned to acting, but by that time the play was not the thing; it was the images on the screen that people wanted to see.

Lugosi appeared in numerous Hungarian and German movies before deciding in 1921 that America would not only be more politically stable than his native land but it would also be a more fertile ground for an experienced actor. By the time he played a slimy spy in his first American picture, *The Silent Command*, the die had already been cast: here was a man audiences loved to hate.

1927 and 1928 were particularly busy years for him as he was not only making films but also starring as the lead in *Dracula* on Broadway and on tour. 1929 proved to be a significant year for it marked his first appearance in a talkie (*Prisoners*), a chance to play a criminal investigator instead of a criminal instigator (*The Thirteenth Chair*), and a part in a film whose title described his screen persona perfectly (*Such Men Are Dangerous*).

It offended Lugosi to know that other actors were being considered to portray Dracula in the film version of "his" role, but once chosen he played the part enthusiastically and in so doing put his indelible stamp on the vampire legend. The sets of the castle in Transylvania and the abbey in England showcase some of the most forbidding staircases and crypts ever filmed, but, because the screenplay was based on the play and not the novel, the movie becomes stage-bound and static after Dracula leaves his homeland. In England only the scenes in which the Count confronts the groveling Renfield and the sly Van Helsing crackle with the intensity presented in the supernatural tale Bram Stoker created. Lugosi never looked more aristocratic or powerful than he did in *Dracula*, no mean feat considering that he was forty-eight years old and had already passed the age when he could play swashbuckling or romantic leads convincingly.

Dracula, released in February of 1931, proved so successful that Lugosi was groomed to play the monster in *Frankenstein*, which was to begin filming that summer. A number of reasons have been given for his withdrawal from the production: lack of dialogue; the makeup was too heavy and took too long to apply; his image would be hurt by the role. Whether all or none of these were valid excuses, one fact remains clear: Lugosi alone purposefully removed himself from *Frankenstein* and by stepping aside he gave Boris Karloff the role that jump-started a career which eclipsed his.

Even though he had overlooked a peach, Lugosi picked some choice plums from the Poe tree. Bela made the most of his first chance to play the mad scientist in *Murders in the Rue Morgue* (1932), then teamed with Karloff in *The Black Cat* (1934) and *The Raven* (1935). These three features are not very scary or faithful to the works of Poe, but they ooze with great atmosphere and contain at least an aura of malevolence about them. It is still great fun to see Karloff and Lugosi glaring at one another and exchanging dialogue fraught with veiled threats. Those two actors really knew how to smile and smile and be a villain.

Lugosi pretends to be putting a spell on Karloff in this gag shot.

White Zombie (1932) is one of Lugosi's most effective horror pictures. This landmark "living dead" film presented Bela as the aptly-named Murder Legendre, a sorcerer who used an army of walking corpses to carry out his orders. These creatures, with their fixed stares and rigid movements, are some of the most frightening and yet tragic figures from the early sound era. Much has been made of the poetic aspects of the dialogue, of the symbolism inherent in the white and black clothing, and of the fairy tale nature of the plot. But it is chiefly Bela's commanding presence that makes *White Zombie* unforgettable. The widow's peak, those hypnotic eyes, and the delicately-trimmed beard (no actor ever looked more sinister when bearded than Lugosi) made him the satanic figure without peer.

Bela kept delivering the shivers in film after film during the thirties, even in those movies in which he served as a red herring. He also found time to appear in five serials, the best being *The Phantom Creeps*. But during 1937 and 1938 pickings were slim because Universal had shifted its focus away from horror and the British Board of Censors had become critical of such motion pictures. Lugosi was forced to go on relief after it became clear then that the doors in Hollywood would open wide for him only if he said, "Boo!"

Fortunately, in 1939 Universal resurrected the Frankenstein saga with *Son of Frankenstein* and Lugosi was eager to be hired to play the crippled Ygor even though he only received the same salary he had earned for *Dracula* ($500 a week). He didn't have much to say in the film, but his gestures and expressive eyes provided action enough to make his onscreen time memorable. When Bela reprised the role in *Ghost of Frankenstein*, he stole the picture with his portrayal of Ygor's feverish desire to have his brain placed inside the monster's head.

Anyone looking at a list of Lugosi's credits through 1940 will see the names of stars like Garbo, Rathbone, W.C. Fields, Lionel Barrymore, Loretta Young, Laughton, and Hardwicke; notable directors Browning, McCarey, LeRoy, Kenton, and Lubitsch; and the studios of Universal, Paramount, MGM, Twentieth Century-Fox, and Columbia. Beginning with *The Devil Bat* made in 1941 for Poverty Row's Producers Releasing Corporation, he appeared principally with second-rate casts in low budget films churned out by journeymen directors like William "One Shot" Beaudine. Rather than take what amounted to cameos in better movies, Lugosi chose the lower road that offered meatier roles with cheesier surroundings.

That he had slipped from doing A films was obvious, but it is also apparent that to rate his minor features a B- would be an act of kindness. Few campier scenes have ever been filmed than the one of Lugosi walking bent over like a hirsute Groucho Marx in *The Ape Man* or the one in which Bela as *The Voodoo Man* speaks mystical gibberish while George Zucco chants "Ramboona" in the background to the accompaniment of John Carradine playing the bongos like a demented Desi Arnaz. Yet Lugosi seemed more at ease in these unintentionally silly movies than when he had to endure the antics of the East Side Kids twice for Monogram and the tomfoolery of Carney and Brown in a pair of RKO programmers.

Lugosi managed to pull himself out of the quagmire of schlock a couple of times during the war years. In 1943 he portrayed the character he had refused to play twelve years earlier, that of the monster, in *Frankenstein Meets the Wolf Man*. Unfortunately, the makeup did little to disguise his features and, because the creature had become blind and mute, his part consisted mainly of stumbling around with his arms out as if looking for the light switch. He was more convincing as the gypsy/fortuneteller/werewolf who inflicts Lawrence Talbot with the cursed lycanthropy in *The Wolf Man* (1941). In 1944 Bela had his last opportunity to play a vampire in a serious role in *The Return of the Vampire*.

Because no film offers came to him after the middle of 1946, Lugosi took his show on the road, playing in *Dracula* to half-empty houses in places light years from Broadway. A few years later he had become little more than a sideshow attraction as he toured theaters with a gorilla. That he had fallen so low must have hurt his pride, but he always kept the stiff upper lip for the press and the public. In March of 1948 he told an interviewer that he had not been asked to do anything in a new Abbott and Costello picture that was unbecoming to Dracula's dignity. "There is no burlesque for me," he said. "All I have to do is frighten the boys, a perfectly appropriate activity. My trademark will be unblemished."

Abbott and Costello Meet Frankenstein proved to be Bela's last hurrah, although it took some persistent arm-twisting by his agent to secure the part for him. The darkening of his hair and the layers of makeup were very obvious, but so was the realization that no one else should be playing Dracula. Bela had hit the stake right on the head: Dracula *was* his trademark. He seemed to relish every word he spoke and even took an extra beat on the pauses so as to increase their ominous significance. His performance might have been a fitting swan song for there are worse ways to exit than by going into the sea in the clutches of the wolf man.

Alas, in the name of earning money, Bela found some of those worse ways. One was to confront Old Mother Riley in England. Another was to meet a Brooklyn gorilla along with a bargain basement version of Martin and Lewis. But when Lugosi met Ed Wood Jr., director and writer of some of the most execrable films of all time, he had reached the bottom of the abyss.

Bela can be found in three of the atrocities Wood engineered. In *Glen or Glenda?*, a picture about a transvestite, Lugosi sat in a room that resembled a funhouse chamber of horrors and intoned cryptic warnings about green dragons and little boys. In *Bride of the Monster* he wrestled with a rubber octopus that displayed less animation than a bowl of oatmeal. Lugosi had no dialogue in his final film, the infamous *Plan 9 from Outer*

Space, because he died on August 16, 1956, just a few days after shooting had begun. We are left with the impression that if Lugosi had lived and Wood had presented him with more scripts, Bela would have answered the call of the clapboard again and again.

Bela Lugosi was a trouper in every sense of the word. He quietly fought his addiction to morphine and methadone for years, winning the battle when he committed himself for treatment in 1955. The failure of four marriages did not diminish his jest for life or dissuade him from making it five in August of 1955. But, most importantly, acting was in his blood (and vice versa). He virtually threw himself into the parts he played, even to the point of overacting. He seemed to be saying to us, "I know this is dreadful rubbish, but look at me! I'm acting my heart out!"

Why Lugosi remains such a powerful presence today is due in part to the fact that he is inextricably connected with the main creatures of the horror mythos. He was the definitive Dracula, the best of the deformed and mildly-deranged helpmates to the monster and the Frankensteins, and the spark that ignited the legend of the wolf man. No one played a madder mad scientist than Lugosi did and, after a dozen appearances as such, it is doubtful that anyone played it as often. He knew where he belonged, nestled in his niche. That was his blessing and his curse.

Even with all his faults Bela Lugosi remains the purest symbol of menace and evil Hollywood has yet produced. He is our bogeyman, the one who in sundry forms haunts our sleep with those piercing eyes, that commanding voice, those claw-like hands. And even while the nightmare is fresh and the sheets are still clammy some voice inside us cries out with the plea that perhaps Bela was answering all those years: "Go ahead. Scare me again."

Vincent Price looking suspiciously sinister in this publicity photo for *The Bat*.

Prince of Players

RIGHT NOW SOMEWHERE ON CLOUD NINE one harpist may be saying to his companion in life, "I still can't understand it. We gave him everything. Culture. Trips abroad. An Ivy League education. We encouraged him with his legitimate stage career. We applauded his reputation as a gourmet and an art critic. And what is his claim to fame? Scaring people!"

Father knows best: Vincent Price, that handsome sophisticate who for years looked like he belonged in the den or library with a glass of claret in his hand as he gazed knowingly at a painting above the fireplace, is the same man who frightened two generations of moviegoers. Away from the camera there were few actors more urbane; on the screen in his genre roles he delivered more shivers than the iceman.

The making of Vincent Price the gentleman is an easy path to trace. He was born May 27, 1911 into an affluent St. Louis family. While still a teenager he cultivated his interest in art by traveling abroad. He graduated from Yale in 1933 and earned an M.A. from the University of London in 1935. While in England he began acting in operettas and plays almost as a lark and he found the diversion much to his liking. Even at the beginning there was undoubtedly a touch of the ham in him which he barely controlled throughout his career, but in that respect he is in good company with John Barrymore, Charles Laughton, and other actors who sometimes tried to out-herod Herod.

After performing in *Victoria Regina* opposite Helen Hayes both in London and New York, Price assumed major parts in a few more productions before turning his attention to films. His first role of consequence was as Sir Walter Raleigh in support of Bette Davis and Errol Flynn in *The Private Lives of Elizabeth and Essex* (1939). Soon he appeared in other historical pictures such as *Brigham Young* and *Hudson's Bay* and also took the lead in his first real horror film, *The Invisible Man Returns* (1940). Even though Claude Rains played the invisible man in the original, Vincent also became identified with the part and it is his voice and not that of Rains as the unseen smoker who provides the final lines in *Abbott and Costello Meet Frankenstein* that causes the comedy duo to abandon ship.

Throughout the 1940s his work gave little indication of the direction it would take later. His two best movies of the decade paired him with Gene Tierney: the mystery *Laura* with its haunting story and theme song and *Dragonwyck*, a costume drama in which he was moderately nasty. He had another chance to hone his villainous skills in *Shock* (1946) when he portrayed a psychiatrist torn by guilt after murdering his wife.

The years following the end of World War II found him engaged in a variety of parts, most of them far removed from the gruesome. Vincent was downright hilarious as a bombastic thespian in *Curtain Call at Cactus Creek* and the neurotic sponsor of a quiz program in *Champagne for Caesar* (both 1950), sagacious as Omar Khayyam in *Son of Sinbad* (1955), and sleazy as a newspaper magnate in Fritz Lang's *While the City Sleeps* (1956). His lone entry into the horror genre during this period proved to be a significant one. As Henry Jarrod, the disfigured sculptor who opened a *House of Wax* (1953), Price was a menacing force, particularly when the heroine cracked his false front and revealed his scarred face in 3-D, causing audible gasps in theaters across the country.

The release of *The Fly* in 1958 swerved Vincent's career in the direction of the Grand Guignol for keeps. The next year he kept on the wing in the sequel, *The Return of the Fly*, and *The Bat*.

Also in 1959 Price appeared in two pictures directed by William Castle, *House on Haunted Hill* and *The Tingler*. Castle, king of the gimmicks, employed just about every trick imaginable to get people into theaters: insurance policies for those dying of fright, skeletons dangling over the heads of the audience, mild electric shocks in the seats, and specious film processes called Emergo and Percepto. Somehow Vincent managed to keep a straight face through the hokey business, and if both films seem a bit silly now it is not because he was unconvincing but rather because Castle failed to heed the advice Gertrude gave to Polonius: "More matter, with less art."

Going from movies packaged by William Castle to those helmed by Roger Corman might have seemed to be a step sideways or backwards in 1960, but neither Price nor American International Pictures regretted that decision. Corman's credo can best be summarized in a few words: quickly make films that make money. In six years Corman and Price reinterpreted Edgar Allan Poe to a new generation. *House of Usher* led off with a hit, followed by *Pit and the Pendulum, Tales of Terror, The Raven, The Haunted Palace, The Masque of the Red Death,* and *The Tomb of Ligeia.*

Most of these AIP films were built around this scenario: put Price in a castle or mansion, surround him with atmosphere and a few actors, and then have him either get mad or go mad. It was during this series that Vincent perfected that glint in his eyes that told us "He's going off the deep end again." To see Price and scream queen Barbara Steele playing hide-and-seek in *Pit and the Pendulum* or to follow him on his scenery-chewing march through the multi-colored chambers in the climax of *The Masque of the Red Death* is just as much fun as watching Boris Karloff, Peter Lorre, and Price stealing scenes from each other in *The Raven* and *The Comedy of Terrors*.

Price made four pictures for American International in England at the end of the decade, the best being the first, *The Conqueror Worm*. Then he returned to America to portray his most famous villain, *The Abominable Dr. Phibes*, who disposed of those associated with his wife's death in a ritualistic manner that mirrored the plagues of Egypt. In this film and the follow-up, *Dr. Phibes Rises Again*, Price had to let his eyes do the acting because his "face" was a mask for the hideous skull it covered.

Theatre of Blood, a 1973 United Artists release, provided a slight twist on the original *Phibes*. Vincent played a much-panned thespian who used

Price, Barbara Steele, and Antony Carbone in *Pit and the Pendulum*.

the works of Shakespeare to find nine ways of eliminating his critics. This proved to be Price's last chance to reign uncontested in the modern horror arena. In *Madhouse* (1974) he took on an autobiographical part much like Karloff did in one of his last efforts (*Targets*), that of an aging horror actor who is more the hunted than the hunter.

The suave Vincent Price as *The Abominable Dr. Phibes*.

The fact that Price appeared in few motion pictures after the mid-seventies was simply a matter of time. By the 1990s Vincent looked his age and acted it. Tales of terror demand leads who have the vivacity to enact their nefarious intrigues. The clock had also run out on subtlety in horror films. *Halloween, Friday the 13th,* and their sequels and clones with their emphasis on slashings, gore, and special effects rendered superfluous actors who could express malevolence with just a lifted eyebrow.

Though his appearances in films became infrequent, Price returned to his first love, the stage, and scored a singular triumph as Oscar Wilde in a one-man play from 1977 to 1982. He hosted the PBS *Mystery* series from 1978 to 1987 and could be heard as the voice of the dastardly Professor Rattigan in Disney's *The Great Mouse Detective* in 1986.

Fans of Vincent Price who witnessed his brief appearance in *Edward Scissorhands* (1990) were probably more disappointed with what they heard than with what they saw. That unique voice which was quite capable of being mellifluous one moment and malefic the next was almost absent; only a shadow remained. The diminished quality of that gifted tongue seemed a special loss to those who remember him as having one of radio's best voices.

As *The Saint*, that model of suave efficiency, Price made some of the other crime-busters on the air sound almost illiterate. Simon Templar, unlike his contemporaries, could not be considered a gumshoe out for a buck. He just encountered people in trouble and helped them as the "Robin Hood of modern crime."

Templar was not above slipping repartee into his interviews:

> Templar: One of us is in a bad way. Either you're dead or
>   I'm crazy.
> Carter: I assure you I'm not dead.
> Templar: I'll see my psychiatrist in the morning.

But just about anyone can deliver a wisecrack. No other radio investigator would ask a question like "*Whom* have they in mind for Carter's murder?" or quote Hamlet's "king of infinite space" speech to a cabdriver. Templar flew above his contemporary sleuths solely on the wings of Vincent Price's wit and style.

Most of Price's other notable work on radio could be heard on *Escape* or *Suspense*.

One of his most memorable episodes on the series designed to "help us get away from it all" was "Blood Bath" which aired June 30, 1950. In this version of "thieves fall out" Vincent's character narrated the story of how greed and the steaming South American jungle claimed the lives of members of an expedition until he alone survived.

Another tale of *Escape* from that year, "Three Skeleton Key," was deemed highly appropriate for that series and also for *Suspense* in 1956 and 1958. On all three occasions Price narrated the terrifying tale of rats that cover a lighthouse and hold its inhabitants captive. Vincent is totally convincing as the lighthouse keeper who tries to retain his sanity and at the same time describe the claustrophobic environment above the incessant chattering of the ravenous rodents. Any list of the most frightening shows in the history of radio is incomplete without "Three Skeleton Key."

Of Price's twelve appearances on *Suspense* none is more chilling than "Fugue in C Minor" broadcast on June 1, 1944. That evening Vincent starred as Theodore Evans, a widower so obsessed with organ music that he built the pipes of an organ into the walls of his house. When he brings home a woman he is courting, his two children confess to her their fear that their father murdered their mother and that her spirit still lives in the pipes. It turns out that the children are right about Evans and before the program is over Price gets a chance to pull out all the stops in more ways than one. This episode is doubly significant. No other single broadcast of radio drama demonstrated a more perfect marriage of story and music. More importantly, this "phantom of the opera" plot complete with the unveiling of his genteel facade was a precursor of the type of role for which Price would become famous later.

It is ironic that Vincent Price never had a chance to play Dr. Jekyll and Mr. Hyde for few actors could play both gentleman and madman so credibly. In fact, even his maniacs have an air of refinement about them. That is an element that Price was never able to completely submerge regardless of whether he portrayed a baron of Arizona, a Dutch patroon, an Egyptian architect, or Dr. Goldfoot; breeding willed its way out. With just a tilt of his head or a roll of syllables across his velvet throat he could make a derelict sound positively patrician.

Somehow Price managed to survive the girl bombs and cinematic bombs with aplomb. Those misfires pale beside his accomplishments, not the least being that he was the featured player in some of the most memorable if not the best horror films of three decades. The success of these movies is chiefly attributable not to Corman's exploitative powers or the magic of 3-D or Richard Matheson's considerable skills as a screenwriter but rather to the presence of a star who knew how to carry a picture.

Even though Price died October 25, 1993 he is still very much with us for just his appearance in a vintage movie or on a rerun of a television program conjures up in us images of dark passages, stormy nights, bubbling laboratories, torture chambers, and foggy graveyards. If that signifies that he is best known for scaring people, so be it. Even art connoisseurs and gourmands are fairly common, but classy frightmeisters are rare and worth their weight in gold. When it comes to delivering the thrills in eerie movies and on suspenseful radio shows, aficionados of the macabre do not count the cost. They just look for the Price.

Karloff: A name and a face that could upstage the stars of a film on a lobby card.

The Face of Fear

IN 1941 BROADWAY AUDIENCES WATCHING what has become the warhorse of stage comedies, *Arsenic and Old Lace*, howled with laughter when the man playing gangster Jonathan Brewster claimed that he strangled one of his victims because "he said I looked like Boris Karloff." What made that line so hilarious? The actor speaking those words was Boris Karloff.

Even then Karloff had become so associated with scaring people that just the mention of his name was a cause for shuddering or nervous giggling. The name he was born with on November 23, 1887 in Dulwich, England was more prosaic: William Henry Pratt. Because his father had been a civil servant, William was groomed for a career in consular service, but he developed an interest in acting at an early age and went to the theater every chance he could.

He took a bold step for a person barely out of his teens when he emigrated to Canada in search of his identity as much as anything else. By the time he answered a newspaper ad in Vancouver for a character actor he had already decided to take his mother's maiden name as his own last name.

Boris thought he did reasonably well in his first role in which he played a man of sixty and he probably looked the part better than others his age. Examining photographs taken during the early years of his career confirms what the camera showed later: the shape of his cheekbones, the set of his jaw, and the creases by his mouth along with those bushy eyebrows lead one to speculate that he never looked very young as an actor. Karloff's appearance may have eliminated him from playing callow swains, but it certainly helped him to convincingly portray most other male roles. No acting school could have taught him more than he learned by appearing in scores of stage productions. By the time he began knocking on the doors of studios in 1919 he could play everything from a prospector to a priest.

In going from a talking medium to a silent one in those early days of cinema how a person looked was of utmost importance so Karloff usually found himself typecast as a villain or cad. In *The Bells* (1926) he demonstrated how expressive his face could be when he played a hypnotist locked in a battle of wills with criminal Lionel Barrymore, but the silents were really not golden for him. Lon Chaney, another actor who could hardly be considered the handsome hero type, advised Boris to find his own niche by doing something "no one else can or will do." In 1931 he did just that. When Bela Lugosi said no, Boris said yes and his career was off and stomping.

It was director James Whale himself who wanted Karloff for the part of the monster in *Frankenstein*. He saw something in the actor's face that he liked and so did makeup man Jack Pierce who exaggerated Karloff's features into a flat-headed, slimy-haired, heavy-lidded, scar-faced creature. Pierce's additional touch of green-gray greasepaint brought out the cadaverous nature of that face better in black and white, making the monster look like something who had both feet in the grave.

Karloff's experience in dozens of silent pictures helped him immensely in rendering a variety of emotions as the mute creation of Henry Frankenstein. The initial revulsion that audiences may have felt upon seeing the monster for the first time altered a bit as Boris convincingly registered confusion, torment, pity, amusement, and even gentleness under all that putty and rubber.

But *Frankenstein* is one of those movies in which actors and plot are not the only attractions; *where* is almost as significant as *who* and *what*. It is difficult to concentrate on Colin Clive's interpretation of his role as creator when he is upstaged by the pyrotechnics of a laboratory whose vertical dimensions seem boundless. The expressionistic sets with their odd angles and rough-hewn stones seem to steal any number of scenes from the actors who are dwarfed by them. *Frankenstein* definitely was the foundation upon which Karloff's reputation was built, but, more importantly, it (more so than its predecessor, *Dracula*) was the progenitor of horror films in which settings mingled with story to achieve that hard-to-define but unmistakable Universal touch.

One immediate benefit from the popularity of *Frankenstein* occurred when Universal offered Karloff a contract which assured him some security during the Depression. In his next major role for the studio he played Imhotep, better known as *The Mummy*, who is brought back to life after 3,700 years to search for his long lost love. Karloff is effective in his portrayal of a relentless force who appears unstoppable until struck down by supernatural means. Unlike later films in this series the titular figure is not under wraps for very long. Boris appears bare-faced but leather-skinned for most of the seventy-two minutes. But just to get prepared for the early scenes in the film Karloff had to put himself in Pierce's hands for eight hours of bandaging, wetting, and drying, twice as long as the torture he endured for *Frankenstein*.

In 1934 Universal decided to play both their aces, Karloff and Lugosi, at the same time in *The Black Cat*. Boris had an unsympathetic role as a sadistic Satanist who battled psychiatrist Bela for the lives of innocent bystanders. What makes Karloff's performance so chilling is that he underplayed the part by speaking words of reason and reconciliation that masked the machinations lying just beneath the surface. It has been suggested by some critics that the roles could have been reversed, but restrained performances were as anathematic to Lugosi as crosses were to his favorite count. For proof one need look no further than their next pairing, *The Raven*, in which Lugosi's mad doctor went over the top to reach those in the balcony with his fiendish dedications to Poe as he attempted to execute most of the cast. Conversely, Karloff, as a prisoner on the lam who earnestly wanted to change his appearance and instead was disfigured by the doctor, touched a responsive chord in ugly ducklings everywhere.

Bearded Bela and bewigged Boris in *The Invisible Ray*.

Karloff, now a name to be feared, rode high in the credits and on posters. His own studio as well as others like Columbia and Warner Brothers used him in films with spooky titles like *The Old Dark House*, *The Black Room*, *The Invisible Ray*, *The Walking Dead*, *The Man Who Lived Again*, *The Invisible Menace*, and *The Man They Could Not Hang*. Even if the plots were not particularly scary, Karloff's baleful glares sent temperatures to zero at the bone.

In 1935 the matchmakers at Universal decided it was time to marry off their profitable offspring so the *Bride of Frankenstein* was created. It has almost become a platitude to claim that *Bride* is the rare sequel that is better than the original, but if it is an improvement Boris deserves a good share of the credit for that accomplishment. In the scenes with the blind hermit who teaches him to talk, he reacted with a simple-minded glee totally in keeping with the monster's limited intelligence. That ability to speak soured Karloff on playing the part because he believed that the best monster was the inarticulate one and feared that changes from the original concept made the creature more comic than tragic. Boris stepped into those twelve-pound boots one more time in *Son of Frankenstein* before turning to more palatable projects.

Although Karloff appeared in only seven movies during the war years, he kept busy with *Arsenic and Old Lace* in New York and on road tours as well as radio work. Unlike Lon Chaney Jr. whose dull delivery was an inherent liability and Lugosi whose thick accent made precise enunciation difficult, Boris was a reigning horror star whose voice proved to be eerily effective on the airwaves. Just a whisper from him that ended abruptly is the vocal equivalent of the creaking door on *Inner Sanctum*.

He stepped inside that famous door often, taking part in two of the more notable episodes, "The Wailing Wall" in which a man's conscience rather than a woman's spirit haunts him for decades and "Birdsong for a Murderer," a tale of blackmail and a deranged killer involving a couple that is skillfully constructed to lead listeners to suspect the wrong spouse.

Karloff, a superlative narrator, could fill an interrupted threat such as "I think I'm going to …" with so much dire portent that we didn't want him to go on, and he knew how to pause after a description like "The moon cast a glimmer over the room and …" so the shivers that had been running up our back could shift into high. His well-modulated delivery contributed much to the effect of the famous *Lights Out* story in which he played a man who watches in horror as his shrewish mate turns into a "Cat Wife."

Karloff's visits with comedians Fred Allen, Jack Benny, and Jimmy Durante on radio and later on television with Red Skelton and Jonathan Winters revealed a good sport who was not above lampooning his image as bogeyman. He could follow a threatening promise with a quip adroitly and knew what to do with a punch line. Comparing his exchanges with Baggy Eyes on a 1945 show or with the Schnoz in 1947 with the off-key, faltering misreading that Lugosi gave in a 1948 sketch with Abbott and Costello demonstrates clearly that it was not just before the cameras that Karloff was the better actor. Among the titans of terror only Vincent Price demonstrated a better sense of comic timing than Boris.

When Karloff returned to the screen after three years on the stage, he made some forgettable films like *The Climax* and *Lured* but also starred in a pair worth remembering, *House of Frankenstein* (1944) and *The Body Snatcher* (1945). In the former, the first "all-monster rally," Karloff performed capably as mad Dr. Niemann who wanted to use Dracula, the wolf man, and the monster to carry out his plans of vengeance. In Val Lewton's adaptation of the story by Robert Louis Stevenson, Boris portrayed a cold-blooded grave robber who apparently returns from the dead in one of the most electrifying climaxes ever filmed.

Beginning at this point in his life in the middle and late forties it seemed that Karloff was attempting to stretch his range, to prove to himself if to no one else that he could not only assume different kinds of roles

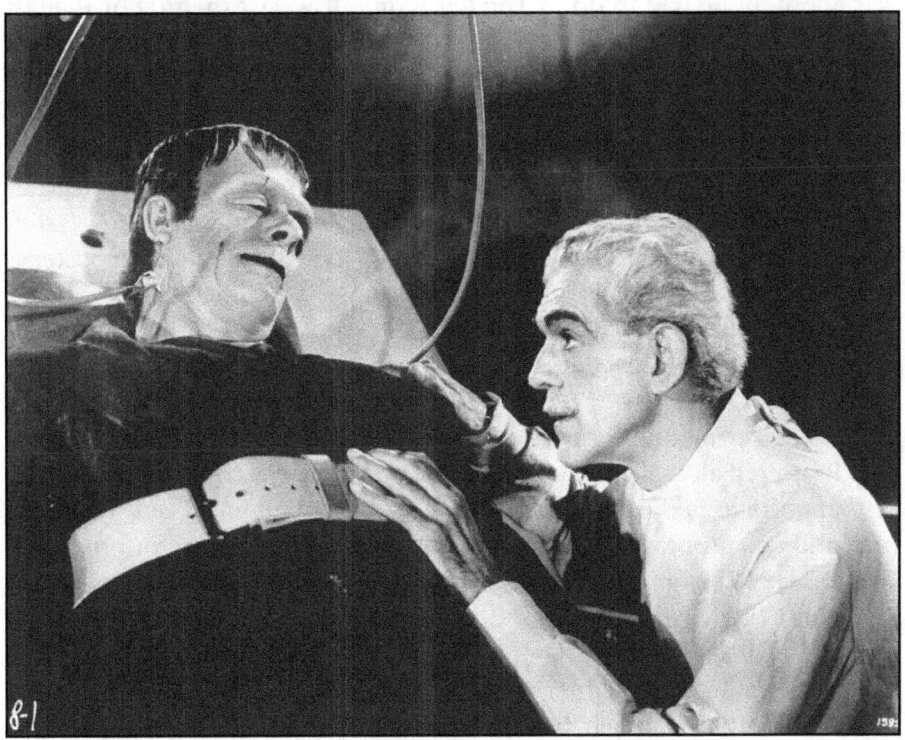

Karloff with the monster (Glenn Strange) in *House of Frankenstein*.

but also excel in them. He played an American Indian in *Unconquered* and *Tap Root*, a faithful servant in *The Strange Door*, and a good, "unmad" doctor in *The Black Castle*.

Drawn back to the stage in 1950 to walk the decks as Captain Hook in *Peter Pan*, he enraptured audiences and critics who loved both his acting and his singing. Five years later Boris reached what he considered the zenith of his career when he returned to Broadway in *The Lark* as Bishop Cauchon, a part that allowed him to reveal those aspects of personality that he did so well: anguish and vulnerability.

The series of horror films made in England by Hammer rekindled an interest in that genre, calling Karloff back into service on both sides of the Atlantic. The only distinction about these films is that Boris Karloff appeared in them. Surrounded with casts of nobodies, Boris had to carry the films on his seventy-year-old shoulders. He got to rub sutures with an old friend one more time in *Frankenstein 1970* in 1958, this time as the doctor and not the monster. As *The Haunted Strangler* he proved to be quite frightening just by contorting his face and biting his lip. Unfortunately, some moguls must have thought Karloff could raise goose bumps by merely standing around and reacting to eldritch events which was about all he had to do in *Voodoo Island*. It wasn't the first or the last time he was used or misused to beef up the gate. Back in 1949 when he acted as a red herring while Abbott and Costello met the killer, *Boris Karloff* was shoehorned in at the end of the title just because that name meant good box office.

One man who did know what to do with Boris was Hubbell Robinson, producer of *Thriller*. From September 1960 to April 1962 Karloff narrated (and sometimes starred in) sixty-seven episodes of this mystery-horror series. Some of the early offerings barely qualified as whodunits, but bone-chillers like "The Devil's Ticket" and "The Grim Reaper" are creepy even when viewed today. Outside of his role as a vampire in *Black Sabbath* in 1964, his work on *Thriller* marked the last time Boris could send us cowering under the covers.

Scattered along the rest of the route one can find trifles such as *Ghost in the Invisible Bikini*, mild parodies like *The Raven* and *Comedy of Terrors*, and an autobiographical role as an aged veteran of horror movies in *Targets*. He developed a case of double pneumonia while shooting night scenes for *The Crimson Cult* and, although he never fully recovered his strength, still kept acting even if it had to be from a wheelchair. He looked deathly ill in an episode of *The Name of the Game* in late 1968 and lived only a few months longer before the end came in his native England on February 2, 1969.

Since his death the pretenders, impressionists who have lisped to talk like him and actors who have tried to stalk like him, have met with indifferent success. With Boris Karloff the cliché has to take a new twist: the face is familiar and we can't forget the name. That's as close to immortality as a movie star can get this side of paradise.

Lon Chaney Jr. and Evelyn Ankers with the cane that also plays an important role in *The Wolf Man*.

Far As the Curse Is Found

HE AND SHE ARE SITTING ON THE PORCH SWING looking at a full moon. She snuggles close and whispers dreamily, "What does that moon make you think of?" Without a moment's hesitation he replies, "Lon Chaney Jr."

That nameless beau can hardly be blamed for his impulsive answer even if he gets the cold shoulder the rest of the evening. Lawrence Talbot, the character Chaney played in five motion pictures, dreaded lunar beams as much as Dracula disliked the dawn's early light. In *The Road to Morocco* moonlight became Dorothy Lamour; in moonlight Lawrence Talbot became the wolf man.

Just as Talbot's lycanthropy was a curse not of his own making so Chaney had a burden thrust upon him early in life: he was in the shadow of a father whose leading roles in *The Phantom of the Opera* and *The Hunchback of Notre Dame* are legendary.

Although Lon Chaney's son from his birth on February 10, 1906, he wasn't always Lon Chaney Jr. Creighton Tull Chaney, shuttled around from boarding houses to stepmother to grandparents during his youth, grew up healthy and strong enough to pick baskets of fruit all day for three cents a bushel. The elder Chaney lived until 1930, long enough to see Creighton married and gainfully employed as a boilermaker.

But the sound of banging metal is nothing compared to the sirenic enchantment of the casting call. Chaney followed the advice of a director who, after hearing him sing at a party, suggested that he try the Hollywood studios. By 1932 he had a contract with RKO and began appearing in westerns and other adventure films.

Because neither of the Chaneys qualified for the "pretty boy" parts, they usually portrayed villains or social outcasts in those days of typecasting. In the thirties Creighton played the same type of role so often he felt he had a patent on the line "So you won't talk, eh?"

During the middle of the decade he became Lon Chaney Jr. in the credits but not in his heart. He later claimed that he had been coerced into making the change in order to continue working in movies. To keep from starving he allowed the studios to use the new name that certainly had more marquee value than the old one.

Another disappointment occurred when Lon's screen test for *The Hunchback of Notre Dame* was shelved, thus depriving him of a chance to recreate the role of Quasimodo that his father made famous. However, in that same year of 1939 he landed one of the best parts of his career.

Chaney, who had played Lennie, a slow-thinking but humane migrant worker, in the dramatic adaptation of *Of Mice and Men* on the West Coast, seemed a natural choice to star in the United Artists version of John Steinbeck's novel. Critics weren't the only ones awed by the pathos Lon brought to the character. Lennie's innocence and unfulfilled dreams touched the heartstrings of audiences across the country. But even this success had a downside to it because some producers who had formerly seen him as a meanie now only wanted him to be a dimwit.

Even if Lon still battled stereotypes at least he had achieved credibility as an actor and steady employment with a contract from Universal. Although he was the title character in *Man Made Monster*, his first film for the studio, Lionel Atwill got top billing as a mad scientist intent on using a carnival worker's tolerance for withstanding jolts of electricity as the first step in creating a race of zombies. Fifteen years later Chaney would be the featured player in a similar movie called *The Indestructible Man*, but in early 1941 he seemed content to take second billing just to keep the wolf from the door. Later that year Lon opened that door and let him into his life.

The Wolf Man is a landmark horror film for any number of reasons. Few motion pictures in the genre can boast of having a better cast than this one that featured Claude Rains, Warren William, Ralph Bellamy, Bela Lugosi, Evelyn Ankers, and Maria Ouspenskaya in support of Chaney. The music and mist-shrouded sets create an atmosphere that can chill even when the creature is not stirring. The dialogue written by Curt Siodmak, author of *Donovan's Brain*, is as close to poetry as can be found in any spine-tingler. This movie established the folklore surrounding werewolves (e.g., the mark of the pentagram, effect of the moon, aversion to silver) that persists to this day. The wolf man embodied a horror that was truly horrific; a pale count or a monster made from cadavers may seem more dead than alive, but this was a normal man who became a snarling beast right before our eyes, kindling that fear of being chased by a wild animal that lies within us.

The Wolf Man marked the beginning of Chaney's ascent past Lugosi and Boris Karloff during the war years to become Universal's leading frightmare. As such he left behind the appendage that had been forced on him, now being billed simply as Lon Chaney.

When Universal decided to remake *The Phantom of the Opera*, Chaney wanted to be the phantom, but after Claude Rains won the job Lon consoled himself by stepping into the big shoes of the monster in *Ghost of Frankenstein* (1942). To become the wolf man Chaney had to sit for five hours a day under the hands of makeup wizard Jack Pierce. Although it took less time to shape the head of "old sew and sew," Lon developed an allergy to the rubber base Pierce used, sidelining him for a week.

Chaney continued to work undercover in his next film, *The Mummy's Tomb*. He played the mummy twice more in *The Mummy's Ghost* and *The Mummy's Curse*, but all three movies failed to live up to earlier titles in the series for any number of reasons: the move to less exotic locales like sleepy New England towns or the use of bland starlets whose fates seemed of little consequence or it could have been the ludicrous prospect of a limping, prune-faced, unraveling refugee from a first aid kit being somehow menacing. Lon himself disliked the role because he had nothing to say and had no identity under all that makeup.

In 1943 he was back as the doomed Talbot in *Frankenstein Meets the Wolf Man*. Originally some thought had been given to having Chaney play both major parts through the use of doubles and trick photography, but this proved unwieldy so Lugosi took over as the stumbling monster. Though the two creatures were allied for a while, audiences knew it wouldn't be long before they were engaged in hand-to-claw combat.

During the next two years Talbot sought cures for his affliction at the *House of Frankenstein* and the *House of Dracula*. With each film audiences were drawn to feel more sympathetic toward his plight because Chaney made his fear of the approaching night seem very real. At the conclusion of *House of Frankenstein* Talbot appears to find both romance and release from his predicament when he is shot by a silver bullet "fired by someone who loves him enough to understand." When he showed up hale and hairy at the *House of Dracula*, he found a doctor mad enough to cure him and closed the picture by taking a moonlit stroll with the leading lady. But there seems to be an unwritten rule that monsters cannot live happily ever after so he suffered a relapse into his feral state when Abbott and Costello met Frankenstein and company in 1948.

Chaney did have a chance to go almost completely without makeup through one creature feature, *Son of Dracula* (1943). The character he portrayed was actually Dracula because his name of Alucard proved to be a ruse to hide his identity as he sought new blood in Louisiana. This movie, with its foggy cemetery and spooky mansion, earns higher marks for mood than for story, but that was what made the films from Universal so appealing. The veiled threat did not frighten us as much as the prospect of what might be lurking behind the decaying headstones or in that cobweb-covered coffin. Chaney's vampire was more calculating and relentless than Lugosi's, although the comment is often made that he looked too healthy for a parasite. Perhaps it was his bulk that made him so formidable a figure: here stood a vampire who looked like he could tackle Bronco Nagurski.

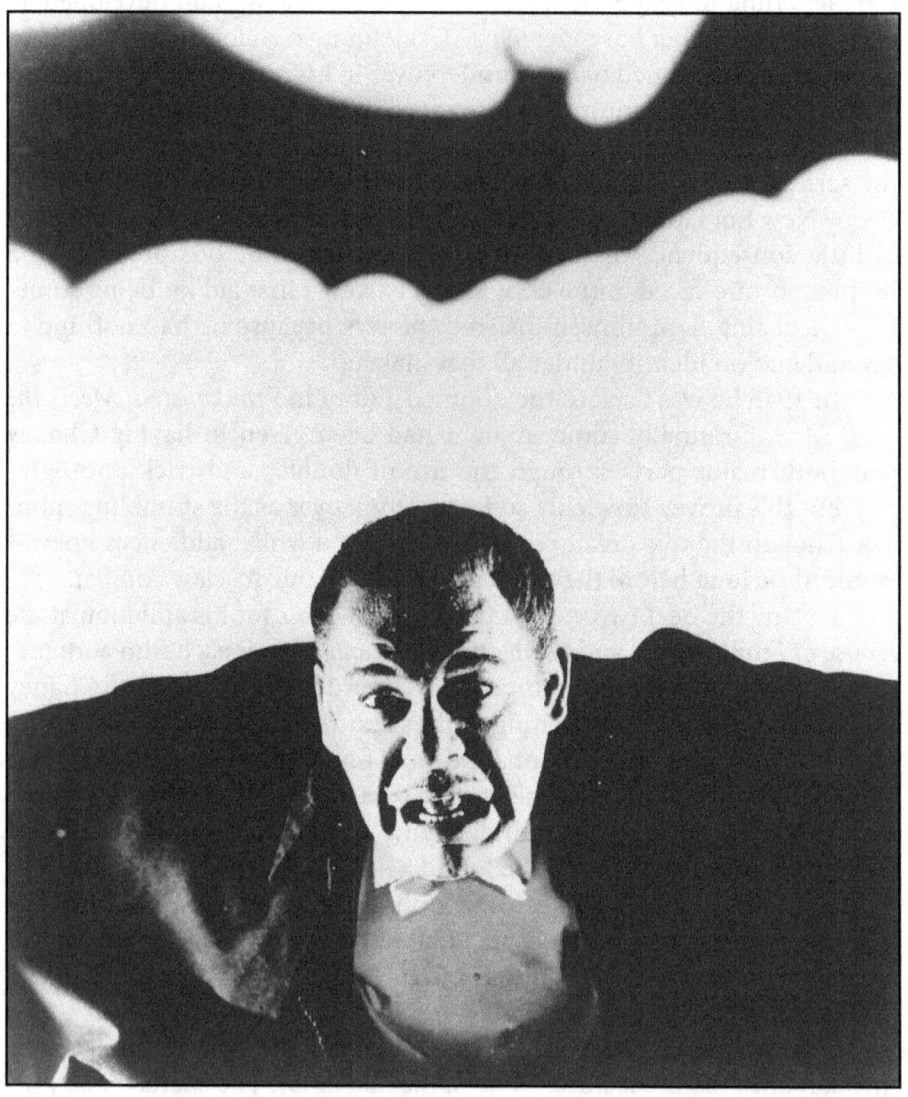

Chaney as the *Son of Dracula*.

Universal allowed Chaney more opportunities to show his face in a sequence of six mysteries based on the *Inner Sanctum* radio program, but these low-budget efforts with lurid titles like *Weird Woman* and *Calling Dr. Death* turned out to be predictable melodramas that barely qualified as features. After releasing *Pillow of Death*, the last picture in the series, the studio shifted its focus away from horror films in 1946 and Chaney found himself once again relegated to character actor rather than star.

Of all headliners in the field of horror Chaney seemed to age the fastest. Karloff and Lugosi were at least in their mid-forties when they started scaring people in talkies. Chaney was only thirty-five when he first bayed at the heavens ten years later. In 1952 while Bela cavorted with Old Mother Riley and Boris solved crimes as Colonel March Lon played a spineless, aged sheriff in *High Noon* who is of little help to Gary Cooper, a man who was born five years before him in 1901. Bags under his eyes, puffy cheeks, and a hangdog expression had set in early and grew more pronounced as Chaney approached his sixties. His appearance suggested a hard-drinking man so more roles as drunks were offered to him. He had already begun to drink like a hard-drinking man.

Chaney still performed capably in a few respectable movies like *The Haunted Palace* and *Welcome to Hard Times*, but with increasing frequency his roles consisted mainly of making token appearances as warlocks or madmen in exploitation films. Cult status has been conferred on some of these oddities as the curious still seek out videos of *Hillbillys in a Haunted House* to discover what business Chaney and John Carradine had in the same frames with Joi Lansing and Ferlin Husky and also *Spider Baby* to hear Lon sing the title song.

The years that had not been kind to him turned more vicious near the end. Throat cancer, gout, and beriberi as well as hepatitis made his last days unpleasant ones. He died "in agony" on July 12, 1973.

He lived in agony as well. He was reminded of the distant father whose achievements he could never hope to match every time he signed his name or looked in the mirror. The profiles, mien, and diction of Basil Rathbone or Lionel Atwill worked both in the laboratory and the drawing room; Chaney knew well what limitations his face and tongue had placed on his career. The tortures that his father inflicted upon himself in order to become a skeletal phantom and a truly deformed hunchback were equaled by the torment the son endured. The transformation from human to werewolf that takes only seconds on the screen required Chaney to be virtually immobile all day while he endured twenty changes of makeup. The easy way was not the Chaney way.

"The way you walked was thorny through no fault of your own," the words Maleva speaks in *The Wolf Man* over the dead Talbot, could have been Chaney's epitaph. Although he alone accomplished the grand slam of horror, Lugosi and Karloff had first dibs on Dracula, Frankenstein's monster, or the mummy. Even Henry Hull had gone hirsute before him in *Werewolf of London*. Let the others have their day. For as long as "the wolfbane blooms and the autumn moon is bright" Lon Chaney Jr. will haunt the night.

In the still of the fright: No other photo conveys the story line of a motion picture more thoroughly than this composite shot for *Mad Love*.

A Little Terror

ALL TOGETHER NOW: PINCH YOUR NOSTRILS and put a guttural tone into the emphasized words: "I have this *anger* that comes from somewhere *way down* inside of me that drives me *on and on and on.*" Congratulations. You have just done a perfect Peter Lorre.

Professional impressionists will confess that Lorre is one of the easiest voices to copy, but the fact that mimics still include him in their repertoire is a tribute to the staying power of a man who, though small in stature, stands tall among the most unforgettable actors of all time.

It should surprise no one to learn that a celebrity not known for a beaming demeanor as an adult did not experience much happiness as a youth. His mother died not long after his birth in Rosenberg, Hungary on June 26, 1904 and he was soon uprooted in a move to Vienna. He did not get along with his father and ran away at the age of seventeen to join a German theatrical troupe. He barely scratched out a living during the 1920s, but he became so convinced that acting was his calling that he abandoned his given name, László Löwenstein, for one simple enough for audiences to remember.

That name became famous in 1931 when Fritz Lang, who had seen Peter at work in a Berlin theater, chose him to star in *M*. Lorre's portrayal of a child murderer who has no place to hide because he is sought by both the police and the underworld is so effective that viewers are torn between feelings of pity and disgust. The role was a definitive one in his career for it was the paranoiac, the man who is both haunted and hunted, the possessed one who cannot help himself that Lorre did better than anyone else. In 1935 he assumed a part that played right into his strength as an actor, that of Dostoevsky's guilt-ridden Raskolnikov in Columbia's version of *Crime and Punishment*.

Lorre delivered one of his best performances in another 1935 film, *Mad Love*. For this atmospheric horror film, Lorre played bald Dr. Gogol, a surgeon who becomes obsessed with an actress named Yvonne (Frances Drake) who is married to pianist Stephen Orlac (Colin Clive). When Orlac's hands become useless after an accident, Gogol agrees for Yvonne's sake to graft the hands of an executed knife-thrower onto Stephen's arms, then tries to make Orlac and the police think the musician has committed a murder with them so can have the woman for himself. Just after he tells Yvonne that "every man kills the thing he loves," Gogol is about to put his words into action when Orlac, arriving with the police, kills the doctor with a dagger.

Perhaps the best word to describe Lorre's first characterizations is *creepy*. With the bulging eyes of the eggheaded Gogol he best exemplified the wild psychopath that women dreaded. His hands just *had* to be cold and clammy, his panting breaths like those of a mad dog. In the early thirties Boris was sometimes billed as Karloff the Uncanny; at the same time Peter very easily could have been called Lorre the Loathsome.

Alfred Hitchcock, who had admired Lorre's work in *M* and had hired him for *The Man Who Knew Too Much* even before the actor knew any English, cast him as the General in *The Secret Agent*. Although John Gielgud and Madeleine Carroll were the stars, Lorre stole the film playing what a reviewer for the *New York Times* called "one of the most amusing and somehow wistfully appealing triggermen since Victor Moore, a homicidal virtuoso."

His work for Hitchcock earned Lorre a contract with Twentieth Century-Fox. Out of this union came the Mr. Moto movies which proved beneficial for both parties: the series gave Peter a chance to play one of his most memorable characters and also provided the studio with a string of eight B pictures that turned a nice profit. As the laconic Japanese detective Lorre did a capable job of underplaying a part, something that was against his natural tendencies.

In 1940 he again put on the villain's mantle as a sadistic warden in *Island of Doomed Men* and also joined Lugosi and Karloff in throwing a few scares into Kay Kyser and crew in *You'll Find Out*. In 1941 he appeared in his first film for Warner Brothers, a mystery that is the stuff screen legends are made of.

The Maltese Falcon is most assuredly not Peter Lorre's picture, but it isn't Humphrey Bogart's or Mary Astor's or Sydney Greenstreet's either. Credit the sum of all their parts under John Huston's skillful direction for creating movie magic. Lorre demonstrated that he could be a credible menace whether mincing or conniving for his curly-haired, sleepy-eyed, effeminate Cairo is as far removed from his part as Gogol as Boise is from Bermuda.

You'll Find Out is the only film teaming Lugosi, Karloff, *and* Lorre.

Peter's role as a doomed black marketeer in *Casablanca* the following year was small, but it is probably not just a coincidence that within thirteen months he appeared in two of the greatest motion pictures of all time. Certainly Bogart deserves some credit for this fame, but there was something about the contributions of Lorre and Greenstreet, integral like bushes on a landscape painting, that would detract from the work of art if they were not there. Greenstreet and Lorre complemented each other so well that they were teamed again in *The Verdict, Passage to Versailles, Three Strangers,* and *The Mask of Dimitrios*. Whenever those two got together, audiences could look forward to scenes of intrigue, double crosses, and suspense.

Largely overshadowed by these significant films is *The Face Behind the Mask*, a 1941 Columbia release that might reveal more facets of Lorre's talent than any other picture. This tale of immigrant Janos Szabo who moves into a life of larceny after becoming disfigured in a fire, finds love with a blind woman who is killed by a bomb meant for him, and enacts a revenge that seals his own doom allows Peter to convey feelings of innocence, hope, anger, tenderness, depression, affection, bitterness, exuberance, and remorse in less than seventy minutes. People then and now who see stills of Lorre in makeup showing Szabo's scarred face or the wording "What fiendish fury turns man into monster?" on the one-sheet poster mistakenly want to slot *The Face Behind the Mask* into the horror genre when it should be remembered as a crime film with a twist, a twist that wrenches the heart.

During the war years Lorre also appeared in two farces, *Arsenic and Old Lace* and *The Boogie Man Will Get You*. In *Lace* he got to ham it up as a tipsy and forgetful Dr. Einstein. In the latter film he played a mad scientist who, along with henchman Karloff, tried to profit off experiments with dupe Maxie Rosenbloom. Lorre, even more than Karloff, came to be known thereafter as the bogeyman. A 1944 *Abbott and Costello Show* took full advantage of his scary reputation as Bud took Lou to Peter's rest home which turned out to be as restful as a spook house on Halloween.

Lorre's appearances on *Suspense* from 1942 to 1945 gave him six opportunities to split personalities. No other actor jumped from sniveling whiner to raving psychotic as quickly as Peter Lorre. His characters, like Joe Reese in "Nobody Loves Me" broadcast August 30, 1945, developed persecution complexes that hounded them all their lives.

Reese, after calmly chatting about books, would suddenly be ranting that "I had to get her to look at me in that beautiful, *naked* way from back *deep* in her head." When Peter went off the deep end on radio, it could hardly be called overacting because going overboard every few minutes was just his style like Al Jolson when the singer belted out certain lyrics with gusto. Paul Frees, the Lorre mimic who played with fire on the Spike Jones parody of "My Old Flame," wonderfully captured the "now he's crazy, now he's not" flavor of Peter's delivery.

When Abbott and Costello took their summer break in 1947, Peter starred in an NBC series entitled *Mystery in the Air*. In dramatizations of works by famous writers like Poe, Pushkin, and Maupassant, Lorre played a variety of demented criminals. He received excellent support from radio veterans such as Joseph Kearns and Agnes Moorehead, who played a suspicious landlady in "The Lodger," the tale of a Jack the Ripper character tailored perfectly for the actor who was at his best when on the spot. Near the end of he series in September Peter reprised his role as Raskolnikov in a sanitized adaptation of the Russian classic.

It is unfortunate that a recording of the first episode of *Mystery in the Air* has not survived for if ever there was an actor born to speak the ravings of the murderer tortured by conscience in "The Tell-Tale Heart" Peter Lorre was that man. He toured the United States giving readings of the story during 1947 at the same time *The Beast with Five Fingers* played in many theaters around the country.

Beast is one of those oddities in which the title is better than the picture. Even the poster art showing a huge clutching hand promised more terror than the movie produced in the story of a pianist's disembodied hand that appeared to be the source of malevolence stalking those gathered in a lonely villa for the reading of a will. Although Lorre was billed beneath Robert Alda and Andrea King, audiences almost certainly came to see him chew the scenery and create some tension as he chased the hand around a room.

Lorre appeared on the screen infrequently during the late forties and early fifties and even when his film work increased in 1954 his parts were usually little more than cameos. He played a servant in *20,000 Leagues Under the Sea*, a slave trader in *Five Weeks in a Balloon*, a raving Nero in *The Story of Mankind*, and a drunken clown in *The Big Circus*. At that time in his career he may have had to take whatever came his way. He told one interviewer, "I'll do anything they want me to do—ghoul, goon, or clown—as long as it's necessary." Necessary for the motion picture or necessary to make a living, he didn't say.

In the early sixties American International Pictures, riding the wave of renewed interest in Edgar Allan Poe brought about by the Roger Corman-Vincent Price collaborations, gave Lorre his final chances to strut and fret in front of the cameras. In "The Black Cat" segment of *Tales of Terror* he played a besotted cuckold who, after imprisoning wife and her lover, was tormented by the image of the cat. He got an opportunity to stretch his wings in *The Raven* as Dr. Bedloe, yet another inebriated character who served as pawn or, more appropriately, as rook in a game of spells cast between sorcerers Karloff and Price. The three actors were featured as undertakers in *The Comedy of Terrors*, a spoof that gave all the major players including iron-lunged Joyce Jameson and indestructible Basil Rathbone some great moments.

Both Price and author Richard Matheson admitted that the lines coming out of Lorre's mouth were only an approximation of what had been written. This improvisation did not bother the scenarist much and Vincent claimed that some of the ad-libs were better than the original dialogue, but Karloff and other actors were not amused when the cues became lost in Peter's translation. However, the people who signed the checks at AIP had no regrets that Lorre was just in the middle of a four-year contract which called for him to make five more pictures by the end of 1966. But all plans for future projects ended abruptly when Lorre died after suffering a stroke on March 23, 1964.

Vincent Price delivered the eulogy for Lorre at the Hollywood Memorial Cemetery. Price genuinely liked his little buddy, who at 5'5" had stood nearly a foot beneath him. In those last three films together Price got to know Lorre well and what he saw was an unhappy actor who had been hopelessly typecast.

But part of the web that ensnared Lorre he had spun himself. He did not extend the boundaries of his terrain as Price and Karloff had. We cannot picture him at the age of fifty playing an insurance salesman or steel magnate or advertising executive or rancher or architect. Instead he portrayed the villain, drunk, or madman over and over again.

Peter Lorre the actor may have been effective playing persecuted miscreants simply because he was capable of assuming exaggerated versions of Peter Lorre the man who believed that his size kept him from getting better parts. Of his eighty-two features he achieved top billing only in some of the early films and the Moto series. He appeared in just a handful of pictures that can truly be called horror films, yet he was saddled with the label of bogeyman. Even his voice did not belong to him; he had to share it with copycats appearing on TV and in nightclubs and with hoods who threatened radio detectives Sam Spade and Richard Diamond. Long before Lorre died he had been eclipsed by his sinister image which Hollywood created and the public expected.

But he was wrong if he thought, like killer Joe Reese, that "nobody loves me." We love you, Peter. It's a love that comes from *way down* deep inside that keeps driving us *on and on and on…*

Mary Philbin cringes as Lon Chaney gloats in *The Phantom of the Opera*.

The Phantom (Yikes!) Again

IT MAY COME AS A SURPRISE to modern moviegoers accustomed to following the gory trail of slashers that quite possibly the most horrifying moments ever filmed occurred over eighty years ago without a sound made or a drop of blood shed. In *The Phantom of the Opera* when imperiled heroine Christine pulled the mask off the Phantom to reveal a hideous, skull-like head, time and hearts and stood still. Beneath that loathsome disguise stood the man of a thousand faces, Lon Chaney.

Chaney's star, unlike that of many of his contemporaries, was still ascending when the silent era ended. He had an advantage over others in his field in that he did not have to learn how to express himself with his face and body; he had had been doing it virtually all his life.

It was his luck and not his curse to be born to deaf-mute parents in Colorado Springs, Colorado on April 1, 1883. Almost from the cradle he communicated with gestures and before his fourth birthday had already appeared in a pantomime play.

Shortly after the turn of the century his brother talked Lon into performing in comic operettas for a local stock company. Chaney possessed a natural clowning ability and a flair for broad comedy with exaggerated reactions. It had to be a love of the greasepaint that kept him going during those early days when he was making less than fifty dollars a month.

Chaney saw the handwriting on the wall that would be replaced by the moving figures on the screen. He started at five dollars a day as an extra sitting in saddles or train seats. Gradually his roles in two-reel westerns and slapstick comedies increased so that by 1916 he had become a regular in Universal feature films. When Chaney's request for a raise and a contract was rejected by Universal, he began to freelance with Paramount, Goldwyn, and other studios to give him bigger parts and more money.

It was with the release of *The Miracle Man* and *The Penalty* that Chaney finally became a leading player. His characters often had aptly descriptive names like Frog and Blizzard. The legless Blizzard in *The Penalty* proved to be the first of any number of roles that caused Chaney considerable discomfort as he had his calves and feet folded up and bound behind him so that when he appeared to be bouncing around on stumps he was actually painfully abusing his knees.

In the climax of *Outside the Law* he pulled the neatest trick of the year 1920 when gangster Ah Wing (Lon) murdered Black Mike (Chaney).

Although Chaney was often cast as a villain in melodramas, three of his early films were adventures from literature: he played a blackguard in an adaptation of Joseph Conrad's *Victory*, a pair of pirates in *Treasure Island*, and the crafty Fagin in *Oliver Twist*.

Chaney's appearance as a mad scientist in *A Blind Bargain* (1922) was the first of his archetypal roles that would reappear again and again in frightening films of the next three decades. He not only played the madman possessed by the idea of implanting monkey glands into humans to prove his demented theories but he also shuffled about as an ape-man. Three years later in *The Monster* his Dr. Ziska tried to bring the dead back to life in a sanitarium. In between these turns as deranged men in white he starred in *While Paris Sleeps*, the first of numerous movies to use a waxworks as a setting for nefarious doings.

In 1923 Chaney returned to Universal to give one of his most poignant performances as Quasimodo in *The Hunchback of Notre Dame*. He was touching as the deformed bell-ringer trying valiantly to save the beautiful Esmeralda who had brought a little kindness into his life of scorn and shame. Lon reached deep into his makeup kit to alter his features with a hideous eye, growths on his cheeks like huge sebaceous cysts, and a mop of hair more frightening than a fright wig.

His next picture after *The Monster*, *The Unholy Three*, marked the first time Chaney worked at MGM with Tod Browning, the man who would later direct Bela Lugosi in *Dracula* and *Mark of the Vampire*. Browning and the macabre went hand-in-hand so it was quite natural that he and the actor best-known for playing sinister characters would team up seven more times in the next few years.

The unholy three were a midget, a strongman, and Lon, who doubled as a ventriloquist and a woman. After the thieves fell out and the two others were killed, Chaney threw his voice around a courtroom to exonerate a man on trial for murder. Doubters considered Edgar Bergen foolhardy for bringing Charlie McCarthy to radio; imagine what acting ability was needed to play a ventriloquist in a silent film!

Chaney came back to Universal in 1925 to become a phantom more ghastly than anything dreamt in a nightmare on Elm Street. Even though he remained in the shadows for much of the first thirty minutes and wasn't seen in all his shocking repulsiveness until nearly half the action had unfolded, Erik/Chaney took over after the unmasking and captured all the great moments whether disguised in the masked ball scene, eavesdropping with fluttering cape from a treacherous perch atop the opera house, forcing Christine to demonstrate her courage, or employing the cunning devices in his underground horror chambers. Even in those final scenes after the frantic chase through the streets of Paris when he appeared to be cornered, Erik had one more trick up his sleeve: the threat to throw the bomb that wasn't there. That's the way for a villain to bow out, showing the mob their fear in a handful of dust.

Having played lame or legless characters several times, it was only a matter of time before Lon would assume the part of an armless man in another Chaney-Browning collaboration. In *The Unknown* (1927) Chaney, as a circus charlatan who had his arms bound to his sides to fool the public, committed a murder to protect his secret and then had his arms amputated to win the love of a woman who eventually married someone else. Acting without arms was a real challenge in a medium where everything had to be conveyed through facial expressions and gestures. Chaney did more than reveal his soul on film; he seemed willing to sacrifice part of his body every time the cameras rolled.

One Chaney-Browning film, *London After Midnight* (1927), might be considered their best—if someone can find a copy of it. Although it is considered a lost film, the story survived and there are enough stills around to attest to its existence. The photographs show Chaney in two roles: sporting a fedora as Inspector Burke of Scotland Yard and also in costume as a piranha-toothed, long-haired vampire wearing a Mr. Hyde outfit under a top hat. Near the end of the picture it was revealed that Burke had disguised himself as the vampire to help solve the case which must have bewildered audiences because the square-jawed Burke did not look anything like the unearthly creature of the night.

By 1930 people wanted to hear their favorite stars as well as see them. For his first speaking film Chaney decided to remake *The Unholy Three*. He demonstrated clearly that he could do some magic with his vocal chords just as he had done previously with his face by using a falsetto for the woman and lowering it for his principal role which, as a ventriloquist, allowed him to employ several more voices, including that of a parrot. There was no doubt that Lon had made a successful transition to talkies as *The Unholy Three* earned almost three million dollars for MGM.

Lon Chaney with some of the tools of his trade.

Unfortunately, Chaney's first talking picture was also his last. He died of cancer on August 26, 1930, shortly after the movie had been released. Douglas Fairbanks, Rudolph Valentino, and even the Keystone Cops could thrill audiences, but Lon Chaney could chill them as well. He was the trailblazer of terror, the actor who starred in the first American vampire film and who put the *mad* in mad scientist.

But Lon Chaney cannot accurately be called a horror star. He was a master artificer who assumed a multitude of identities through skillful use of his own makeup and a dedication to his craft that placed performance ahead of pain. Cowboys, crooks, clowns, creeps, conjurers, Orientals, soldiers of fortune and misfortune, buccaneers, freaks of nature, biddies—they were all putty in his hands with putty on his cheeks. The best of the nostalgic lines about the days of silent films is "They had faces then." True, and Lon Chaney had most of them.

THE RELIABLES

That smirk told moviegoers they were in good hands with Gabby Hayes.

How the West Was Fun

PICTURE AN AUDIENCE WATCHING a western movie. There before them are all the ingredients they have come to expect: the stalwart hero and his faithful horse, the beautiful damsel who needs help, the villain and his henchmen, the Indians and the cavalry, a herd of cattle, and perhaps even a posse thrown in for good measure. But wait! Somebody's missing. A western just isn't a western without that bumbling, muttering character known as the sidekick.

Westerns never suffered from a shortage of humorous sidekicks. Smiley Burnette, Pat Brady, Fuzzy Knight, Andy Clyde, Pancho, Pat Buttram, and Andy Devine rode wide or snide next to the two-fisted idols of our youth. But there was one confederate who cantered head and whiskers above all the others: that sputtering, cantankerous curmudgeon, Gabby Hayes.

George Francis Hayes was born on May 7, 1885 when the West was still wild, though he started life as a tenderfoot in Wellsville, New York. He ran away from home before finishing eighth grade and joined a traveling repertory group. After an apprenticeship in burlesque and success in vaudeville, Hayes was tempted to retire at forty-three when the Crash wiped him out and woke him up. He began looking around for work in California and found it in that novelty called the talkies.

Hayes began his film career with bit parts in musical comedies like *Rainbow Man* and *Smiling Irish Eyes*. He also appeared in two serials, *The Lost City* and *The Lost Jungle*, and a pair of the better 1930s comedies, *$1,000 a Minute* and *Mr. Deeds Goes to Town*. But once he tried on western duds as one of the *Riders of the Desert* in 1932 he knew he belonged where the buffalo roam.

For a couple years he played heavies, but in *The Lucky Texan* (1934) when he got his first chance to play a comical sidekick he milked it for all it was worth, hamming it up during the final chase that featured horses, a railroad handcar, and a Model T Ford. In another 1934 film, *Blue Steel*, while playing a sheriff he unveiled two of his great scene-stealing techniques: chewing a mouthful of tobacco and scratching that bird's nest of a beard.

The first cowboy hero he appeared with regularly was John Wayne in the Lone Star/Monogram series, although he did not have a continuing role; he might appear as an editor in one and a rancher in the next. Even in the first few Hopalong Cassidy pictures he had no permanent identity, and his character even bit the dust in the initial offering, *Hopalong Cassidy* (1935). But after being dubbed Windy Halliday in *Bar 20 Rides Again* he became Hoppy's steady partner for nineteen films until he left the series in 1939.

There were hundreds of people both in and out of show business who complained that they could not find work during the Great Depression. George Hayes was not one of them. In fact, 1932-1939 marked his most productive period. Many actors do not log a hundred films during careers that span two generations. For example, Melvyn Douglas appeared in seventy-five movies dating from 1931 to 1981, the year of his death. Gabby Hayes galloped through 105 features in *eight* years.

From 1939 to 1946 Hayes was under contract to Republic, feeling very much at home working for the studio most identified with B oaters. He rode most frequently with Roy Rogers during those years, though he also aided Gene Autry, Bill Elliott, and Buck Jones. Somehow he found time to be seen with Ken Maynard, Tim McCoy, Bob Steele, Don Barry, Allan Lane, Sunset Carson, Bob Livingston, and other good guys of the second rank. The only western actors more popular than Hayes in 1943 were Rogers, Burnette, and William Boyd. He stayed with the last cowboy star he supported, Randolph Scott, through his 170th and final picture, *The Cariboo Trail*, released in 1950.

Not only did Hayes rub elbows with most of the Hollywood cowboys but he also met just about everybody in the who's who of the West. The leading characters in *Man of Conquest* (1939) consisted of Sam Houston, Andrew Jackson, Jim Bowie, and Davy Crockett. *Young Bill Hickok* and *Jesse James at Bay* were early Rogers-Hayes films. In *Badman's Territory* (1946) he encountered the James Gang, the Dalton Boys, Sam Bass, and Belle Starr, and when they came back in *The Return of the Badmen* two years later they brought the Sundance Kid, the Youngers, and Billy the Kid with them. These horse operas may not have been historically accurate, but, as one reviewer remarked, the all-important business of westerns consisted of "hard riding and fast shooting."

Amid all the gunplay, fights, rustling, and robbing there was still time for comic relief. How did they spell relief in those sagebrush sagas? G-a-b-b-y. Oh, he answered to Breezy, Pop, Hap, Juke, Hardtack, Desprit, Pesky, Grizzly, and even just plain Gabby Hayes, but no matter what they called him he was always cut from the same shabby bit of cloth.

Although some of the humor Hayes provided resulted from pratfalls or ludicrous chases, more often than not the laughs came as a result of his irascible disposition. Quite frequently the antics of his temperamental jackass Hannibal or the temerity of some rascal set off that toothless wad of hair. He tossed distinctive curses like "You dad-ratted coyote," "You gol-darned son of a prairie varmint," "You dad-burned scalawag," and "Consarn your ding-blasted mangy hide" at man and beast alike.

Even when agreeing with Cassidy or Rogers with his trademark "Yer durn tootin'" or the tamer "Yessiree bob" it is difficult not to smile at this marble-mouthed man of the mountains. More than a few of the chuckles he generated came simply from his edentate manner of speaking which resulted in quaint expressions such as "Eggsacly. Tomorrey is Sattiday," "Shore reminds me o' th' time that loco idjit kerlapsed up in Montanny," and other forms of geriatric baby talk. Just listening to him stretch the truth with a twinkle in his eye rendered him as playful and harmless as Fibber McGee. He was a real character but a credible one in spite of or because of his idiosyncrasies. A *New York Times* critic reviewing the 1947 Bill Elliott film *Wyoming* wrote that "the bewhiskered George (Gabby) Hayes, as Elliott's partner, is entirely plausible."

Once, during a break in his film schedule, Hayes decided to let a barber remove that famous beard. He regretted it immediately because he thought his bare face made him look twenty years older. He snuck in the back door of his house and informed his wife that they were going to their home in Palm Springs. He never recanted his claim that he didn't leave their desert home until the whiskers grew back.

Hayes did little professional work after his film career ended. William Boyd, who owned the rights to the Hopalong Cassidy movies, edited a number of these features for television in 1949 and 1950 so a new generation could see Hoppy and Gabby together. George had a television series of his own from 1950 to 1954 in which he brought back a bit of the Old West for the younger set. Gabby's face showed up in a number of other places during the fifties, most notably on comic books and cereal premiums.

Anyone who claims to have been born old could be speaking for the King of the Sidekicks. George Hayes, who played grizzled galoots most of his career, did not even reach sixty-five years of age until he was through with movies at mid-century. His wife of forty-five years died in 1957, and

One of the benefits of eating Quaker Oats in 1951.

Gabby officially retired in 1960. He died February 9, 1969 in Burbank and is buried in Forest Lawn.

The legacy of Gabby Hayes upon the consciousness of Americans is probably greater than most people realize. Visualize a prospector with a mule or the Old Man of the West coming down from the hills. Now picture the coot squinting out from under the turned-up brim of that flea-bitten hat as he sits impatiently on a saddle next to Hoppy or Roy. It's the same person, riding out of our reel past into our real one.

Hayes once told an interviewer, "Gabby is a lying, bragging old codger, but everybody loves him." Yer durn tootin'!

Ronald Reagan and Frank Lovejoy on *The Winning Team* in 1952.

Never the Groom, Always the Best Man

THERE IS NO DENYING THE FACT that in all walks of life some people are going to be underrated. Among the personalities of the twentieth century Nellie Fox, Wendell Willkie, John Havlicek, Jerry Kramer, Bo Diddley, Aldous Huxley, Reginald Marsh, and Nikola Tesla were not accorded the plaudits given to their more celebrated contemporaries. Actors and actresses like Lionel Atwill, Ida Lupino, Jeff Chandler, Judy Holliday, and Agnes Moorehead will also very likely never be granted the full recognition they deserve. Frank Lovejoy, too, has stood in the wings for a long time and it is only fitting that he be called forth to take a long overdue curtain call.

Never a star in the same class as other actors of his era like Tyrone Power, Errol Flynn, and Robert Taylor, Frank Lovejoy was a lesser light even when playing first or second lead in films, yet he was comfortable in more avenues of entertainment than many of the luminaries who outshone him as he distinguished himself not only on the screen in thirty features but also on the stage, radio, and television. He was an actor who consistently produced realistic characterizations because he received his primary training not from studying actors but from observing events around him. The lessons of his youth remained with him all his life.

Lovejoy was born March 28, 1912 in New York, the son of a salesman for Pathé Films. While working as a runner on Wall Street during the Crash, he learned "how people react, what shows on their faces and what doesn't." He began his acting career with some stock companies and made his Broadway debut in Edgar Rice's *Judgment Day* in 1934. He got his first taste of radio acting in Cincinnati before returning to New York to embark upon the network career that would be his livelihood until the late forties.

Lovejoy's claim that he performed on 4,000 radio shows may seem like an inflated boast until one realizes that he toiled in the casts of *As the Twig Is Bent, We Live and Learn, Bright Horizon, Stella Dallas, This Day Is Yours, Young Widder Brown, Valiant Lady,* and other soap operas. An actor who had continuing roles on some of these daily dramas could log several hundred shows a year. One veteran of the soaps who appeared with Frank any number of times over the years was Joan Banks who also happened to be Mrs. Lovejoy.

An early adventure series gave him a change of pace from the sudsers. *The Blue Beetle* fluttered through a brief run in the late thirties as a syndicated answer to *The Green Hornet*. Frank played Dan Garrett, a novice policeman who, under a secret identity, wore a mask and blue chain mail to thwart dope peddlers, saboteurs, and other assorted criminals. After triumphing over the scofflaws, the Beetle cackled fiendishly and sprayed his vanquished foes with taunts like "Let that be a lesson to you." Lovejoy seemed to relish this hokum and played it to the hilt to please the juveniles who were enthralled by his daring exploits.

If *The Blue Beetle* did nothing else, it should have shown Frank that he belonged where the action is. Through the forties and fifties he appeared on just about every crime and adventure series including *Gangbusters, Mr. and Mrs. North, This Is Your FBI, The Amazing Mr. Malone, Calling All Detectives,* and *Mr. District Attorney*. Some of his more memorable radio work was heard on the best adventure program, *Escape,* and *Suspense,* "radio's outstanding theater of thrills."

Of all the episodes aired in the twenty-year history of *Suspense* perhaps only the famous "Sorry, Wrong Number" had more emotional intensity than the thrice-broadcast "On a Country Road." On January 4, 1954 Frank and Joan played a couple who, while stranded on a deserted road during a storm, learn from their car radio than an insane female killer had escaped from a nearby institution. The tension that arose when a distraught woman appeared in the rain is a credit to the Lovejoys' ability to make us believe they really were that terrified pair sitting in the front seat awaiting rescue or death.

Other roles on *Suspense* and *Escape* suited Frank's style even better than the melodramatic ones because he often had parts which required him to narrate the story or present it in a stream-of-consciousness manner that took the listeners into his confidence. Lovejoy, who sounded like an ordinary Joe, was an Everyman often caught in circumstances over which he had little control. In "Treasure, Inc." "Danger at Matecumbe," and certain other episodes of *Escape* he played pliable men who were led by the charms or machinations of women into webs of deceit and murder

Frank played Lt. Weigand on *Mr. and Mrs. North*.

that either endangered or ruined his life. Radio noir never had a more credible actor to roll with the punches of life than Frank Lovejoy.

Because Frank had demonstrated repeatedly on programs like *Columbia Workshop* and *Lux Radio Theatre* that he was adept at conveying the humanity of average people, he became a logical choice for the role of Randy Stone on *Night Beat*. *Night Beat* only ran from 1950 to 1952 on NBC, but it is the benchmark by which other human interest dramas should be measured. As a reporter for *The Chicago Star*, Stone was touched by the lives of old ladies, frightened runaways, punchy ex-boxers, alcoholic losers, wheeler dealers, and all the other creatures of the night who walk the urban streets. A few of the episodes in this series contain some of the most moving moments ever produced on the air because the understated acting of Lovejoy and his supporting cast was so exemplary, so natural, that we believed in and cared for the people passing before our ears and eyes. *Night Beat*, rather late radio, is truly great radio.

When radio gave way to television, Lovejoy stepped from one medium to the other in one graceful stride. Just as he sounded like one of us on radio, he had the face of the man on the street on the small screen. Although ruggedly handsome, Frank certainly wouldn't make many women swoon. He looked like an iron-jawed, two-fisted man ready for action, and there was plenty of that to be found on TV.

His first work on television was for the dramatic anthology programs *Stage 7, Four Star Playhouse,* and *Lux Video Theatre*. One of his notable efforts on *Lux* in 1954 which won him an Emmy nomination for best actor in a single performance was a version of "Double Indemnity" in which he played the malleable insurance salesman ensnared by femme fatale Laraine Day. He also earned critical acclaim for his performance as Lieutenant Maryk in "The Caine Mutiny Court-Martial" on *Four Star Playhouse*. Another *Four Star* production in which Lovejoy played a man named McGraw who protected Audrey Totter from her ruthless husband became the pilot for *Meet McGraw*, a series that ran during 1957-1958 on NBC and rerun under the title *The Adventures of McGraw* the next season.

McGraw, like radio's Pat Novak, became involved in cases either because people just showed up and asked him for help or else he started snooping around just to be snooping around. On his dangerous assignments McGraw seemed more willing to use his fists than a gun. Lovejoy did play a private detective of the hard-boiled school, Mike Barnett, in *Man Against Crime*, one of the rock 'em, sock 'em offerings of that period.

During those twilight days of network radio and the early years of television, Frank also found ample work in motion pictures. His first film, *Black Bart* (1948), and his last one, *Cole Younger, Gunfighter* (1958), were westerns. He played military officers eight times, most notably as the understanding Sergeant Mingo in *Home of the Brave* and as the tough colonel in *Retreat, Hell!* who drove his men relentlessly but who still showed concern for them. His performance in the lead of *I Was a Communist for the FBI* was lauded by a *New York Times* critic as "a model of light and efficient resolution, ingenuity, and spunk." His acting in a handful of these spy and crime dramas was so authentic and done with such apparent ease that another *Times* reviewer, after viewing his work in *Finger Man*, stated that "if Mr. Lovejoy can walk through a part like this in his sleep, he still does a good job." And he did a good job when called upon to be a heel in *The Americano*, a detective watching an edgy Humphrey Bogart in *In a Lonely Place*, an acerbic songwriter in *I'll See You in My Dreams*, and a peppy Rogers Hornsby playing on *The Winning Team* with the actor who would one day win his way into the White House.

One of Frank's better performances can be seen in *Try and Get Me* (aka *The Sound of Fury*), a grim tale of hapless Howard Tyler who falls into a life of crime and eventually becomes a victim of mob violence. Contrasted with the ravings of psychotics Jerry Slocum (Lloyd Bridges) in this film and Emmett Myers (William Talman) in *The Hitch-Hiker*, Lovejoy's characters of Tyler and Gil Bowen may seem to some viewers to be too phlegmatic when actually Frank was doing the more difficult job of conveying natural emotions of trapped men caught in desperate situations. The brief, protective embrace and blessing of the little Mexican girl by Bowen in *The Hitch-Hiker* and the expression on conscience-stricken Tyler's face as he stands by the bedroom window credibly convey the torment of caring fathers who know that any minute they may never see their families again.

In 1953 Lovejoy appeared in two of the early 3-D motion pictures, *House of Wax* and *The Charge at Feather River*. In the latter film when Lovejoy's character, Sergeant Baker, unleashed a stream of tobacco juice toward the camera at a rattlesnake, members of the audience either ducked or raised their arms to protect themselves. Now that's real acting!

That same year Frank supported Virginia Mayo in *She's Back on Broadway*. In 1960 *he* was back on Broadway, this time in one of the triumphs of his career. Lovejoy's portrayal of unethical candidate Joseph Cantwell in Gore Vidal's *The Best Man* was one of that season's most distinguished performances. Brooks Atkinson, by no means the easiest critic to please, wrote that "Frank Lovejoy gives an extraordinary portrait of a bigot and charlatan who believes his own propaganda." It seemed that this would be a natural role for Lovejoy to assume when the play moved to the screen, but it was not to be. Cliff Robertson played Cantwell in the 1964 film for by then the best man was no longer around.

In the fall of 1962 the Lovejoys were appearing in a road version of the Vidal play in New Jersey. On October 2 Joan found Frank dead in bed in their room at the Warwick Hotel in New York. She called in a physician who pronounced the cause of death to be a heart attack. Frank had gone full circle: Gotham to Gotham, stage to stage, big city, bright lights. It had been an active life, but one that was far too short.

Melvyn Douglas, Lee Tracy, and Lovejoy in the play that ran for over 500 performances on Broadway in 1960 and 1961.

The footlights were turned out early on other actors such as Alan Ladd and Montgomery Clift, but they had entered self-destructive tunnels from which they could not escape with their best work clearly behind them. For Frank Lovejoy life might truly have begun at fifty because he was right at the top of his form at the end.

No amount of praise or wishful thinking will alter the virtual certainty that Lovejoy would never have become a star of the first magnitude. It must be with some mortals that their destiny is to barely touch the brass ring and never to hold it in their hands. For every John Wayne there is a Forrest Tucker, for every Henry Fonda an Ed Begley, for every Gary Cooper a Dennis O'Keefe. Frank Lovejoy never had his day in the sun and he will probably always remain in the shadow, but that isn't such a bad place to be. After all, the shadow knows and so do we.

Alan Ladd as Shane.

A Prisoner of Doubt

IF WILLIAM SHAKESPEARE COULD HAVE STUDIED the life of Alan Ladd, he might have changed one of his most famous speeches to read "The fault, dear fans, in our stars is not in the gossip columns, but in themselves, that they are unstable." The tragedy of Alan Ladd is that he never overcame the feelings of insecurity which followed him from rocky cradle to premature grave.

The seeds of discontent were planted not long after his birth on September 3, 1913 in Hot Springs, Arkansas. He spent much of his youth moving from place to place, first with his widowed mother and then with her and his stepfather. Not having any place to call a real home damaged his fragile psyche just as years of improper nourishment while on the road took a toll on his body. When his family settled in California and Alan started school, he had the embarrassing distinction of being both the oldest and shortest boy in his class. The students called him "Tiny" Ladd.

At North Hollywood High School he excelled in two activities for which size did not matter: swimming and dramatics. He won medals for his prowess in the pool and might have entered the 1932 Olympics had not his confidence been shattered by an errant dive that resulted in a head injury. Fortunately, his success in *The Mikado* and other productions had the opposite effect by bolstering his self-image.

Alan got up the nerve to enter the Universal Studios acting school and, even though he washed out after a few months, he learned much about using voice and manner there. By working as a grip for Warner Brothers, he observed how movies were made and became more convinced than ever that he wanted to step in front of the cameras.

While waiting for his big break into pictures, Ladd found that practice at improving his diction paid off with small parts on the *Lux Radio Theatre* and other dramatic radio shows. A talent agent, ex-actress Sue Carol, liked what she heard and, when the handsome blond visited her office, she liked what she saw. It was truly a labor of love for her to find work for this client who would become her husband in 1942.

Sue went out of her way to find parts for Alan, even to the point of keeping costumes on hand so if, for example, she learned that a studio was casting a western or a naval adventure, he could make a quick change and show up suitably garbed for that film.

Her resourcefulness paid off. Even if Ladd's name appeared far down in the credits at least he was working steadily in his medium of choice supporting Douglas Fairbanks Jr., Victor Mature, Clark Gable, and other stars. At this time Sue's strategy seemed to be "Don't worry about the size of the role. Just get your face seen often enough and good things will happen." Many people who have seen two notable films of 1941, Laurel and Hardy's *Great Guns* and the magnificent *Citizen Kane,* are unaware that Alan Ladd appeared in both pictures.

It might have been a combination of his death scene in RKO's *Joan of Paris* and Sue's power of persuasion with director Frank Tuttle that earned Alan the part of a cold-blooded killer in *This Gun for Hire*. Even though he was fourth-billed, Ladd's performance as Raven clearly outshone the efforts of Veronica Lake, Robert Preston, and Laird Cregar. He did have a moment of redemption at the end but no romantic interludes with Veronica.

Ladd and Lake, who also appeared together in *The Glass Key, The Blue Dahlia,* and *Saigon,* were barely speaking acquaintances in real life, yet on the screen their good looks and underplaying meshed perfectly. Her small stature also made them a natural couple for any setups because camera crews did not have to resort to the gimmicks (deceptive angles, trenches for the women, or boxes for Alan) employed when he played opposite taller actresses.

Paramount, pleased that *This Gun for Hire* made millions at the box office, gave Ladd a bonus, raised his salary, and rushed *The Glass Key* into theaters to take advantage of his sudden fame. One fight in this story of political corruption contains possibly the most realistic right hook ever thrown in a movie. William Bendix, playing his patented thick-skulled hood, accidentally knocked Ladd unconscious, but both men later came to regard it as a lucky punch because it marked the beginning of a close friendship between the two actors.

Ladd played likable rogue *Lucky Jordan* who foiled Nazi agents and then decided to join up with "an outfit that will pay me fifty a month and

Ladd and Lake in *The Blue Dahlia*.

throw in a uniform free," a speech that coincidentally described his personal life because during most of 1943 he served in the Army.

Riding the crest of popularity, Alan seemed to be everywhere: his face on the covers of movie magazines and on screens in theaters, his dulcet tones on radio shows when Bob Hope broadcast from camps, and his name on the lips of a growing body of fans. Throughout his career Ladd regarded his admirers fondly and always honored requests for photos and autographs.

When Alan returned to the Paramount lot after his discharge, his star was still brightly shining. In *The Blue Dahlia* he reunited with Bendix and Lake in a tale of murder and dissimulation written by Raymond Chandler that was just what post-war audiences wanted to see. Ladd showed that he was capable of more sensitive portrayals outside of crime dramas as the lead in adaptations of two literary landmarks, *Two Years Before the Mast* and *The Great Gatsby*, but he had not escaped the low opinion of his own abilities. "I can't act," he would confide to friends. "I don't have the training those other guys do. What if I can't make pictures anymore?"

Sue provided the initiative that Alan lacked. She convinced him to take a "leave of absence" from Paramount until they paid him what other top revenue-producing actors were earning. It took considerable prodding to get him to attend parties and ceremonies and, although she convinced him that they were a necessary part of a star's life, no one could make him comfortable in society. Ladd's shy taciturnity became so much a part of his personality that, had he been seated next to Gary Cooper at one of those functions, he might have responded to Coop's famous "Yep" with "You've stolen my dialogue for the rest of the night."

It would have been a stretch for Ladd to make such a comment because he seemed out of his element with humor. His sketches with Abbott and Costello, Burns and Allen, and Ed Gardner went over the airwaves like a lead vacuum tube. Even on his own show, *Box 13*, the jests between his character, Dan Holiday, and Suzy, Dan's addlepated secretary, were painfully forced and uniformly witless. The rest of *Box 13* made for good listening as Ladd's resonant voice recounted the dangerous situations that confronted Holiday, a mystery writer who advertised for adventure and got all he could handle every week. In the movies Ladd wisely steered clear of comedy except for cameos; he knew be belonged in the world of suspense and intrigue reflected in the titles of his films: *Appointment with Danger, Chicago Deadline,* and *Thunder in the East.*

In the late forties and early fifties he starred in several westerns including *Whispering Smith* and *Branded* which were above average and in one that is an unqualified classic. His performance in *Shane*, especially in the scenes with Brandon De Wilde, Jean Arthur, and Van Heflin in which he convincingly registered compassion and anguish over a misspent life, vividly demonstrated that he was an actor and not a pretender. The sequence with Brandon that closed the picture is a strong contender for the most poignant moments in the history of cinema not only because of the boy's plaintive cries but also because the heartfelt sincerity of Shane's advice and the remorse on Ladd's face were perfectly executed by a man who had learned his craft well.

It is ironic that by the time *Shane* was released and winning praise in 1953 Ladd was not even in the country to appreciate the upswing in his popularity. He left Paramount after completing *Botany Bay* for a more lucrative contract with Warner Brothers that allowed for some freelancing. Money also motivated the Ladds to move to England where Alan could make films without paying taxes providing he stayed at least eighteen months. Although Ladd later regretted leaving his old studio and disliked being away from home for such a long time, financial security became one of the driving forces in his life despite the fact that he had invested wisely in property and had plenty in the bank. The fear that his wealth would disappear in a moment kept pushing him on to make pictures even when infections and illnesses were telling his body to rest.

When he returned to America, Ladd found that he was still in demand. The westerns produced by Warner Brothers and MGM (*Drumbeat, The Big Land, The Badlanders, Guns of the Timberland*) with the expectation that some of the magic of *Shane* would rub off on them turned out to be fairly routine. When given a change of pace, Ladd rose to the challenge. In *The Deep Six* (1958) he played a conscientious Naval Lieutenant during World War II who was torn between duty for his country and his Quaker beliefs regarding nonviolence. That same year he delivered a balanced performance in *Proud Rebel* as an ex-solider embittered by his experiences in the Civil War yet softened by love for his mute child (played by his real son, David). If Alan looked at home in the cockpit scenes of *The McConnell Story*, it is a testament to his acting ability because he had a pathological fear of flying.

Ladd could still reel in some beauties, but the one that got away in 1956 tormented him the rest of his life. After he rejected an offer to play Jett Rink in *Giant*, the part went to James Dean. George Stevens, director of *Shane,* also had cause for second-guessing because he did not get along with the headstrong Dean and would have preferred to work with Ladd who listened to rather than rebelled against advice, but at least he won an Oscar for directing *Giant* that helped him forget those skirmishes while Alan had to live with the thought that Dean's nomination for best actor might have been his.

By the time the war story *All the Young Men* appeared in theaters in 1960 the years of nonstop work and worry along with frequent illnesses, irregular eating patterns, and growing reliance on the bottle had left their marks on Ladd's face. The good scripts that once poured into his box were now being offered to Paul Newman, Gregory Peck, and Burt Lancaster. To get top billing he had to go to Europe in a sword-and-sandal turkey called *Duel of Champions* for which he almost did not get paid. If that fiasco did not suggest to him that the curtain on his career was descending, his brief appearance in *The Carpetbaggers* would have convinced him that the end was near had not the end already come. On January 29, 1964, five months before the premiere of *The Carpetbaggers*, his butler found the lifeless actor in bed, a victim of a fatal and possibly accidental combination of alcohol and sedatives.

It was a sad conclusion to a life that should have been a rags-to-riches story with a happy ending. Instead, memories of childhood poverty haunted him with suspicions that disaster waited around every corner. Ladd proved that a leading man need not be tall and dark, yet remained sensitive about his height and could not escape the feeling that producers and other studio executives treated him like a boy. Despite evidence of notable performances in *Shane* and at least four other pictures, he could not shake off the self-doubts about his talent.

Behind that talent was one of the nicest human beings who ever became a major Hollywood star. Humble, conscientious on the set, gracious to interviewers, accessible to fans, honorable in business dealings, loyal to friends and family, he was almost too ingenuous to survive in that jungle of inflated egos and rampant deception. The bittersweet story of Alan Ladd is one of a good man who yearned to be up there on the screen but who didn't want to stand in the limelight and realized too late that he couldn't have one without the other.

Jack Carson, the serious actor, with Zachary Scott and Joan Crawford in *Mildred Pierce*.

Mr. Reliable

THERE IS A LIMBOLAND BETWEEN THE MOUNTAINTOP where the screen legends reside and the plain which is home to the character actors. Perpetually stuck in the middle are those performers who were frequently cast as second leads such as Preston Foster, Dan Duryea, Evelyn Keyes, Ralph Bellamy, Van Heflin, Claire Trevor, Marjorie Reynolds, Eddie Albert, and Diana Lynn.

Perched high on a ledge somewhere within sight of the peak sits Jack Carson all alone muttering to himself "So near and yet so far."

No one could have predicted that John Elmer Carson born October 27, 1910 in a small town in Manitoba, Canada would have even reached those heights. His family moved to Milwaukee when he was still a child and he attended St. John's Military Academy in Delafield from 1923 to 1928.

At Carleton College Jack excelled in football and swimming and he dabbled in a few dramatic productions, but he seemed more interested in pulling pranks than in pulling grades. He then sold insurance for a year until an acquaintance named Dave Willock suggested that they get an act together and go on the stage. Just like the fabled team of McGee and Nitney that Fibber always bragged about, Willock and Carson hit audiences with an assortment of quaint sayings, snappy jokes, soft-shoe dances, and bouncy songs.

By 1935 vaudeville was dying and, as Jack freely admitted, "We helped kill it." When the act split up, Carson became master of ceremonies at a theater in Kansas City, but he never forgot his friend even after he left the stage for Hollywood in 1936.

The standard joke of self-deprecating comedians, "I started at the bottom—and stayed there," is only half-true in Jack's case. He did begin slowly with uncredited parts like filling Henry Fonda's car with gas in *You*

Only Live Once and doing his bit as a cop in Wheeler and Woolsey's *On Again-Off Again,* but at least his face was now before the public in theaters all over the country.

Producers at RKO liked what they saw of him so they put him in seven of their best features in 1938 alone. In *Law of the Underworld* Carson gained notice as a henchman of Chester Morris, and he drew more attention as a droll criminal named Red Jenks who gets bumped off in *The Saint in New York.* His vaudeville training served him in good stead aiding Joe Penner in two farces, *Go Chase Yourself* and *Mr. Doodle Kicks Off.* He acted as the right-hand man to Ginger Rogers in *Vivacious Lady, Having Wonderful Time,* and *Carefree,* though he was usually left out at the end and soon became known as the bounder left out cold by the right hand of the other man. Somebody had to be the brash suitor of the sweetheart who took it on the jaw from the hero before the fade-out and Jack obligingly kept sticking his chin out time after time.

Even though he occasionally found himself in significant films such as *Destry Rides Again* and *Mr. Smith Goes to Washington* and had moved up in the credits, more often than not Carson was stuck in B pictures supporting the likes of Jed Prouty, Stu Erwin, and Bob Burns. Of the dozen movies in which he appeared in 1940 most are forgotten or forgettable except *Love Thy Neighbor,* an effort to bring the Jack Benny-Fred Allen feud to the screen, and *Lucky Partners,* which might be regarded as his breakthrough film because, though he loses Ginger once more, he grabbed third billing behind her and Ronald Colman.

Perhaps it was the uneven nature of the projects he did bouncing between RKO, Paramount, Universal, and Fox that convinced Carson to sign a contract with Warner Brothers. At least by regularly appearing with the major actors of Warner's, audiences would say, "That's the same guy who kissed Ann Sheridan and took a shot at Edward G. Robinson" instead of "Who's that chump who got socked in the kisser?"

Right away in *The Strawberry Blonde* (1941) he made an impression as the genial villain who steals Rita Hayworth away from James Cagney who in turn romances Olivia de Havilland. But even when Jack's character wins he loses for it turns out that Rita is a shrew and Olivia a darling so Cagney gets the last laugh after all.

Playing a comedic heel became Carson's customary role as he provided some of the sparks that came between Myrna Loy and William Powell in *Love Crazy* and between Cagney and Bette Davis in *The Bride Came C.O.D.* In the service comedy *Navy Blue* he was on the receiving end of soap, eggs, and pail of water tossed by Jack Oakie. As Joe Ferguson, a gridiron hero and former beau of the wife of a university professor in

The Male Animal, he threatened to disrupt the marriage of Henry Fonda and Olivia de Havilland. Carson's beefy frame and expert delivery of fatuous remarks enabled him to give an impeccable performance in this adaptation of James Thurber's play and earn best acting honors from the National Board of Review of Motion Pictures.

Carson proved to be a versatile actor who could still play it straight when he assisted Robinson in *Larceny, Inc.* and befriended Errol Flynn in *Gentleman Jim*. But the most fortuitous pairing with any Warner player came in 1942 when he squared off against Dennis Morgan for Ann Sheridan's hand in *Wings for the Eagle*.

The camaraderie between Morgan and Carson became apparent when the pair sang and danced their way through "Tiptoe Through the Tulips" and "Am I Blue?" in *The Hard Way*. During the filming the two ex-Milwaukeeans cemented a friendship that lasted long after the cameras stopped rolling. Once a week Jack, his wife (singer Kay St. Germain), Dennis, Marie Wilson, and old pal Willock put on a vaudeville show at an army camp near Los Angeles. Carson gave generously of his time to entertain troops during the war and eagerly accepted parts in the patriotic movies *Thank Your Lucky Stars* and *Hollywood Canteen*.

Dennis, Jack, and Ann reunited in *Shine on Harvest Moon* (1944) in which Carson as a hammy magician named Georgetti and Marie Wilson as his dotty assistant provide the comic highlights. Just Carson's wild-eyed expressions and the manipulation of his mustachioed lip were enough to send audiences into paroxysms of laughter.

His flexible features were spotlighted in his next film (the first to give him top billing), *Make Your Own Bed*, in which he played an inept detective helping and hindering Jane Wyman and also in *The Doughgirls* when he never seemed quite certain as to whether he was married, single, on foot, or on horseback. When Carson was stumbling around in a fog of uncertainty, his perplexed face seemed to be saying, "Will somebody tell me what's going on around here?"

In 1945 he took a break from lightweight fare when he assumed the part of Wally Fay, a brassy realtor who is of dubious aid to Joan Crawford in *Mildred Pierce*. As Carson demonstrated often later in his career, he could be an oily creep if the part called for it.

It was in the postwar pictures with Morgan that Jack reached the peak of his popularity. In *One More Tomorrow* he played a butcher who stood up to some bigwigs and got the girl at the end. The *Two Guys from Milwaukee* were Dennis as a prince and Jack as a cabbie, although Carson made most of the humor and had one reviewer raving that he could "get more muscular energy into a comedy role and edge it with a finer degree

Carson, the comic actor, with Ginger Rogers in *The Groom Wore Spurs*.

of mental lassitude than any six screen comedians we can think of …the boy's very, very funny."

The Time, the Place, and the Girl featuring the duo hit theaters shortly thereafter and *Two Guys from Texas* in 1948, but neither proved to be as amusing as *Milwaukee* or *It's a Great Feeling* (1949) in which the pair, playing themselves, engaged in some double crossing à la Hope and Crosby as they each tried to win a movie part for (and the affections of) waitress Doris Day. (Jack and Doris played virtually the same roles in another 1949 effort, *My Dream Is Yours*.)

Many people today are unaware that during the 1940s Carson hosted his own radio program. After doing some work on *The Signal Caravan* with veterans Hal Peary and Jane Morgan, he headlined a CBS program with support from Arthur Treacher, Dale Evans, and Willock. During the 1947-1948 season he switched to NBC to host *The Sealtest Village Store*.

The Village Store featured kidding between Carson, Eve Arden, Willock, and bald-pated bandleader Frank De Vol, usually followed by a skit parodying specific films or stock characters often seen in pictures like cowboys, pirates, and gangsters. The laughs frequently came from confusion over complicated names such as Flooglefleegle and a steady stream of corny gags along the lines of "Who are you, k-nave?" "Who wants to k-now?" Carson aptly described the program when he said, in response to one of Dave's inanities, "That's not funny, but it's silly." Silly or not, it is still a joy to hear to Eve and Jack display their talents at mimicry while tossing dialects and foreign accents back and forth.

When television replaced radio as the public's medium of choice, Carson was there as well, sharing hosting duties on *The Four Star Revue* with Danny Thomas, Ed Wynn, and Jimmy Durante from 1950 to 1952. During the next decade he appeared on *Ford Theatre, U.S. Steel Hour, Playhouse 90, Studio One, Lux Video Theatre, Screen Director's Playhouse*, and other dramatic programs of merit as well as *Bonanza, Thriller, Zane Grey Theatre, The World of Disney, Alfred Hitchcock Presents*, and other popular shows. Of special note is his appearance in a seriocomic episode of *The Twilight Zone* as a used car salesman who suddenly can't help telling "The Whole Truth."

Though his work on TV and radio kept him busy, Carson still found time to appear in films. *The Good Humor Man* (1950) is one of his more humorous roles as he dodges policemen and crooks for eighty minutes while managing to take a pummeling from fists, flour, soot, water, and pies. The movie was derivative of and inferior to Red Skelton's *The Fuller Brush Man* and is perhaps most noteworthy for teaming Carson with Lola Albright who became his third wife in 1952.

Jack again took it on the lam in *The Groom Wore Spurs* (1951), but at least as a phony cowboy star the humor focused on what he did and not the damage done to him, and old screen mate Ginger Rogers added to the merriment by acting as his lawyer. In 1954 Carson ambled about amusingly as another cowpoke, this one full of arrogance and bluster, who gave Rosemary Clooney all the headaches she could handle in *Red Garters*.

In the mid-fifties his parts in movies diminished and were almost exclusively dramatic. Carson was in top form as a cynical press agent in *A Star Is Born*. He demonstrated a forceful presence playing the loud-mouthed neighbor in *The Bottom of the Bottle,* conniving sheriff in *The Tattered Dress*, obnoxious heir in *Cat on a Hot Tin Roof,* loyal mechanic in *The Tarnished Angels*, and corrupt politician in *King of the Roaring 20s.* Even when he assumed a lighter role like the loutish captain sent into space at the end of *Rally Round the Flag, Boys!* his shady characters usually got their just desserts.

It seems that Jack Carson, however, never got what was coming to him. He died too soon, of stomach cancer that stuck him down on January 2, 1963 at the age of fifty-two while he was rehearsing to appear in a production of *Critic's Choice,* a fitting title for a finale because Carson was the critic's choice, the director's choice, and the people's choice to be the dependable role-player who stirred the plot. He could fill the screen with those massive shoulders and that broad grin and be convincing whether behaving obstreperously or treacherously.

Jack Carson could act circles around comedians and clown better than most actors. Awarding him the title of "Hollywood's All-Around Mr. Reliable" may not seem like much of a consolation prize to Jack sitting up there on that aery perch unless he looks up some night at the sky and realizes that some of those heavenly bodies shine brightly and some just glimmer but they all are stars.

William Bendix with Riley's TV family: Peg (Marjorie Reynolds), Junior (Wesley Morgan), and Babs (Lugene Sanders).

The Lovable Lug

DEEP IN THE FILES OF THE COLUMBIA Broadcasting System a card contained these words about an actor written after his radio audition: "Excellent—a bet for *Gangbusters* and *Skyblazers* …Specializes in mugs, tough guys, gangsters, policemen." An interviewer described the man's expression as being "very like the puzzled look you see on the face of a dumb fighter as he comes out for one more battering in the tenth round."

For a time William Bendix rebelled against typecasting and considered his face his misfortune until he met a character who taught him to accept life's vicissitudes with a philosophical "It's a losing fight."

To young Bill Bendix who grew up in a tough New York neighborhood fighting became a way of life on the streets, although he credited his mother's firm hand with keeping his name off police blotters. Because his father held a variety of jobs from musician to stevedore, Bill hardly had time to get into any trouble in one place as he passed through ten different schools in eight years.

Bendix, who loved playing stickball, passing a football, or swimming off the docks more than hitting the books, left school in 1920 at the age of fourteen to engage in a series of odd jobs, none of which brought him more satisfaction than working at the Polo Grounds when both the Giants and Yankees played in that stadium. There, in the shadows as locker boy and in the sunlight as batboy, he got to know some of the legendary players of the time. Bendix claimed to have seen a hundred of Babe Ruth's 714 home runs and to have contributed to Ruth's indigestion when he brought the slugger handfuls of hot dogs. Bill filed these memories away and later retrieved them when he assumed the title role in *The Babe Ruth Story* in 1948.

In the 1930s Bendix engaged in a series of jobs including running a grocery store, massacring sentimental ballads as a singing waiter, counting automobiles crossing a bridge for the WPA, and selling cheese, a position he lost for eating too many samples.

His first nibble of show business came as a member of the Federal Theater where, for $17.50 a week, he performed in gymnasiums, cellars, and school auditoriums located light years away from the Great White Way. In 1939 as part of the New York Theatre Guild he appeared in several minor productions on Broadway and gained additional experience by playing summer stock in New England.

Later that year his breakthrough role, that of a policeman named Krupp in William Saroyan's *The Time of Your Life*, allowed him for the first time to support his wife and daughter with a respectable salary of $100 a week and, more importantly, brought him to the attention of producer Hal Roach, who signed Bendix to a movie contract.

Although *Woman of the Year* is fondly remembered today as the first pairing of Spencer Tracy and Katharine Hepburn, it also marked the screen debut of William Bendix, cast in the role that would soon become his trademark, a tough cookie on the outside who talked with a snarl but who everyone knew was a softie at heart.

Because Bill's face naturally looked like that of a battle-tested veteran, he seemed right at home playing soldiers in the war pictures *Wake Island* and *Guadalcanal Diary*, his work in the former earning him an Academy Award nomination for Best Supporting Actor in 1942. In *Guadalcanal Diary* he purloined the plaudits that might have gone to top-billed Preston Foster and Lloyd Nolan and earned one critic's praise for his impressive performance that "adds humor and meaning to every scene in which he appears."

As the dimwitted detective Brannigan in Abbott and Costello's *Who Done It?* Bendix proved to be an adept scene-stealer in comedies as well. His antics during the handcuff bit, according to Bob Thomas in his book *Bud and Lou*, prompted Costello to storm into producer Alex Gottlieb's office and demand that Gottlieb never again "put anybody who's funnier than me in a picture of mine!"

If the histrionics of a shackled Bendix brought laughs in a supporting part, his dual role of a poetic marine and a chorus girl in *Abroad with Two Yanks* generated twice as many guffaws two years later in 1944. The sight of the corseted, burly Bendix singing "I Need a Man" while dancing sedately amazed the character played by co-star Dennis O'Keefe and amused audiences who welcomed such wartime fluff in their local theaters.

Although Bendix had some funny moments as a gangster who won't say die in Fred Allen's *It's in the Bag*, his métier continued to be dramatic roles. As the one person who had to endure more pain than any of the other survivors floating in *Lifeboat*, he earned one of the highest tributes given to an actor when a critic for the *New York Times* stated that "William Bendix, who never has been bad in a film, has never been better."

In the title role as *The Hairy Ape* (1944) he brought some sensitivity to a brutish stoker in the adaptation of Eugene O'Neill's play, prompting one critic to call it "his all-time high performance" and to claim that his work in the film "rarely falls below excellent." As Hank, a man bent

Bendix and Alan Ladd on their guard in *China* (1943).

on a course of murderous revenge against a woman who insulted him, Bendix brought authenticity to the part because in real life slights and ridicule wounded him deeply due to his inherent desire to please everyone. Bill took adverse criticism perhaps too seriously, though conversely he never nurtured a Hollywood ego over the puff pieces distributed by Paramount.

At Paramount he developed a friendship with Alan Ladd and also an image as a tough guy in the Ladd vehicles *China*, *The Glass Key*, *The Blue Dahlia*, *Two Years Before the Mast*, and *Calcutta*. The disparity between the blond good looks of the one actor who spoke in carefully-worded sentences and the plain features of his stocky colleague who delivered lines in his characteristic Carnarsie dialect made for a natural contrast on the screen even in movies that didn't cast them as adversaries.

Of all the films Bendix made the one that turned his career in a different direction and eventually gave him a lasting identity was a now-forgotten B picture called *The McGuerins from Brooklyn*. Irving Brecher, who had written screenplays for Marx Brothers comedies and MGM musicals, saw in Bendix's performance as a strong-willed schmo the embodiment of the oafish character who would blunder through *The Life of Riley*, a comedy show he planned to produce. The audition was a mere formality and in January 1944 Bendix stepped into the lead role in a radio series that would become his steady meal ticket until 1951.

Unlike other situation comedies in which geography and social status remained anonymous or of little import, *The Life of Riley* set the scene virtually every week by reminding listeners that the Rileys, solidly entrenched in the working class, lived in a bungalow within coughing distance of smoggy Los Angeles. From that home Chester A. Riley, lunchbox in hand, trudged daily to and from his work as a riveter at an aircraft factory.

Even though listeners could identify with the economic struggles of a middle class family, the writers took the sting out of the similarities by making Riley not only arbitrary and stubborn but also nearly illiterate and clearly obtuse. Every week they placed self-revealing words in Riley's mouth that we understood but he apparently did not such as "It's time you learned that if you don't ask me questions, you won't get a foolish answer" or "You can't win an argument with a moron and I ought to know" or "I'll dig around in my head and come up with something concrete." The barbs with which he cut himself deepest sometimes came when the voices of Alan Reed or Frank Nelson as his conscience haunted Chester by claiming to be in his head to which Riley angrily replied, "That's a lie! There's nothing in my head."

Bendix perfected his delivery of these and other lines to the point where he squeezed more laughs out of simple statements than the jokes merited. When Riley enigmatically claimed to neighbor Jim Gillis, "I'm engaged to be married…but don't tell my wife," we can almost see Gillis doing a double take. When wife Peg forgave him for "all the nutty things I've done," Riley blithely added, "Now I know why we make such a nice couple. You're even nuttier than I am," a punch line Bendix served up so delectably that it is still funny after hearing it numerous times. Anyone who listens to Bill's reading of this half-hearted ad which, at the insistence of his conscience, Riley placed in a newspaper for a fur he found and doesn't smile belongs in the Buster Keaton Stone Face Club: "If you think I found something you think you lost, try and prove it."

Being fatuous and funny week after week is no easy matter as listening to the puerile chatter emerging from the mouths of Jerry Lewis and Marie Wilson fifty years ago proves. Somehow Bendix imbued lines like "Hand me a piano" with an air of spontaneous asininity before launching into some treacly lyrics about mothers that induces us to chuckle and say, "Yes, that's something that nitwit Riley might really blurt out on the spur of the moment."

Bendix made Riley such a good-hearted lummox that we forgave him for stumbling weekly into predicaments which were exacerbated by his obstinate behavior. Paula Winslowe capably played Peg, the patient wife who tolerated the hot-tempered but soft-headed klutz, and John Brown did double duty as Jim Gillis, who often laid traps for his gullible neighbor, and as Digby O'Dell, the friendly undertaker who dispensed good advice and whose entrance could be predicted when the soliloquizing Riley, in the midst of one of his dilemmas, tossed out a straight line such as "I'll never be in any deeper than I am right now."

Versions of O'Dell's famous signature lines, "You're looking fine, Riley. Very natural" and "I better be shoveling off" became the "in" ways to begin or close conversations across the country, and Bendix through Riley also contributed to the colloquialisms of the time with his remarks of "My head's made up," "It's a losing fight," "You're hanging an innocent man," and "What a revoltin' development this is." If such a book as *Bartlett's Familiar Expressions* existed in the post-war years, *The Life of Riley* would probably have earned as many entries in it as any other radio program. Bendix, who routinely exhibited his range as Riley by going from pigheaded autocrat to whimpering weakling in seconds, continued to appear in a variety of movies while working on the series including a musical fantasy (*A Connecticut Yankee in King Arthur's Court*), a western (*The Streets of Laredo*), comedies (*Kill the Umpire*, *A Girl in Every Port*), message pictures (*The Time of Your Life, Johnny Holiday*), and crime melodramas (*The Dark Corner, Detective Story*).

Of course, when Brecher wrote the screenplay and planned to direct *The Life of Riley*, there could be no one else to take the part of Chester Riley than William Bendix. Ironically, it was because Bendix had contractual commitments to complete *The Life of Riley* and other films that prevented him from being part of the cast of the initial TV version of *The Life of Riley* starring Jackie Gleason which ran from October 1949 to March 1950.

Late in 1952 with a lull in his movie career and no radio show to prepare for, Bendix began filming episodes of *The Life of Riley* which premiered in January 1953 and became an NBC Friday night regular until the end of the run in August 1958. Changes from the radio cast included Marjorie Reynolds as Peg and Tom D'Andrea as Gillis. Neither John Brown nor the character Digger O'Dell appeared in the televised version of the Riley saga during the Bendix years.

The Chester Riley viewers saw on the small screen did not disappoint for just as Bendix sounded like a blue-collar stiff so his craggy appearance might easily have prompted those at home in front of their sets to say, "Now there's a guy who looks like he works in a factory."

The plots still centered on Riley's mismanagement of the family's affairs including sticking that prominent nose into the activities of his children, although complications involving Riley's eccentric friend Waldo Binny (Sterling Holloway) figured in a number of episodes. When prognathous Bendix appeared head-to-head with Holloway whose husky voice often gave way to squeaks better suited to the throat of Henry Aldrich, viewers might easily have said aloud, "There's a guy who looks like he works in a factory listening to a guy who sounds like he swallowed the factory's whistle."

Throughout the 1950s Bendix made guest appearances on comedy-variety shows and performed on a number of televised dramatic programs including two of historic note. On September 29, 1952 he starred as "The Hollow Man" on the last episode of *Lights Out*. In 1958 during the first season of the *Desilu Playhouse* he played a man who experienced a recurring dream which placed him back in December 1941 trying to warn people about the coming attack on Pearl Harbor. That episode, "Time Element," written by Rod Serling, sold CBS on the idea of a new series that would eventually be called *The Twilight Zone*.

Bendix appeared at least once on virtually all the prestigious anthology programs including *Playhouse 90, Schlitz Playhouse of Stars, Fireside Theater, Screen Director's Playhouse, Robert Montgomery Presents*, and

Philco Television Playhouse. In the summer of 1959 he played one of the unfortunate kidnappers in a special adaptation of O. Henry's story "The Ransom of Red Chief." Later that year he returned to thugdom one more time as a leader of the Tri-State Gang who found out it's a losing fight to tangle with Eliot Ness and *The Untouchables.*

Early in 1960 Bendix starred in his only other TV series, *The Overland Trail*, which attempted to follow in the tracks of the other westerns riding television's crowded range at that time. The premise of a Civil War vet and a dexterous youngster played by Doug McClure interacting with different passengers in their stage every week made for a type of *Grand Hotel* on wheels, but after seven months it became just another desert drama to bite the dust.

Bendix tried several more times to score with a series. A 1961 episode of *Mister Ed* misfired as a pilot for *The Bill Bendix Show* and an unaired pilot for *Rockabye the Infantry* was produced in 1963. When CBS cancelled *Bill and Martha*, a proposed series teaming Bendix with Martha Raye, the actor sued the network for breach of contract. Although Bill received a sizeable amount for settling out of court, his alter ego Riley might have appraised the situation with a pithy "I got the dough but no show."

To an old trouper like Bendix the show had to go on even if it meant taking minor parts in featherweight films like *Law of the Lawless* and *For Love or Money* or appearing in summer stock productions of *Take Her, She's Mine* in venues so far removed from the bright lights that his most severe critics might have been strident crows in nearby cornfields.

He continued taking the roles that came his way until pneumonia claimed him at the age of fifty-eight on December 14, 1964, less than three months after his last television appearance on an episode of *Burke's Law.*

Four years before his death Bendix took stock of his accomplishments in an interview in which he said, "I've had a long, varied, eventful career. I don't hate anybody and I don't have any bitter thoughts. I started out without any advantages, but I've been lucky and successful and I've had fun."

He lived the life of Riley so we could have the time of our lives.

J. Carrol Naish as a French-Canadian guide in *Saskatchewan* (1954).

A Man of Many Parts

ASK THE QUESTION "Who played a criminal in more movies: Humphrey Bogart, Edward G. Robinson, James Cagney, or J. Carrol Naish?" and the likely response from many people today is "Who is J. Carrol Naish?"

J. Carrol Naish, who charted more often on filmdom's underworld hit parade than Bogie, Eddie, Jimmy, and a raft of Hollywood heavies, belonged to that caste of character actors which included such familiar faces as Alan Mowbray, James Gleason, Franklin Pangborn, and Walter Brennan whose presence in movies of the thirties, forties, and fifties added color and depth to the story lines. A distinction that separated Naish from most of his confreres is that he could dip into his arsenal of dialects so that both the sound tracks and the images flickering on the screen bore a strong note of verisimilitude.

The one glaring irony in his life is that of all the nationalities he portrayed in pictures which included Arabs, Spaniards, Native Americans, Russians, Mexicans, Frenchmen, Greeks, Chinese, Indians, Poles, and Japanese, Joseph Patrick Carrol Naish, born January 21, 1896 in New York City as the great-great grandson of the Lord Chancellor of Ireland, never played an Irishman.

More interested in learning from life rather than from books, Naish dropped out of school in his teens and earned a meager living as a promoter of new songs at vaudeville theaters and nightclubs. After serving overseas in World War I, he decided to stay in Europe after the Armistice. As Naish toured the Continent in the early 1920s singing and doing odd jobs for room and board, he began to absorb the culture of the countries he visited. By the time he returned to the United States in 1926 he could speak eight different languages.

After serving as a stunt man and extra in silent films, Naish landed the part of a Japanese prince in a touring company of *The Shanghai Gesture*. One member of that company, Gladys Heaney, became his wife in 1928 and remained so right up until his death on January 24, 1973.

After appearing in several more plays, Naish tested for a small role in the early talkie *Cheer Up and Smile*. Before long he became Public Enemy #187, appearing frequently in crime pictures with lurid titles like *Ladies of the Big House* and *Homicide Squad*. Sometimes he labored in anonymity, but by 1932 he had earned a spot in the credits as well as roles that promised more than bit parts.

As Loretta Young's Chinese father in *Hatchet Man*, he performed capably under William Wellman's direction until the title weapon cut short his character's life in one of those cops-and-robbers films that Warner Brothers did better than any other studio.

Because of Naish's swarthy countenance, he quickly became typecast in villainous roles. Even when appearing in the comedies *The Kid from Spain* and *Elmer the Great* his job was not to throw straight lines to Eddie Cantor or Joe E. Brown but rather to menace the heroes or their friends.

Whether cast as a bootlegger in *The Mad Game*, a poisoner in *The Devil in Love*, a corrupt lawyer in *No Other Woman*, or a cheating gambler in *Frisco Jenny*, Naish might have been a candidate for the title of Hollywood's ruffian-in-residence of 1933 had he not already earned the honor of busiest actor for he showed up in eighteen features that year plus a serial, *Mystery Squadron*. In fact, this period marked the most active portion of Naish's career as he appeared in an average of fourteen movies a year from 1932 through 1936.

In 1934 he assumed the guise of a real person for a change, Leon Trotsky, in *British Agent*, and when he played a blackmailer in *Upperworld* who bumped off a chorine played by Ginger Rogers, it marked the only time Ginger was killed in a picture. The same couldn't be said for Naish's characters because in most of his movies that year, including *One is Guilty, Return of the Terror, The Defense Rests*, and *Murder in Trinidad*, they paid dearly for their crimes. Naish could have answered the title question posed in one of his films that year (*What's Your Racket?*) with "Playing hoods and getting caught or killed before the end credits roll."

In the mid-1930s both the quality of his pictures and of his parts improved. He assumed the role of Grand Vizier in *The Lives of a Bengal Lancer*, buckled some swash as a pirate in *Captain Blood*, portrayed a hoodlum in the Bette Davis crime meller *Special Agent*, and played an Indian Major in *The Charge of the Light Brigade* and a French officer in *Anthony Adverse*.

Even when producers placed him back into the world of crime Naish had stepped up a notch during 1936 and 1937 when he took on three notable detectives. As a snake charmer in *Charlie Chan at the Circus*, moody scofflaw in *Bulldog Drummond Comes Back*, and sly shopkeeper in *Think Fast, Mr. Moto*, the outcome was clear: guilty as cast.

He solidified his tough guy image as the *King of Alcatraz* and, in *Persons in Hiding*, joined with Patricia Morison on a criminal rampage inspired by the exploits of Bonnie and Clyde. Alluring, saronged Dorothy Lamour could do nothing to curb the malicious tendencies of the natives he played in *Her Jungle Love* and *Typhoon* who planned to make the white visitors crocodile fodder.

In *Beau Geste* (1939) Naish bit into his meaty party as Rasinoff who, as thief and informer, got his comedownance in a fall from a watchtower. His gangsters now traveled in royal company: if he wasn't trying to corner the oriental rackets in *King of Chinatown*, he was abetting the *Queen of the Mob*.

He assumed a sympathetic role in *Blood and Sand* (1941) as the matador-turned-mendicant who found favor with the current king of the cape (Tyrone Power). For his portrayal of a confused Italian prisoner of war in *Sahara* Naish received an Academy Award nomination as Best Supporting Actor of 1943.

When given a chance to work on the right side of the law, Naish slipped on a trench coat and performed admirably as detectives solving mysteries in *Calling Dr. Death* and *Enter Arsene Lupin*. But, more often than not, he walked by night and stepped into the shadows to do dirty deeds in *The Whistler* or, in the xenophobic war years, played Japanese or Nazis in a slew of movies including *Behind the Rising Sun*, *Waterfront*, and, most notably, in the *Batman* serial as the nefarious Dr. Daka.

In the mid-1940s Naish began doing occasional guest shots on radio programs, most notably on *Suspense* in the episodes "Footfalls" (1945) as a blind father reluctant to believe his son committed a murder, and later in 1952 as the unfortunate bloke who found "The Treasure Chest of Don Jose."

Perhaps the high point of Naish's cinematic career came in 1945 when he rendered an endearing performance as a Mexican accepting a posthumous Medal of Honor for his son in *A Medal for Benny*. For his efforts he earned his second Academy Award Best Supporting Actor nomination by the Academy of Motion Picture Arts and Sciences. (He won the Golden Globe award in that category.)

In 1946 he played another anxious father as he tried to steer son John Garfield away from a musical career in *Humoresque*. In *Carnival in Costa*

Alan Reed looks on as Naish makes a point with *Life with Luigi* director Mac Benoff.

Rica (1947) and *The Kissing Bandit* (1948) he assumed patriarchal duties again for the benefit of Vera-Ellen and Frank Sinatra, respectively. Naish took playing fathers to fully-grown children while barely nudging the age of fifty in stride for by that time he had tried his hand at everything from an artist in *Gentleman at Heart* to a hunchback in *House of Frankenstein* to an ape-man in *Dr. Renault's Secret*.

In 1948 Naish began making fewer pictures because in September of that year he assumed his most famous role, that of Luigi Basco in the CBS radio program *Life with Luigi*. Every week on this heartwarming show, listeners followed the adventures of immigrant Luigi as he grappled with understanding the complexities of American life and making a living in his humble antique shop in Chicago. Naish played Luigi with such sincerity that the audience knew his naïve honesty would win out over the machinations of crafty Pasquale, who repeatedly attempted to ensnare Basco in traps from which the only escape was to marry Rosa, Pasquale's giggling, obese daughter.

Life with Luigi, with its unique framing device of Luigi writing a letter to his mother in Italy, with the important civic lessons learned in quaint fashion by Basco, Schultz, Horowitz, and Olsen in night school, and with its unabashedly patriotic messages spoken by a sometimes bewildered newcomer who demonstrated more wisdom than jaded natives, successfully accomplished what other situation comedies seemed afraid to attempt, namely mixing humanity and humor. Not just any actor could make audiences shed a tear and laugh out loud in the same thirty minutes; J. Carrol Naish accomplished this feat regularly until the show left the air in March of 1953.

When *Life with Luigi* moved to television in September 1952, most of the radio cast came along with Naish: Alan Reed as Pasquale, Jody Gilbert as Rosa, Mary Shipp as teacher Miss Spaulding, Ken Peters as Olsen, and Joe Forte as Horowitz. Sig Ruman replaced Hans Conreid as Schultz. *Life with Luigi* had a short run on TV, concluding on December 22, 1952.

In 1954 Naish won the title role in *Sitting Bull,* a natural choice after portraying that tribal leader in *Annie Get Your Gun* (1950) and a Nez Perce Chief in *Across the Wide Missouri* (1951). The actor considered his favorite screen role to be an Italian police detective in *Black Hand* (1950).

In the fall of 1955 he returned to the theater in the Broadway production of Arthur Miller's *A View from the Bridge*. In the first portion of the drama Naish portrayed a German immigrant named Gus and after the intermission he returned as Alfieri, an Italian lawyer. A critic for the *New York Times* called his performance "particularly good."

In 1957 and 1958 Naish filmed thirty-nine episodes of the syndicated series *The New Adventures of Charlie Chan*. He starred as the famous investigator using London as his home base with support from James Hong as Number One son Barry.

In Naish's final series, *Guestward Ho!*, he stole the show as Hawkeye, a canny Native American whose ironic remarks garnered most of the chuckles in this sitcom which ran during the 1960-1961 season.

Naish, who freelanced throughout his long motion picture career as he selected the roles he wanted, took an eclectic approach to television as well. He reprised his role in "A Medal for Benny" on *Lux Video Theatre* in 1954, played a gambler in "Key Largo" on *Alcoa Hour* in 1956, and also appeared on the *Schlitz Playhouse of Stars* and *Desilu Playhouse*. He popped up in offbeat roles on the western series *Wagon Train, Wanted: Dead or Alive, Bonanza, The Restless Gun, The Texan,* and *Cimarron City*. He could also be seen having fun with the casts of *Green Acres, I Dream of Jeannie,* and *Get Smart*.

There wasn't much fun to be found in his last project. Somehow Naish was enticed out of retirement into playing Dr. Frankenstein in *Dracula vs. Frankenstein*, an odious exploitation film that escaped into theaters in 1971. Performing in a wheelchair and reading his lines from cue cards, Naish looked as if he and co-star Lon Chaney Jr. couldn't wait for "The End" to come. Two years later it did, for both men.

There are those who claim the end had already come earlier for actors like J. Carrol Naish who relied on ethnic characterizations for their livelihood. Such criticism, raised as early as 1952 when objections to the representation of Italians shown in the television version of *Life with Luigi* may have contributed to its hasty exit, are not without validity. But Naish proved that he didn't need a dialect to affect a credible performance. He was the product of an industry that not only tolerated stereotyping but avidly propagated it.

Regardless of whether he played a crook or a cowpoke, a papa or a peasant, a major or a matador, a trapper or a Trappist, a gaucho or a guard, a composer or a count, a publisher or a prospector, a sleuth or a spy, J. Carrol Naish treated audiences to realistic portrayals that merited the simple accolade "What a character!"

Ida Lupino, Howard Duff, and Stephen McNally in a tense scene from *Woman in Hiding* (1950).

King of Spades

ALTHOUGH THE MOST FAMOUS NUMBERS in radio may have been the 39 of a parsimonious comedian and the 79 of the fun-loving couple who lived in and on Wistful Vista, another set of digits, usually spewed out in rapid succession by a detective as a preface to the story of his latest adventure, also brings back the glow of yesteryear for many people. When Sam Spade dished out his license number 137596, listeners eagerly pulled up close for a big helping of a capered caper served exquisitely by the man playing the detective, Howard Duff.

Duff, who late in life admitted that it seemed like he had always been in radio, actually didn't earn his first job in the medium until after graduating from a Seattle high school. By that time he had abandoned his early ambition of becoming a cartoonist and had turned his attention to acting in *Volpone, Private Lives*, and other productions with the Seattle Repertory Theater.

Duff considered some of his early work on Seattle station KOMO to be that of a disc jockey because his duties consisted mainly of playing records, reading commercials, and tossing in patter to fill time until the newscasts which he also read. Later he moved to KFRC in San Francisco where he served as relief announcer.

His first real acting on the air came as the *Phantom Pilot*, an airborne champion of justice who, with the help of a plane called Skyball, swooped down on crooks and captured them like a cowboy hero corralling outlaws with his trusty steed. A lasting benefit of the overblown series was that one of the cast members, Elliott Lewis, became a lifelong friend.

After the *Phantom Pilot* had been grounded, Duff found work during the Depression when Arch Oboler cast him in some of his plays. Oboler certainly proved to be a friend in need then, but later, after America entered World War II and Duff received his induction notice, could not deliver on a promise which was quite in keeping with the power the author believed he had. Oboler told Duff he would have the draftee out of the army in twenty-four hours. Duff did indeed receive his discharge—four years later.

However, another radio contact, Ted Sherdeman, writer of *Latitude Zero*, a landmark but short-lived science fiction show on which Duff had appeared, used his influence to find a spot for the actor with the Armed Forces Radio Service. Besides editing out commercials from the discs sent to stations for rebroadcast to the military, Duff tapped into his experience as a DJ by introducing prerecorded musical numbers inserted to fill out the shortened programs.

Howard tailored his dialogue to fit the program so that, for example, after Archie finished his weekly sign-off with his employer, Duff fractured a little more English in the same style: "Now, before we leave Duffy's Tavern, leave us put a couple nickels in Duffy's jukebox. Duffy's jukebox, where the feet meet the beat. Well, the platter is spinning, the needle's in the groove, and here's the foist number coming up."

After the war ended, he found work on dramatic shows and also on lighter fare. In a bit of fluff for *Hollywood Preview* called "Slightly Sixteen" Duff demonstrated that he could insert a little life in the "man must marry in a hurry to inherit a fortune" plot by playing nicely off Jane Withers and, judging from the audience's reaction to a scene with another actress, putting his heart (and lips) into the romance.

His appearances on *Suspense* acquainted him with William Spier, the program's producer-director, and may have given him an advantage when Spier held auditions for a series to be based on the exploits of Dashiell Hammett's famous private eye. Rather than try to imitate Humphrey Bogart, who had starred as Sam Spade in the best-known screen version of *The Maltese Falcon*, Duff decided to read the lines with a devil-may-care air which convinced the bearded director that having a tough guy who was also a wise guy might be just what post-war Americans wanted to hear.

The Adventures of Sam Spade lived up to its title. Spade didn't handle cases in the conventional sense; he ventured off on chases that veered in capricious directions and we went along, holding on tight for the bumps and curves Sam inevitably encountered.

There are few, if any, "serious" programs more pleasurable to listen to than *The Adventures of Sam Spade*, and perhaps the principal reason why it is so entertaining is that Duff and Lurene Tuttle, who played Spade's secretary Effie Perrine, enjoyed the roles so thoroughly their enthusiasm imbued the show with a sense of fun unequalled along Gumshoe Row.

Certainly writers Bob Tallman and Gil Doud deserve some credit for the witty lines, but the banter between Spade and the gallery of eccentrics he met could only be accomplished by an actor who knew how to turn from playful joker to two-fisted pragmatist on a dime. Duff delivered some of the opening teasers, like the one for "The Prodigal Daughter Caper," with the slickest slice of ham this side of John Carradine. He preceded his dictation of "The Death Bed Caper" by launching into "Many brave hearts are asleep in the deep," started down the scale with "so beware, b-e-e-e-e," gave the date (June 20, 1948) as if beginning his report to Effie, reverted back to the song with a discordant "ware," and added a bold-faced "I have no shame" that made listeners slap their knees and gleefully say, "That's our Sam!"

Indeed, it was Spade's (and Duff's) inherent honesty that won our hearts. Usually the discovery of a corpse or a clue preceded the break for the middle commercial, but on "The Hot Hundred Caper" Sam noted wryly that nobody was directing bullets or taking swings at his head and then grimly confessed, "Not much of a cliffhanger, but the best we could do this week."

The best they could do ranks as some of the best radio programming produced after WWII. If the part called for him to play Spade relatively straight in a tale of betrayal like "The Dick Foley Caper," Duff adopted a world-weary, "sour racket" mode appropriate for radio noir. Conversely, the farcical "Flopsy, Mopsy, and Cottontail Caper" remains delightful even after repeated playings as Spade manages to keep his wit and dignity intact dressed as a white rabbit chasing red herrings.

The mingling of mystery and mirth constituted a delicate balance and Duff juggled them effortlessly. His tongue-in-cheek remarks never let us forget that he was portraying a gun-in-holster detective who meant business, not funny business.

Duff carried the Spade magic to all three networks at one time or another from 1946 to 1950 and even to other programs. Very likely the best of the hour-long *Suspense* episodes is "The Kandy Tooth," a caper which pitted Spade (Duff) against Kasper Gutman (Joseph Kearns), his old adversary from *The Maltese Falcon*. One of the most amusing *Burns and Allen* shows is the episode in which Gracie could not separate Duff from the character he played and had Howard arrested. The night Duff capered with Joan Davis he solved a murder (and got the show's biggest laugh) by announcing that the victim had been fed jumping beans instead of kidney beans and had "been kicked to death from the inside."

Despite the popularity of the program, *The Adventures of Sam Spade* was kicked to death from the outside. Because Hammett, who, according to intimate friend Lillian Hellman, never listened to the show and Duff, who had signed a document in support of the Hollywood Ten, had been deemed Communist sympathizers, the sponsor of the show, Wildroot, decided to cancel the series. A letter-writing campaign brought the show back to NBC in November 1950, but without Duff as prime mover the series limped along for six months before expiring.

Unlike others who had been stung by the Red Scare and could not find any kind of employment in the entertainment industry, Duff simply walked around that temporary roadblock in his career and right through the open gates of the studios whose producers could always use handsome actors who looked like they knew their way around the block.

After debuting in the prison film *Brute Force* in 1948, he moved up to second billing and won accolades as a con man in *The Naked City*, then advanced to the head of the class in the stark crime melodramas *Illegal Entry* and *Johnny Stool Pigeon*.

One of the early highlights of Duff's movie career was as Jack Early in *Shakedown* (1950). As an unscrupulous photographer who used his camera for extortion and blackmail, Duff still conveyed enough humanity so that audiences felt a trifle sorry for Early when he was shot by a thug and redeemed himself somewhat before dying by snapping a photo of his killer.

Duff and Shelley Winters looking shifty-eyed in *Johnny Stool Pigeon* (1949).

The forthrightness that marked Duff's portrayal of Spade came across on the screen as well. Even if his characters were dishonest, his assessment of his own character was not. When he told Coleen Gray "We're no good" in *Models, Inc.*, he spoke with the honest candor of a heel we could trust to tell it like it is.

Although Duff saddled up in the westerns *Red Canyon, Calamity Jane and Sam Bass,* and *Blackjack Ketchum, Desperado*, he seemed out of place in the wide open spaces as if he had taken a wrong turn where the sidewalk of the mean street ends. But when cast in *Women's Prison* as a conscientious doctor or a helpmate for a *Woman in Hiding* or a dedicated police lieutenant in *While the City Sleeps* or a waffling detective in *Private Hell 36*, he was back on his beat with his perspicacity still honing in with unflinching accuracy as in *Private Hell 36* when his Jack Farmer told Cal Bruner (Steve Cochran), "You're sick, Cal. You don't care about anyone or anything."

Another reason he appeared right at home in these films is that his co-star in all four pictures was Ida Lupino who became his wife in 1951. (Ida admitted, "I fell in love with his voice on the radio before I even met him.") They also teamed up in the CBS-TV comedy series *Mr. Adams and Eve* in 1957 and 1958 as married and sometimes harried movie stars. Just as Tuttle's and Duff's affection for their parts on the Spade program shone through their performances, so on television husband and wife genuinely relished lampooning their images on both sides of the camera and taking swipes at the studio system as Eve Drake and Howard Adams.

Throughout the 1950s Duff appeared in a number of TV anthology series including *Ford Theater, Climax, Schlitz Playhouse of Stars, Front Row Center, Science Fiction Theater, Crossroads,* and *Alcoa Theater*, and he also put in an appearance as Mark Twain on *Bonanza*.

He began the following decade as star of *Dante* on NBC. For one season as Willie Dante, a suave nightclub owner with a mildly shady past, Duff traded quips with his bartender (Tom D'Andrea) and maitre d' (Alan Mowbray) and punches with assorted scofflaws.

Although he appeared on almost every dramatic program of note during the 1960s including *I Spy, Burke's Law, Mr. Novak, Judd for the Defense, Arrest and Trial, The Twilight Zone, Combat,* and *The Alfred Hitchcock Hour*, his meatiest part came as Sgt. Steve Stone on *Felony Squad* (1966-1969).

As the gray crept into his temples and seeds of jowls formed along his chin line, Duff moved smoothly from leading roles in which he supported the laws into guest shots where he bent or broke them. Whether appearing on *Mannix, Police Squad, The Streets of San Francisco, The Rockford Files, Shaft* or working with a longer leash in made-for-TV movies such as *Tight as a Drum*, *Snatched*, *The Heist*, or *A Little Game*, his characters were often on their way to dusty death or at least a prison cell.

When *Dallas* hit the jackpot in the late 1970s and Americans became infatuated with watching the unsavory rich dealing deceit at every hand, Duff knew they were singing his song: "Having a Grand Old Crime." As Sheriff Titus Semple on *Flamingo Road* he knew where all the bodies and secrets were buried. On *Knot's Landing* he played Paul Galveston who used his millions to manipulate for his purposes and to degrade for his amusement. As Senator Harry Harrison O'Dell on *Dallas* he had more power than money but no more scruples than the other wheeler-dealers he played.

He continued to find steady employment on *Murder, She Wrote*, *Scarecrow and Mrs. King*, *Detective in the House*, *Magnum, P.I.*, and other crime shows almost to the end of his life as well as land choice roles in the acclaimed films *Kramer vs. Kramer* and *The Late Show*.

Howard Duff died of a heart attack July 8, 1990 at the age of seventy-six. In an action that proved the hard-boiled actor was really a soft-hearted person, Duff had been up late the night before his death at a telethon to raise funds for residents of Santa Barbara who had lost their homes in a recent fire.

Although Duff admitted that his early love was the stage and that he enjoyed making motion pictures, he never lost his affection for radio. He first stepped in front of a microphone in the mid-thirties, could still be heard half a lifetime later on *Zero Hour* in 1973 and *The Sears Radio Theater* in 1979 and 1980, and it is one role in radio that overshadowed all his other accomplishments as an actor.

If some student wants to write a paper about Duff's place in show business history, the words spoken weekly by announcer Dick Joy would be instructive: "And now, with Howard Duff as Spade, Wildroot brings to the air the greatest detective of them all in *The Adventures of Sam Spade*." Period. End of report.

Errol Flynn and Basil Rathbone facing off in *The Adventures of Robin Hood*.

A Well-Graced Actor

A SCULPTRESS WORKING ON A MALE BUST she would call "The Actor" started with a distinctive profile not unlike that of John Barrymore, then, after adding a little of William Powell's urbanity, stepped back to view her work. "Why," she said, "it's Basil Rathbone!"

The result should not have come as a surprise. No composite portrait put on canvas or computer monitor could improve on that sculpture. Few men looked more like a distinguished thespian than Basil Rathbone did. Fonda, Lancaster, Cooper, Bogart, Mitchum, or even Gable would not have seemed out of place driving a truck or building homes, but Rathbone had the face of one born to tread the boards.

He certainly was not acting when he cried after the doctor slapped life into him on June 13, 1892 in Johannesburg, South Africa, but his tearful response to a cue three years later may have saved the lives of his family. His father, a mining engineer who was suspected of being a British spy by the Boers, put his family on a train that was to take them to safety. Before he hid himself under a seat behind his wife's skirts, he gave her instructions to make the child cry if questioned by the Boers. When an armed soldier began interrogating the mother, she started pinching Basil and it was his wailing that hit a sympathetic note in the soldier who gave her his blessing and left them unarmed.

There was even a bit of drama after they reached the coast. Basil's mother, after experiencing a discomforting dream in which she saw a storm-tossed ship sinking as a band of Scottish Highlanders stood by, persuaded her husband to delay sailing for England until the following week. The ship they would have taken did indeed go down in the Bay of Biscay with a band of Highlanders on board, an incident Rathbone always brought to mind whenever he heard or spoke Hamlet's words "There are more things in heaven and earth, Horatio, than are dreamt of in your philosophy."

After such early brushes with death, the rest of his childhood in England seemed tame in comparison. From 1906 to 1910 he attended Repton School where he proved to be an indifferent scholar because his mind was usually on the playing fields when his body wasn't. But even then the stellar athlete who was nicknamed Ratters nurtured a love of the theater and secretly wrote a play he called *King Arthur* when classmates thought he was studying.

When he left Repton, the Rathbones made a deal: if, after a year in a business position Basil still wanted to become an actor, his father would not stand in his way. Basil served his allotted time with the Globe Insurance Company, but just as at school the play was the thing as he would spend his lunch hours in the office attic reciting lines to the cobwebs and rafters.

On the very day his year of service was up he met with a cousin, Frank Benson, who ran a theatrical company. Rathbone was hired immediately and put in Benson's number two company to gain experience which he certainly got acting in towns and villages all over the British Isles. In the summer of 1913 he was brought up to the first team. By the time he entered the military during World War I he had assumed forty-seven different roles in twenty-two of Shakespeare's plays.

After the war he stepped back on the stage in *Peter Ibbetson* and *The Czarina*, although he never strayed far from the Bard. With mixed emotions Rathbone recalled that during one performance of *Othello* he had an awful spell of hiccups that was transformed from embarrassment into triumph when a reviewer praised him for his novel idea of playing a tipsy Iago.

Although Rathbone always made it clear that the theater was his first love, in the 1920s he was slowly drawn into motion pictures. He believed that acting in front of an audience is more difficult than on the screen because there the actor is completely visible and therefore must be totally convincing. Because Basil was stage-trained, he made the transition to talking films much easier than some movie actors of the 1920s. His first talkie, *The Last of Mrs. Cheyney*, gave him a chance to work with Norma Shearer who became a lifelong friend.

People accustomed to seeing Rathbone with the deerstalker and calabash pipe may forget that he was known more for villainy than heroics in his early roles. In 1930 he did play a very Sherlockian Philo Vance who amazed a colleague with his powers of deduction in *The Bishop Murder Case*, but he was more frequently cast as an antagonist with a sneer on his lip and a weapon in his hand confronting Tyrone Power in *The Mark of Zorro*, John Barrymore in *Romeo and Juliet*, and Errol Flynn twice in *Captain Blood* (1935) and *The Adventures of Robin Hood* (1938). With that lean and hungry look and cold steel in his grip, Rathbone made such men as Esteban, Tybalt, Captain Levasseur, and Sir Guy of Gisbourne dangerous indeed.

He remained hissable when wielding a cane as the insensitive Mr. Murdstone in *David Copperfield*, and equally unsympathetic as the callous Evrémonde in *A Tale of Two Cities*. As Karenin opposite Greta Garbo's Anna in *Anna Karenina* he was not really nasty, yet audiences felt more affection for Anna's lover, Vronsky (Fredric March), than for Basil as the betrayed husband.

But no matter whether Rathbone played arrant knave or haughty cold fish he brought a certain class to any film. *Son of Frankenstein* (1939), sometimes lauded for its expressionistic sets and lighting, has a different flavor to it than others in the series and Basil's stylish mien certainly contributed to the overall tone of the film. His Wolf von Frankenstein was one of the least mad scientists in any horror film. In jaunty hunting jacket or well-tailored suit he carried himself like a living ad torn from *Esquire*; in lab coat, listening with his stethoscope for signs of life in the monster, he looked the part of a sane man who simply had been bitten by the same bug that had infected his father. In 1941 when he did play *The Mad Doctor* even then he wasn't mad in the Lionel Atwill-Bela Lugosi style; he behaved more like a Bluebeard who married rich women and then disposed of them.

Whether appearing as scoundrel, soldier, or king, critics recognized Rathbone as one of the most capable actors in England and United States. He was nominated for best supporting actor for his work in *Romeo and Juliet* and for his portrayal of doddering Louis XI in *If I Were King*. He also won accolades for his role as a doubt-torn British officer in charge of doomed members of *The Dawn Patrol*. His Richard III in *Tower of London* remains a textbook example of how to underplay a villain who lets his actions speak louder than words.

1939 is considered one of the high points in Hollywood history because *The Wizard of Oz, Gone with the Wind, Stagecoach, Wuthering Heights,* and other notable pictures were playing in theaters then. Two of Rathbone's films released that year entitled *The Hound of the Baskervilles* and *The Adventures of Sherlock Holmes* added more than a little screen magic of their own. Basil Rathbone and Nigel Bruce, Sherlock Holmes and Dr. Watson; the pairings go together as naturally as bread and butter. Sherlock Holmes *was* Rathbone's bread and butter for fourteen films and for a radio series that ran from 1939 to 1946. Though purists find Bruce too bumbling and some Sherlockians prefer Jeremy Brett to Basil, there

Rathbone, Ida Lupino, and Nigel Bruce in *The Adventures of Sherlock Holmes*.

was little in Rathbone's portrayal of Holmes that was not consistent with the detective Sir Arthur Conan Doyle created. Rathbone most certainly fit the description Doyle included early in *A Study in Scarlet*: over six feet, excessively lean, sharp and piercing eyes, thin, hawk-like nose, an air of alertness and decision, a prominent chin marking a man of determination. Basil looked like Holmes and, for millions of moviegoers and radio listeners, he *was* Holmes.

Late in life Rathbone expressed his belief that the timing for the Sherlock Holmes movies was wrong, that the pictures should have been made earlier so they did not seem so out-of-date. The real problem, however, is that, except for the two pictures released by Twentieth Century-Fox in 1939, they weren't *dated enough*. When Universal took over the series in 1942, Holmes and Watson were brought out of the Victorian era where they belonged into a contemporary setting where they were expected to match wits with Nazis and spies. These films may have been topical and the chemistry of Rathbone and Bruce made them moderately entertaining, but by 1946 the formula had become pretty much cat-and-mouse. Basil felt that by playing the same part too many times he had been confining his growth as an actor so he turned his back on Hollywood to return to the theater.

For a short period he did some radio work on *Theater Guild of the Air* and made guest appearances with Fred Allen and other comedians until being asked to perform in *The Heiress*, an adaptation of *Washington Square*, the novella by Henry James. Before the play's run on Broadway and on tour was finished, Rathbone had assumed the identity of callous Dr. Sloper 672 times and had earned a well-deserved Tony award.

During his hiatus from motion pictures Basil, like virtually every other performer, was drawn as if by magnetic attraction to videoland. Rathbone later wished he had been more discriminating in accepting offers to work on television for he would appear as the Duke in a version of *Huckleberry Finn* one month and be seen joking with Sid Caesar or Milton Berle the next. He grew to distrust that medium because he believed it fostered mediocrity and stifled the imaginations of viewers.

Basil also felt some misgivings about selling his services to Madison Avenue. The magazine, radio, and TV ads were lucrative, but not very satisfying and a bit degrading to an actor of his stature. He took pride, however, in the literary recordings he made for Caedmon Records. Anyone who comes upon these treasures in a thrift store or at a flea market is in for a treat because his mellifluous readings of works by Nathaniel Hawthorne and Edgar Allan Poe do for the spoken word what George Gershwin did for music.

In the mid-fifties with no theatrical opportunities in sight and his distaste for television growing, Rathbone decided to return to movies after an eight-year absence, first as worthy foil to Bob Hope in *Casanova's Big Night* and later to Danny Kaye in *The Court Jester*. In *The Black Sleep* (1956) he played sinister Doctor Cadman whose use of human guinea pigs to find a cure for his comatose wife's condition resulted in a houseful of mutants who eventually turn on him. In 1958 as a snobbish Boston banker Basil proved to be a thorn in the side of Spencer Tracy's Mayor Skeffington in *The Last Hurrah*. He wasn't often given leading roles any more, but when presented with a juicy part like the wily sorcerer in *The Magic Sword* (1962) he shone brightly as the sun around which the other players revolved.

In 1959 Basil demonstrated his versatility in Archibald MacLeish's play *J.B.* After playing the character who symbolized God for ten weeks, he took over Christopher Plummer's part as the devilish Mr. Nickles and was commended by critics for the ease with which he assumed both roles.

In 1962 he set his feet back on familiar ground with old friend Poe in *Tales of Terror*. In "The Facts in the Case of M. Valdemar" segment Rathbone was quite effective as the diabolical hypnotist. His part in *The Comedy of Terrors*, released the following year, seems small in comparison to the on-screen time given co-stars Vincent Price and Peter Lorre, but Rathbone almost steals the picture as landlord J.F. Black who refuses to say die. No matter what means undertakers Price and Lorre devise to kill him, Black, as well-versed in Shakespeare as the man who played him, awakens from his death-sleep and intones sonorously, "What place is this?" It was a marvelous comic performance that allowed Basil to ham it up gloriously.

In the early sixties Rathbone hit the road again, taking his one-man show to the people. During this tour his presentations consisted of reading poetry and performing selected scenes from plays. These appearances were notable for his impassioned, spellbinding interpretations and amusing asides. Rathbone sometimes stopped the proceedings to give the audiences an opportunity to examine both profiles and recount how in his early days on the stage an actress had referred to him as "that young actor with a face like two profiles stuck together."

Basil appeared in a few more films, but his heart wasn't in them and he probably wished the same could have been said for the rest of his body. *Ghost in the Invisible Bikini* is tolerable only because Rathbone and Boris Karloff are in it, but what Basil was doing in *Hillbillys in a Haunted House* may perplex his fans forever. Perhaps just as he thought that Holmes was dated so too actors of his caliber were out of fashion and, if he wanted to work in pictures at that time, he had to appear in drive-in dreck. In view of his railing against mediocrity it must have galled him to be a part of some of it. His fatal heart attack on July 21, 1967 spared him the mortification of seeing his final film performance as a guitar-strumming spirit in the obscure *Autopsy for a Ghost*.

With his death the world lost an actor whose eloquence and noble carriage brought dignity and professionalism to every medium he touched. His absence is one that is still apparent for no one has been able to play a cunning villain with his brio or a hawkshaw with such splendid aplomb. In his time Basil Rathbone played many parts. He made all the world his stage and the stage his world.

THE MOVIES

Even the losers back then are still winners today.

Fascinating Rhythms

WHEN WAS THE LAST TIME YOU WALKED OUT of a theater humming a song from the movie you have just seen? I asked a friend that question about the time I was writing this article during the summer of 1997 and, after he came up dry, he said he would mull it over and get back to me. He later timorously confessed that he thought it last happened when the "Gonna Fly Now" theme from *Rocky* was running through his head—over twenty years before our conversation.

It is likely that discriminating moviegoers today have to search the crannies of their craniums for memorable film tunes. If they were born after about 1970, they may not even realize that there was a time when motion pictures often left audiences singing in the aisles. Examining the Academy Award nominees for Best Original Song since the inception of that category in 1934 reveals that Hollywood, which once hit the high notes consistently, is in danger of losing its voice completely.

The influence of the Fred Astaire-Ginger Rogers musicals was considerable in the early years of the award. "The Continental" from *The Gay Divorcee* copped the first Oscar, besting "The Carioca" from *Flying Down to Rio*. Two years later *Swing Time*'s "The Way You Look Tonight" edged out Cole Porter's "I've Got You Under My Skin." In 1935 and 1937 songs from *Top Hat* and *Shall We Dance* had to settle for runner-up, but it could be argued that Irving Berlin's "Cheek to Cheek" and George and Ira Gershwin's "They Can't Take That Away from Me" have stood the test of time better than the winners, "Lullaby of Broadway" and "Sweet Leilani."

But there can be no quibbling over the choices for the next three years. When Bob Hope and Shirley Ross sang "Thanks for the Memory" in *The Big Broadcast of 1938*, all other songs in that film and others released that year paled in comparison. Cinema reached a high-water mark in 1939, a year any melody would have had to go "Over the Rainbow" to beat out what became Judy Garland's signature song. In 1940 people left theaters after seeing *Pinocchio* in a euphoric mood, convinced that their dreams would come true if they wished upon a star.

The competition intensified during the war years. In fact, a case could be made for the assertion that some of the best music for the movies was written from 1941 to 1945. Whether the reason for this is "adversity produces greatness" or the popularity of musicals or composers concentrating on boasting morale or merely coincidence is a matter of conjecture. Just the number of songs nominated each year would give credence to the belief that these five years represented a peak period for movie melodies. Nine songs were in the hunt for the prize in 1941, ten in both 1942 and 1943, eleven in 1944, and a never-equaled fourteen in 1945.

Giving the award to the Jerome Kern-Oscar Hammerstein tune "The Last Time I Saw Paris" in 1941 seems fair, although "Blues in the Night," "Chattanooga Choo Choo," and the bouncy, topical "Boogie Woogie Bugle Boy of Company B" are still toe-tappable today. There is also no valid reason to contest the selection of perennial favorite "White Christmas" which snowed under the likes of "I've Heard That Song Before" and "I've Got a Girl in Kalamazoo" in 1942.

Just as "White Christmas" is inextricably connected with Bing Crosby so "You'll Never Know," the winner the following year, became attached to the star of *Hello, Frisco, Hello,* Alice Faye, who needed every ounce of her charm to counteract the power of "That Old Black Magic" from *Star Spangled Rhythm.*

When Crosby came back in 1944 "Swinging on a Star" in *Going My Way*, he helped push the Jimmy Van Heusen-Johnny Burke ditty past the stiff competition of "I'll Walk Alone," "Too Much in Love," "The Trolley Song," and the haunting "Long Ago and Far Away."

In 1945 the team of Richard Rodgers and Oscar Hammerstein, who had already made their mark on Broadway, brought their only original film score to the screen in *State Fair* and it took all the talent they could muster for their "It Might as Well Be Spring" to top the likes of "Accentuate the Positive," "Love Letters," "I'll Buy That Dream," and "So in Love."

After reaching such heights for several years in a row, it seemed only natural that screen music came down to earth. The next two winners, "On the Atchison, Topeka, and the Santa Fe" and "Zip-a-Dee-Doo-Dah," were likely to stir audiences into singing along with the actors as they decidedly outdistanced their challengers for that honor. Doris Day's beautiful interpretation of "It's Magic" in her first film, *Romance on the High Seas,*

1944 was Bing's big year.

certainly surpassed Bob Hope's warbling in *The Paleface*, but the catchy rhythm of Jay Livingston's music and the easy-to-remember lyrics penned by Ray Evans made "Buttons and Bows" the indomitable tune of 1948. The following year *Neptune's Daughter* gave birth to "Baby, It's Cold Outside," the perfect duet that became a standard for countless couples from Phil Harris and Alice Faye to Steve Lawrence and Eydie Gorme.

The 1950s began strong with a banner year in which the lovely "Mona Lisa" edged past the operatic "Be My Love," the playful nonsense of *Cinderella*'s "Bibbidi-Bobbidi-Boo" and the clippity-clopping of "Mule Train."

In 1951 Bing showed that he could still ride home a winner, "In the Cool, Cool, Cool of the Evening," from *Here Comes the Groom*, although it certainly helped to have Hoagy Carmichael and Johnny Mercer providing the horsepower. The laudable "A Kiss to Build a Dream On" finished out of the money.

Just as Gary Cooper loomed larger than life throughout *High Noon* so Dimitri Tiomkin's pounding, hypnotic chords and Tex Ritter's mournful rendition of "Do Not Forsake Me, Oh My Darling" had the other best song nominees shaking in their boots. Oscar stayed out west for another year when Doris Day as *Calamity Jane* revealed her "Secret Love" in 1953.

By the mid-fifties it became clear that releasing 45 RPM records and albums of soundtracks enhanced the chances of music makers winning the big prize. Customers buying Doris Day's "*Que Sera, Sera* (Whatever Will Be, Will Be)" in 1956 may have been carried away with the infectious tune to the point where they forgot or didn't care that it came from an Alfred Hitchcock thriller, *The Man Who Knew Too Much*. Pat Boone's version of "Friendly Persuasion (Thee I Love)" and the Crosby-Grace Kelly take on Porter's "True Love" reminded people listening to their phonographs of what they had seen recently on the screen.

Similarly, singles recorded by the Four Aces of "Three Coins in the Fountain" and "Love is a Many-Splendored Thing" helped to escort those two themes to the finish line in 1954 and 1955 ahead of notables such as Berlin's "Count Your Blessings," Cahn and Van Heusen's "The Tender Trap," Mercer's "Something's Gotta Give," and two of the most moving compositions of that or any other decade, "Unchained Melody" and Tiomkin's "The High and the Mighty."

1957 marks a watershed in movie music. That Hollywood had shifted its aim toward the younger generation now going to theaters was evidenced in nominees like "April Love" and "Tammy." Bing Crosby had become passé; Frank Sinatra singing "All the Way" in *The Joker is Wild* (and, two years later, "High Hopes" in *A Hole in the Head*) was now the pop star delivering the Oscars. Lerner and Loewe scored a knockout with "Gigi" in 1958, just before the musical film in its traditional form started to wobble on its last legs. Instead of hiring people like Berlin, Porter, Betty Comden and Adolph Green to write half a dozen numbers to supplement the plot, producers began seeking songwriting duos like Van Heusen and Cahn, Henry Mancini and Mercer, and Burt Bacharach and Hal David to supply one song with a "hook" that hangs around long after the picture is over.

There is no denying that these talented teams knew the right buttons to push. Many Sinatra movie tunes bear the Van Heusen-Cahn stamp, including a nominee in 1964 that became one of Frank's most popular numbers on the nightclub circuit, "My Kind of Town." They also were responsible for "The Second Time Around," "Pocketful of Miracles," and 1963's best song, "Call Me Irresponsible." Mancini and Mercer won back-to-back Academy Awards in 1961 and 1962 for "Moon River" and "Days of Wine and Roses." Bacharach and David had more success on the *Billboard* charts than on the screen, but "The Look of Love," "Alfie," and the ubiquitous Oscar-winner in 1969, "Raindrops Keep Fallin' on my Head," played well both in record stores and at box offices.

Of the movies made in the last three decades of the twentieth century, one would be hard-pressed to find many which have produced original songs likely to become standards with the possible exception of "The Way We Were" which by its very nature is a paean to nostalgia. Who, for instance, can sing even one stanza of the winner for best song in 1979, "It Goes Like It Goes," or "Let the River Run" from 1988, when only three pathetic tunes were nominated?

The sorry state of contemporary movie music was graphically illustrated when *The Little Mermaid, Beauty and the Beast, Aladdin, The Lion King,* and *Pocahontas* not only won the Oscars for best song but also dominated the nominations as well. [Since the article appeared add *The Prince of Egypt, Tarzan,* and *Monsters, Inc.* to the list of animated winners.] Yet how many youngsters who have seen these pictures can carry even one of those limp tunes across a room? Treat those same children to a viewing of Disney's *Snow White and the Seven Dwarfs* from 1937 and they will be heigh-hoing, whistling while they work, and hoping that their prince will come.

Those partisans who harbor memories of the winners by default in 1987 and 1997, "(I've Had) The Time of My Life" and "My Heart Will Go On," should be reminded that their enduring popularity is due in no small part to the tidal wave of merchandizing which turned *Dirty Dancing* and *Titanic* into cash cows that are still being milked. One suspects that in 2050 when those two melodies have vanished into trivia books Fred and Ginger will still be whirling through the consciousness of music lovers to the strains of "Night and Day," "Let's Call the Whole Thing Off," "Pick Yourself Up," "Smoke Gets in Your Eyes," and "A Fine Romance," timeless numbers from their films that weren't even nominated for best song.

Of course, the compositions for Best Original Song represent just a fraction of the enchanting music that entertained us in those popcorn-scented dream palaces. From dramas such as *Dark Passage, Clash by Night, Casablanca,* and *To Have and Have Not* came the incidental bonuses of "Too Marvelous for Words," "I Hear a Rhapsody," "As Time Goes By," and "How Little We Know," and comedies like the Road pictures of Hope and Crosby produced memorable ballads ("Moonlight Becomes You," "But Beautiful,") and the pleasing "Personality." The scores of *Oklahoma!, Show Boat, Kiss Me Kate, South Pacific, Annie Get Your Gun, The Sound of Music, The King and I, My Fair Lady*, and numerous other musicals certainly made for some enchanted evenings that lifted our spirits so high we left theaters wanting to climb every mountain or at least the nearest lamppost so we too could be singin' in the rain.

It seems there are very few films being made today that would prompt me to sing their praises let alone praise their singing. The music now permeating soundtracks appears designed by composers to stupefy the senses rather than to bewitch the intellect. But those unforgettable melodies and soothing lyrics from years ago that keep floating through my mind…

The memory of all that, no, no, they can't take that away from me.

Warren William as Perry Mason at the scene of the crime in *The Case of Howling Dog*.

The Case of the Overlooked Series

NEARLY EVERY DEFENDER OF JUSTICE worthy of the name has been heralded on the screen and honored later by film historians and authors in print. Sherlock Holmes, The Saint, Charlie Chan, Boston Blackie, Mr. Moto, Ellery Queen, The Falcon, James Bond, and other detectives/agents have all their chance to shine. It is time to turn a flashlight on a neglected series and bring Perry Mason out from the shadows to have his day in court.

Between 1934 and 1937 Warner Brothers released six adaptations of Erle Stanley Gardner novels to capture the audiences who were solving mysteries with urbane Philo Vance and that convivial couple, Nick and Nora Charles. Warren William, who had just taken over from William Powell as Vance in *The Dragon Murder Case*, was selected to play Perry Mason.

Like Basil Rathbone, William presented one of those finely-chiseled faces that seemed appropriate whether he wore villain's cape or hero's robe. As Mason he looked and acted like a fox, using his prominent nose to sniff out important clues to help win cases for his clients.

In *The Case of the Howling Dog* (1934) Mason begins observing keenly soon after Arthur Cartwright (Gordon Westcott), a man bothered by a yelping German shepherd belonging to neighbor Clinton Foley (Russell Hicks), asks Perry to make Evelyn, the woman living with Foley but who is actually Cartwright's wife, his heir. When Mason visits the Foley grounds, he notices that Foley is building an addition to his garage that he doesn't appear to need and that his housekeeper, Lucy Benton (Dorothy Tree), seems reluctant to talk about the bandage on her right hand.

After Foley receives word that the Cartwrights have reunited and run off together, he is sent a wire by a woman whose face is hidden telling him not to "do anything that will cause more scandal." The telegram is signed "Evelyn."

One night Bessie Foley (Mary Astor) confronts her husband with a gun while he is shaving. After Foley unleashes a dog that attacks and is shot, he grabs a letter opener and advances on Bessie before he too is stopped by a bullet. Some doubt is raised in the viewer's mind as to the identity of the shooter because Bessie looks to an open French window after each report.

At the scene of the crime Mason is more deductive than District Attorney Claude Drumm (Grant Mitchell) and atrabilious Sgt. Holcomb (Allen Jenkins) who want to pin the murder on Cartwright because of the obvious motive of a cuckolded husband seeking revenge. Shaving cream found on a towel suggests to Perry that Foley had not been surprised by a jealous intruder bent on quick retribution.

After he talks with Bessie, who claims to be innocent of Foley's murder, Mason agrees to handle her defense and advises her to admit nothing to anyone. Deciding that the three keys to solving the crime are the handwriting on the telegram, the dog, and the whereabouts of the Cartwrights, Perry lures Lucy Benton into a trap by pretending to be a newspaper editor offering her $10,000 for her diary and dispatching two of his operatives who come away with a page ripped from that book.

At a critical juncture in the trial Mason manages to move the proceedings to the Foley home where he proves that the shifty-eyed, ambidextrous Lucy was sinister in more ways than one when she wrote left-handed as Evelyn under Foley's instructions. Immediately after this revelation workmen digging in the foundation of the garage discover the bodies of Arthur and Evelyn Cartwright, victims of Foley's wrath and cunning. The hasty entombment of Evelyn was what had prompted the dog to yowl, and Perry convinces the jury that Bessie is innocent of Foley's death because the real family dog would not have attacked her.

Bessie, of course, did kill her husband in self-defense, but because Mason would not let her testify and because she could not be tried again for the same offense she walks out of Mason's opulent office a free woman with the titular pet whose howling had caused Foley to switch dogs.

Why Foley did not add the dog who knew where the bodies were buried to his concrete cemetery rather than place him in a kennel where Mason could find him probably did not concern moviegoers who undoubtedly were just satisfied that a murderer and flagrant philanderer had paid for his misdeeds. Director Alan Crosland kept the action going in his usual workmanlike fashion, pausing only to take a slow pan of the courtroom during the opening remarks.

Donald Woods and Margaret Lindsay in *The Case of the Curious Bride*.

William cuts a roguish figure as Mason, a man who is not above using Della Street (Helen Trenholme) for ruses and for romance. Early in the picture when he paints a portrait of Della taking care of him in later years, he speaks in the flippant tone of a jesting roué who knows it is a pipe dream. In the clinching closer Della murmurs, "You're a cross between a saint and a devil" to which Mason replies, "How do you like it?"

Enough people liked it that Warners brought Mason back the following year to solve *The Case of the Curious Bride*. The bride is Rhoda Montaine (Margaret Lindsay) whose first husband, Gregory Moxley, presumed to be dead, is alive, putting her marriage to wealthy Carl Montaine (Donald Woods) in jeopardy.

When Mason has the coffin of Moxley opened by his pal, coroner Wilbur Strong (Olin Howland), and discovers a wooden Indian instead of a corpse, he suspects that Gregory is still alive which he is—but not for long. By the time Perry finds Moxley he is dead in an apartment where signs of a brawl are evident. Rhoda becomes the chief suspect.

Mason takes charge by orchestrating Rhoda's surrender to the authorities and ordering Carl, who obviously knows more about the murder than he admits, to "say nothing and plenty of it," reminding him that a husband cannot testify against his wife. When Montaine's father attempts to clear that legal hurdle by having the Carl-Rhoda union declared illegal because of Rhoda's first marriage, Mason goes him one better by having his right-hand man, Spudsy Drake (Allen Jenkins), produce a woman named Florabelle (Mayo Methot) to claim that she had wed Moxley first. Under intense grilling by policemen Florabelle admits the deception, but Spudsy does come through with Doris Pender (Winifred Shaw), who actually was married to Moxley.

Perry wins the case not in a courtroom but at a cocktail party he is hosting. There Doris's brother confesses that he was at the apartment on the night in question and ran into the person he believes committed the murder: Carl Montaine. As Carl recounts his actions, a flashback reveals how Moxley (Errol Flynn) struggles first with Rhoda who flees the scene and then with Montaine whose haymaker sends Moxley against a fireplace mantle which holds a lethal shard of broken mirror. Mason promptly declares the death as accidental and, with a tap on the senior Montaine's well-padded checkbook, promises to defend Carl.

The Case of the Curious Bride is a worthy candidate for best of series because it deftly mixes mystery and merriment. The shifts in tone from light-hearted to deadly serious might be attributable to the crackling dialogue written by Tom Reed and Brown Holmes, but surely director Michael Curtiz deserves credit for putting his stamp on this entry.

While Mason picks up crumbs of evidence, the diversions tossed in for laughs work more often than not. In the phone booth scene in which Mason is concealing Rhoda below sight of the police, the cracks by the cops about how much Mason pays per month for renting the booth are followed by the physical comedy of Spudsy, in order to create a diversion, attempting to pick a fight first with a bruiser who scares him away and then with a squirt who quickly floors him.

The repartee between Mason and Della (Claire Dodd) generates a sexual chemistry that approaches that found in the Thin Man series. Della saucily tells Perry that his French accent is lau-zay and placidly tops his order to take down important remarks in shorthand by saying, "I will—if any turn up." After Mason tells her to cancel his trip to China, she indicates that the steamship company will be "glad to know that. The boat sailed this morning," prompting William to execute two perfectly-measured double takes, one over each shoulder. Dodd even got to close the picture with a twist on a cliché that might have had matrimonial implications: "If only you couldn't cook."

Flynn, in his first American film, had nothing to say and precious little to do except prove his character could not win a fight with a man or a woman. He would later team with Curtiz numerous times in movies such as *Captain Blood* and *The Adventures of Robin Hood* which would solidify his image as a romantic leading man.

Curtiz put an indelible mark on the picture for *Curious Bride* looks like no other film in the series. Early changes of scene are accomplished by going out of focus on one object and then converging on a similar object in another part of San Francisco. A chase in which Mason and Della flee a police tail does not end with the typical sequence of car stopping—men exiting car—men opening door of building—cut to interior pattern but rather by viewing everything from the hallway where the car stops in an arched doorway and the two men rush toward the viewers to enhance the urgency of their mission.

Later, in the visiting area of the jail, the cut from Mason talking to the jailer to a scene in a prison cell with the brother of Florabelle is so quick and seamless it appears that the camera had merely moved to the left in the very same room.

Curtiz, like Mason, seemed in control at all times, being careful not to let the wisecracks and slapstick detract from the story line. When Drake and Mason sit on some steps and wax lachrymose after sniffing a handkerchief of tear gas, Curtiz knew just how long to let Jenkins and William go on with their crying jags before the comical would have become ridiculous.

Unfortunately, Curtiz was not at the helm during the production of the next Mason film, *The Case of the Lucky Legs* (1935), and the result is a screwball mystery. A tip-off that the tone would be considerably lighter appeared during the opening credits when William was shown in a straw hat, looking more like a song-and-dance man than the snap-brimmed lawyer of the first two movies.

The first glimpse of Perry in the picture is his unlucky legs sticking out from under his desk where he is sleeping off the effects of a hangover. The owner of a department store, Mr. Bradbury (Porter Hall), whose name the groggy lawyer keeps mangling, wants Mason to find Frank Patton (Craig Reynolds), a con artist who promotes leg contests purportedly sponsored by hosiery companies but who skips town without paying off. Two winners of the gam parades, Margy Clune (Patricia Ellis) and Thelma Bell (Peggy Shannon), are also after Patton.

Having seen a photograph of Margy, Mason recognizes her coming down the stairs of Patton's apartment building shortly before he finds that Patton has been murdered with a scalpel. Margy's suitor, Bob Doray (Lyle Talbot), is a leading suspect because he is a doctor.

Margy and Thelma admit to Perry that they were in Patton's apartment, but both profess to be innocent of the crime. Mason deduces that

Bradbury is the killer whose unrequited love for Margy drove him to steal the surgical instrument from Doray so the physician would be implicated in the murder.

That the plot had pointed a guilty finger at Bradbury rather early may have contributed to the need for humorous diversions. An ice cube is used by Mason three times to induce laughs: on his forehead, on Bradbury's neck, and in Perry's mouth while his doctor (Howland) takes his temperature, does a take, and then declares, "Perry Mason, I now pronounce you dead."

As Della, Genevieve Tobin, who showed a flair for comedy before retiring from pictures several years after marrying director William Keighley in 1938, cracks wise, perches sexily on a desk with crossed legs, and outsmarts the police by locking them in Perry's office.

The slapstick is repeated later when Margy keeps the cops at bay by throwing bottles from Mason's well-stocked bar. Perry, acting like a caricature of John Barrymore, is more concerned with rescuing a prized bottle of booze than he is in the current status of Clune vs. the gendarmes.

Mary Treen is introduced as Spudsy's wife solely to show that she can throw crockery and a punch line. When Mason points to items on the table and says, "I've got the real dope here," she taps her husband (Jenkins) on the

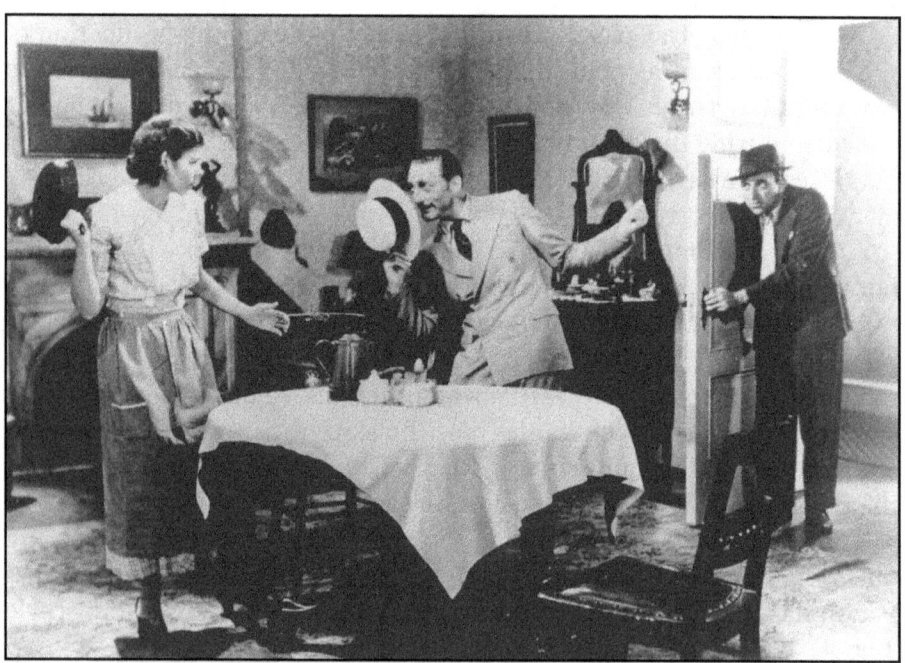

William caught between Mary Treen and Allen Jenkins in
The Case of the Lucky Legs.

shoulder and repeats Perry's words. (Treen's brief appearance as a telephone operator in *Curious Bride* was principally so she could tell Sudsy, "I generally don't accept invitations from gentlemen, but I think you're pretty safe.")

What could have saved *Lucky Legs* from lapsing into the ludicrous might have been a more subdued performance by William, but apparently the direction of Archie Mayo and the script provided by Brown Holmes and Ben Markson gave him no choice but to go for the ham. He cringes from his dissipated reflection in a mirror like W.C. Fields, reads an address off Spudsy's shirttail like Oliver Hardy browbeating a chagrined Stan Laurel not just once but in two different scenes, and engages in a finger-reading routine with an elevator operator worthy of Groucho and Chico.

The climax is also played for laughs as Perry, while undergoing a physical examination, drags the principals from his suite to the doctor's examination room for a fluoroscopic test so a gibe about his kidneys can be delivered before they head back to his office for the wrap-up.

Although Mason is too much of a buffoon and the padding shows, *Lucky Legs* is a pleasant diversion, enjoyable even when Mayo's heavy hand leaves fingerprints. The scene showing the feet of the murderer and victim is risible because it looks as if the men are dancing. When Thelma goes to admit Mason into her apartment, her dressing gown is no more than a few inches above her ankles. After she opens the door and Mason falls in, he stares from the floor at her legs which are suddenly bare to the middle of her thighs, yet when he stands her legs are again covered by the gown. Perhaps the best way to view *Lucky Legs* is to follow Jerry Colonna's advice: "Don't ask questions. Just have fun."

In 1936 Perry Mason was back in *The Case of the Velvet Claws* and Della Street (Claire Dodd) got him—if not to the altar at least into night court where they are married by a judge. Their plans to honeymoon at Pinehurst Lodge are interrupted when Eva Belter (Winifred Shaw) convinces Mason at gunpoint to help her stop a compromising article about her and a politician from being printed in *Spicy Bits*.

When Eva learns that husband George (Joseph King) owns the scandal sheet and has ordered the story published as revenge for her infidelity, she shoots at him and leaves the house. Actually, her bullet missed, but Belter's nephew, Carl Griffin (Gordon Elliott), employs the gun she dropped to kill his uncle after learning that he will inherit the estate.

Perry uses the clue of a second bullet he found to implicate Griffin before rushing into night court once again to prevent neglected Della from annulling the marriage. The couple set out at last to leave the city, although the honeymoon is apt to be short-lived for the final scene shows a thug ordering a taxi driver to take him to Pinehurst Lodge.

Claire Dodd, William, Eddie Acuff, and Winifred Shaw in
The Case of the Velvet Claws.

At barely over an hour *The Case of the Velvet Claws* zips right along and ties up the loose ends nicely (except for the title which is never explained). The humor of the Masons being repeatedly interrupted from consummating their marriage is balanced by Perry's rugged determination to find the truth in the Belter matter.

That Mason had returned to form as lawyer first and wit second is apparent when he questions Eva. He coolly indicates that he means business when, in a speech Sam Spade might have tossed at Brigid O'Shaughnessy, snaps, "It's curtains for you, baby, unless you stop double-crossing me for at least five minutes," then, after hearing her confession, lightens up by promising that he won't use the statements against her because "I'm your attorney and have a code of honor to say nothing of a code in the head."

That cold becomes a running (or sneezing) gag throughout the film. For some reason the malady seems particularly contagious because Mason is seen passing out tissues to the people he has summoned to the scene of the murder. Naturally, it would be too routine to wind up matters there; everyone has to pile in cars so he can unmask the culprit with pizzazz before entering the courtroom in a flourish.

Of course, the other recurring element makes *Velvet Claws* as much of a willtheydoit as a whodunit. As soon as the newlyweds embrace and Mason swears that "I'm here now and I'm not going to leave again" the police are heard pounding on the apartment door. Watching Dodd trudge around in her satin pajamas muttering, "Such air. I've never been given so much of it" and William quoting Shakespeare while in sexual frustration as he dangles from the fire escape will not make anyone forget Carole Lombard, Myrna Loy, and William Powell, but it should help us remember that those three stars were not the only ones capable of teasing and pleasing audiences during the Depression.

Tom Reed's script is satisfactory and the direction of William Clemens adequate. Only one setup shows any inspiration and Clemens tips his hand there by showing Mason entering the murder room at a low level, signaling that it would only be seconds before Perry bends over to examine the floor and, no surprise, finds the incriminating bullet.

Eddie Acuff as Spudsy lifts weights, tails a blonde while in drag, and looks foolish while getting leveled by Griffin after telling the killer, "I've got you in my viselike grip." Wini Shaw, who delivered the showstopping "Lullaby of Broadway" in *Gold Diggers of 1935* and a routine number in *Curious Bride*, had nothing to sing but plenty to say as the erring wife with the errant aim and she said it credibly. Gordon Elliott, before his cowboy days as "Wild Bill" Elliott, did what he could with a part that called for him to be either drunk or devious.

When William left the Warner lot to work for Paramount and MGM, Ricardo Cortez took over as Mason in *The Case of the Black Cat* (1936). June Travis, who had a bit part in *Lucky Legs*, became the new Della Street. What the studio had joined together with *Claws* had been rent asunder by *Cat* so Perry and Della played the field as singles again.

The most accurate name for the picture would have been *The Case of the Caretaker's Cat*, which was both the working title and the title of Gardner's novel. Certainly alluding to a black cat suggested furtive deeds done in darkness. The real mystery, then, is why the actual cat seen in the movie is white with a handful of spots.

Both caretaker Ashton (George Rosener) and his cat Clinker are favorites of millionaire Peter Laxter (Harry Davenport), who mentions them in the new will Mason drafts for him. Grandsons Frank Oafley (Craig Reynolds) and Sam Laxter (Gordon Elliott) are chief heirs. Granddaughter Wilma Laxter (Jane Bryan) is to be left out because Peter believes her boyfriend Douglas Keene (Carlyle Moore Jr.) is a fortune hunter who knew she stood to be wealthy under the terms of the earlier will.

Mason's suspicions are aroused when Peter apparently dies in a fire and Ashton appears in his office with plenty of money to hire the lawyer to represent him and Clinker, but any doubts about the caretaker are allayed when Perry finds him dead in bed. The body count grows when Mason discovers the corpse of Peter's nurse Louise Devoe (Nelda Harrigan), who had just become Mrs. Frank Oafley, on the floor of her apartment next to the remnants of Ashton's crutch. Because blood is found on Keene's shirt, he is charged with both murders and also implicated in the death of Peter Laxter.

During the trial Mason produces Peter at an opportune moment and reveals how Ashton and Laxter faked the latter's death by burning the body of a vagrant in the old man's bed. Peter, fearing that Frank or Sam would kill him out of greed, beat them to the punch and disappeared with most of the cash.

A flashback shows how Ashton, who had the valuable Koltsdorf diamonds in his crutch, is strangled for them in Louise's apartment by the powerful Oafley who carries the caretaker back to his bed so it will appear that he died naturally. Before Frank returns, Peter confronts Louise, demands the return of the diamonds which legally belong to him, and clubs her when she attempts to pull a gun on him. The blood on Keene's clothing belongs to Sam who purposely cut himself to transfer suspicion away from himself because he also had been in Louise's apartment on the fatal evening.

Mason completes the case by boldly announcing that he will defend Peter Laxter and plead self-defense, a move that might buckle the knees of lesser attorneys considering that the defendant is the only witness to Louise's death and is also a confessed body snatcher and arsonist.

Cortez comes off as a rather bland Mason who at times seems as concerned with filling in the blanks on his crossword puzzle as filling in gaps in the mystery. His delivery of "No!" upon being introduced to the man who married Frank and Louise and of "Ashton…dead" at the caretaker's bedside are so theatrical one wonders if the avocation of William McGann, who had taken over the director's chair after Crosland's death in an automobile accident, was woolgathering.

The script by F. Hugh Herbert keeps Perry and Della at more than arm's length. The closest Mason comes to noticing Della as something other than his secretary occurs at the very end when, in a booth at a restaurant, she asks coquettishly, "Are you tickling my leg?" Clinker is revealed to be the tickler before Cortez admits with a chuckle, "No, but it's a very good idea." William would have flicked out the words with a Mephistophelian leer.

Hypnotic title card for the penultimate film in the series.

Despite these sustained objections, *Black Cat* is the first picture in the series with the distinctive flavor of a Perry Mason mystery. For all of Warren William's wily charm his Perry Mason was more bloodhound than barrister, a sleuth in legal garb who closed cases much like Charlie Chan by rounding up all the usual and unusual suspects and then reconstructing the murders until the guilty party confessed or tried to escape. When Cortez's Mason with the help of reliable Paul Drake (Garry Owen) dispenses with the fact-finding and Perry prepares to match wits with persistent Hamilton Burger (Guy Usher), the sound of the gavel is like the ringside gong telling us the preliminaries are over and the main event is about to begin.

Courtroom pyrotechnics, however, cannot disguise the corners that had been cut. Nearly every scene is tied to a soundstage and convertibles are used frequently to manufacture a sense of airiness. Rather than shoot an exterior of a cemetery to verify that Peter Laxter is presumed dead and buried, the studio inserted an artist's rendering of an engraved headstone in a sylvan setting that looks very much like a Charles Addams cartoon.

The gowns by Milos Anderson may be the picture's only extravagance, although when Louise greets Drake and Mason in a black dress with more white plumage on her sleeves than found on an adult ostrich, viewers are apt to stop thinking about the investigation and begin wondering why a nurse would be dressed as if she was going on stage in five minutes, an impression supported by the fact that her sparsely furnished apartment resembles nothing so much as a dressing room recently inhabited by gold diggers in other WB productions.

In the final entry in the series, *The Case of the Stuttering Bishop* (1937), a mustachioed Donald Woods assumed the lead role. After listening to a stammering bishop's story, Perry agrees to aid Ida Gilbert (Mira McKinney) who avers that the girl claiming to be her daughter and heir to the fortune of her father-in-law, Ronald Brownley (Douglas Wood), is an imposter. Mason visits Ida and her friend Stella Kenwood (Helen MacKeller), then learns from Brownley that he intends to draw up a new will leaving everything to the young lady living with him in the house known as Janice Alma Brownley (Anne Nagel) whether she is actually his granddaughter or not.

In an attempt to prove that Janice Seaton (Linda Perry) is the real heiress and that she is actually Janice's mother, Ida offers to meet Brownley near the waterfront and show him a watch that belonged to her husband. Brownley is shot in his car by a woman wearing a light-colored raincoat. Although a body is not found in the automobile when it is hoisted out of the bay, Ida is implicated in his disappearance because her gun and the note proposing the rendezvous are found on the blood-stained front seat. When the body is recovered, Ida is arrested for murder and Mason agrees to defend her.

In court Perry manages to cast doubts in the mind of an eyewitness who admits that he could not be certain Brownley was dead after being shot. On a hunch Mason calls for a coroner's report which reveals the cause of death to be drowning, meaning that the person who shot the millionaire was not necessarily the killer.

While Mason is relentlessly questioning Janice Brownley on the stand, Stella rises to confess that she shot Brownley with Ida's gun, hoping that with Ida out of the way the deception could continue so her daughter could inherit the estate. The bishop (Edward McWade) makes a belated reappearance to announce that he had observed Stella's henchmen, who had provided an alibi for the false Janice, push the car into the water, technically making them guilty of murder which will be of small consolation to Stella and her daughter even if they share the same cell in prison.

Woods presents a dedicated, single-minded Mason, focused on getting to the bottom of the mystery and doing his very best. When he tells the bishop, "I'd fight for a client of mine against the devil himself," he says it with the conviction of Daniel Webster getting ready to take on Old Scratch.

Woods is less effective in humorous sequences like the one requiring him to feign drunkenness. Fortunately, Tom Kennedy was around to provide comic relief as Jim Magooney, a detective from the Nat Pendleton school of oafs, who cannot slap a steering wheel or kick a fender without hurting himself.

Thanks to writers Don Ryan and Kenneth Gamet, Della (Ann Dvorak) does more than take notes and answer phones. She dons a wig to set a trap and knocks the gun from a ruffian's hand at a critical juncture. It is also Della who trips the right switch in Perry's brain when she mentions Stella Kenwood during lunch.

Director William Clemens didn't drag his feet once the characters had been introduced and the crime committed. After the car and note are found, Mason mutters to Paul (Joseph Crehan), "Get me into town quick. I've got work to do." One second later Mason is seen in the hallway of an apartment building and shortly thereafter is ordering Ida and Stella to bed so it will look like they have been asleep when the police arrive.

The charm of these movies is that our attention remains so focused on the larger mysteries that we don't immediately concern ourselves with minor enigmas such as how Woods's Mason knows there is a Murphy bed

Joseph Crehan, Ann Dvorak, and Donald Woods in
The Case of the Stuttering Bishop.

behind a mirrored door in Ida's apartment or how Cortez's Mason senses a nosy landlord is listening outside the door to Keene's apartment or why William's Mason is wearing a tuxedo and top hat while eavesdropping from a perch above a ceiling in *Velvet Claws*.

Nor is it vital to our enjoyment which of the three actors is leading us on the merry chase. William is the most volatile Mason, the man of action who is likely to lose his temper or use his fists as he does in *Lucky Legs* when he knocks out Doray with one punch. Cortez prefers the cool-headed approach as he puffs on his pipe and tracks down his quarry in Sherlockian style. Woods, the earnest Mason, won't let anything, be it women or waffles, divert him from his mission for even a moment. All three Masons demonstrate the ratiocination we expect from our favorite defense attorney.

What Gardner expected was greater fidelity to the Perry, Della, and Paul he created. Despite the fact that in *Black Cat* and *Stuttering Bishop* the "friends, not lovers" relationship between Mason and Street and the role of Drake as trusted aide rather than comic sidekick had been transferred rather faithfully from page to screen, Gardner decided that his books told his stories better than Hollywood did and refused to sell more movie rights. (Warner Brothers toyed with their one remaining property, *The Case of the Dangerous Dowager*, until 1940 when it emerged Perryless as *Granny Get Your Gun* starring May Robson.)

Viewing the films today reminds one how important telegrams were in 1930s pictures. Significant clues hang on disguised handwriting used on telegram blanks and alibis are destroyed because messages could not be delivered. When we peek over shoulders to read "Await your final answer five o'clock extreme limit," the plot thickens as we wonder about the answer and the identities of both sender and recipient. A wire Mason sends to a ship headed for Australia not only demonstrates that telegraphy reached out and touched everyone everywhere in those days but the reply indicating the surprising news that the bishop was not on board sets the stage for his dramatic entrance during the trial. T-mail was even be used for a light touch in *Stuttering Bishop* when one evening Mason sends his regrets for not being able to meet with Della in a pithy message, causing her to express her displeasure at being awakened just to read "Good Night."

Seen as a unit the six pictures, made under B movie constraints using mainly character actors or contract players and journeymen directors, are models of low-budget filmmaking and concatenated storytelling. After brief credits, we are introduced immediately to a yowling dog, stretching cat, or lovely legs, or within the first few minutes to a tongue-tied cleric or inquisitive bride. From then on par for the course is five: establish characters, provide motive, produce corpses, sort suspects, solve crime.

Frank S. Nugent captured the essence of the Perry Mason series in his review of *The Case of the Curious Bride* for the *New York Times* when he wrote that "the pace is swift, the solution well hidden, the comedy good and—but isn't that enough?"

Yes, it is. Beyond a shadow of a doubt.

Fred Allen had high hopes for *It's in the Bag*.

2 Wits, 2 Pics, 0 Hits

OF ALL THE RADIO COMEDIANS, the two who seemed most attuned to the same wavelength were Fred Allen and Henry Morgan. Supreme satirists of the contemporary scene who viewed events through the jaundiced eye of the skeptic, neither was afraid to lash out at targets regardless of consequences. Allen frequently lampooned network executives who interfered with his broadsides or took offense at his ad-libs while Morgan became known as the "bad boy" of radio for his relentless needling of sponsors which cost him his job more than once. The two nonconformists joined forces several times on *The Fred Allen Show* to take swipes at anything within their reach. Morgan considered Allen his hero and mentor, and in 1949 Fred returned the favor by being instrumental in convincing NBC to slot the unsponsored *Henry Morgan Show* immediately after his program on Sunday evenings.

The admiration was mutual and the temperaments similar, yet the two men had something else in common that is not often mentioned: each starred in one film, a picture that, despite impressive casts, writers, and production staffs, failed at the box office and then went back to working on what Allen called the treadmill to oblivion on radio.

The two movies, *It's in the Bag* (1945) and *So This Is New York* (1948), themselves teeter today on the brink of oblivion. Examining both films reveals that they don't deserve obscurity, though neither could be called a hidden treasure.

It's in the Bag opens with Fred interrupting the credits to make sardonic comments about why audiences have to put up with a barrage of names before the beginning of each motion picture. He avers that a number of those credited are relatives of producer Jack Skirball. He even takes a shot at himself when his name appears as one of those who toiled over the script, indicating that the writers listed are "now out of work. You'll see why in a minute."

The action commences with Frederick Trumble altering his will in favor of his grand-nephew, a change his attorney, unctuous Jefferson Pike (John Carradine), tries to dissuade him from making. After Pike leaves, we deduce that the heir is going to be our boy Fred because a photograph taken from the safe by Trumble features a bald-headed baby with Allen's face.

No sooner does Trumble insert a sum of money in the bottom of one of his chairs when he is shot by a shadowy figure from the window who then places the gun in the millionaire's hands so the death will be ruled a suicide.

The scene changes to the brightly-lit exterior of a flea circus owned by Fred Floogle (Allen) who pauses in his barking for customers to bark at Parker (Robert Benchley) about the on-again, off-again romance of Floogle's daughter and Parker's son. Fred's wife Eve (Binnie Barnes) adds to Fred's aggravated condition by complaining about their miserable lot in life. Only son Homer (Dickie Tyler), the genius in the family with his nose usually in a book, seems content with his state. After Fred voices his opinion that he sometimes doubts if Homer is indeed his child, the boy takes off his glasses to reveal Allen-sized bags under his eyes. Floogle does a take and asks the audience "What do you think?" So far the only laughs after the credits have come at the expense of Allen's appearance.

Shortly after Floogle's bookmaker Monte (Ben Welden) arrives to inform the astonished debtor that he now has unlimited credit with him, Fred discovers why when he examines a newspaper story pronouncing him heir to a twelve million dollar fortune. Soon the Floogles are ensconced in a hotel suite spending money they don't even have. This scene has a *Hellzapoppin'* flavor with everybody showing up including members of an Indian tribe who present Fred with a blanket complete with price tag. Then comes the greeting of "How?" to which the Chief replies, "Never mind how. Give me the seventy-two dollars" which precipitates Floogle's second double take of the scene.

Fred and Eve are brought down to earth when Pike informs them that the legacy in Trumble's will consists mainly of five chairs. Now further in debt, the Floogles are anxious to mend fences with Parker, unaware that he is also trying to put the bite on them. Benchley takes over the next several minutes of the picture in a scene that is reminiscent of *The Treasurer's Report* and other shorts he made for Fox and MGM as he describes the Rube Goldberg workings of a fanciful mousetrap. Fred signs a rubber check for $25,000 to finance the half-baked idea.

When the chairs arrive and Fred is reluctant to pay the delivery charges, bright Homer suggests selling them to an auction house for $300. No sooner do Homer and the deliveryman leave than Detective Sully (Sidney Toler) strolls in to inform Floogle that he is under suspicion for murdering Trumble. After Sully departs, a record from the deceased uncle arrives. Upon playing the record and listening to a bit of Frank Sinatra singing a ballad, Eve utters her best line: "It could have been worse. It could have been one chair and five Sinatras."

However, the plot spins faster on the B side with Trumble's own voice indicating that he plans to hide $300,000 in one of the chairs before his demise. By the time Floogle calls Homer, the chairs have been sold and the boy memorizes the list of buyers before the auction house and all its records are destroyed in a fire bomb hurled by the shadowy figure.

Homer remembers the address of the first purchaser, Mrs. Nussbaum (Minerva Pious). Pious and Allen stand in a static two-shot outside her apartment like they are conversing in Allen's Alley until they finally move down the hall a few yards as if someone on the set suddenly remembered this was a movie and not radio. The scene drags and has little point because she had already sold the chair to Jack Benny. The sequence seems set up primarily for the clincher delivered by Fred as he descends the apartment steps looking like Humphrey Bogart at the end of *The Maltese Falcon*, muttering, "If Jack Benny ever finds out there's $300,000 in that chair, he'll divorce Mary Livingstone and marry the chair."

Before Fred arrives at Benny's apartment, Jack, while writing jokes for his show, addresses the audience to slam home the effect of a pun. The faked animosity between the two comedians that made up their long-standing rivalry is scuttled in this meeting, but the Benny affinity for a dollar is played upon with a hat-check girl in the closet and a cigarette machine in the living room. In hopes of getting the chair, Floogle pretends to be a member of the Jack Benny Fan Club and asks for a souvenir to take with him. Before leaving, he is coerced into buying Benny's tie for $2.60 and can only have the chair if he is willing to pay $10.00 a day to rent it.

Outside the apartment building Floogle is almost run over by a car before he can examine the chair. However, the thugs who emerge from the auto do that for him. Pike, who has been masterminding all of the malevolence and who is obviously the villain, approaches Fred for little reason other than to provide one more slap at the Benny character by announcing that he has been trying to collect a fee for the doctor who delivered Jack—seventy years ago.

Flowers and flattery accomplish little when Fred visits Jack Benny's apartment.

The Floogles take Homer to Dr. Greengrass (Jerry Colonna) to see if the psychiatrist can help the boy remember the addresses of the other buyers. Colonna is slightly more subdued than in other pictures and his appearances on *The Bob Hope Show*, but just as wacky, complete with the eccentric habit of slapping himself on the face because he thinks he is being attacked by tsetse flies. Fred's suggestion of "Have you tried flypaper?" is met with the scene-closer that begged more for a rimshot than a fade-out: "Since when can a fly read?"

What follows next almost seems like a reel from another movie inserted by mistake. Fred and Eve see a marquee advertising *Zombie in the Attic* and decide to go in after hearing a man outside announcing immediate seating. After being told by usher after usher "next aisle to the right," the couple find themselves out on the street. They cajole their way back in, take an elevator to the crowded stratosphere level, descend again, complain to the assistant manager, then to the manager who, thinking quickly, decides that the wording on the ticket stub entitles Fred to a seat and produces from a closet (you guessed it) the second chair. If this were a silent movie, a card might have appeared reading "And now back to the picture you were watching ten minutes ago."

The chair is dismantled and flung out of a taxi by the Floogles in a throwaway scene of fifteen seconds as if to make up for time wasted while they lost it at the movies.

Homer recalls that two chairs went to a nightclub. At Phil's Naughty 90s the backstage manager, distraught because the bass singer in his quartet is in his cups, quickly hires Floogle to take his place. (Veteran radio announcer Harry Von Zell plays the uncredited manager and several other radio actors, John Brown, Walter Tetley, and Dave Willock, have bits in the theater sequence.)

Fred discovers his partners on stage are Don Ameche, Rudy Vallee, and Victor Moore who have fallen to this level of show business because they ran out of inventions, megaphones, and breath, respectively. The quartet's song is interrupted when a melee breaks out. The feeble attempts at humor during this scene, Ameche's reading of poetry and Moore's milquetoast bravado, misfire and mercifully end when Floogle is arrested for a second murder.

Just when Fred thinks that jail is the safest place for him to escape from both the murderer and his creditors, Sully announces that Pike has secured his release and suggests that the killers might be members of the Bendix gang, prompting Homer to remember that those crooks have possession of the fifth chair.

A usurper in the Bendix mob has wired the chair so that when Bill sits down he will get the hottest seat outside of prison walls. Whether planned or not, the writers save the best for last because William Bendix provides the funniest moments in the picture. His scare takes after being surprised by his cohorts in the dark and after asking for a knife to cut a cake, and his reading of an annual report of the hoodlums' profits listing holdups, amount of counterfeit money printed, and sundry misdeeds make us wish he had appeared twenty minutes earlier and stayed around. When the juice is flowing through his chair, his galvanic reactions and that of Floogle who is under the desk after finding the money in the chair provide the best physical comedy in the movie.

All that is left is a little more cat-and-mouse, a brief tussle in an alley in which Homer again saves the day, and a hot-foot confession from Pike and his cohort.

Now that the Floogles are really in the chips they once again move into the hotel suite and we join them on the day of the Parker-Floogle wedding, complete with more double takes, Colonna on a stretcher, the Indians again, a brass band, and Fred's closing invitation to come see the wedding at the next showing for which he promises immediate seating.

That line may have been a teaser pointing toward a Floogle follow-up. The closest Allen ever got to a sequel was a radio adaptation of *It's in the Bag* on *The Screen Director's Playhouse* broadcast February 17, 1950. This half-hour version is more ingenious and funnier than the 87-minute film.

Allen, in typical unconventional form, opens and tries to close the show in a couple sentences: "*It's in the Bag* is a murder mystery and the name of the killer is Monte the Gonif. Well, that's all there is to the story. Thank you, ladies and gentlemen, and good night." His hasty exit is stalled by Monte (veteran heavy Sheldon Leonard) who says he has to kill somebody because he has a contract with Murder, Inc. and they will pull out of every crime show on radio if the agreement is not honored.

Fred gives in and in less than five minutes the play is in full force. Parker and the romance of the young couple, which added little to the movie, are scrapped so the hunt for the chairs remains the focus of the

William Bendix passes out the treats to his gang and his viewers.

story. The phonograph record alone gives Allen a better line than he had in the whole picture: "With my luck, it'll probably be Margaret Truman singing 'Mule Train.'"

Allen, whose ratings slipped dramatically at the end of his radio days when he was up against *Stop the Music* and who regularly parodied quiz programs, was right on the money when one of the chairs turned up as a prize on a show he called *Break the Sponsor*. Back in his element of topical kidder, he was up to every comment presented by the quizmaster (Frank Nelson), reacting to the compliment of "You're funnier than Arthur Godfrey" with "Who isn't?" and responding to the question "Where is the capital of the United States?" with "Most of it is in Europe."

Fred proceeds to buy one chair from psychiatrist Dr. Klutz (Hans Conreid) who decides to take up upholstery as a profession and another from Sarah the Psychic who reads both Floogle and the chair. In rapid succession Fred, Monte, Public Eye Perkins (Alan Reed), and Pike (John Brown) arrive at the site of the chair that holds the hidden money. When Floogle reveals that Pike is the murderer, the accused protests that Monte was announced as the culprit at the beginning of the program to which Fred says that was just a ruse to throw the guilty party off his guard.

Allen has one more trick up his sleeve: the chair has no money, just a letter saying that the $300,000 is tied up in a murder story that can be sold to the movies which begins with a man standing in front of a flea circus…

At the end of the program Allen joked with the director of the film, Richard Wallace, who said that he hadn't seen the comedian in any films since *It's in the Bag*. Fred replied, "Hollywood had me, Hollywood threw me back to radio, and that's how people started watching television."

In 1948 a few of the people who were not watching television paid to see a film with a title which sounded like a travelogue. Just as *It's in the Bag* begins with Allen's name above the title, so Henry's screen debut starts with "Henry Morgan in *So This Is New York*" superimposed over a freeze-frame of Morgan standing in front of a cigar store.

This film also opens with the star commenting on motion pictures as Ernie Finch (Morgan) watches a silent film flicker before him in a movie theater. Finch, a cigar salesman who lives in South Bend circa 1920, reflects back to what happened after his wife Ella (Virginia Grey) and her sister Kate Goff (Dona Drake) each inherited $30,000 from their rich Uncle Fergus. Kate is loved by local butcher Willis (Dave Willock), but Ella wants her sister to test the matrimonial waters of New York in hopes of finding a rich husband. Ernie, who is against the idea, reluctantly agrees because the women hold the purse strings.

Virginia Grey and Henry Morgan in one of the hotel scenes.

On the train to Big Town they meet bachelor number one, debonair Francis Griffin (Jerome Cowan) who makes advances and proffers indirect proposals such as "Two can live as cheaply as one" to which Ernie replies, "Not my two." It turns out that Griffin is after Ella, not Kate, and soon pays for his lustful pursuit with a sock on the jaw in separate scenes from both Mr. and Mrs. Finch.

In New York some humor is milked from the excessive demand for tipping, answered in part by Ernie's decision to wear a coin dispenser attached to his pants. The vernacular of the streets takes a ribbing in a vignette in which a cabbie's mutterings of expressions like "Hey, mac, I can't wait all day for ya to chew the fat. Ya wanna hack or don't ya, hey?" are explained in subtitles: "This vehicle awaits your pleasure, sir."

As Ernie watches the women spend $1600 on clothes so they can resemble glamorous flappers, he offers snide commentary, some of which seems casually delivered as throwaway lines. "I never drank this much before prohibition" disappears amidst the marital blather.

An amusing bit occurs when Finch wants to send a one-word telegram to Willis imploring him to come to New York with just the invitation of "Now." Arnold Stang, a regular on Morgan's radio program, plays the Western Union clerk who strives unsuccessfully to get Finch to use some of the other nine words to which he is entitled.

Meanwhile Ella has scouted Mr. Trumbull (Hugh Herbert), a rich explorer who has filled his apartment with heads both mounted and shrunken. Herbert, in a restrained performance, looks as baggy-eyed as Allen and utters nary a one of his patented woo woos even when Trumbull and Kate are caught doing the hula by Mrs. Trumbull who had returned unexpectedly from a hunting trip.

Next on Ella's list is Herbert Daly (Rudy Vallee), a wealthy horse-owner. Kate is attracted not only to the millionaire but also to his jockey Sid Mercer (Leo Gorcey) who has ridden prize horse Coyote to repeated victories. Vallee's southern dialect stands up well for a Yalie and he plays it straight, even sternly reminding a tippling Ernie "That's against the Volstead Act." Finch's rejoinder: "So am I."

After Mercer's chances with Kate are dashed when Daley reveals the jockey's criminal past, tipsy Sid confides to Ernie that his boss has fixed the upcoming race in Coyote's favor. To get revenge on Daley, Mercer confesses that the jockeys have a surprise planned and advises Finch to wager on Honor Bright.

Morgan and Stang together again, this time on a lobby card.

At the track Ernie is in a quandary over which horse to bet on. In one of the film's subtle satiric moments, seconds after being discovered by his boss who had followed him from South Bend and summarily fired for being caught in a lie, Finch decides to place his money on Honor Bright.

During the race it appears that his choice is going to finish last until all the other horses start moving in slow motion. Thanks to that gambit and the other jockeys vigorously whipping Honor Bright, he wins the race with Ernie providing the cynical commentary: "What a fighting heart! What a lucky thing the fix was in." Daley is last seen fleeing the gunshots of crooks who lost money when the fix became unfixed.

Because their resources are dwindling, Kate and Ella lower their sights to ham actor Jimmy Ralston played by Bill Goodwin in a broader version of the vain character he portrayed on *The Burns and Allen Show*. Ralston, an egotistical, uncouth four-flusher, convinces the women to finance his play, *Bridget Sees a Ghost*. The portions of this awful play we see on stage are actually the funniest moments in the movie. Kate delivers her lines hilariously as if she is reading them for the first time, doors do not open in the right direction, wrong props are used, and even the critics watching the atrocity are lampooned.

Just when it seems that all is lost because the inherited money is gone, Willis shows up to claim Kate and the boss appears to reinstate Ernie in his old position. Back in South Bend, Finch wonders what Uncle Fergus would do if he knew about all this. Fergus (Will Wright) comes alive in the portrait on the wall long enough to grumble "Drop dead" and bring down the shade worded "The End."

Fred Allen could not blame the material for the failure of *It's in the Bag* for he and Louis Foster worked on the screen treatment from a story by Morrie Ryskind, who had penned the screenplays of several of the better Marx Brothers films, *My Man Godfrey*, *Stage Door*, and other notable pictures. Alma Reville (Mrs. Alfred Hitchcock) co-wrote the screenplay with Jay Dratner. Director Richard Wallace was no stranger to comedy either, although most of his lighter films featured female leads like Deanna Durbin, Shirley Temple, and Joan Bennett. But neither the writing nor the direction demonstrate much sparkle or originality. The premise was obviously borrowed from Ilf and Petrov's *The Twelve Chairs*. Reaction shots abound as if double takes are supposed to replace repartee or punch lines in generating laughs.

So This Is New York also had impressive names on its roster. Carl Foreman, who later brought gritty dialogue to such films as *Champion*, *High Noon*, and *Home of the Brave*, captured a little of the spirit but not much of the bite of Ring Lardner's *The Big Town* in his screenplay. Producer Stanley Kramer would later add *The Caine Mutiny, Guess Who's Coming to Dinner, On the Beach,* and another all-star comedy, *It's a Mad, Mad, Mad, Mad World*, to the list of films he produced or directed. The name of director Richard Fleischer would one day be seen on the credits for *20,000 Leagues Under the Sea, Fantastic Voyage,* and *The New Centurions*. Two threads are apparent in these overviews: these men were primarily known for action or message pictures, not comedy, and in 1948 all three were in the early, learning stages of their careers.

For Allen and Morgan their movie careers were virtually over after their starring vehicle was released. Allen, who had small roles in two 1930s musicals and some feuding words with Benny in *Love Thy Neighbor* (1940), appeared briefly in two omnibus films in 1952: bickering with Ginger Rogers as one of the six couples who learn *We're Not Married* and pairing off with Oscar Levant in "The Ransom of Red Chief" section of *O.Henry's Full House*. Morgan's only other movie credit was a serious role in the 1960 crime drama *Murder, Inc.*

The reviews for *It's in the Bag* were generally favorable. Bosley Crowther in the *New York Times* called it a rat's nest of nonsense, a crossfire of gags, and commended the credit sequence for its "superlative spoofing." Mori in *Variety* found fault with the continuity and thought the production came off as a series of vaudeville sketches but did single out the Benny sequence as notable. *Time* admitted that the film was not in the same class with the funniest movies ever made but added that it was "funny enough to do very well until a better one comes along which is likely to be quite a while." Its review also cited the credit sequence as the best part of the film. It is telling that a number of critics felt, in essence, the best part of the film was over before the picture itself began.

In the early stages of the project Allen exuded optimism about its success. In August of 1944 he indicated in a letter to Bill Morrow that he and Ryskind were working on a film treatment and that "most of it seems pretty funny to me." But in 1945 after the movie had been released he wrote Morrow "in my opinion it isn't too hot." Later in 1945 he wrote to Abe Burrows that the "trade papers gave it good notices but the picture is pretty weak" and to actor Charlie Cantor he admitted that "it burns me up as we had Bill Bendix and other wonderful people and should have had a smash."

Variety took a rather cautious view of *So This Is New York*, calling it a "fast mix of subtle gags and brittle situations" and suggested that it could be a sleeper. The racetrack sequence was commended as being the funniest in the film, though the reviewer thought Morgan came off as either wry or nasty. In his 1994 autobiography *Here's Morgan*, Henry wrote that

New York Times critic Vincent Canby told him in Sardi's that he liked the film, then added with a dollop of vitriol that Canby had kept that opinion to himself for forty years.

In its review *Time* cataloged the difficulties Kramer and colleague George Glass had in getting financing for the picture after securing rights to the Lardner material. After inking Morgan and getting backing from Enterprise Productions, most of the remaining capital went into landing big-name actors. Kramer recalled that $100,000 of the $600,000 raised for the picture went for Morgan's salary, money the producer believed was well-spent on the man he called "the reigning genius in terms of comedy." The *Time* review commended the horserace scene and thought Lardner himself might have approved of the deadpan humor.

The fact is that both movies show signs of being top-heavy in name appeal and skimpy on production values. *So This Is New York* abounds in newsreel and stock shots of exteriors. A shot of three pairs of walking feet is as close as we get to seeing the principals traversing Gotham's sidewalks. *It's in the Bag* conveys the impression that the actors never moved off the sound stage. The music is unremarkable or derivative (anyone familiar with Dimitri Tiomkin's work would be hard-pressed to find much that is noteworthy about his contribution to *So This Is New York*) and the

At the racetrack with Leo Gorcey, Rudy Vallee, Virginia Grey, Dona Drake, and Morgan.

sets are undistinguished. The lesson Allen learned from his experience was summarized in a letter to Charlie Cantor: "the moral is…don't make an independent picture."

Allen laid some of the blame at the doorstep of producer Skirball for not only how the movie looked but also for how it was backed and promoted by Manhattan Productions. He complained in his letters about the delayed opening in New York and how the film was being distributed. Fred himself did everything he could to push the movie like appearing on the October 29, 1944 *Jack Benny Program* to tell Benny he had just completed a new picture called *It's in the Bag* and to "take one for the team" by rolling with the punch of Jack's stinging comeback: that it ought to be a success because "you're advertising it under each eye."

In his autobiography Kramer lamented the trouble in distributing *So This Is New York* and claimed that United Artists never showed the picture in a first-run theater in New York. Still feeling the effect of some disdainful reviews and the negative responses from preview audiences decades after the film was released, he called the movie "a colossal failure" and "about the biggest bomb made in the history of the film industry."

More recent assessments of the films reveal less harsh evaluations. In *5001 Nights at the Movies* Pauline Kael called *So This Is New York* "a deadpan farce that's uneven, but frequently very funny." Leslie Halliwell in *Halliwell's Harvest* may have presented the most perceptive comments on *It's in the Bag* when he called it a rambling, cheaply-made farce shot on the barest number of sets, a unique curiosity that with "a little more work all around might have become a comedy classic."

Both black-and-white films, released through United Artists, feature episodic, sometimes disjointed sequences showcasing a parade of guest stars with the most amusing scenes occurring at the end. The plots were triggered by an inheritance and fueled by a search involving five chairs or suitors. And each film reduced the main star to being either an irascible malcontent mugging for laughs or a smug spoilsport sniping from the wings. Each wit was playing out of position and, after one notable strikeout, both the industry and the comedians knew it.

It wasn't just the mediocre returns at the box office. Amidst Vallee and the other cinema veterans, neither Morgan nor Allen had a chance to establish a comic persona like Danny Kaye or Bob Hope did and thus came across more like bystanders than star attractions who could carry a picture. So they went back to radio where the mavericks play to cast their satiric gibes.

It's in the Bag is not a bad way to spend an hour and a half, but if one wants to hear Allen handle a murder mystery with aplomb listen to his spoofs with Basil Rathbone broadcast on *The Fred Allen Show* in 1948 and 1949. *So This Is New York* is no worse than *Good Sam, You Gotta Stay Happy*, or a number of other comedies released in 1948, though the mordant wit of the real Henry Morgan can be found in his radio parodies of commercials and motion pictures and his barbed exchanges with Stang.

The best way to view Allen's and Morgan's records in the field of entertainment is not to mark the scorecard solely on what appeared on the screen. They had little success when they played on the road in Hollywood, but when they returned home to the airwaves they were in a league of their own.

Warner Oland starred in *Charlie Chan in Egypt* with player Rita Cansino, who later changed her last name to Hayworth.

B's, Please

A PRIMARY BENEFIT OF GOING TO THEATERS years ago was a bonus that many people took for granted: a double feature which often teamed a highly-touted A production with a B picture that made up its lack of big stars with fast-paced action, songs, or laughs. For some of us, the bottom half of these double bills were the tops.

During the golden age of movies, studios like Metro-Goldwyn-Mayer, Paramount, Warner Brothers, Twentieth Century-Fox, Universal, and Columbia released a plethora of "quickies," black-and-white, low-budgeted films made in less than three weeks which ran for little over an hour. Because a number of the studios owned the theaters where their films were playing, the moguls figured they might as well use the existing sets and the contract players they had to pay whether they were working or not to produce extra magnets to attract people to the ticket booths.

Fringe players on the Hollywood scene such as Monogram, Republic, and Producers Releasing Corporation rarely made it to the big leagues, producing almost exclusively B pictures. (Cynics claim some of their movies merited letters closer to the end of the alphabet.) These companies earned profits because they could manufacture a package of thrills or chuckles for $100,000 or less. Republic rode on the steady shoulders of Gene Autry and Roy Rogers through outdoor settings which cost nothing and past facades of carpentered western main streets. At Monogram the Bowery Boys engaged in horseplay before backdrops that changed little from picture to picture. Although PRC had the reputation of being the bottom of movieland's barrel, from time to time it issued a keeper like *Detour*, one of the best examples of film noir which was shot in six days with a credited cast of just seven players. But audiences didn't expect staggering production values from the economy line, just plots that didn't plod.

One of the unexpected bonuses of a B picture was seeing those talented performers who provided supporting roles in main features finally getting a chance to shine. The best parts of *Hold That Ghost* occurred when Joan Davis clowned with Lou Costello, yet she never appeared with Abbott and Costello again and rarely had such a juicy part in a big picture. But she starred in a number of B movies for Columbia and Universal that allowed her to take pratfalls and throw her delectable double takes left and right. To see Joan and rubber-legged Leon Errol cavorting in *She Gets Her Man* might have made people holding their sides from laughter march toward the theater manager's office to demand that *She Gets Her Man* appear first on the marquee because the unbridled slapstick alone was worth the price of admission. Anyone who remembers the way Joan could deliver a funny line with a poker face can appreciate one of her responses in this film: "That was a very intelligent question. Has anybody got any stupid ones?"

Keenan Wynn and Frank Morgan, members of the MGM stock company, stood front and center in the 1946 fantasy *The Cockeyed Miracle*. The twist in this comedy was that, while both actors played ghosts, dapper Ben Griggs (Wynn) who died young returned as the father of gray-haired Sam Griggs (Morgan) which resulted in amusing dialogue like Ben admonishing his son to "treat your father with more respect" to which Sam replied, "Why, I'm twice as old as you."

Hugh Herbert, often given little more to do in A movies other than to throw in a "Woo woo" now and then, scored in leading roles in both *Ever Since Venus* for Columbia and Universal's *There's One Born Every Minute* which allowed him to not only drive the action but also provoke giggles with speeches such as "The other side has been robbing you for years. Why not give us a chance?"

In addition to giving the veterans an opportunity to flex their muscles, B pictures also served as a training ground for Anthony Quinn, Jane Wyman, Glenn Ford, Elizabeth Taylor, Dan Dailey, Robert Mitchum, Rita Hayworth, Donna Reed, Dennis O'Keefe, Susan Hayward, and other performers who would soon graduate to the A team. O'Keefe demonstrated so much natural ability for physical comedy in *I'm Nobody's Sweetheart Now* and *Good Morning, Judge* that it seems almost a shame he moved into crime melodramas. Hayward, so breathtakingly beautiful in 1941 that she almost stole Republic's *Sis Hopkins* from Judy Canova just with her face, did top the star in one scene by perfectly intoning the Canova-ism "You're telling I" after Judy admitted, "I'll be a real dummy."

But the B movies that bring back the fondest memories are those the studios released periodically as part of a series. The principals usually remained the same; just the villains, bit players, and story lines changed from year to year.

Sometimes the titles didn't even undergo much alteration. If the new movie advertised on store windows was *Spook Busters, Ghost Chasers, Spook Chasers, Spy Chasers, Jail Busters, Blues Busters, Fighting Fools,* or *Feuding Fools,* we knew Leo Gorcey, Huntz Hall, and the Bowery Boys were on the loose again in a neighborhood theater with their brand of knockabout comedy featuring Hall's asininity and Gorcey's malapropisms.

From 1938 to 1950 Penny Singleton and Arthur Lake starred in twenty-eight *Blondie* films for Columbia Pictures. It didn't seem to matter if the large print on the posters told us Blondie hit the jackpot, went to college, or took a holiday; we knew somehow she would have to correct the effects of Dagwood's bungling.

Popular radio shows spawned a few series in the 1940s. Although Jimmy Lydon didn't have Ezra Stone's adenoidal quirkiness, his Henry Aldrich stumbled through the same kinds of romantic entanglements and clouds of confusion that made each weekly visit with the Aldrich clan a nightmarish scavenger hunt. Harold Peary appeared as the Great Gild-

Dagwood is also on the campus when *Blondie Goes to College.*

ersleeve in four RKO pictures made between 1942 and 1944. Columbia released eight films in the middle of the decade built around the Whistler who walked the streets by night tingling spines with the eeriest thirteen notes ever heard. On six occasions the cameras rolled into the Jot 'Em Down Store and each time Chester Lauck and Norris Goff answered the casting call as Lum and Abner.

The lovers of belly laughs who knew when their favorite characters had returned just by checking the newspapers had no advantage over the mystery fans who did not have to be great detectives to know a new case was afoot. They loved to tag along with the hawkshaws to see if the crime would be solved with brains or brawn.

In thirteen films Boston Blackie (Chester Morris) proved to be as quick with a wisecrack as with a gun. Sometimes Blackie seemed more intent on twitting Inspector Faraday with comments like "those lousy cigars are ruining your wind" than in capturing the crook, but he always delivered the goods along with the gibes.

The Falcon as portrayed by George Sanders or his brother, Tom Conway, used more urbane wit and less force than Blackie to crack thirteen cases for RKO. (Three featherweight entries by Film Classics with John Calvert as the Falcon were released in 1948 and 1949.) Ellery Queen, the Lone Wolf, Bulldog Drummond, and the Saint also sorted out clues during those years. Peter Lorre's tenure as Mr. Moto proved to be a short one: eight movies for Fox from 1937 to 1939.

But another oriental detective, Charlie Chan, stands as the all-time champ of culprit-chasers on the screen. His record: 44-0 in bouts with sundry miscreants from 1931 to 1949 for Fox or Monogram. Warner Oland, Sidney Toler, and Roland Winters played the imperturbable Chinese sleuth who always produced an apt maxim for any situation. The important lesson of this series could be stated as "Criminal who tangles with Charlie Chan like man who wants to serve drinks: both end up behind bars."

Just as for Sherlockians "it is always 1895," so for many movie fans Basil Rathbone will forever be Sherlock Holmes. From 1939 to 1946 Rathbone and Nigel Bruce as Holmes and Dr. Watson battled a variety of foes from the fiendish Hound of the Baskervilles to the nefarious Professor Moriarty and wily Spider Woman.

For those who craved more exotic adventure than cat-and-mouse games Monogram delivered a series about Bomba, the Jungle Boy, ex-Tarzan Johnny Weissmuller garbed as Jungle Jim rescued exploited natives and endangered damsels on Columbia's soundstage version of Africa, and Paramount and United Artists saddled up William Boyd sixty-six times as Ho-

One-sheet poster for the first film in the series.

palong Cassidy during the same years Cesar Romero, Gilbert Roland, and Duncan Renaldo were playing that western Robin Hood, the Cisco Kid.

The deluge of B movies that had flowed during the thirties and forties began to dry up after the studios were in essence told, as a hoodlum in a Boston Blackie film might say, "I got a message from the feds: 'If you know what's good for you, you better stop playing monopoly and sell your flick joints.'"

Once divested of their showplaces where they had dictated booking policy, there was no longer any financial reason for these companies to churn out dozens of pictures in order to fill seats every night of the week. Since the downfall of the studio system many independent quickies have been made, but they don't have the same recurrent characters and piquant flavor of those treats served by the moviemakers who followed the motto of Warner's B unit: "Make 'em fast, make 'em loud, make 'em fun."

And what fun we had. Whatever our favorite characters happened to be, whether they were goofy guys, gorgeous gals, galloping gunslingers, or glib gumshoes, bargain basement movies gave us pleasant escapism every week. When they played at our local theater, it was like welcoming old friends back to town. Those films may have been B pictures, but for many of us who loved them they rated an A in entertainment.

THE RADIO SHOWS

Jim and Marian Jordan, showing smiles here in 1943, are still getting chuckles in the 21st century.

Fibber McGee and Molly: Always Good for a Laugh

On April 16, 1935, Jim and Marian Jordan began a new program on radio. On September 6, 1959 that couple's final broadcast was heard on *Monitor*. Between those two dates listeners were treated to one of the most exquisite pleasures radio had to offer: *Fibber McGee and Molly*.

In the beginning the McGees were nomads, but once they settled in Wistful Vista a pattern soon developed. The formula that writers Don Quinn and Phil Leslie concocted changed very little during the vintage years. The ingredients were almost always the same: give Fibber a problem, let him simmer for a while, drop in three or four bits and half a dozen characters, then get him out before the tag. Fibber sometimes had a bitter pill to swallow at the end, but things finally came to rest at the McGee house.

And what a house it was: 79 Wistful Vista, the most famous address in radio. We know that property as well as our own: the hall where the couple welcomed their guests; the closet; the horsehair sofa and Fibber's well-worn chair; the living room rug spotted with paint and ink from ill-fated projects; a kitchen which was the scene of misguided efforts to make vase, fudge, and cake; and the yard, site of fights with Gildersleeve, aborted barbeques, and a singular attempt to extract maple syrup from an elm tree.

The parade of characters who walked through the front door of that house contributed no small part to the charm of the program. The Old Timer had more old gags than a gang of kidnappers. Nick and Ole regularly donated their time and their jokes. Windbag Gildersleeve blew in long enough to ignite his short fuse. Horatio K. Boomer could find his way in and out of the house but seemed incapable of locating that missing card or paper among all the gewgaws he carried with him. Doctor Gamble and Teeny might stop by just to tease or aggravate Fibber. Henpecked Wallace Wimple used the house as a refuge from his formidable stronger half. The McGees trimmed more than a little of the upper crust off Mmes. Uppington and Carstairs. Try as he would to remain calm, LaTrivia usually could not refrain from flying off the handle (or hying off the fandle, as he might say at the height of his tantrum).

Fibber McGee and Molly boasted one of the strongest lineups of any comedy program. Harold Peary, Shirley Mitchell, Bea Benaderet, Gale Gordon, Dick LeGrand, and Arthur Q. Bryan possessed some of the better-known voices on the air; Bill Thompson alone owned a handful of them. The show wasn't complete until everyone had been heard from. Even Fibber would poke fun at their standard practice of marching the cast before us by asking Molly, "Who hasn't been in yet?"

If Teeny hadn't been in yet, Marian Jordan could have answered, "Me." Not only did she vividly portray Molly as a long-suffering, good-natured housewife but she also was just as convincing as Fibber's nemesis, the little girl who outwitted him so consistently that he thought she was a midget. Marian also played characters named Cornelia Wheedledeck, Bedelia Wearybottom, and Geraldine, particularly in the early days of the show.

But it was Jim's Fibber that was the program's sine qua non. Fibber McGee is sui generis; there never has been anyone like him. There is a line of descent from Chester Riley to Ralph Kramden to Archie Bunker. Irma, Lucy, and Gracie could have been sisters. But there was only one Fibber, a garrulous know-it-all and lovable bungler, an inveterate teller of tales and dreamer of dreams with no visible means of support. He certainly remains one of the most distinctive characters to have appeared on any comedy program on radio or television.

The characters were memorable, but so were their favorite sayings. The show left us singing its phrases. "'Tain't funny, McGee" has been squelching punch lines for over sixty years. Almost to her dying day in 1984 my mother would say things like "Old Motor Mouth he was known as in those days," an echo of the preludes that Fibber delivered before embarking on his tongue twisters. "That ain't the way I heered it" is still the way I hear it from time to time. "Heavenly days!" may not have been original with Molly, but she made it hers and we made it ours. "You're a harrrrd man, McGee" we would say to a friend in jest, to which he or she might reply, "Hard, my clavicle!"

The stock phrases were just part of the fun for the whole show lifted our spirits. The teasing introductions by Harlow Wilcox whet our appetite for the visitors who were shuffled in and out between bouncy musical numbers. Even the middle commercial seemed painless because we, like the McGees, were drawn into Harlow's web and it was over before we knew it.

The program was both fun *and* funny. Some sitcoms of past and present are as mirthless as *Murder at Midnight*, but Fibber and Molly were always good for a laugh. Presented with a smorgasbord of word play, sarcasm, hyperbole, banter, riddles, shaggy dog stories, malapropisms, running gags, wheezes and twists on wheezes, one-liners, and non sequiturs prepared by Quinn and Leslie, there had to be *something* we liked. Marian knew what her husband was going to say, but no one can blame her for sometimes breaking up when Jim read his lines. Even after hearing Fibber fume and sputter on dozens of shows, it is still a delight to listen to him blurt out a torrent of nonsense like "You haven't ever been sued for fifty grand by a guy that it wasn't your fault if he got bit by a dog that didn't belong to you so how can I be legally liable anyway, have you?" To listen to the exchanges between Fibber, Molly, and the characters played by Cliff Arquette on episodes broadcast during the early fifties is to hear the best badinage of confusion since the heyday of the Marx Brothers.

None of this brief encomium is to claim that *Fibber McGee and Molly* was perfect. The running gags limped at times, but so did those employed by Jack Benny and Bob Hope. Although some of Fibber's predicaments were downright silly, they never seemed as contrived as those entangling the Aldrich and Bumstead families. Once the listeners bought Fibber, they bought the whole package.

And it was quite a package that came gift-wrapped to us through three decades and which is still is available on tape or disc. When it opens before us, we see a magical place where every business is located at 14th and Oak, all calls have to go through a smooth operator named Myrt, streetcar conductors speak in garbled tongues, and the only drink in town is hot-buttered root beer. Over there on the back steps there's a short man saying, "Oh, no, you don't" and a little girl replying, "Oh, yes, I do." But isn't that him by the side of the house telling his wife that if their neighbor doesn't keep his dadratted lawn mower in better shape he'll borrow one from somebody else? And that's the same gabby fellow on the front sidewalk who's boring a portly doctor with a story about some Fred Nitney that he used to have a vaudeville act with back in Starved Rock, Illinois. It seems that no matter which way we turn we can't get away from Fibber McGee and Molly. May it always be so.

If Randy Stone had played his cards right, he might have come across these two some night in a penny arcade.

Watchman, Tell Us of the Night

It ran only two years and it appeared late in the game, at a time when most programs were losing the good fight to the other medium. Mention it to ten people at random and it is likely that none of them will remember it. Yet *Night Beat* remains a favorite not only among collectors but also with listeners to shows that feature vintage broadcasts. What is there about these tales of a newspaperman's adventures that attracts such a loyal following?

The primary asset of the program is that the write person was played by the right person. The character of Randy Stone, reporter for *The Chicago Star*, required an actor who could convey the honesty, sincerity, compassion, and vulnerability of an everyday fellow, and nobody could portray those traits more convincingly than Frank Lovejoy did. Frank played dependable characters in the movies and a stalwart detective on television's *Meet McGraw*, but Randy Stone was the role of his career.

We are naturally drawn to Randy because he isn't just a scribe and narrator; he is one of us. We are walking the cold and windswept streets of Chicago with him in search of a story. When he tries to return a hat to a pedestrian or finds a good home for a cat, we feel he is merely doing what we would do. Even when he does something less than admirable like running away from a man who claims to be pinned in a condemned building because he suspects the man is the one who wrote him a threatening letter, Stone is only guilty of being human.

One of Randy Stone's most endearing qualities is his kinship with the little guy, the eccentric, the castoff. As Stone admitted at the top of one episode, "I seem to have a knack at getting mixed up with offbeat characters." It doesn't matter if it's an old man with a system to beat the roulette wheel or a farmer who wants to love a crook out of town or a scared girl from Kansas who doesn't belong in a police lineup or a punch-drunk ex-fighter who wants to see his old flame one more time or a lover of art who claims that someone has killed Vincent (van Gogh); no matter what their circumstances or mental capacity, Randy Stone becomes their champion.

Although many episodes were devoted to these studies in human nature, some of the scripts would have been right at home on *Suspense*. The "race against time" theme was used to great effect a number of times. In the first show of the series broadcast February 6, 1950, Randy rushes to the top of the Wrigley Building to save a man from committing suicide. In other episodes he searches for contaminated butter to prevent a typhoid epidemic, stages a last-minute rescue of a woman slated for execution, and spearheads a manhunt for a probable carrier of rabies. The most inventive of the suspenseful episodes is "The World at Your Fingertips," a telephone drama somewhat reminiscent of "Sorry, Wrong Number." Stone dials a number at random and gets a distraught woman who had been locked up in an office by her mentally-ill husband who has gone for a gun so he can kill her. The rest of the show chronicles Stone's efforts to locate the woman or her husband *and* keep his line clear so she can call back.

Stories in the series about crime or revenge are superior to those written for programs like *Gangbusters* and *This is Your FBI*. "My Brother's Keeper," which tells about an escaped convict who holds a couple and Stone captive before being gunned down by the police, contains the kicker that elevates it above the level of crime melodrama: neither the husband nor the convict could kill the other because they were brothers. In "Firebug" our attention during the search for an arsonist is not directed to the fires and their consequences but rather to the suspicions of a father and son and the anguish of the lonely wife and mother who started the fires because "nobody talked to me." In "Juvenile Gangster" a confrontation between two thugs in a roadhouse is designed not to demonstrate dishonor among thieves but rather to show a boy what his father was really like. A heavy-handed approach to the oft-told variations of Chaucer's "The Pardoner's Tale" could have resulted in the typical "crooks kill each other off" finale, but at the end of "Molly Keller" the emphasis is on bitterness and wasted lives as a widow sends two men to find the third member of a robbery, the man who framed her husband. In "The Football Player and the Syndicate," William Conrad gives a brilliant performance as a gambler who can't pay his debts; his fear is so palpable that we can see the beads of perspiration on his face and his eyes darting back and forth as his end approaches. For a program in which the threat of death loomed often, *Night Beat* showed remarkable restraint. More often than not, murder and suicide were left waiting in the wings.

A few episodes are unique. "Old Home Week" is the only one that is not set in Chicago or its environs and, even though there is an attempted murder and an accidental shooting, it is one of the lighter efforts complete with puns and garrulous characters. "His Name Was Luke" approaches fantasy as it unfolds the story of a Christ figure who does not appear to us or Randy but who changes the lives of four disparate people for the better. Perhaps the most touching episode is "Anton's Return" which tells of a prisoner and his wife who not only die at the same time in different places but with same final words on their lips. Achieving poignancy without becoming maudlin has never been easy, but the writers for *Night Beat* accomplished it as well as anyone on radio.

Russell Hughes wrote a number of the scripts as did director Warren Lewis and editor Larry Marcus, but whoever did the writing followed the unvarying pattern: teaser, story, moral. This tight, unified structure contributed significantly to our enjoyment of the series. We looked forward to Stone luring us into his net with lines like "This one began in the shattering turmoil of a manhunt and ended in the quietness of the morgue" or "That night my story began with the innocent ringing of my telephone...I didn't know that at the other end of the line was death" or "This one began with the story of an execution and ended with the death of a man's soul." Who could turn off the radio or switch stations after hearing leads like that?

The stories themselves are filled with realistic dialogue and vivid descriptions. Several episodes, particularly "Byline for Frank," begin with graphic images of Chicago that are much more sensuous than Carl Sandburg's poem about the city. It doesn't matter if Stone is engaging in raillery with a short-order cook, exchanging veiled threats with a ruffian, or cajoling policemen; all the conversations ring true. The mark of verisimilitude is also on the portraits Randy paints for us. When he mentions souls eaten away by loneliness like "the lone drinker in a plush bar who toasts his reflection in the mirror and wishes he was too drunk to see it," we know that we have seen his counterpart all too often. The description Randy gives of a woman named Stella could have come from the pen of Raymond Chandler: "I'd met her type before. The gals that were beautiful once but who don't care too much anymore. She was fighting a losing battle with weight, and her hair, in spite of a mass of small blonde curls piled over the part, showed at least two weeks behind on the bleach." Randy Stone calls them like we see them.

After the denouement, Randy always stepped forward to deliver his final comments on *la condition humaine*. Following the suicide of a misunderstood but great painter, Stone aptly adds that "we never appreciate the sane people until it's too late." Some of his closing thoughts analyzed either love or hate, and on one show he combined them: "Let someone get up and talk about hate and he's hailed as a new leader. Let him speak of love and he's ridiculed, he's spit upon, and…even nailed to a cross. Love is the greatest thing, the oldest yet the greatest thing." That last sentiment is revealing for, despite the assorted characters with devious and dubious motives that we meet, *Night Beat* is life-affirming. Yes, Randy says, this is a rat race we're in, but "just because you didn't come in first doesn't mean you're last." After the aphorism, all that remained for Stone to do was deliver his familiar signature, a call for the copyboy to pick up his completed story.

The scripts were written for an intelligent, sentient audience. It is entirely appropriate that the writing is literate for our storyteller is not a street-educated Broadway from Runyonland but rather an experienced newspaperman whose livelihood is words. Allusions to the Bible, Dante, Shakespeare, and Pope do not come as a surprise when spoken by a journalist. What other program would begin with a quotation from Juvenal? As Fred Allen might say, "It's not *The Green Hornet*, kiddies."

The quality of the writing was complemented by superb sound effects. When Stone steps out of a building, we hear the el, car horns, police whistles, even the ticking of a taxi meter. The crowds that he meets are distinct: appreciative in a jazz club, raucous in a burlesque theater, savage at a prize fight, apprehensive during a hostage crisis. We expect to hear thunder in a death scene or a car smashing a police barrier or a roller coaster, but what demonstrates the attention to detail are the subtle touches like hesitant footsteps and the hum of an elevator. A scene in an operating room is so realistic that we hear the labored breathing of the patient, the passing of the instruments, and the irrigation as counterpoint to the dialogue between Stone and the surgeon. *Night Beat* clearly was not a program devoted to cutting corners.

Nowhere is the quest for quality more apparent than in the casting. Every week some of radio's standbys could be heard aiding or frustrating Randy. Right before our ears Ed Begley became an embittered industrialist, Richard Crenna a guilt-ridden jockey, Sheldon Leonard a hardened gangster, Bea Benaderet a concerned mother. Peter Leeds, Bill Conrad, Jack Kruschen, Gerald Mohr, Ben Wright, Larry Dobkin, Bill Johnstone, Ted de Corsia, and Tudor Owen made multiple appearances playing shady or misunderstood characters. Veterans Jeanette Nolan, Joan Banks (who appeared with husband Frank on numerous shows), Betty Moran, Jeanne Bates, Barbara Fuller, Lurene Tuttle, and Georgia Ellis handled most of the important female roles, although Virginia Gregg deserves honorable mention for doing double duty as landlady and spurned lover in "The Search for Fred." It is no wonder that actors and actresses returned to the program; everyone in the cast was given credit at the end of most episodes.

It really then should be no mystery why followers of old-time radio regard *Night Beat* with so much affection. It starred a fine actor who played his role the way a reporter writes a story: the reporter is not the subject of an article, he only interacts with the subject and then tells us what he has seen. Give the actor a first-rate cast to work with, well-written scripts, and solid production values, and the result is choice radio drama.

Well, that's it. Mix the ingredients anyway you want, rearrange the paragraphs, and it would still come out the same. It's a story of people and a show that just won't die. You can't change that. But none of us is perfect. We all need help now and then. Copyboy!

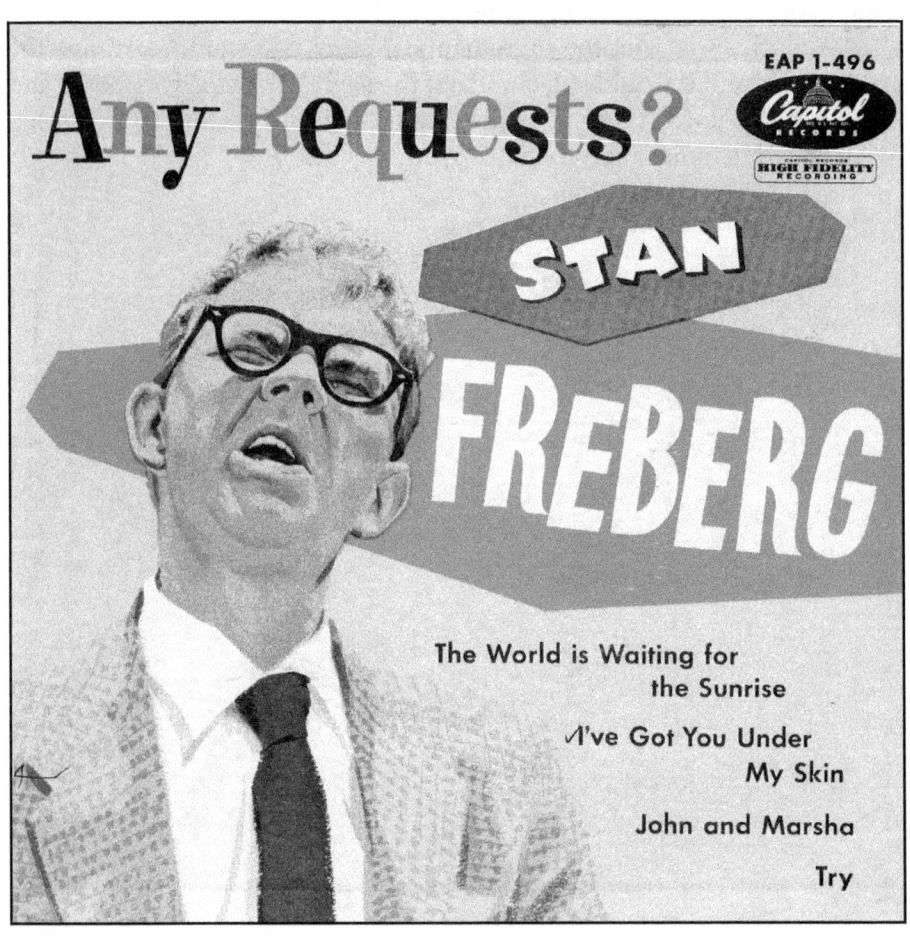

Just one request: CBS, give that wit who's been making all those funny records his own radio show.

The Best Zings in Life Are Freberg's

When the subject of the moment turns to parodies done on radio, immediately the names of Bob and Ray, Fred Allen, and Jack Benny come to mind. Very few subjects escaped the keen gaze of Bob Elliott and Ray Goulding, Allen took on everything from game shows and detective programs to musicals, and Jack used the second half of his programs to poke fun at movies and mysteries. And there was one other show so filled with notable parodies that it still gives off a warm glow over thirty years after it flashed briefly before us. That program was *The Stan Freberg Show*.

The CBS series ran as a sustained feature for fifteen weeks on Sundays during the summer and fall of 1957. The fact that the show could not attract a sponsor became a running gag and by the fourteenth episode Stan decided to be his own patron. He took a good-natured swipe at Pepsodent and himself by having Jud Conlon's Rhythmaires sing the jingle, "You'll wonder where the Freberg went if you tune in two weeks from now."

Just hearing the first episode might have scared potential sponsors away for good. What kind of comedy show was this with a twenty-minute sketch about a rivalry between two Nevada nightclub owners that satirized greed, one-upsmanship, and meretriciousness? The episode concluded with a vision of Armageddon after one owner tried to out-Herod the other by booking the hydrogen bomb: "I wonder if the boys were still counting their profits when time ran out and the man pushed the button." Then, nothing but the eerie sound of the wind passing over the post-atomic wasteland. No credits, no applause, no audience laughter fading in the background. It was a daring debut, an anti-war fable for Cold War America.

The second and subsequent episodes sounded a bit more conventional than the opening one, but the show was still unlike anything else on the air since Henry Morgan left that corner in front of the cigar store. Freberg couldn't resist slapping his listeners awake by offering challenges like "Just in case there is someone we haven't offended, this will do it" before launching into a rock ditty entitled "Jeannie with the Light Brown Wig." Indeed, the musical parodies are some of the most memorable moments from the series, especially "The Banana Boat Song" with Peter Leeds as the bongo player with the sensitive ears, "The Yellow Rose of Texas" with the runaway drummer, and the mumbled lyrics on "Sh-Boom." Recordings of these songs preceded the series and their popularity did much to bring about *The Stan Freberg Show*.

What makes the lampoons wear so well is that Freberg hit the target every time. When he was wailing "Day-O," he sounded like Harry Belafonte. When chasing the dragon, he *was* Joe Friday. When awash with bubbles and schmaltz, he became Mr. Wunnerful. In those days Stan was a gifted mimic with a deadly aim.

He also must have been a bit of an enigma to some listeners who were probably scratching their heads over the sounds coming through their speakers. Exhibit A: a tuned sheep chorus that rang their bells to "The Lullaby of Birdland." Exhibit B: acrobats (on radio!) Exhibit C: a woman at Mount Rushmore who carved oleomargarine busts of Mary Margaret McBride, Wyatt Earp, and Fats Domino. Exhibit D: a number from the Skin Divers Mandolin Club. And that's only from the first three shows!

During those few months on the air Freberg aimed at all aspects of the American scene. He satirized Ralph, Alice, and Ed in "The Honeyearthers." *Gunsmoke* became *Bang Gunley, U.S. Marshall Fields*. The *Lox Audio Theatre* was sponsored by the "salmon-shaped bar of soap that swims up tub." Twice listeners endured the absurdities spoken by members of a panel who held postgraduate degrees in Little Orphan Annie and Tarzan. Censors, do-it-yourself kits, actors, the flying saucer craze, abominable snowmen, pedants, demigods of U.S history, Good Humor men, interviewers; they all felt the sting of Stan's irreverent barbs.

Even though Freberg knew before the thirteenth show aired that it would all end in two weeks, he didn't coast. In fact, the thirteenth and fourteenth episodes may be the best entries in the series. (The final episode merely repeated favorite sketches and songs.) The highlight of episode thirteen, "Gray Flannel Hatful of Teenage Werewolves," is a devastating satire that rakes both horror movies and advertising agencies over the coals. Freberg was at his best when wielding two-pronged weapons as he did when he spoofed westerns and psychiatry in "The Lone Analyst."

In the penultimate episode he satirized detective shows and commercials when he became Sam Splade, a seedy gumshoe who spouted ludicrous similes like "he bit off his words like a rattlesnake striking a radish" and "she screamed and fell like a sack of wet spaghetti at a noodle festival." Anyone who thinks the overwrought language and gratuitous violence are far-fetched has never heard an episode of *Pat Novak for Hire* or read a novel by Mickey Spillane.

And anyone who ever listened to *The Stan Freberg Show* knows that it was a genuinely funny, well-written program. It had talented comic performers like Daws Butler, who had such a gold mine in his throat that Hanna-Barbera staked a claim there, and June Foray, who possessed a raspy voice that always provoked laughter. It had critical acclaim from the press. What it didn't have was a large audience and a sponsor, and that combination killed the show.

Stan Freberg rose from the ashes of that program to become one of the most inventive minds in advertising. It is ironic that the man who could not find a sponsor now has clients from all over the country eager to tap his fertile imagination. Over the years he has created campaigns to sell chow mein, encyclopedias, prunes, sound systems, tea bags, albums, lawn mowers, and dozens of other products. His unconventional brand of humor is still very much in evidence as it is one of the trademarks of his commercials. Even the name of his production company, Freberg Ltd., seems to be yet another of his running gags for if there is one word that applies to the wit and creativity of Stan Freberg it is definitely the opposite of *limited*.

Alice Faye and Phil Harris on the job in 1949.

A Joker and a Queen

To determine what show was the funniest program on radio would not be a simple task. Some might select one that produced the most jokes per half hour or one that generated the longest laughs from the studio audience or one that kept the chuckles rolling for twenty seasons or more. But if the criterion for funniest show is which one could make us laugh out loud both then and now, a leading candidate for that honor is *The Phil Harris-Alice Faye Show*.

Credit for the funny lines on the program should be given first to Ray Singer and Dick Chevillat. Singer and Chevillat belong in the pantheon of radio comedy writers with Paul Rhymer, Fred Allen, Don Quinn and Phil Leslie, and the Jack Benny team, all of whom richly deserved the billing they received at the beginning or closing of the program. Singer and Chevillat's special talent was tailoring wisecracks to character, loading characters with foibles so an infinite number of gags could be hung upon them.

Much of the humor on the program revolved around Phil's character or lack of same. Vanity about his looks and singing could be cashed in for jokes about curlers, mirrors, gold records, and southern cooking. His affinity for the bottle floated to the surface every time he expressed distaste for water or milk. Phil's propensity for getting into ridiculous situations stemmed from his bullheaded pride and gullibility, both of which seem to have no bounds.

One fascinating aspect of the Phil Harris on this show grew out of the brash character he played on Jack Benny's show: he had become a glib illiterate. He spelled *blood b-l-u-d* and thought the Eiffel Tower could be found in New York City. Words like *inpecnably, indubinably,* and *Apa-*

protamaz regularly tumbled out of his mouth. He issued malapropisms like "split an subjunction" and "optical delusion" without blushing. Yet at the same time he could be a smooth conversationist with a line of self-confident patter followed by a sobriquet. Nobody possessed a greater reservoir of cognomens than Harris stored in his arsenal. *Clyde* and

Phil's big novelty hit was a real novelty: the title appears nowhere in the lyrics.

Myrtle remained his favorites, but those around him were just as likely to be called *Oglethorpe, Hastings, Winston, Levi, Casper, Herman, Thelma, Ruby, Cletis, Louella, Mercedes, Hershel,* or *Bernard*. Ed Wynn claimed to be the perfect fool; Phil Harris was the perfect *cool* fool.

The wealth that Alice had supposedly amassed from her career as a screen queen and her age served as fodder for numerous jokes. Periodically the writers raked up the ashes of *Fallen Angel* for laughs when Alice probably wished they would have left the film that virtually killed her movie career buried and forgotten.

Alice might have proved to be a sensible balance for the unstable Phil had not Frank Remley been brought in to tip the scales in the direction of lunacy. If Remley, Phil's left-hand man in half-baked schemes, had to honestly list his vocation on a job application he might write, "Playing the guitar—badly." His avocation was straining the Harris/Faye marriage. Irredeemably irresponsible, Frankie loved cards, booze, and women, and most of his business associates just happened to be conmen. In short, he filled the bill as just the sort of foil needed to stir the plot.

It would probably annoy Frankie to be called a *foil*. In one episode he said, "Curly, you're the star of this show, but it must burn you up on Sunday when I get all the laughs." Phil replied, "But the fire's put out on Monday when I get all the money."

Elliott Lewis, an accomplished actor, producer, and director who worked on a score of radio programs, played Frankie so convincingly that when we hear his voice on any other show we are tempted to say, "Why is Remley playing it so straight?" Lewis acted the part with relish, delivering his lines just the way a lovable rascal should. If awards had been given for best supporting actor on a comedy series, Elliott Lewis would have won at least a couple of them.

His chief competition for that honor might have come from Walter Tetley who played Julius Abbruzio, the quintessential wise guy, the kind of imp whose entrance speech consisted of endearing sentiments like "I heard youse guys were writing a song and I hurried right over so I could be the first one to say, 'It stinks.'" The barrage of insults he hurled at Remley and Harris sometimes took the form of asides like "I know everybody's got a right to be a moron, but these guys are abusing the privilege." He served primarily as unwilling guinea pig for bizarre experiments or reluctant rescuer of the maladroit pair. When Julius fell into their hands, he released his "seal cough" or sent out impassioned calls for help, but as often as not he outwitted his elders and left them with a sardonic "So long, suckers."

Rounding out the regular cast were Robert North as Willie, Alice's brother, and Anne Whitfield and Jeanine Roose as the Harris daughters.

Willie aggravated Phil simply because he was everything Harris was not: effeminate, efficient, well-mannered, and parsimonious. Phyllis and Little Alice could have been called Little Phil and Little Phil II because they frequently delivered lines not only in the style of their father but with the very same cadence (e.g., "It ain't been easy, Clyde").

Everyone in the cast proved to be a master of timing and delivery. The questions "This is a wrestler?" and "Are you kiddin'?" are not particularly amusing unless someone like Tetley can give them just that right touch of skepticism. North's smug expressions "Good morning, Philip" and "Yes, indeed. Um-hmm" touched a nerve in Harris and the laugh button in listeners. When Lewis said, "Some people are nearsighted. You are nearreared," he had a way of making such inanities sound perfectly logical. After Remley reveals that he has a total of thirteen cents to get the Harris family into the circus, Phil unloads two sentences of priceless sarcasm: "You think it's safe to carry that kind of money around? Somebody might roll you for the whole wad." On one show when Phil says, "This'll take brains" and Remley adds, "Let's put our heads together," Alice delivers the perfect squelch: "That ain't gonna do it."

But, of course, even Groucho or W.C. Fields could not produce guffaws if given fluff. Singer and Chevillat handed the cast a bountiful supply of ludicrous situations and snappy one-liners. They made Frank and Phil the ultimate klutzes, a pair of bumblers who repeatedly dismantled the Harris house or poured money into dubious ventures. The banter that flowed between the duo made for some of the best lines on the program as this sample from the June 26, 1949 episode demonstrates:

> Harris: I've got a good band.
> Remley: So has Lombardo.
> Harris: So far we're even. Let's go to point two. Lombardo ain't a comedian.
> Remley: You're still even.
> Harris: Point three. Lombardo don't sing the way I do.
> Remley: That puts him ahead.

It wasn't just in the exchanges with Harris that Frankie got the big laugh. He liked to tease Curly about being henpecked ("Sometimes I'm sorry we married her") and his appearance ("I think it's very attractive the way your chins cascade into your chest. I imagine that when you drool it looks like a babbling brook"). Nothing could faze him. Even after Mr. Scott (Gale Gordon) told him "I don't want you on the show. I wouldn't have you if you paid me and you can start looking for a new job because you're fired," Remley still had the last word: "Undecided, huh?" Confronted with the problem of disguising a sway-backed horse from Alice, he recommended turning it upside down and telling her it was a camel. Julius soon topped him: "How can I win a race with a thing like that? Every time he takes a step his stomach bounces along the ground like a basketball. I can't ride him. I'll have to dribble him around the track." Then Harris tossed in one more nag gag as the plug was clip-clopping his way around the track and started to snore. "I'd wake him up," Phil said, "but I believe he's going faster this way."

That series of jokes exemplifies the technique the writers used week after week: start with a predicament and build a fortress of jokes around it. The structure became so predictable that the audience anticipated entrances or catch phrases. When Phil asked Remley a question like "Who can you get that will be willing to jump out of a second-story window?" everyone knew that Julius would appear immediately. When Harris asked his pal where he could buy a steer or a boat or a mink coat or anything alive or dead, Remley was sure to say, "I know a guy..." On the June 5, 1949 episode after Frankie declared that after an operation "I couldn't eat any solid food. I was on a liquid diet," the audience began laughing without waiting for the punch line because his dissolute reputation rendered any further comment superfluous.

Some of the most sustained laughs came not from scripted lines but from bloopers and the ad-libs that Phil made after the blunders. On April 24, 1949 after Harris answered the telephone Alice asked, "Who was that the cone fall was from?" Phil wouldn't let it pass: "You better get your teeth fixed before you go back to pictures. If you walk in there with that revolving bridge...Take it one more time, but let me stand back." When one of the girls mumbled a line on another night Harris quipped, "Why do you have to come in here every morning with a mouthful of mashed potatoes?" After Frank Nelson stumbled over a word on a 1953 show, Phil had a line ready: "*I'm* the one that's a test pilot for Seagram's." He also made the best of his own mistakes. On the October 2, 1949 episode he said, "The one with the silery-silery-silery-celery sticking up inside the garbage can," and then quickly added, "This program has been transcribed for earlier broadcast." On a night when a crow figured prominently in the script, Phil followed a slight flub with "I might do the crow before the show's over." It's no wonder that Rexall and RCA sometimes lost part of their final commercials; they couldn't count on the unexpected happening, but perhaps they should have for extended laughs were apt to come from any source.

And the program remained funny right up to the last 1954 broad-

Alice and Phil on the links in 1991.

cast. The best episodes in the series are probably those done during the 1948-1950 seasons, but the later shows are amusing even after Willie had virtually disappeared, Lewis began playing a Remleyesque gent named Elliott Lewis, and the Singer-Chevillat team had been replaced by writers like Ed James and Jack Douglas. The pattern of the show changed little from season to season: the problem presented along with some familial persiflage, Lewis brought in to advance the story, a Harris number and a Faye song, complication of the problem with Julius, and then the inevitable failure of Phil's plans.

Audiences liked the taste of that recipe and kept lapping it up and laughing it up week after week. It was a delicious mixture of one part picaresque characters, one part farce, and two parts zesty dialogue with a pinch of exquisite delivery tossed in to give it just the right flavor. It's the kind of tempting dish that even today makes us come back for seconds. Or thirds. Or…

Gildersleeve (Harold Peary) and Birdie (Lillian Randolph), right at home in Summerfield.

The Human Comedy

WHEN THROCKMORTON P. GILDERSLEEVE left Wistful Vista on a train in 1941, no one would have predicted that he would be riding the airwaves until 1957. But when one listens to episodes of *The Great Gildersleeve* spread over that time period, it becomes clear that the show succeeded because of its cast filled with people much like the folks we knew well. *Vic and Sade*, probably the only other radio comedy that presented a more vivid picture of small-town America, was house-bound most of the time with much of the action being reported by the three principals. In *The Great Gildersleeve* we get out and mingle with our neighbors.

Undoubtedly the most conspicuous person to be found on a tour of Summerfield would be the great man himself. As a water commissioner Gildy was a washout. He habitually got to work late, knew little about his job, and couldn't bring himself to fire his incompetent secretary because "I'm not tough. I'm just lovable." And, he might have added, love-addicted. Over the years he chased belles Leila Ransom (Shirley Mitchell) and Adeline Fairchild (Una Merkel) and professional women like Eve Goodwin (Bea Benaderet) and Kathryn Milford (Cathy Lewis) almost to the altar. If we caught him sighing, it was probably because he had just fallen in or out of favor with another woman. If we found him muttering, it might have been due to stumbling over a roller skate left by his nephew Leroy.

That scamp with the dirty hands and the shirt hanging out is the culprit. Leroy as played by Walter Tetley was Everyboy. He broke windows, loved sports and comic books, read his sister's diary, didn't like girls, struggled with schoolwork, pouted or cried when he didn't get what he wanted, and bellowed with "the soul of a train announcer." His answers to questions bore the stamp of youthful logic. When his uncle found a bird's nest under his bed and asked what it was doing there Leroy replied, "It must've got lost." He once tried to get Gildy to go fishing by citing a newspaper article about a man who caught a ninety-pound swordfish. After being reminded that that event had occurred in Florida and not at nearby Grass Lake, Leroy's shook that fact off with a typical reply: "Sure, but it shows they're biting."

If Leroy fell victim to all the fits that affected boys, his sister Marjorie seemed possessed by all the fancies that attracted teenage girls. If she had a faraway look in her eyes as she sat in the swing, it was because she had a boyfriend or a crooner on her mind. If a boy like Marshall Bullard happened to be sitting next to her on that swing, we would hear very authentic dialogue filled with hesitant questions and awkward silences. When she got married and became a mother of twins she lost some of her sparkling allure, but when in high school Marjorie Forrester, even more than Corliss Archer or Judy Foster, was the girl next door for millions of listeners.

If an astrological sign ruled Gildersleeve's life, it had to be Capricorn for he would almost always encounter that old goat, Judge Horace Hooker who proved to be both friend and nemesis. As Gildy's rival in love, Hooker enjoyed taunting his pal with insults and the purest cackle ever heard on radio. When Harold Peary's "dirty laugh" confronted Earle Ross's rat-tat-tat chortle, it made for the best duel without words since the grunt of Frankenstein's monster met the growl of the wolf man.

When Throcky wanted balm for wounds of body and soul, he usually avoided the sardonic Hooker and instead turned for solace to Richard Peavey (Richard LeGrand). Quite often his visits to the drugstore were ostensibly for the purchase of cigars, although more often than not he merely sought advice from the friendly pharmacist. But of all people in the community to ask, Peavey represented the worst choice for he was the Great Equivocator, a fence-sitter who if asked by St. Peter at the pearly gates "You want to come inside, don't you?" would probably respond with his standard "Well, now, I wouldn't say that." Peavey also served as the town fuddy-duddy, a dullard who would spend several minutes tracing his sales of hot chocolate through the seasons when he could have stated the obvious in a few words: he sells more when it's cold, little or none when it's warm. By the time Gildersleeve left the store he frequently departed with more nostrums or stogies and less patience than when he entered.

Going to Floyd Munson's barbershop to regain his composure sometimes brought no relief. Floyd's palaver proved to be less soporific than that dispensed by the druggist, but his incessant chatter and teasing got on the nerves of the man he addressed as the commish. Munson (Arthur

Q. Bryan), a crafty clipper, appealed to Gildersleeve's vanity in order to supply him with shaves, shampoos, massages, and anything else flattery would sell.

On his way home Gildersleeve might stop to chat with Rumson Bullard if his snobbish neighbor deigned to converse with him. Like most characters played by Gale Gordon, Bullard displayed a hair-trigger temper and a blustery manner. Two blowhards living across the street from each other made for a volatile powder keg and all it took to set it off was Bullard shouting, "Gildersleeve, you're a nincompoop!"

If Gildersleeve took a stroll after supper and found himself out of luck with Cupid, his destination would likely be the room above the barbershop. In this clubhouse of sorts, incomplete with a badly-tuned piano and worn furniture, the Jolly Boys played cards, told stories, and sang standards. Police Chief Gates (Ken Christy) joined Gildy, Munson, Hooker, and Peavey to form a barbershop quintet who, though not always melodic, at least belted out their ballads fervently.

By taking us around Summerfield almost weekly the writers created a small world that leaves an ache in our hearts because we know that we now have teeming airports, shopping malls, cinema complexes, and impersonal clinics where we once had railroad stations, vibrant downtowns with soda fountains and theaters that resembled opera houses, and crusty, no-nonsense doctors who made house calls. The family hour wasn't a time determined by network executives when people should take their places in front of the hypnotic eye of a television like robots; it was the time after supper when families actively entertained themselves with games, songs, reading aloud, and reviewing the day's activities. Although Gildersleeve failed sometimes in his efforts to convince Marjorie and Leroy to keep the home fire burning, he gave it his best shot.

Peary in close harmony with Bryan, Christy, Ross, and LeGrand.

Listeners also felt they were getting the best every week when they tuned in to this program because, unlike other thirty-minute shows that shortened or interrupted the narrative to make room for musical interludes by singers and orchestras, *The Great Gildersleeve* was a true situation comedy, packed with incidents from introduction to tag. An example is the June 9, 1946 episode that looked back on the previous Fourth of July. Gildersleeve wakes up to the sound of firecrackers, enjoys some holiday chitchat at the breakfast table, has a window drop on him while hanging the flag, converses with Leila, confronts the neighbor boy and his toy cannon, joins the Jolly Boys on a hayride, argues with Hooker and Munson over who will be chef at the picnic, engages in horseplay at the swimming hole, and concludes the day by singing "In the Good Old Summertime" with the Boys on the ride home. Every episode seemed so loaded with details and scenes that we never felt cheated.

Another trait that separates *The Great Gildersleeve* from other comedy shows is that the humor comes not so much from the lines written as from how those words are spoken. Cook Birdie (Lillian Randolph) repeated the same phrase over three or four times and still got guffaws. Leroy's doubting laugh preceded Gildersleeve's "Leeeroy" like clockwork. If Throckmorton promised to pay Leroy as much as he was worth to do a job, Tetley could bring a whine to "Is that all?" that earned more laughter than the question merited. Richard LeGrand's dry delivery provoked chuckles just by speaking his opening "Hello, Mr. Gildersleeve." Both Willard Waterman and Harold Peary could sputter and pontificate just the way an impulsive windbag should. When Leroy shook his head and exclaimed, "What a character!" he said a mouthful because it truly were the characters and not just what they said that brought us back week after week.

Even today we want to come back again and again to *The Great Gildersleeve*. Each time we listen is like a visit to that place we called home and a chance to meet one more time those very human people we knew then. Thornton Wilder may have called it Grover's Corners in his famous play, but many of us have come to think of Summerfield as our town.

The only comic book Connie might have allowed in her classroom.

In a Class by Herself

WHEN WE LOOK BACK AT OUR SCHOOL DAYS, most of us can recall one special teacher who made a difference in our lives. But no matter how affectionate we feel toward that individual we never use a possessive pronoun when referring to him or her. That unique honor was bestowed upon only one educator, a person who, although she taught fictitious students in an imaginary high school, will always be remembered as *our* Miss Brooks.

As we were reminded at the beginning of many episodes in the series, Constance Brooks taught English at Madison High School. One of the unusual features of this program about teachers is that we rarely found Connie actually teaching. Most of the action took place before school, after a class had ended, after school, or at lunch. Yet no program about teachers has captured the essence of school rivalries, faculty-administrative relations, and the drudgery of academic routine as well as *Our Miss Brooks* did.

Most episodes followed a rigid pattern: Connie started things cooking with her landlady, Margaret Davis; the plot thickened when Walter Denton arrived to pick her up; and finally the pot got stirred up by Mr. Boynton and Mr. Conklin at school. The menu was predictable, but it allowed us to savor each course separately to enjoy the full flavor of the program.

Some of the breakfast conversations between Connie and Margaret (Jane Morgan) bordered on the surrealistic. Mrs. Davis occasionally complained about her absentminded sister, though her own train of thought became derailed so frequently that sometimes even Connie's best efforts could not get her back on the track. Connie often hurried off to school rather than sample some of Margaret's culinary experiments such as watercress-and-cucumber omelets, blubber burgers (whale meat fried in seal fat), and parsley-and-banana sandwiches. Even Walter Denton, possessor of a cavern for a stomach, passed on these exotic dishes in favor of tamer fare like toast and eggs.

Richard Crenna played Denton with an adenoidal fervor that made him almost as memorable as those other hobbledehoys, Henry Aldrich and Homer Brown. Conklin described Denton's voice as sounding "like a canary who had just caught a rancid batch of birdseed." Crenna gave the character a playful snicker that once caused Connie to remark, "I wish you'd stop auditioning your sinuses." Walter, like most boys, favored sports, cars, and girls over schoolwork. For some reason known only to the writers, Denton sometimes appeared at the front door with a grandiloquent speech like "during that one breathless, rapturous moment right before twilight, that moment like the hush of a giant wave ere it pounds mightily upon the golden beach, that timeless moment of promised ecstasy, culminating in a crescendo of clamorous, amorous bliss." Such a torrent of words left Miss Brooks (and us) wondering how such poetic phrases could emanate from a student who struggled to score 29 on an exam. Fortunately for Denton, as long as his pal Stretch Snodgrass remained at Madison he would never have to wear the dunce cap.

Mortimer Snerd and Stretch Snodgrass: one of these two was a real dummy and the other one wasn't much brighter. Stretch, Madison's star athlete and prize numbskull, fit Connie's description of him: "the body beautiful and the head empty." Mrs. Davis thought that somewhere along the line the boy's development had been arrested. "Arrested?" Connie said. "It's been sentenced and shot." Leonard Smith's Snodgrass, a little less obvious than Charlie Cantor's Clifton Finnegan, relied more on malapropisms than the denizen of *Duffy's Tavern*, though they both stumbled around in the same fog. Because Stretch represented the school's chief hope on the gridiron and basketball court, keeping him both eligible and happy became the chief concern at Madison on a number of occasions.

Connie got most of the carries with the two running gags that kept the program moving week after week: running out of money and running after Mr. Boynton. Almost every episode contained at least one allusion to the penurious state of teachers. Miss Brooks remembered that even at the age of seven "I was already planning my career—poverty." She claimed that "every mirror in the house has bad luck because I'm always broke" and once turned down a position that paid double her present salary because she couldn't afford to work that cheap. Brooks always owed Mrs. Davis back rent, had items in the pawn shop, and owned a "late 1935" Nash parked perpetually in the repair shop. Regular mix-ups involving small amounts of money added to her financial woes.

Complicating Connie's life was that handsome hunk of inertia known as Philip Boynton, a bashful biologist whose idea of a romantic line on a moonlit evening consisted of a question: "Isn't it a keen night for trapping gophers?" Upon seeing mistletoe above a willing Miss Brooks, he overlooked the obvious and instead seized that moment to comment on the parasitic characteristics of the plant. He once asked Connie for a lock of her hair not as a remembrance but so he could put it in cheesecloth to make a pillow for his pet frog, McDougall. His favorite spot to take Miss Brooks on a date was the zoo. It might seem that such a square would be a drag on a comedy program, but the reserved hesitancy of Jeff Chandler and, later, Robert Rockwell served to be a perfect foil for the wisecracks delivered by that master of the snappy comeback, Eve Arden.

Some of the most precious lines on the program came from exchanges between the two love-crossed teachers. Once Boynton confessed, "I used to be a Boy Scout, you know." Miss Brooks replied, "What do you mean, used to be?" Another time Philip accused Connie of finding another man before the biologist had left town and asserted that "you could have waited until the body was cold." Her response: "When was it warm?" One New Year's Eve as Connie snuggled up to him while they looked over a record collection Boynton said nervously, "I'm a little off balance. I don't want to break any records." Connie's deadpan reply: "Don't worry. You won't." What followed this bit is a truly inventive sequence written by writer-director Al Lewis in which the pair read actual titles of songs that consciously or subconsciously revealed their feelings:

> Brooks: If I Could Be with You One Hour Tonight.
> Boynton: I'm a Lone Cowhand.
> Brooks: Baby, It's Cold Outside.
> Boynton: Don't Fence Me In.
> Brooks: I'm in the Mood for Love.
> Boynton: It's Too Late Now.
> Brooks: I Can Dream, Can't I?
> Boynton: All Right, Louie. Drop the Gun.
> Brooks: Everything I Have is Yours.
> Boynton: I've Got Plenty of Nothing.

Amusing exchanges between teachers and students captured some of the humor implicit in the school environment, but if an autocratic windbag of a principal played by Gale Gordon is added to the mixture, big laughs are guaranteed. Osgood Conklin regarded the faculty as his army, often giving them orders like "Halt!" and "At ease but remain alert."

Gordon and Arden made visits to the principal's office a joy.

He treated his daughter and wife in a similar fashion. Once when his spouse called him on the phone and said, "This is Margaret, dear. Your wife," his responded with "I know your title. I conferred it on you." If he called school into session on a Saturday, he made it strictly optional: come or die. But, like many taskmasters, he could be fawning to his superiors like Mr. Stone, head of the board of education. He also proved to be an easy mark for blackmail. All it would take is "I wonder if the school board knows about…" and he would be willing to negotiate or capitulate.

What made Conklin such a funny character was that Gordon generated guffaws whether he underplayed the part by speaking in a restrained manner or bellowed in disbelief. One day when Connie couldn't do anything right in his presence, she knocked his tray against him in the cafeteria. When she offered to replace the spilled pea soup, she asked how much he would like. Gordon's reply was delivered in an even, dry tone: "About as much as is now in my vest pocket." His patented, shrieking double takes often received the loudest response from the audience, although the most sustained laugh in the program's history came after Conklin had been temporarily deafened by a cannon's roar. Later, while the principal sat in his office, the cannon exploded again and Osgood calmly said, "Come in." The audience roared for over twenty seconds.

Even today no one can be blamed for laughing loud and long at *Our Miss Brooks* for it was definitely one of the funniest shows during radio's twilight years. It had more hilarious throwaway lines per half-hour than you could shake a laugh-meter at. These exchanges did little to advance the story but contributed much to the enjoyment and satisfaction of the total package. Six exchanges from different episodes are samples of this form of incidental humor:

> Boynton (in cafeteria): It isn't as bad as it used to be. I think the food's picked up.
> Brooks: They don't want you to step in it.
>
> Conklin: How could a hurricane possibly get this far into the United States?
> Brooks: Smugglers?
>
> Harriet Conklin (about a hideous handkerchief): Isn't it the end?
> Brooks: I hope so.
>
> Harriet: How can you stand there and shiver like that?
> Conklin: I study nights.
>
> Boynton (after telling a joke): Didn't you get it?
> Brooks: Oh, I got it, Mr. Boynton. It's just that I've had all I want of it.
>
> Davis: I'm going to give Minerva [the cat] a bath.
> Brooks: Why? Are the mice complaining?

Even these morsels that fall alongside the main path of the story usually slanted toward Connie for, despite the gifted supporting cast, this was Eve Arden's show. Arden, a talented mimic who could copy Conklin's bark and Stretch's dopey delivery, also echoed the nuances in lines spoken by veteran character actresses Mary Jane Croft and Sandra Gould. She was a versatile performer who could scream convincingly on cue, cover actors' blunders smoothly, and even sing competently when the situation called for it.

Arden captured our attention and affection from the time she addressed us as confidants at the beginning of the program right up to the closing when she tied up the loose ends just before the tag gag that frequently involved Boynton or Conklin. During each episode she tossed in asides intended for our ears only such as commenting on Osgood's fiendish chuckle: "I'm glad he doesn't hold my mortgage."

We empathized with Miss Brooks because Eve made her such a believable person. It seemed perfectly natural that everyone at school turned to her for advice and, in some cases, took advantage of her soft-heartedness. It is a credit to Eve's acting ability that she could convey a warmth and vulnerability behind the shield of jests. She hurled insults like "if the girdle fits, wear it" at Daisy Enright, her rival for the affections of Boynton, not out of spite but because Daisy's snide remarks about Connie's clothes and appearance hurt and she was simply striking back in self-defense. When Boynton repeatedly ignored her in favor of his animals, her acerbic quips came out so the tears wouldn't. Even her asides after getting tyrannical orders from "Old Marblehead" Conklin were appropriate reactions to unrealistic demands designed to break her spirit.

It is no small accomplishment to play a character as a multi-faceted person who was sympathetic, sarcastic, helpful, resourceful, diplomatic, and witty all in the course of thirty minutes. Eve Arden did just that from 1948 to 1957 on radio and from 1952 to 1956 on television. *Her* Miss Brooks was a human, humane, and humorous teacher we were glad to know and proud to claim as *our* Miss Brooks.

  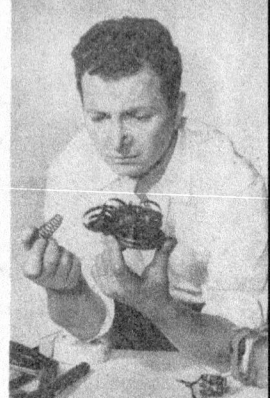

Our Henry goes to work. He once put on a campaign not to be nominated for President. It was successful in all details.

Is he a social outcast? "I never had a circle of friends," says Henry pitifully. "I only had enough to form a triangle."

Henry's a mastermind. By the time he was 12, his IQ was that of a man of 21—and vice versa.

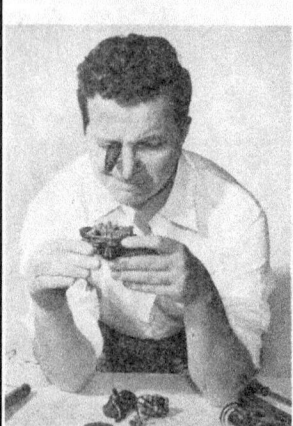 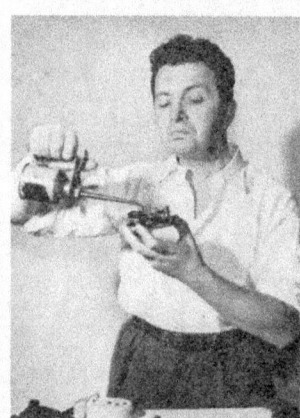 

"Feed your children enough 'Oh Henrys' and they'll get sick and die,", was the way Henry attempted to sell that candy bar.

Heaven help the clock if Henry can't fix it. He once slung a watch across a restaurant because it had stopped running.

Rebellious Henry advises kids to leave home, become smugglers. "It's exciting, it's healthy!"

Henry Morgan with time on his hands.

For He's a Jolly Bad Fellow

LOU COSTELLO FREQUENTLY TOLD US "I'm a b-a-a-a-d boy," but we didn't really believe him. Even though Red's Junior acted like mischief personified, we recognized such antics constituted just another page torn from the Skelton scrapbook of satire. Only one person could truly claim to be radio's bad boy to the core of his irreverent soul: Henry Morgan.

Morgan had a reputation as a sponsor-baiter in the New York area on WOR and WJZ, but it was not until 1946 that the entire country could hear his slings and arrows on ABC. No sponsor took that bait for a few weeks until Eversharp bit off a mouthful that proved hard to swallow. In the months that followed more than one executive probably considered drastic uses for the Eversharp Schick razor.

When Morgan was permitted to handle the commercials, he rarely delivered them according to form. He sometimes began like he was going to read it straight and then when it came to the "push-pull, click-click" feature, directed the sound effects crew to insert sounds appropriate for a construction site. Another time, after commenting that commercials were too serious and that they deserved a lighter touch, he laughed after every assertion which seemed to cast doubt upon the quality of the razor. Other spots portrayed disastrous things happening to people during the minutes saved shaving with the speedy razor as well as a hapless man who got bloody fingers from picking up the blades.

Even when the sponsor went to the trouble of recruiting men for a shave-a-thon on stage using various razors, Henry threw a shadow over the validity of the contest by insinuating that the winner using a Schick razor was a child. One night he even told the audience outright that the sponsor didn't particularly like the commercials. "They don't like me," he added. Small wonder.

It wasn't just the commercials that struck the gong with an unorthodox bo-ing. Right from the beginning when the announcer asked instead of proclaimed the title of the program to the unique rendition of "For He's a Jolly Good Fellow" to Henry's devil-may-care greeting of "Good evening, anybody. Here's Morgan," listeners somehow got the idea that the sounds coming out of their radios during the next thirty minutes would not be anything remotely akin to *A Date with Judy*.

In fact, *The Henry Morgan Show* wasn't really like anything else on the air. Milton Berle's program also consisted of a string of sketches built around a theme like housing or recreation, but like Jack Benny and Skelton he exchanged sarcastic remarks with his announcer and usually had one domestic scene that played like a mini-sitcom. Morgan's shows took the form of free-wheeling skits that were sometimes related, sometimes not. Whatever amused Henry went on the air whether it made sense to the rest of the universe or not.

Many of the bits began with a "What if…" premise. What if people in the year 2000 looked back at the artifacts of New York of 1946? What if an old jokes home existed where gags like Pat and Mike wheezes could go to die? What if a reserved coach from England presented a pep talk at halftime to the losing team? What if a Frenchman broadcasting a boxing match acted according to stereotype and became preoccupied with a beautiful woman in the crowd?

Some of the pieces fit together nicely, others misfired badly. Combining baseball with the worlds of symphonies and operas hit the mark as did the glimpse into the private lives of businessmen who talk adspeak even at home. Conversely, the adventures of Peter and the landlord and also the march of science feature sputtered each time they were used.

Morgan, an innovator who rarely played it safe, even took swipes at the KKK and the needless violence of comic strips.

Henry had a better batting average in the parodies than he did in the speculative brand of humor. The man who had an innate distaste for commercials certainly invented some beauts like "One-a-Minute vitamin. Pop one in your mouth. Do this every minute, every day. You'll agree you were never more active in your life," and "Nicoteenies, the cigarette dipped in cough medicine" that rots the lungs.

Morgan was at his very best when lampooning radio shows and movies. His version of an Anglicized quiz program called *Take It or If You'd Rather Not You Needn't* scored with categories like "Famous Prime Ministers who've been hit by cricket balls." As Jimmy Morgan he mimicked

Jimmy Fidler's delivery of such tidbits as "Bulletin—The Marx Brothers are related." His soap operas presented teasers like "Can a woman of sixty-five find happiness with a man twice her age?" Non sequiturs flowed all around his Question Man:

> Announcer: Who played first base for the Baltimore Orioles in 1902?
> Question Man: *The Mill on the Floss* was written by George Eliot.
> Announcer: Our next question. George Eliot asks ...

The motion pictures that bore a passing resemblance to those we saw locally flashed before us at the Henry Morgan Theater of Coming Attractions. A promo for a Bogart and Bacall film consisted principally of his guttural mumbling and her sultry muttering. One movie starring Betty Gargle had a supporting cast of "Richard Moey as Doey, Robert Joey as Moey, Doris Doey as Floey, Florence Floey as Doey, and Lassie as Chloe." They don't make pictures like that anymore—or at any time.

Other bits of nonsense thrown in from time to time consisted of interviews with Morgan in a variety of guises and also exchanges with Arnold Stang. Henry, more than adequate with dialects, regularly appeared as either a Russian or the Austrian-German Heinrich Von Morgan, resident expert on everything. Arnold and Henry as Gerard and Hank conversed in laconic New Yorkese that either got the show off to a running start or a walking lull.

What better way to liven up a dull moment on an unconventional program than presenting some of the most off-the-wall music this side of Spike Jones. Have a gent play "The Man on the Flying Trapeze" on the bagpipes. Introduce "Sitting Bull" who chants "a combination of all the Indian stuff he's ever heard." Produce a singer who does "Old MacDonald Had a Farm" in five languages. Allow a man to out-Lauder Sir Harry with a Scottish ditty. Permit a woman and her cocker spaniel to warble through "Sugar Blues." When Bernie Green and his musicians played midway through the show, the audience probably expected kazoos to pop out of nowhere.

Green should have considered himself fortunate for he alone got billing next to the star. ("*The Henry Morgan Show* featuring Bernie Green and his Orchestra and a few surprises.") *The Henry Morgan Show* of 1949-1950 that did give credit to Stang, Minerva Pious, Art Carney, and other performers was a slicker product but more predictable, usually fitting this pattern: routine with Stang, an interview with athlete Carney, a song from the Billy Williams Quartet, another bit, a band number, and a sketch. Some of the sketches like the one in which Hamlet is a detective (more precisely, a private orb) hit the right note, but the whole program came wrapped in too nice a package that made it look like others on the air. There was no jack-in-the-box or rubber snake to jump out and startle us.

The Henry Morgan Show of 1946-1948 delivered what the title promised: except for the occasional Hortense and Gerard routines, all the comedy revolved around the writer and star. If ratings dropped or the jokes fizzled, there was only one person to blame. Unlike the remarkably consistent scripts written for Benny and for Marian and Jim Jordan, the Morgan opus was very erratic. The October 15, 1947 show, which led off with a lame joke that was resuscitated later for no other reason than Morgan considered it a goody and wanted it to get a laugh, featured a lethargic sketch on the history of pretzels that went nowhere. The following week the cast raked quiz shows, child psychiatry, and movies over the coals in fine style.

Another flaw in the program arose from Morgan's penchant for letting his personal gripes get in the way of entertainment. When a congressman criticized the way New Yorkers talk, Henry opened a show with a rebuttal that featured a senator who spoke with a southern drawl and concluded with the host saying, "Well, I got that off my chest." When a joke died, Morgan would laugh it off and say, "Some of this seems awfully funny to me," as if the rest of the world was out-of-step. The ultimate failure of Henry Morgan to stay on the air stemmed not from his conflicts with Schick or Rayve or any other sponsor but because Henry chose to play to the man inside him beating his own different drum rather than to the folks listening at home.

Though stubborn and opinionated, Henry Morgan offered a refreshing voice in those post-war years. What a pleasant change to hear the sound of honesty running through every episode. To the people who greeted a joke with a hand he said, "Oh, I don't think it deserves applause." Who else would have encouraged listeners to shop around on the other stations while the band played? Instead of opening a show with bombastic promises he calmly stated that "Tonight's program is going to be different. Not better, just different" or admitted that "Last week's show was a little disjointed, but this week—chaos." And, of course, he couldn't help giving a most appropriate admonition to a clap-happy audience: "Never applaud a commercial. You'll ruin radio forever."

Contrary to what some individuals on Madison Avenue might have thought, Henry Morgan did not ruin radio forever. In fact, he saved it from drowning in a sea of conformity. Today Henry Morgan is remembered as a rebel with some claws whose satire and candor cut mercilessly through the hyperbole and inanity of advertising and entertainment. That alone should fill us with a warm glow every time we pass a cigar store on a corner.

Red Skelton could be protecting Bill Thompson from a blooper in this gag shot.

We Interrupt This Program to Bring You a Blooper

WHILE LISTENING TO THE GREAT COMEDY SHOWS we are apt to be so entertained by the brilliant timing and the fast-paced gaiety that the minutes fly by like a speeding train. But what adds to the enjoyment of these programs is that once in a blue moon or when the moon got in somebody's mouth like a big pizza pie, the well-oiled machine got derailed for a few riotous moments that became the highlight of the show. Out of the mouths of babes, guys, and dolls came the words that no one wrote but that we love to quote more than the scripted lines.

Jack Benny and his writing team knew better than anyone else how to make the most out of bloopers. Don Wilson's famous corruption of Drew Pearson's name was reprised gloriously when Frank Nelson broke Jack up with his own Dreer Poosen. One night Benny himself almost topped Harry Von Zell's mispronunciation of Herbert Hoover by mentioning the "Houvier Vacuum Cleaner Factory."

Although Don and Rochester stumbled occasionally, Mary Livingstone seemed to scramble words more than anyone else on the show. She was the one who ordered a chiss sweeze sandwich and wondered how Jack could possibly hit a car when it was up on the grass reek. The audience was on the same page as the Benny team; they got the joke even if Mary mangled the line:

> Jack: To win an Academy Award you gotta do a picture with absolutely no laughs.
> Mary: Well, your darn one last near made it.

Perhaps Mary's well-documented nervousness accounted for her flubs. Her spontaneous giggle made us forgive her immediately. We were tempted to say with a Benny twinkle in our eyes, "Watch it, Doll, or you'll be back at the May Company."

Jack's nemesis, Fred Allen, the acknowledged master of the ad-lib, also squeezed the maximum yuks out of fluffs because he could generate apposite words in the very next breath. His ready wit was displayed in every show, even back in the *Town Hall* days when, during an interview with a train porter, he said, "And as you look down back near—back down memory's tracks, Mr. Cooper...You'd have to have been cross-eyed to look the way I was saying it."

Some performers like Harold Peary played over mistakes with barely a passing glance. In a 1943 *Great Gildersleeve* episode Peary said, "I wish I could see Leila's face when she casts a sight on all that chickenware ... kitchenware." Two years later his description of *Carmen* hit a snag, but Hal knew where to place the blame: "He no sooner arrives and starts make loving...Well, who wrote this?"

Phil Harris, however, would not let misreadings go by without a comment. Walter Tetley as impish Julius had a terrible time expressing the simple thought that Phil was losing his sponsor and "going in the beat—neat—meat business." Harris let him have it: "Wait a minute. I ain't leaving Rexall and I ain't going in the neat business either." In a 1951 show the effect of a minatory remark uttered by a crook (Sheldon Leonard) was lost when he warned that "jokes like that make my tringer finger itch." Phil used that slip as a running gag that night and weeks later after Elliott Lewis as Remley recommended his "pickled pig's nickels."

Although Jim Jordan is not widely regarded as a master of the snappy comeback, his responses after muffs were right up Allen's Alley. On the January 21, 1941 show Jim as Fibber McGee proudly announced that "here we had this piano all the time and I never knew the—thou—than now that I was a musician. It's hard to play the piano and talk at the same time."

Without a doubt the most famous howler in the history of Wistful Vista's prominent pair occurred on the night of November 6, 1948 when Jim launched into one of his tongue-twisters that did exactly that to his tongue: "We had about as beat-up a bunch of bakers as ever balled up a bunch of batter, but the reason my batter baked better was because I beat my batter in a platter which made a better batter, splattered the bladder, scattered the patter...[laughter. Door bell.] Come in, come in, quick!"

Two weeks later the sound effects man suffered through one of those nights. Fibber dropped a light bulb from a ladder to the Old Timer. We heard the sound of a hammer hitting a bulb, but it wouldn't break. Finally

We Interrupt This Program to Bring You a Blooper • 373

"'Twas funny, McGee" when Marian would break up after one of Jim's bloopers.

Bill Thompson as the Old Timer said, "I missed it, Johnny." *Then* came the smashing of the bulb. Shortly afterwards Fibber told a policeman who came by to look out for broken glass because "I dropped a light bulb down there. It finally broke."

During the last years of the thirty-minute episodes Jim took errors in stride by repeating the line correctly and taking the audience along with an aside. In a 1952 show, for example, his first words were "I'm as hungry as a last year's bird nest. I'm as empty as a last year's bird nest. We better do 'em all twice." Marian's ebullient laugh which accompanied the fluffs and Jim's impromptu remarks add even more to the listening enjoyment of *Fibber McGee and Molly*, one of radio's best comedies.

Edgar Bergen, another entertainer whose ability to improvise is underrated, knew (as did Jack Benny) that the show worked best if the star took most of the jokes on the chin so he had the dummies bat his blunders right back into his face. Even the dim-witted Mortimer Snerd had to remind his master in a 1953 show that "you gave me the line wrong."

One evening in 1945 Charlie McCarthy, when conversing with Louis Bromfield about chickens, stated that he wouldn't pay eighty cents a dozen for eggs because "I guess that makes them the sleetest least ... Bergen, will you try to stay awake? What was I going to say before Bergen's gums got going wild?"

The single episode that probably disturbed Edgar's dreams in his later years was the one broadcast on January 29, 1956. Near the beginning he tried to ask Charlie a question that just wouldn't come out:

> Bergen: Why do you think sometimes ... ah ... Why do you think the sweaters make ... ah ... ah ... I can't read this.
> Charlie: I noticed that. Do you want to try it once more or do you want me to sit up there?

Later the lines were still jumping around on the page:

> Bergen: You're not allowed to raise rabbits in our neighborhood.
> Charlie: Don't tell me. Tell the rabbits.
> Bergen: That isn't the right answer.
> Charlie: Well, then why did you make me say it?

The last of his three stooges, Effie Klinker, had an appropriate reply when the great man stumbled on another night in 1956:

> Bergen: You might enjoy *The Man in the Gray Fannel...*
>   Flannel Suit.
> Effie: Would you like to take that over...Flannelmouth?

One of the funniest flubs Lucille Ball ever made required no comeback. In the vacation episode of *My Favorite Husband* broadcast April 29, 1949 Lucy as Liz Cooper explained to a local gent that she would like to know the way to Goosegrease Lake. He asked her, "Whatcha gonna do there?" Her response: "We're gonna goose a grease." After the laughter subsided, the actor playing the rustic could barely get his next line out. Talk about a showstopper!

But the show had to go on. Performers made the best of it by making jest of it. After all, they were just small errors that everyone makes now and then like the actress who, as a stewardess in a 1952 show, told passengers to "fasten your selfty bates, er, safety belts." That night Red Skelton had his standard joke ready for anyone who blew a line: "We're gonna miss you around here."

Actually the people who muffed lines should have gotten a bonus instead of the sack because they were responsible for some of the most memorable moments of radio comedy. Their mistakes don't come back to haunt them; they come back to entertain us. As long as there are rewind buttons on tape recorders or CD players we will be able to retrieve and enjoy the unwritten words that sound so tweet, er, so sweet to our ears.

The Great Gildersleeve could also claim the title of Radio's Quote King.

Brush Up Your Gildersleeve

When the subject of the most elusive program is raised, fans of old-time radio will cite their favorite quarry which has been on their most wanted list for years. They may, for instance, be yearning to hear Groucho and Chico wreck havoc with Flywheel, Shyster, and Flywheel or Marvin Miller solve cases as Peter Quill or Arthur Q. Bryan pontificate as Major Hoople. But if the topic of the moment happens to be which show is the most *allusive*, *The Great Gildersleeve* sticks out just like the titular character's stomach.

The Great Gildersleeve gives listeners the impression that John Whedon, Sam Moore, John Elliotte, and Andy White may have written the scripts with a book of quotations handy. While other writing teams probably said, "How can we twist a wheeze to fit this situation?" the duos of Whedon and Moore and Elliotte and White may have wondered, "What quote can we toss in here that seems appropriate for this situation?"

Seasonal references were employed to set the scene. In the fall Gildersleeve described the brisk air by reaching for the handy "frost on the punkin" line from James Whitcomb Riley or, with niece Marjorie's assistance, remind everyone of Helen Hunt Jackson's assertion that we "cannot rival for one hour/October's bright blue weather." On a day when her uncle has spring fever and wants to cavort barefoot in the grass Marjorie has some suitable lines from Robert Browning's *Pippa Passes* ready: "The year's at the spring/And day's at the morn/Morning's at seven;/The hillside's dew-pearled…"

In other episodes the announcers told us the time of day or the state of Gildy's temperament with the help of the immortals. As "the curfew tolls the knell of parting day," the great man plods his weary way like

Thomas Gray's ploughman in "Elegy Written in a Country Churchyard." But if he is introduced to us with euphoric lines beginning with "Breathes there the man, with soul so dead" from Sir Walter Scott's *The Lay of the Last Minstrel*, we know Throcky is in an upbeat frame of mind.

But Gildersleeve himself seemed to be the best barometer of his moods. When his bluster or bungling didn't convey his feelings, he let the bards speak for him.

In the lap of tranquility he recited from Longfellow's "The Village Blacksmith": "Something attempted, something done/Has earned a night's repose." Heeding the call of the beach, he echoed John Masefield when he admitted "I must go down to the seas again." When feeling on top of the world, he burst forth with an apt line from Byron's *Childe Harold's Pilgrimage*: "On with the dance! Let joy be unconfined!"

At other times Gildersleeve became more philosophical. In a Gray mood he dips into the elegy again to remind one and all that "the paths of glory lead but to the grave." Trying to look for the silver lining in the clouds, he reaches for the sentiment that can be traced all the way back to Euripides: "The darkest hour is just before dawn." When the Jolly Boys thought Judge Hooker was knocking at death's door, Gildy tried to put up a brave front by tapping into some Tennyson to indicate the way he wanted to go: "Let there be no moaning at the bar when I put out to sea."

In Walker Percy's novel *Lancelot* the narrator declares that "Death's banal, but fiberglass in the neck is serious business." For Gildersleeve being lovesick became the pain in the neck that put him in darker moods than the prospect of facing the Grim Reaper. When he uttered the famous "It is a far, far better thing that I do, than I have ever done" from *A Tale of Two Cities* or adapted Longfellow's "The Day is Done" so he could fold his "tents like Arabs and silently steal away," he infused the lines with so much self-pity we have to laugh at the incongruity of this whimsical windbag treating an apology or humiliation like a life-threatening illness or tragic disaster.

Horace Hooker, like Gildersleeve, used literature to make a point, but the point was usually part of a needle designed to get under the water commissioner's thin skin. "Why so pale and wan, fond lover," the opening line of Sir John Suckling's "Song," followed by Hooker's derisive chortle stung the recently-rebuffed ladies' man. On another occasion Gildy's conscience rather than his pride became the target when the Judge quoted from Richard Brinfield's "Address to the Nightingale" to remind his chum of those he should trust: "Every one that flatters thee/Is no friend in misery./Words are easy, like the wind;/Faithful friends are hard to find."

Richard Peavey dispensed a few quotations in addition to sundaes and sundries when Gildersleeve stopped by the drugstore. The pharmacist once described his home life as being like that portrayed in "The Shooting of Dan McGrew": "So cramful of cozy joy and crowned with a woman's love." Peavey's history of being henpecked might be traced back to the day he heard a speaker deliver the stirring "I am the captain of my soul" portion of William Ernest Henley's "Invictus." Peavey thought the orator had directed the words at him, but because his stronger-willed wife believed the man was looking at her the druggist settled for being the captain's mate.

Nearly everyone on the show got a chance to wax poetic from time to time. Leila Ransom and Floyd Munson showed they could be Whittier if not witty when the former drawled out Barbara Frietchie's "Shoot if you must, this old gray head" and the saucy barber of Summerfield recalled the "barefoot boy, with cheek of tan." Even surly Rumson Bullard could quote the classics to suit his purposes as he did when he ranted against the younger generation by repeating the "As the twig is bent" maxim from one of Alexander Pope's moral essays.

For Birdie and Leroy it would have been out of character to be spouting epigrams. Birdie learned her lessons from life, not from books, and Gildersleeve's nephew reacted to life's vicissitudes not with memorized couplets but rather with distinctive ejaculations like "Oh, for corn's sake!" If Leroy started quoting Keats or Milton, listeners would have stared at their radios and copied Walter Tetley's patented "Are you kiddin'?"

But when Marjorie dreamily recited the verses of Rupert Brooke or Robert Herrick or when Hooker moralized by delivering part of the "quality of mercy is not strained" speech from *The Merchant of Venice* or the "proper study of mankind is man" aphorism from Pope's "Essay on Man," it sounded perfectly natural on this show, one of radio's more literate comedies. When Throcky or Marjorie read aloud from *Little Women, A Christmas Carol,* or *Ivanhoe,* they just reinforced the belief that the audience already had, that this program placed a high value on both language and literature.

The repeated use of allusions was ideally suited to *The Great Gildersleeve,* the leisurely-paced comedy that unashamedly took time for the plaintive sighs and awkward pauses which portended more than words could express. Quotations were also used for ironical effect such as the night Gildy sententiously preached that "Procrastination is the thief of time" (one of Edward Young's "Night Thoughts"), an axiom rarely heeded by the speaker who habitually put off finishing water reports and asking women for dates until the last minute. Just as the speakers usually did not provide attribution for their literary quotations, the bits of dialogue in which the characters unconsciously revealed themselves were sometimes left with no pointed remark to underscore the message so the audience could fill in the gap with a line of their own from *Don Quixote*: "The pot calls the kettle black."

Recognizing pertinent allusions unobtrusively integrated into the narrative is just one of the pleasures of listening to *The Great Gildersleeve*, a program that, because it relied on characterization rather than on jokes for its humor, seems to improve with the passing years. Age cannot wither it, nor tape squeal stale its infinite variety. Whether the credit for its enduring charm belongs mainly to the actors or to the writers is a moot point. All that matters was best expressed by Shakespeare in *As You Like It*: "The little foolery that wise men have makes a great show."

The Jack Benny Program played thousands of jokes many different ways.

The Sweetest Music This Side of Waukegan

WHEN SOMEONE MENTIONS THE SUBJECT OF MUSIC on *The Jack Benny Program*, most people will think about the vocals performed by Dennis Day, the singing commercials done by The Sportsmen, the band numbers of Phil Harris and the orchestra, or perhaps the theme songs of "Love in Bloom" and "Hooray for Hollywood." But the sweetest sounds heard on the show were the melodies that came from the dialogue.

In their scripts the writing team of John Tackaberry, Milt Josefsberg, George Balzer, and Sam Perrin (with some late help from Hal Goldman and Al Gordon) created a pattern of metrical speech that became an integral part of the program. By using repetition, catch phrases, pauses, anacoluthons, and running gags, the Benny team produced rhythms that, instead of prompting audiences to tap their feet, had them rolling in the aisles.

The writers took full advantage of Jack's wonderful sense of timing every chance they could. After Don Wilson or Phil Harris pulled a corny joke, Benny inserted perfectly-timed repetitions of their names followed by an insult along the lines of "Don…Don…Moby Dick" or "Phil…Phil…Denatured Boy." The tune stayed the same, only the last part of the lyric changed: after the first name spoken twice came the sarcastic cognomen intended to squelch the joker.

Two was also the magic number when Jack invited trouble by hailing a character portrayed by Frank Nelson. Whenever Benny said, "Oh, waiter…waiter," "Floorwalker…floorwalker," "Usher…usher," "Doctor…doctor," or just "Mister…Mister," we knew the next word spoken would be a rapacious "YESSS!" delivered with the glee of a vulture about to descend on its prey.

The edgy exchanges between Benny and Nelson frequently headed down a road that allowed both men to employ one of their pet expressions. Jack would pose a "you asked for it" question like "Are your eggs fresh?" or "Do you enjoy aggravating me?" and Frank would let him have it with his elated squeal of "Ooo, are they!" or "Ooo, do I!" after which Jack might provide counterpoint with his indignant "Now cut that out!"

The Sportsmen also annoyed the star of the show with commercials that veered from delivering the sponsor's message into silly patter songs. Benny's attempts to stop them took the form of "Wait a minute" repeated usually four times, ending in a crescendo of frustration that sometimes generated the biggest laugh of the half-hour. The routine became so well-established that on the January 19, 1947 broadcast as Jack alone listened to the quartet on the phone, members of the audience used their imaginations to "hear" the song spin out of control until Benny reached the boiling point.

Another of Jack's famous exclamations emerged when he was on the receiving end of a tirade. After Don castigated him for his cheapness with a tongue-lashing that began "You are without a doubt the most parsimonious…" or an auto dealer called the Maxwell "without a doubt the oldest, worst, most beat-up piece of junk I have ever seen," we knew it was the storm before the calm that would be culminated by an offended "Well!" delivered with all the finality of a stick hitting a kettle drum.

Jack employed a different tactic whenever Mary Livingstone needled him by simply repeating the last part of the comment twice in a derisive chorus. Mary's gibes usually focused on his tight-fisted reputation or his age and sometimes she hit both targets with one shot as on the Thanksgiving show in 1949 when her claim that "You haven't paid for a turkey since you chipped in with the Pilgrims" was echoed by "chipped in with the Pilgrims, chipped in with the Pilgrims."

Eddie Anderson in his role as Rochester also used a line of skepticism that he delivered in his characteristic rasp. If Jack told his valet to go through his suit before sending it to the cleaners to make certain he did not leave any money in the pockets or suggested that Errol Flynn might star in a movie about his life, a refrain of four words said what everyone was thinking: "Oh, boss, come now!"

Although Mel Blanc did not belong to the regular cast, his versatility as the man of a thousand voices made him so valuable that his frequent appearances were always welcomed with pleasure by audiences. His entrance as Professor LeBlanc, Benny's long-suffering violin instructor, seldom varied: scratching of a bow on strings followed by a "No, no, no, Monsieur Benny" spoken metronomically. When his ears and patience could not take any more dissonance, he unleashed the expletive "*Sacrebleu!*" enunciated lyrically and sounding so much like a blessing that Jack responded to the curse with a "Thank you."

The litany between Benny and the Mexican characters Blanc assumed never failed to tickle Jack. These bits hinged on the same simple questions:

Jack: What's your name?
Mel: Sy.
Jack: Sy?
Mel: *Si.*

Back and forth the pair would go in a seesaw rhythm that might also include similar-sounding *s* words such as *soy* and *sore*. The duet became a trio on the nights when Bea Benaderet joined them as Sy's sister Sue who liked to sew.

Whenever Benny walked into a railroad station, it served as a downbeat signaling Mel to assume the role of the announcer proclaiming "Train now leaving on track five for Anaheim, Azusa, and Cucamonga," a triad of cities as euphonious as Atchison, Topeka, and Santa Fe. The variations on this theme seemed endless with the writers occasionally having Blanc stop after "Cuc—," giving Jack a line of dialogue, and then letting the other shoe drop with "—amonga." One of the best Benny shows ever is the December 11, 1949 program on which Mel announced departures in the bouncy rhymes "Train leaving on track one for Baltimore and Washington,/It's leaving now so you better run," "Train leaving on track three all the way to Schenectady,/Just one stop at Kansas C," and "Train leaving on track two for Asheville, Nashville, Kalamazoo,/Takes on water at Waterloo," which were punctuated with "shave-and-a-haircut" drum riffs.

Blanc's ability to vary delivery in his roles as Polly the parrot or as bakery personnel in the "Cimarron rolls" routines hit the right note with audiences, and the writers knew he would be right on key in other roles as well. As Punchy, a boxer who sniffed between words, Mel used that peculiarity to provide a highlight of the May 22, 1949 episode. After Jack doubted the fighter's claim that he had played with a well-known musical group by stating, "You were never with Lombardo's band," Punchy replied, "Oh, yes (sniff), yes (sniff, sniff), yes I was," perfectly mimicking the schmaltzy coda of the Royal Canadians.

Other supporting actors who appeared on the show played virtually the same arrangements every time they appeared. As the tout, Sheldon Leonard's opening chord rarely deviated from "Hey, bud, bud." His response to Jack's course of action took the form of a definitive "uh-uh." By employing terms of the racetrack the writers rode the nag gags through many variations on a theme, occasionally providing a switch by having Jack get the horselaugh such as on March 21, 1952 when he declined coffee even though "it's a sleeper" in favor of tea because "it's in the bag."

Artie Auerbach's Mr. Kitzel had music in his speech if not in his heart right from "Hello, Mr. Benny," which he sang as much as said. Even when he wasn't reciting versions of his "Pickle in the middle with the mustard on top" pitch or saying "hoo hoo hoo" as if ringing his version of the NBC chimes, the patterns of Auerbach's Jewish dialect had a rhythmic rise and fall that made his persiflage with Benny sound like a well-orchestrated chorus.

Conversely, Jack's dialogue with the characters assumed by Benny Rubin hit the same note in a composition that might have been titled "No Information Please." The pattern never varied: Jack asked three related questions such as "How much weight is Our Fancy carrying?," "What is the name of the jockey?," and "How long is the race going to be?" The answer to each question was the same: "I don't know," often delivered in a slur that sounded like "I dunno." Jack then exploded with a fourth question such as "If you don't know anything about the races, what are you doing behind the desk?" Rubin completed the bit with his reason for being: "I had to get behind something. I lost my pants." Today this seems like a long way to go for a punch line and a quick exit, but as long as Rubin got laughs the writers kept playing that old familiar strain.

Another version of the Three Benny Opera occurred with some regularity in Jack's battle of words with Dennis Day. Day offered overtures that teased Benny's curiosity such as declaring that he was going to have his tonsils removed. After the three queries of "Are your tonsils infected?," "Has your throat been sore?," and "Have you been catching colds?" received negative responses, Jack irritably demanded an explanation, then regretted it every time when he became the recipient of an inanity like "A doctor friend is coming over and I don't know how else to entertain him."

Jack marched to a different tempo when someone else played inquirer. Although Bea Benaderet had a recurring role as Gertrude Gearshift, one of the telephone operators who provided an off-key intermezzo from the plot with nasally gossip tossed back and forth with cohort Mabel Flapsaddle, she also acted as nurses or receptionists who requested information from Benny. The series of questions and answers took on a sing-song pattern that often came back to the same refrain Jack played for years. This dialogue from the January 21, 1951 broadcast is typical of the antiphonal exchanges:

Bea: Your name?
Jack: Jack Benny.
Bea: Your address?
Jack: 366 North Camden Drive.
Bea: Your age?
Jack: 39.
Bea: Your height?
Jack: 5 feet 10½.
Bea: Your weight?
Jack: 155.
Bea: Your age?
Jack: 39.
Bea: Color of hair?
Jack: Brown.
Bea: Color of eyes? Oh, they're blue, aren't they?
Jack: Bluer than the feet of a Sicilian wine presser.
Bea: Complexion?
Jack: Fair.
Bea: Your age?
Jack: 39.
Bea: Your occupation?
Jack: Comedian.
Bea: I thought so.

The figurative imagery of Jack's eyes used in that sketch became a running gag which was brought in out of the blue with dulcet and picturesque similes such as "bluer than the lips of the winner of a huckleberry pie-eating contest" or "bluer than the thumb of a cross-eyed carpenter."

The Benny team loved words and when they found a tune they liked they found ways to play it on their own hit parade for many weeks. During World War II the writers introduced Sympathy Soothing Syrup and, not just content with the music of its alliteration, decided to capitalize on the advertising gimmick of reversing the spelling of a product's name. The writers invented a catchy jingle for "yip-yip yhtapmys" that even spread to Ronald and Benita Colman, Jack's neighbors, who also sang its phrases.

The mellifluous sound of Benny's advertising agency, Batten, Barton, Durstine, and Osborn, was too much for the writers to overlook so they built an entire episode (November 21, 1948) around Jack's attempts to call the agency whose name, as Mary aptly stated, sounded like "a trunk falling downstairs."

Jack, Mary Livingstone, and Eddie Anderson knew how to hit the right notes.

On April 24, 1949 the writers again satirized Madison Avenue in a lilting way when Jim Backus, as car salesman Plain Bill, promoted an automobile's most distinctive feature, a "dynaflex, superflowing turbovasculator which is syncromeshed with a multicoil hydrotension dual vacuum dynamometer." The function of this wondrous accessory? It empties the ashtray. Never ones to waste a good lyric, the writers had Mary and Rochester sing it again that night and brought it back the following week so Harris could wrestle with the melodic mouthful.

Although Phil's character on the show was that of a tippling boor spouting malapropisms, the lines he spoke frequently evinced the flair of a brash illiterate. He would say his way onstage with "OK, fellows, here's Harris the star,/So tear up your passes and staaay where you are," "So far, folks, this show has smelled,/But Harris is here and I'm jet-propelled," "OK, folks, you're all in clover,/'Cause Harris is here and the lull is over," and other couplets that he hammered home with a heavy-handed invitation for applause in the form of "lay it on me." Sometimes after inserting a pun, he laughed it up and blew his own horn with a non-rhyming but still rhythmic boast of the "Oh, Harris, many brave hearts are asleep in the deep, but you're awake every minute" or "Oh, Harris, you may not be the star, but without you the show is nothing, nothing" variety.

One night Jack marveled aloud about Phil's hammy behavior by claiming that "if he was half as good as he thinks he is, he'd be twice as good as he is," then wondered some more with "What kind of a joke was that?" which underlined one of the unwritten commandments of the writers: sound is sometimes more important than sense.

A notable example of nonsense carrying the day (and the show) occurred on April 4, 1954 when Benny, in a sketch as a psychiatrist, stated that his name was "William Jackson Ph.D., B.A., LL.B., M.A.,B.S., M.D.," then added, "Yes, my last name is…," proceeded to wrap his lips around the fourteen letters and, *mirabile dictu*, somehow said the six syllables of gibberish in a lilting fashion which drove home the point that the string of degrees could have been his last name.

Although the writers frequently employed poetic devices (a hillbilly sketch on November 27, 1949 focused on the humor in the rhyming names *Em, Lem, Shem,* and *Clem*), the dialogue itself formed the heart of the symphony that carried *The Jack Benny Program*. Much of the humor came simply from the give-and-take in straight line-punch line form, but the Benny team excelled in setting up jokes to match the peerless delivery of the show's star by devising routines in measures of three, four, or five parts. Most of the episodes contain instances of this structure. Two examples are given here.

On May 11, 1952 Jack asked questions from another room while Rochester and his friend Roy cleaned the living room. Jack asked, "Where's my shoe brush?" and Rochester answered, "Right next to your shoes." Roy and Rochester moved the piano and then Jack said, "Where's my hairbrush?" Rochester's answer of "Right next to your hair" would seem to be the zinger that would end the number, but the Benny boys were not done playing that tune yet. After Roy and Rochester talked momentarily about bathing suits, Jack got the last laugh: "Where's my toothbrush and don't be funny."

On the first show of the 1952-1953 season Benny, while looking at the labels on his various keys, explained to Rochester what the abbreviations on each one meant: WT for wardrobe trunk, DD for desk drawer, and LC for linen closet. Jack then said, "BA," and waited for Rochester to ask the precisely-worded question "What does that one open?" (*not* "What does that one stand for?"). Benny's answer: "Bank of America." After the laugh and applause, there was an encore when Jack read "SM" and Rochester obligingly asked, "What's that?" "Santa Monica branch."

The exchanges with Dennis, Benny's encounters with an assortment of oddballs which began innocently and culminated with Jack's slow burn, the conversations between Jack and Phil about the members of the band that flowed from one offbeat musician to another, Mary's letters from her mother describing sister Babe and other eccentrics on the family tree; all followed the pattern of building routines in three or more parts of harmonic progression that reached a climax as emphatic as the clashing of cymbals.

The cadence of the dialogue became so ingrained in the performers that they adjusted to bloopers or hesitations without missing a beat. On January 20, 1952 Jack paused several times because of audience reaction and Phil played right along:

Jack: What did–What did–What did Fletcher–What did
   Fletcher do this time?
Phil: He–He–He–He didn't do nothing.
Jack: Then why–why–why–Then why did they take him back
   to prison?

The payoff seemed predictable and did not receive the response as the lead-in lines which demonstrates that even when out of sync the two men were playing perfect two-part harmony.

The Benny writers who knew a good thing when they wrote it also knew a good thing when they heard it even if it came out a clinker so they reprised Dreer Poosen, chiss sweese, grass reek, and similar ghostly fluffs weeks after they had first haunted the show. They also brought back the refrains of "What happened to the gas man?," "Did you hunt bear?," the Swiss echo, and other running gags and paid attention to the top hits on the record charts to find ways of squeezing topical laughs out of catchy titles like "Come On-A My House," "Hernando's Hideaway," and "Mule Train."

The musicality of *The Jack Benny Program* is readily apparent when one listens to the parody performed by the Beverly Hills Beavers on the April 23, 1950 broadcast. The children's voices (even the growl of the youngster playing Rochester) do not sound very much like the cast members they are impersonating, yet by replicating the caesuras and cadenzas of the dialogue, Mary's sassiness, Phil's braggadocio, Dennis's goofiness, and Jack's exasperation come through in well-orchestrated strains of parrying and thrusting. Jack and Mary, who were sitting with us in the audience that night, liked what they heard and could have said what we think whenever we listen to the episodes of this beloved series: "They're playing our song."

To call the Benny writing team composers and to label Jack and his supporting cast virtuosos would be presumptuous, but just as many big bands produced a unique style of music, the scripts of *The Jack Benny Pro-*

gram have distinctive patterns tailored to players whose special delivery made that show different from any other on the air. So let the good times roll for the fans of one Benny who snap their fingers to the beat of "Sing, Sing, Sing" *and* for those who favor the other Benny who hold their sides to the rhythm of "Laugh, Laugh, Laugh."

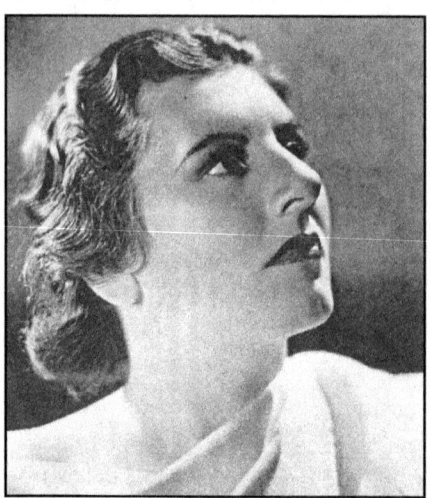

Claudia Morgan, Anne Seymour, and the versatile Cecil Roy were frequently heard on *Quiet, Please*.

The Thing on the Radio Dial

LET ME TELL YOU ABOUT THIS DREAM I keep having. I get out of this Hudson (you know, one of those you step down into) in front of a theater. I go right past this one-sheet for *Sorry, Wrong Number* and the lobby cards for *Out of the Past*. I don't even stop by the candy counter filled with boxes of Welch's Pom Poms, Mason Dots, and Licorice Clix.

I go right inside the swinging doors without a ducat and there's an award ceremony going on. And up on the stage there's this octopus grabbing each statuette as fast as the emcee can announce the categories and winners: "For best music: Albert Berman. For best writer: Wyllis Cooper. For best actor: Ernest Chappell. For best dramatic series: *Quiet, Please*." I start to yell "Hey, give someone else a chance" when the octopus looks at me with those glaring red eyes and wraps one of its tentacles around me and—Well, that's when I wake up screaming.

I'm beginning to suspect that experience is more like payday instead of pipe dream because that show may have deserved those honors, especially considering the cards were stacked against it. *Quiet, Please* only aired from June of 1947 through June of 1949, didn't have a sponsor, and ran up against some pretty stiff competition.

How stiff? Well, at one time in late '48 it was running on Mutual on Monday nights against *Dr. IQ*, *Get Rich Quick*, and *Lux Radio Theatre*. Wait. It gets worse. In the winter and spring of '49 on ABC *Quiet, Please* had to keep up with musical programs and *Strike It Rich* and *Quick as a Flash*. On Sunday afternoons, for crying out loud! It's bad enough to be opposite quiz shows that were as popular then as peanuts at a circus (remember what they did to Fred Allen), but broadcasting a spine-tingling show loaded with atmosphere on the day of rest while families prepared or ate their suppers was like booking Boris Karloff on a wake-up show so he could hobnob about his latest spookfest and dunk doughnuts with Bishop Sheen.

So it's no wonder the show didn't attract many listeners then. Some people still don't even know there was such a program. Some may say those shows have vanished into the dust of antiquity like the Cro-Magnon man. That is what they say. Now I will tell you what I know.

Because most of the episodes have been found, we now have a pretty good idea as to the breadth of Wyllis Cooper's canvas. The comparison to art, by the way, is not a stretch because Cooper painted with words: landscapes, houses, cityscapes, and people were vividly described in poetic imagery. When he set the scene by telling us "the streets were wet with the bitter rain of the waning winter that night" and then described the sounds of tires which resembled striking matches and the subterranean bellow of the subway, he wasn't just knocking on the door of our senses. He was dragging us right outside so we felt cold and damp with the smell of rubber and sulfur in our nostrils as we flinched from the deafening roar of the train passing by. Cooper didn't need clattering chains and moaning spirits to create a mood of foreboding. When we're told lights filled "the night sky with signs and portents of inescapable terror," our hair started flexing its muscles for the sit-ups that were to come.

But enough about laying the groundwork. I have other stories to tell before…before you go. Where was I? Oh, yes. Cooper was an artist with the pen, but he could also be a hard-working craftsman who did his homework. If he wrote about plumbers, he got the jargon down to the last el and t. The same for when his plays dealt with railroads or oil fields or aircraft or steel mills or distilleries. He knew his onions. Come to think of it, Coop could have probably done a good one about a man who smells onions every time someone dies.

That's one thing you could count on with *Quiet, Please*. No matter if the story was set in the past, present, or future or if the tone shifted from tongue-in-cheek to gravely serious, death either sat center stage or skulked in the wings. But what kept the few loyal listeners coming back was how Bill Cooper, that old magician of language and plots, could keep shuffling the same deck of cards for two years and deal a new hand every week.

He could just pluck a number out of the air like "Three" and build a framework around it concerning a man named Sebastian who is hounded by that digit from the groups of people he encounters to the telephone numbers he dials to a bartender named *Drei*. A sense of fatalism builds to the climax when Sebastian foresees that a judge will pronounce a sentence upon him that will have him hanging by the neck until he is "dead, dead,

dead." Or Cooper could put a new twist on the "pact with the devil" legends by spinning a winsome tale ("Kill Me Again") about how a man finds himself ensnared by a loophole in his agreement with one Mr. Hellman.

When Cooper sent us traveling in time, he punched our ticket for both chills and chuckles. The owner of a magic watch finds out that "It Is Later Than You Think." "One for the Book" is just that: In 1937 Sergeant Max Westlake meets Major Max Westlake when the Major exceeds the speed of sound in 1957 and flies "so fast he got here before he started." Sgt. Westlake's query "Have I got to go through all that again?" closes the show on a whimsical note that makes us think about the repetitive lasso that time has thrown around him.

Thoreau once claimed that time was but the stream he went fishing in. Cooper seemed to be saying in his plays that time is the ocean we are drowning in whether we are coming or going. Amnesia victim Ulysses Smith, after seeing "Little Visitor" Jeffrey several times in different places, realizes that the boy is himself as a child and is going to turn himself in after stealing money, thus becoming "the only man in the world that was haunted by himself." In "Pavane" childless Andrew meets a mysterious little girl in the dark who eventually reveals to him that she is his unborn child who will only live eight years.

Coop was really quite adept at confounding our sense of time, space, and reality. In "And Jeannie Dreams of Me" a man named Troy has had a dream lover named Jeannie since childhood whom he visits often in her colonial house throughout his life. She saves his life by sending him back to rejoin his body just before disaster strikes, then later Troy spends years with her while his inert frame lies in a coma in an army hospital. As Cooper bewitches us in this fanciful tale, at times we don't know for certain if we are in Troy's real world, his dreams, Jeannie's dreams, or our nightmares.

And, speaking of nightmares, that man could tell some good ghost stories and other supernatural yarns. Like "Take Me Out to the Graveyard" where everyone this taxi driver meets wants to go you-know-where and that's exactly where they end up. Come to think of it, so will we, which is what the cabbie means at the end when he says he will be calling on us sometime. And in "My Son John" there's a vampire who says he's also coming after us some night with his boy who was bitten by old man Dracula himself. "Some People Don't Die," namely the wizards and mummies dwelling in the cliffs, are ready to claim new victims with rattlesnakes.

I don't blame you for shivering. Something in the other room? You must be hearing things. You know, it *was* all the things we were hearing that made those shows so frightening. Bill McClintock's sound effects of wind whistling or pipes rattling or claps of thunder would give anyone the heebie jeebies. And, if the theme song wasn't creepy enough, Albert would be playing softly in the background like a serenade at a séance and then all of a sudden he'd hit that organ with a sting that would make the skin crawl on the phantom of the opera.

As if Cooper needed any help in scaring us out of our seats. Imagine being down in some Egyptian tomb with a hawk-headed, bloody-billed creature who is definitely not resting in peace. When that archeologist sees his own face chiseled on a slab and rubs elbows with Osiris and Isis, claustrophobics don't wonder "Whence Came You?" but instead holler, "What way out of here?"

Or climb up on an oil rig to meet "The Thing on the Fourble Board" who has an adorable face but a body only a mother arachnid could love. If the mewing and word-portrait of "Maxine," written by Cooper and spoken by Chappell doesn't cause goose bumps, brother, your imagination is in need of a transfusion.

Or stand out in the land of the "Northern Lights" on a desolate, ice-covered wasteland and then return via teleportation covered head to foot with caterpillars. These are not just ordinary caterpillars waiting to become docile tiger moths, mind you, but rather alien beings intent on world domination. The eerie way that one furry thing called "Isabella" says her vowels is enough to send Raymond shrieking right through *Inner Sanctum*'s creaking door into the night.

Even a trip back to gentler times innocently called "Tanglefoot" has sinister implications if the conductor is Cooper and the destination a small town in 1915 where two plumbers raise large, lethal flies. What starts off as a folksy "what if…" story turns into a tale of terror as Chappell, just as he did in "Fourble Board," goes from incredulous observer to crafty entrapper who enjoys luring visitors in front of "Louise" before warning her not to get her "feet stuck in the manpaper."

We also had to be on our toes and ready for sudden changes because Coop, that wily hurler, could throw a mean curve. "Never Send to Know" begins playfully as a private detective pokes fun at some of the clichés in the trade, but when he is confronted by the ghost of a man he killed the mood turns grim indeed. "The Man Who Knew Everything," quite amusing for the first fifteen minutes as Cooper takes aim at quiz shows and other targets and even inserts his own and Chappell's names into the script, becomes deadly serious when the smug narrator who can foresee the how but not the hour of his demise learns that his when is now.

Ernest Chappell seemed to be the right actor to narrate *Quiet, Please* because his versatility allowed him to connect solidly with whatever Cooper pitched at him. If Coop handed him "If I Should Wake Before I Die" and said, "This week I want you to be a cold, calculating scientist to whom knowledge is all and you don't care if your brother dies out in space or if you destroy your rivals," Chappell became a Dr. Anderson who had all the warmth and tenderness of a stalactite. Time and again in poignant love stories such as "The Little Mourning," "In Memory of Bernadine," "The Evening and the Morning," and "Consider the Lilies" he played impassioned men who demonstrate undying love. He could stay in character as both a sober and drunken spirit observing his wife's trial for his murder in "Baker's Dozen" and remain inebriated throughout a shaggy dog fantasy as a "moon man" who poses the question Cooper must have been asked repeatedly: "Where Do You Get Your Ideas?"

Chappell could play highbrows, tough guys, and everything in-between. Take, for instance, this one play called "Tap the Heat, Bogdan" where he became a bigoted bully with an accent thicker than frozen borscht. You can't help disliking the jerk. Ditto for Monk, a ventriloquist and murderer in "3,000 Words." When he was the "Good Ghost," he adopted a more colloquial tone as befit his not-too-bright character and delivered seriocomic lines such as "It's bad enough to murder a guy. Do you have to scare the life out of him?" with a straight voice. And when playing the bombastic, superstitious title character in "The Hat, the Bed, and John J. Catherine," Chappell had more ham in him than Porky Pig.

But Chappy was at the top of his form when speaking from the heart and wrapping his lips around Cooper's poetic rhapsodies. I tell you, that Chappell could get a throb in his throat like a lovesick pup or he could put such a lilt in his voice you thought he was reading measures off a score instead of sentences off a page and you felt you could hang your hat on every note. Man, he was some actor. That's why it seems a shame radio wasted much of his talent by having him push soup and cigarettes or just using him as an announcer. That was like making Jimmy Stewart do weather reports in Washington because he could say "Walla Walla" pretty good or turning Edward G. Robinson into a news commentator because he could punctuate every statement with a "See?" or …

But I'm getting off the subject and I can see it's getting close to meal time. Yes, I know you're not hungry. I was thinking of…

Well, I guess I was thinking of those other voices we heard like those of Anne Seymour, Bess Johnson, and Nancy Sheridan, three outstanding actresses who spent many of their days elbow-deep in the soaps. Claudia Morgan took time out now and then from playing Nora Charles on the air to play opposite Chappy, her real husband. Character actors Ed Latimer and Warren Stevens could be heard occasionally, and once in a while J. Pat O'Malley stopped by to throw his brogue around the kilocycles. With a man like Cooper at the helm who tossed real people like George Custer and Abe Lincoln into the scripts, you never knew what to expect. Why, Jack Lescoulie (that's right, from *The Jackie Gleason Show* and *The Today Show*) took the part of the other plumber in "Tanglefoot." And then there was Cecil Roy who played everyone (and everything) from six to ninety-six (that's both in years and in legs).

And the wonder of it all is that Cooper didn't need a stage filled with players, an orchestra, singers, a big technical crew, and an audience to pull it off. He weaved his magic carpet out of just three or four actors, a sound man, and one musician. Now don't get me wrong. Those people by the mikes certainly did a great job, but if Bill Cooper as writer and director hadn't been there to tell them what to say and how to say it ... Well, *Quiet, Please* might have turned out to be just a curiosity like *The Strange Dr. Weird* or *Dark Fantasy* that could rattle bones but didn't offer much meat to chew and digest.

Sure, Coop could freeze our blood with horror stories, keep us in suspense waiting for retribution in the revenge stories "Come in, Eddie" and "Bogdan," and even tantalize us with unresolved endings or inexplicable deaths when he gave us a whiff of "The Smell of High Wines" and a glimpse of "The Oldest Man in the World." But more often than not Cooper's plays have something to say about prejudice or hatred or the profound depths of real love or the true manifestation of courage or the importance of preserving the earth for future generations.

And, let me tell you, when Cooper set his sights on sending his moral right to our hearts, his aim was better than Cupid's. After listening to his St. Patrick's Day fable "Dark Rosaleen," we are so full of the love for all mankind we want to run out and kiss everyone we meet whether they are Irish or not. The soldiers who are visited by a heavenly guest in "Berlin, 1945" aren't the only ones who come face-to-face with the true meaning of Christmas. But if you want your emotions drained and experience the uplift of a life-affirming message, tune your ears to the moving Passover/Easter story "Shadow of the Wings" about a sickly little girl, her mother, and a celestial visitor. Talk about being touched by an angel! Brother, those last five minutes would bring tears to the eyes of an atheist.

The one recurrent theme that Cooper played during the last ten months of *Quiet, Please* came as a result of him looking into his crystal ball and seeing a sight more horrifying than any of the weird creatures stirring around in the attic of his imagination. In "Portrait of a Character" the tone is somewhat lighthearted as Gabriel, after observing the wickedness of earthlings while waiting for repairs to his horn, is told by the Boss to give the atom to them and stand by to play a big job "any day

In 1950 Wyllis Cooper directed and produced another eerie,
imaginative series, television's *Stage 13*.

now." However, the mood in "Adam and the Darkest Day" is considerably bleaker as we visit a barren place that used to be Chicago where only three people and mutant fish have survived a nuclear holocaust. Bombs that turn the entire planet into a fireball seem to leave no hope for airborne humans until a "Very Important Person" gives them (and us) a way out.

In the final episode of the series ("Quiet, Please") the last man on Mars implores us to learn from their internecine wars and to dwell together in unity. Even the parting words Cooper himself leaves with us at the end of the program's last gasp, "I hope we'll meet again sometime," may be packed with more meaning than we realize if the significant word in that sign-off is *hope*.

Yes sir, Wyllis Cooper had a lot to say and the way Ernest Chappell and colleagues expressed those thoughts…Well, *Quiet, Please* is simply radio drama at its best.

That music? Oh, that's a recording of the show's theme, the second movement of Cesar Franck's *Symphony in D Minor*. I thought it would get you in the mood for …what is to come.

How could I turn on the phonograph in the other room from my chair? Let's just say I have those extra arms that people are always wishing for.

Now why don't you turn on the Philco console just inside the doorway there and we'll see if we can't find a good eerie story like "The Green Light" or that haunting "Sketch for a Screenplay" or—What's that? Yes, there is a big aquarium back there behind the radio and phonograph. That's right. There is something in there. No—stay where you are! Screaming is no way to greet "Olive." I know she likes you. Or at least she will.

You remember me telling you about the dream I keep having? Well, after listening to *Quiet, Please*, it's just like the song says: my dreams are getting better all the time.

Ozzie Nelson and Harriet Hilliard were on the air for CBS in the mid-forties.

The Wizardry of Oz

IT IS COMMON PRACTICE TO DISPARAGE *The Adventures of Ozzie and Harriet* by labeling the program as an unrealistic portrayal of family life. Such criticism is guilty of the same fault often leveled at the show, namely that it ignores the way things really were.

Many episodes of the series began with incidents involving Ricky and David which mirrored similar events found in thousands of American homes such as struggles with homework, plans to raise spending money, involvement with girls, fights after school, and participation in sports. Then Ozzie and Harriet dispensed sagacious advice to the boys on how to resolve their problems just as fathers and mothers across the country did with their children.

A plot device employed by Ozzie and his other writers involved complications arising when parents don't practice what they preach. Ozzie once chastised David for turning down a party invitation for dubious reasons before he became entangled in a dinner engagement with a man whose name he didn't remember. After admonishing David for the boy's needless anxiety over an arithmetic test already taken, Oz became a worrywart agitated about everything from drapes to burglars, although his concern may have been a ploy to ease the minds of Harriet and his older son. Not long after reminding both sons about their promise to do homework, Ozzie's pledge to take them on a hike triggered a series of events that culminated in the Nelsons attending a football game.

More often than not, the opening exchanges with or without the boys merely set the stage for what the show was really about: the battle of the sexes. Harriet didn't even have to throw down a gauntlet; all Ozzie needed was a whisper of a challenge and the war between men and women resumed in full force.

Sometimes a leaky faucet or a burned-out bulb led Ozzie to assert his masculinity in disastrous ways that resulted in flooded bedrooms and plastering jobs. Nelson himself stated the formula on one occasion: "The husband is supposed to be the bumbling, fumbling, stupid one who makes mistakes and the wife is the level-headed one who straightens things out."

Harriet certainly seemed like the patient spouse who, upon hearing her husband castigate himself for panicking over a rumor with the words "I'm a fool. I'm a dope. I'm a moron. I'm an idiot. Well?" blithely urged him to "Keep going, dear. I'll tell you when to stop."

Oz, it seemed, didn't know when to stop when he strapped on his armor. His plan to cure what he perceived to be Harriet's habit of exaggeration consisted of an attempt to embarrass her by grossly inflating the value of their furniture in front of a man Ozzie assumed was a dealer in antiques. Instead, Nelson became the humiliated one when the person writing down the fantastic figures turned out to be a tax assessor.

On another occasion a few innocent questions about his day downtown convinced Ozzie that his wife had become a creature driven by insatiable curiosity. After Harriet mentioned that a friend she would not name had paid Oz a compliment, suddenly the accuser became an interrogator obsessed with discovering the woman's identity. His foray of concocting an amorous interlude from his past, interrupted at a climactic moment, which he had hoped would elicit a curious response from Harriet that he could exchange for the complimenter's name, failed miserably. Harriet ended the skirmish by confessing that the admirer was an artifice, a paper tigress with the improbable name of Constantina Wasselmix.

At times Ozzie became so driven by his desire to compete that he willingly marched into enemy territory like challenging Harriet to a knitting contest. Lest the audience miss the leitmotif, Nelson spelled it out by stating that he "was going to prove that men [fanfare] are superior to women." As might be expected, the sock he knitted looked like a wool funnel that would fit someone with a quarter-inch ankle who wore a size 23 shoe.

The rules for combat became so complicated that only Ozzie could understand them. One day he told his wife that she was pretending to want him around the house so he would leave, "but knowing that I know reverse psychology you try reverse reverse psychology. You say you want me inside so I'll think you want me outside. Actually, you really want me inside but thinking you want me outside I stay inside, but I'm going to fool you. I'm going outside," which was where Harriet wanted him to go in the first place.

Although Oz clearly lost more battles than he won, draws seemed to reinforce the notion that marriages have more truces than surrenders. If Harriet showed a lack of will power in the opening minutes of an episode by buying cosmetics and flannel she really did not need, Ozzie could be counted on to have no sales resistance when he visited the barbershop and bought everything offered from shampoo to manicure. Because Harriet also knew the rules of the game, she would often let her husband fall into his own trap and extricate him at the cost of a dress, coat, or alligator bag. The spoils of war became her Sunday outfit.

David Nelson knew what the final score would be. When his father admitted, "I don't win all the time," David added, "But she does." If Ozzie boasted, "When I really make up my mind to change something about your mother, you know what happens," David confidently replied, "I sure do, Pop, but you might as well try anyway."

Beneath the carapace of this rivalry beat two soft hearts and no amount of jousting could hide the fact that Ozzie and Harriet were better lovers than fighters. Despite the couples' vow to be sensible at Christmas and give each other a radio phonograph, listeners knew that when she expressed interest in a nightgown and he coveted fishing equipment that the object of their affection would get the object of their affection. In typical fashion both of them tried to save face for their moment of weakness by claiming that the gifts came not from each other but from pets in the neighborhood.

For another special occasion Ozzie's plan for finding a unique gift to express his love on Valentine's Day was hampered by his indecision with the result that the only presents he could find at the last moment were a bag of popcorn and a bouquet of violets. Harriet came to his rescue by acting touched as she fabricated a romantic reminiscence involving flowers and popcorn on their first date. The love between Harriet and Ozzie which permeated the show left audiences with a warm feeling about marriage to go along with a sense of well-being caused by laughing at dialogue largely devoid of gags or insults, a twofold accomplishment few comedy programs achieved.

The two neighbors brought in weekly to counsel Ozzie often fell right in line with the marital-martial theme. Thornberry espoused the male point of view in tongue-in-cheek comments along the lines of "I believe every man should be happily married whether he likes it or not." Emmy Lou staunchly defended women by declaring that they "don't exaggerate. It's just that after they finish telling the truth they keep on talking."

Although they had small parts on the program, John Brown and Janet Waldo were at their very best on *The Adventures of Ozzie and Harriet*.

As the teasing opportunist Thorny, Brown spoke in a more natural voice than the Brooklynese he assumed in other roles and the sepulchral tones of Digby O'Dell on *The Life of Riley*. His sarcastic greeting of "Mother Machree!" upon seeing Oz knitting is priceless as is his delivery of a zinger after hearing Ozzie say that he didn't want to be hauled off a baseball field in a wheelbarrow because "that thing's for hauling junk around" and observing Nelson's crumpled form on the ground: "If you could see yourself now, Oz, you'd climb right in."

Janet Waldo's Emmy Lou deserved radio's "mountains out of molehills" award, even topping the calamities characters played by Elliott Lewis laid out for a bemused George Burns. All Ozzie had to do was mention a modern art exhibit and Emmy Lou breathlessly began jumping to conclusions on a set of escalating trampolines, painting Nelson as an artist who lives "in a garret. A tiny cubicle. A niche. A cubbyhole. A dump. Your room is so tiny you have to paint with your hands in your pockets. You have to peek through a keyhole to see your model in the next room. For years you work on your portrait. Day in, day out. Only a few more days and then your masterpiece is complete. What depth! What beauty! Your very soul is in your painting." She carried on in this rhapsodic manner until she spurred Nelson to impetuously ask $5,000 for a work of art that existed only in her fevered imagination. These flights of fancy and Waldo's inimitable ecstatic squeals made Emmy Lou one of the most adorable adolescents on the air.

Amusing as the characters are, *The Adventures of Ozzie and Harriet* truly qualifies as a sitcom for when the situations raised the baton everyone played along. Nelson started with a simple premise like altering the way his eggs were prepared and suddenly he became capricious Ozzie who ordered tutti-frutti ice cream instead of vanilla or chocolate, sat on the floor instead of on chairs, and wiped his hands on the "hers" towel. Even when he acted predictably like delivering his "I-yi-yi" line after confronting one of the voluptuous women played by Veola Vonn who appeared occasionally at his front door, men would chortle knowingly, realizing that they would have also been tongue-tied in such a situation.

Nelson, like Art Linkletter, knew that kids say the darndest things and that their spontaneous outbursts brighten conversations in real homes so he handed some of the funniest lines to David and Ricky even though he did not permit his own sons to play themselves until 1949. When David described how he was kissed by a girl before and after hitting a home run and Ricky said, "Twice, boy. It made me sick," parents across the country laughed because they knew such a comment could have emerged from the mouth of one of their babes.

Because the shows were based upon incidents common to most families rather than on topical events, most episodes of *The Adventures of Ozzie and Harriet* have aged well and some of them can stand unashamedly as notable examples of 1940s comedies. "The Lodge Initiation" (September 16, 1945) is an amusing satire in which Ozzie, seeking to join the Ancient Order of Prehistoric Monsters, faced the stiff initiation test of agreeing with everyone for a day. The conversations at the breakfast table found Ozzie eating multiple helpings of oatmeal he didn't like and changing his mind so often he had to answer "Yes, dear" even to Harriet's question of "Ozzie, are you crazy?"

The real David and Ricky joined the cast in 1949 when the show had moved to ABC.

Nearly every long-running program devoted at least one episode to the subject of paying income taxes, and on March 13, 1949 the Nelson family tackled that annual ritual in memorable fashion. After Ozzie lectured Ricky about being indecisive, he spent most of the day scurrying back and forth between his desk and the mailbox on the corner as he fretted over deductions while Harriet could not decide between buying a gray or blue outfit. The scene of Ozzie lifting Ricky who is holding the envelope with the tax form up and down by the mailbox while repeatedly changing his mind, like the one of Harriet plopping oatmeal on his plate in the lodge episode, is a joy that plays wonderfully on radio but which would lose some of its comic force on television.

The Halloween adventures of the Nelson family presented October 31, 1948 very well might be the best comedy show devoted to that holiday. After Verne Smith's intriguing introduction set an appropriate eerie mood, Ozzie's yearnings to return to the nocturnal prowls of his youth are realized after being cajoled into visiting the forbidding McAdams house. Jack Kirkwood's appearance as a 53-year-old trick-or-treater and Ozzie's choice of lyrics to sing to calm Harriet at the haunted house ("Did you ever think as the hearse goes by, someday you are going to die? There's a spook in the meadow...") are just two of the sparkling facets of this seasonal jewel.

What motivated Nelson to go to the McAdams house was to be a man in the eyes of his children just as his desire to impress Harriet with his physical prowess preceded his collapse on the baseball diamond. After sending Ricky and David away with Thorny for a night in the woods so he could "turn the marriage license to the wall" and spend a romantic evening alone with Harriet, his concern for the safety of his sons during a thunderstorm overcame any personal considerations so the couple drove up to the cabin to be with the boys. Even though his ideas often flopped spectacularly, Ozzie rarely failed in the important aspects of being a father.

Behind ne'er-do-well Ozzie Nelson stood crafty Oswald Nelson, law school graduate, who, to borrow a line from Phil Harris, knew what he was doing every minute. By cultivating an image for himself and Harriet as "America's favorite young couple," he subtly suggested a difference between their brand of comedy and the "older" offerings of Fred and Portland, Jack and Mary, the Aces, George and Gracie, and the McGees. In March of 1949 alone he made sure audiences heard of both The Best Husband and Wife Award from *Radio Mirror Magazine* and also The Good Radio Award presented by *Magazine Digest* for the show's "conscientious respect for its listeners, for attaining an unfrenzied presentation of genuine American humor, understandable and enjoyable to every member of the family from grandma to junior."

As family fare *The Adventures of Ozzie and Harriet* was more than fair. As entertainment it can match the best offerings of *Blondie, Father Knows Best, The Aldrich Family,* and *The Life of Riley.* Ozzie and Harriet came across the airwaves as sometimes erring but always caring parents expressing a sincere interest in the health and social development of their children, who, although sometimes mischievous as all boys are, demonstrated credible respect for their mother and father.

When Verne Smith opened a typical episode with the words "It's a pleasant family scene we find in the living room of the Nelsons at 1847 Rogers Road" and placed Ozzie on the couch, Harriet in an easy chair, and the boys in the kitchen before finishing his introduction with "Ah, this is the life," scoffers may be tempted to ask, "Was it ever like this?" Listeners who listen to the entire show are more likely to exclaim, "Would that it was ever like this!"

Mel Blanc contributed his bit to some of the best Benny shows both on radio and on television.

The Best of Benny

WHEN THE MUSEUM OF BROADCASTING Communications was still located in the Chicago Cultural Center, many visitors who stepped into the MBC's version of Jack Benny's vault undoubtedly wondered, "What would it be like to be trapped in here?" I, too, entertained such a thought and even asked myself, "If the vault door did close and trap me in here, what one Benny episode would I want to hear while waiting to be rescued?"

Picking a favorite Benny show is not easy, but after playing a number of tapes before groups at senior centers, nursing homes, and adult day-care facilities, the reaction of the listeners seems to support my personal choice: the December 11, 1949 broadcast in which Jack prepares for a trip to Houston.

What gives this show a special flavor is what made *The Jack Benny Program* such a steal when CBS's William Paley lured Benny away from NBC at the end of 1948. All the character traits of Jack, Phil Harris, Dennis Day, Mary Livingstone, Eddie "Rochester" Anderson, and Don Wilson were already part of radio folklore, and the supporting contributions of semi-regulars Mel Blanc, Frank Nelson, and Bea Benaderet had become as eagerly anticipated by audiences as the entrances of the stars.

The jokes about Rochester putting thick socks in Jack's suitcase so he can soak up Texas oil, Jack calling reputed boozer Phil "Rudolph the red-nosed reindeer," and Mary's remarks about her peculiar relatives are just appetizers for the one kind of humor the Benny writing team of George Balzer, Sam Perrin, John Tackaberry, and Milt Josefsberg did better than anyone else on the air: the running gag. Three shining examples on this episode raise it to the empyrean of radio comedy.

The first gag occurs when Bea, acting as a distraught wife who mistakenly calls Jack on the phone, warns a man named Charlie that he better leave town because her husband is looking for him with a gun. Little more is made of this until halfway through the show when Jack and Mary step inside a railway station. Running footsteps are heard, followed by a gunshot and Jack's comment: "Poor Charlie. He didn't quite make it."

Day's daffy nature is brilliantly revealed in a sequence at the front of Jack's house in which Dennis says a few words, slams the door, and rings the buzzer repeatedly. Finally an irritated Benny sends Rochester to the door and brings Day inside. The buzzer rings yet again because this time Rochester has been locked out. Jack's observation, "This is like a Marx Brothers picture," is not quite accurate for in our imagination the scene plays much funnier than it could ever be on the screen.

But the zenith of running gags is reserved for the train station. Blanc, whose turn as announcer usually consisted of variations of his "train now leaving on track five for Anaheim, Azusa, and Cucamonga," developed a rhyming cadence to his delivery of departures on this show which were punctuated by a drummer who rapped out a "shave and a haircut, two bits" beat. When Nelson assumed his usual obnoxious character as a sarcastic magazine clerk, he irritated Jack enough to set off this exchange:

> Benny: You burn me up, you stupid jerk.
> Nelson: When you come round, I go berserk.
> Blanc: Train now leaving for Albuquerq. (drum bit)

When Jack yells in desperation, "Now cut that out!" we are thankful that the writers didn't.

Timing is everything and *The Jack Benny Program* had everything: witty dialogue delivered by accomplished performers accompanied by the creative use of sound effects. It seems like an easy formula for success and yet this program was one of the few shows to mix the ingredients in just the right proportions regularly.

Another entry that might qualify for the blue ribbon is the January 25, 1953 show in which Jack and Mary go to the races. This episode features an extended visit to the vault, Day's quaint method of picking winners, Sheldon Leonard as a tout, Blanc as another kind of track announcer, Nelson as an impertinent waiter, and even boss Paley himself as a bettor who regrets taking a tip from Benny about a horse.

And then there is the uproarious show in which Jack and Ronald Colman switch personalities in dreamland or the nights a frustrated Benny tries to listen to the World Series on radio or contact his agency on the phone or the one that begins at his swimming pool and ends at a dentist's office or the time he attempts to sell his decrepit car or …

As Jack often said when doing a slow burn, hmmmm. Maybe picking the cream of the Benny crop is not so simple because much of what he did represents the very best that radio had to offer during those vintage years. The memory of Benny's significant contribution to that medium lived on for many years at the MBC, a place that would have brought a smile to Jack's face because, with no admission charge, it proved that the best things in life are free.

Marilyn Maxwell and other guests had to be ready for anything when Bob Hope got near a microphone.

From Gags To Snitches

WHILE READING THE PORTION of Leonard Maltin's *The Great American Broadcast* dealing with Bob Hope and his writers, one parenthetical statement leaped off the page to my eyes as if it had been trumpeted in bold type: "(Hope never mimeoed his opening monologue, for fear that someone might steal his jokes between Sunday and Tuesday.)" "So that explains it," I said, and not parenthetically.

In 1993 I purchased at auction an actual script of the *Camel Comedy Caravan* for Friday, June 4, 1943. This salute to the Army on CBS was, in the words of announcer Jimmy Wallington, "the first of five special programs dedicated to our Fighting Forces." In subsequent weeks Jack Benny, Rudy Vallee, Bing Crosby, and Fred Allen would host tributes to the Navy, Marines, Coast Guard, and Merchant Marine.

That Hope, who had already taken his show on the road to many camps, was selected to beat the drum for the Army should surprise no one. And Hope certainly deserved Wallington's introduction which, on this script, was written in pencil: "We call on a man who has done more than anyone else we know to entertain our men in uniform…Bob Hope!"

Now I could stop wondering why the first page and pages four to forty-four were typed on bond paper and Hope's monologue on pages two and three were carbon copies on onionskin. The revelation in Maltin's book made it clear that the monologue had been inserted at the last minute and that the other members of the cast never saw it.

The monologue itself is instructive, providing an insight into how "Rapid Robert" delivered a barrage of gags in his inimitable style. Every word is in upper case with no indentions and only ellipses to indicate the end of a joke.

Hope began with his patented "inserted quote and plug the sponsor" gambit: "THIS IS BOB 'GUEST STAR' HOPE TELLING YOU LISTENERS TO USE A CERTAIN KIND OF TOOTHPASTE AND SMOKE A CERTAIN KIND OF CIGARETTE…AND THEN YOUR MOUTH WILL ALWAYS HAVE ENAMEL IN WHICH TO HOLD YOUR CAMEL." The follow-up jape, a subtle reference to Pepsodent, was red-penciled.

In typical fashion Hope moved into topical territory by dropping the names of Mayor La Guardia and Henry Kaiser, then mentioned the dimouts: "AS MY BROTHER SAID, IT'S SO DARK YOU CAN'T TELL WHOSE POCKET YOU'RE PUTTING YOUR HAND IN." As if anticipating that effort would bomb Hope put the blame on same: "THAT'S WHAT MY BROTHER SAID."

The next wisecrack got the red-pencil treatment perhaps because it was deemed a trifle racy: "BUT IT'S SO DARK AND CROWDED ON BROADWAY YOU HAVE TO PINCH YOUR LEG TO FIND OUT IF IT'S YOUR OWN…MY CASE COMES UP TOMORROW."

Par for the Hope course, transitions are hard to find. Right after a jest about the family of a deceased pinball player having his tombstone tilted, from out of left field came "WHILE I WAS HERE I WENT TO SEE THE BROOKLYN DODGERS PLAY" and a comment that the players don't talk back to the umpire anymore because "THEY FOUND OUT THE OTHER DAY HE'S ON THEIR DRAFT BOARD."

A pun about potatoes and being in the chips which led to a remark about automats and the OPA were both eliminated, but one stop at the automat emerged unscathed: "YOU USED TO PUT YOUR MONEY IN A SLOT AND GET FOOD…NOW WHEN YOU PUT YOUR NICKEL IN, A HAND COMES OUT, WIPES YOUR CHIN WITH A NAPKIN, AND SAYS, 'YOU'RE THROUGH BUD. THIS IS WAR.'"

Hope rode shortages over to the subject of transportation. One rib about subways made it to broadcast ("TODAY I GOT ON A SUBWAY AND A PONTIAC GOT ON WITH ME") and another did not ("THE SUBWAYS ARE REALLY CROWDED…I GOT ON AT 42ND STREET AND YOU WHAT HAPPENED AT 43RD STREET? I GOT IN!")

Probably the most judicious excision severed a string of whimsy about the gas pinch getting so bad that Hope saw a taxi driver going down Broadway on roller skates with passengers on his back and the meter in his mouth. Not only did it take too long to unfold; the image was too far-fetched to be very amusing.

The shift to other means of transportation must have been deemed too abrupt for between "BUT" and "THE GAS SHORTAGE IS TOUGH" someone inserted "I want to tell you" in pencil. Those who thought that

Hopeism flew naturally from Bob's lips as a bridge between gags and who might be disillusioned by such a revelation should just laugh it off as did Jack Benny's fans when Mary Livingstone told her husband on one show "You couldn't ad-lib a sneeze."

The onslaught of quips ran on about, and was out of, gas. A policeman inquired if a couple were pleasure driving to which the man replied, "DON'T BE SILLY. WE'VE BEEN MARRIED FOR TEN YEARS." In the final sally Hope literally went to the dogs with a joke about a bus driver who used Chanel #5 instead of gas: "AND IT WAS THE FIRST TIME I EVER SAW THREE DACHSHUNDS AND A GREAT DANE CHASE A GREYHOUND DOWN 42ND STREET."

The monologue is certainly not Hope at his best and for a very logical reason: his writers had just created material for a show broadcast three days previously and had to produce another arsenal of one-liners for run-throughs on Sunday. No matter how much is happening at home or abroad there is only so much newsworthy fodder available in any given week, and Hope and his scribes could hardly be blamed for saving his best swings when he came up to bat on his home turf at NBC.

On that night, however, it must have seemed to Hope, as he confessed in the title of one of his books, like he had never left home because he brought Jerry Colonna, Vera Vague, and Frances Langford with him.

The dialogue between Langford and Hope suffered a number of deletions, but the necessary remarks about soldiers and WAACs stayed out of the red. Vera played her usual man-hungry role to the hilt during a routine after Bob had introduced her to Xavier Cugat; only unfunny insults comparing her to Phil Spitalny and a drawn-out joke about burning Cugie's mustache so the wax would seal his lips were cut. The badinage between Hope and Colonna concerning rationing played as written. A sketch involving Frances and Bob in a taxi driven by Vera to a train station where Jerry sold tickets was too long at 7:30 so it was snipped in several spots, but fortunately the funniest exchange survived:

> HOPE: Tell me...is the 8:31 coming in at 8:31 today?
> COLONNA: Yes and no.
> HOPE: What do you mean, yes and no?
> COLONNA: Well...8:31 *yes*...today *no!*"

A log inserted near the end of the script indicates that considerable trimming was needed because the initial lineup ran over fifty-two minutes, a timing unacceptable for a program given an unusual forty-five minute slot. A notation near the bottom of that page reveals that a later timing yielded a decidedly more tolerable 43:45. Of course, the untouchables on this patriotic program were Bob's version of "Thanks for the Memory" tailored to remind listeners "not to forget our fighting boys" and his tribute to the "fellows who'll roll the tanks across the Rhine and march in the streets of Berlin and Tokyo."

In 1943 Hope and the rest of the world had more important matters to worry about than the pilfering of gags, especially the lukewarm drolleries offered on this show. So I like to think that Bob's fears were unjustified and that the penciled "Emily" on the first page is the name of the typist or script girl, but sometimes I find myself wondering "When did Milton Berle start that shtick of dressing up as a woman?"

Jack Webb starred on ABC radio as morose Pat Novak.

He Walked by Night

ALTHOUGH JACK WEBB'S BEST-KNOWN SERIES was *Dragnet*, more than a few devotees of old-time radio savor his appearances on another show even more. Before Webb walked the streets of Los Angeles as monotonic Joe Friday, he haunted the docks of San Francisco as colorful Pat Novak.

Pat Novak for Hire actually served as Webb's springboard to *Dragnet*. A West Coast version had aired in 1946-1947, but *Pat Novak for Hire* did not reach a national audience until February 13, 1949 over ABC. On June 3, 1949, even before *Pat Novak for Hire* finished its run, Webb had already started asking witnesses and suspects for the facts as LAPD's crime-fighting sergeant on NBC. After the June 25th broadcast, Pat Novak took the proverbial long walk off a short pier and should have sunk into oblivion.

Why *Pat Novak for Hire* keeps bobbing to the surface decades after its demise is not easy to explain to someone who has never heard any of the episodes. Part of the fascination with the program is that, remarkably, its flaws are its strengths. Saturated with hard-boiled characters, hopelessly entangled story lines, ludicrous similes, and dialogue that is often spewed rather than spoken, *Pat Novak for Hire* achieves that rarified level of camp: the show is its own parody.

Another reason the program refuses to go away is that *Pat Novak for Hire* is perhaps the best example of *radio noir* (or, given Novak's proclivity for receiving beatings, *radio noir et bleu*.) A tone of pessimistic fatalism pervades the stories as cynical loners and losers jostle while grabbing for the brass ring which ultimately eludes them all. Foghorns, solitary footsteps, and forlorn theme music convey a mood befitting shallow, devious people moving in a world of shadows and intrigue.

Pat Novak stepped out of those shadows to announce that he rented boats and did "anything else that's cash and carry." For some reason all sorts of nefarious types seemed driven to Novak, who was no detective public or private, to act as an intermediary to pick up a package in a boat, deliver a geranium plant, follow a woman carrying a green bag, find a horse, etc. Invariably bodies started falling and Novak found himself the scapegoat. Week after week villains played Novak for a chump and, stubborn cuss that he was, Pat kept sticking his chin out for more. It's no wonder some folks called him Patsy.

Once corpses, guns, and other incriminating evidence appeared in Novak's apartment it was only a matter of moments before Inspector Hellman (Raymond Burr) arrived on the scene, dragging the hangman's noose he always carried with him which, by no coincidence, fit perfectly around Pat's neck.

Hellman seemed determined to place every murder from the shooting of Dan McGrew forward at Novak's doorstep. "You're a small-time waterfront punk," he snarled. "I don't like you and I'm gonna hang you by your heels." He became so obsessed with capturing his quarry that he often leaped over legalities such as the time he wanted to take Novak down to headquarters shortly after finding a dead woman's body, prompting Pat to bark, "Get out of your haze, Hellman. You don't even know who's dead yet, but you're going to book somebody."

Hellman, a brutish sort who too often employed his fists more than his brain, enjoyed goading Novak into making insolent remarks such as "You couldn't find a moose in a bathtub," "You can't find your back pocket with radar," or "You couldn't track down a live bear in a phone booth," and then cuffed him with impunity, knowing that his adversary could not return the blows without being arrested for striking a police officer.

The verbal sparring between Hellman and Novak became one of the highlights of every program as the two combatants circled each other relentlessly, looking for openings to launch vituperative assaults. The animosity present in the rapid-fire insults and accusations was so palpable one suspects that Burr and Webb themselves might have been close to throwing some punches with their punch lines.

Novak and Hellman were more akin than different. When claiming that Hellman possessed a disposition like a ton of rhubarb and had a heart "big enough to hide behind a piece of birdseed," Novak could have been describing himself. He regarded the living, the dead, and the dying with equal disdain. Seconds after hauling a wounded man into his boat, Pat told him to "pick another place to die. Go back in the bay to die where you'll have company." Finding a body in his apartment, he muttered, "He wasn't a good enough guy to bleed in the living room so I dragged him in the kitchen and left by the back door."

Novak could not even exchange pleasantries with a bank clerk; his response to "Isn't it a good morning?" was "If it's your choice, stay with it."

Novak's choice made him a fitting noir protagonist for his every action seemed founded on one motive: self-preservation. As he walked through his purlieus of rancid alleys, raucous arenas and racetracks, flea-bitten lunchrooms, seedy hotels that "in a good season couldn't draw transient mice," clammy morgues, and tawdry nightclubs lit up with enough neon to "light up a main intersection in heaven," his solitary goal seemed to be to brush up against death almost constantly without getting any of it on him.

When in his usual spot, aptly described by Hellman as "peeking from behind the eight ball," Novak sought help in one of the city's watering holes from "the only honest guy I know," Jocko Madigan (Tudor Owen). What Novak wanted from the ex-doctor, now a full-time souse, was a legman to uncover leads that might extricate him from his predicament, but, before he could spill his story, he was forced to listen to an assessment of his character like an errant son being lectured by a long-suffering father.

For someone in a perpetual stupor, Madigan acutely evaluated human nature. He pegged Novak perfectly in his diatribes: "You have no moral sense. All you have is a small bundle of regrets, something you drag out periodically as proof of your decency...You're hopeless, Patsy. You're like some overripe planet disemboweled from the skies. You don't know where you're going and where you've been...You move in the twilight zone between good and evil without any predisposition toward either one."

After enduring the scolding until Madigan ran out of breath or stopped to refill his glass, Novak explained his dilemma before sending the boozer off to find bits of evidence that might get him off the hook. Some of the missions took the form of simple requests to rifle through the dressers or suitcases of suspects for clues, but other errands assigned to Madigan were so vague (e.g., "Find out about Earl Hayes and see if there's a guy named Max anywhere," "Nose around about tomorrow's election," "Hit all the race rooms") that no sober person would have undertaken them. Given a business card and told, "His prints are on it. Check it out at headquarters. Find out if he's got a record," Jocko blithely started off on his assignment, leaving those at home to contemplate the sight of a tipsy philosopher staggering into a stationhouse where he is given free rein to search through police files.

But, because Novak look listeners immediately back on the trail with him, there was little time to ponder such improbabilities or other questions like what payment Madigan received for breaking into homes and visiting newspaper morgues. Sooner or later Novak encountered a femme fatale intent on seducing him into cooperating with some sultry purring. (Yvonne Peattie and, to a lesser extent, Betty Lou Gerson really steamed up the vacuum tubes with the way they delivered the lascivious innuendoes.) Although Pat often played the sucker for these smoldering women, he was not above using some arm-twisting when cornered. With Novak and his vamps, sweet nothings soon gave way to mean somethings such as a feminine promise to "throw you away like a wad of gum" and his threat to "dirty you up like a locker room towel."

Novak squirmed mightily when on the hot seat and he let everyone know about his discomfort, even when blasting armed thugs with a coarse stream of venom such as "I've met better people in sewers. Now look, meathead, I'm only going to say this once more so make a copy of it. You got the wrong guy. You think I got something. I haven't got it. So you and your pals swing out of here on your tails. I never saw you until three minutes ago and I'm tired of the friendship already."

Scriptwriter Richard Breen, a friend of Webb's, occasionally inserted a humorous line into Novak's exchanges with ruffians that would not have been out of place coming from Bob Hope's lips in one of his spy films. About to be escorted into a car for a ride by gunsels, Pat held back long enough to say, "You boys run on. I'll grab a cab" before being rudely tossed into the back seat.

Breen's most notable contribution to the program, however, came in the form of figurative language designed to capture the flavor of a Raymond Chandler novel, but when the overblown similes and metaphors emerged from Novak's mouth they sounded more like parodies dripping from the pens of humorists S.J. Perelman and James Thurber. A sampling: "It was like chasing a spider with a bowling ball." "He was as sad as a tap dancer in moccasins." "He was smiling like a vulture with a first option on a massacre." "It was like trying to put a smoke ring in your pocket." "It was so quiet you could hear a worm with whooping cough and there were enough shadows around to keep a ghost happy for years." "Her voice reminded you of a furnace filled with marshmallows." "It wasn't going to be easy. You might as well try to French fry a kettle of bones." "It was like trying to weave a rug with a spinning wheel and a bucket of sand." "I might as well have been looking for a stick with one end." "It was like trying to dance the minuet on skis." "I began to get unhappy like a three-legged man at a ballet school." "It was like offering to buy aspirin for a two-headed boy."

No listener dared cackle long over these hilarious non sequiturs because Novak had already moved on to his next set of lumps. Breen

Raymond Burr played Inspector Hellman.

utilized those interludes when Novak took inventory after recovering consciousness to evoke a sense of sordid atmosphere with descriptive portraits: "When I woke up, the rain hadn't helped the alley much. It was like washing your kid's face and finding out he was ugly to start with. The mud had washed up against the walls and there was a thick, sour smell and down the alley across the street there was part of a sign that said, 'Eats.'"

Although Breen excelled at creating mood, at times he seemed so preoccupied with inventing hard-bitten dialogue and setting scenes that he forgot he was telling a story which should follow some rules of logic. In the episode aired April 16, 1949 a gunman forced Pat and a chanteuse outside a nightclub, shot the woman three times, and then knocked Novak out, his thinking apparently being "Novak is the only eyewitness whose testimony can put me in the gas chamber, but I'll just sap him because he has to be back for next week's show."

Breen must have believed that the best way to tie up any loose ends was to kill all the criminals (on only a couple episodes did Hellman actually take someone into custody) no matter how bizarre their deaths appeared to be. Backing up proved to be particularly hazardous: one person stepped into the engine on a boat and another was trampled by a horse. A woman who watched her wounded accomplice go over an embankment decided to join him by taking a flying leap herself.

Those malefactors who lived long enough to deliver last words received no comfort from the dyspeptic Novak. To a former friend he growled, "You're a small-time bum, Sam, and you're better off dead." A woman's request to die in Pat's lap was denied with a terse "You get mercy, not love, baby," although he actually gave her neither. Sometimes he just listened to those crooks who went out in high noir style like Hilda Travers who admitted that she had "No complaints. I've always gone first class. I wouldn't have it any other way. I could've used a little more time, but I'm not greedy. Still raining out, Patsy?"

Hilda didn't live long enough to hear the weather report, but listeners knew it was always overcast in Pat Novak's world. The program concluded as it had begun with Novak walking and talking alone to the accompaniment of a foghorn. In these postmortems he reviewed the action in a series of short statements such as "He offered a cut to Craig for the heavy-duty work. Wendy was supposed to show up at 10:15. Craig would kill her and wait. When Stan showed up at 10:30, Craig was supposed to stage a fight and wound him. That way he'd be in the clear and so would Odom," but after a few sentences the listener became lost in a sea of names and double crosses. A minute or two later when the convoluted plot was totally unraveled, one wonders if Breen himself could have explained who did what to whom.

But it is the how that makes *Pat Novak for Hire* such a pleasure. The wags who insist that the show should have been called *Pat Novak for Ire* or *Pat Novak for Laughs* are not far off the mark for no other program was so intentionally dark and so unintentionally light. Jack Webb and Raymond Burr went on to better parts, but the raw ferocity present in their performances as Novak and Hellman reminds us of a time when they honed a sharper edge to their acting before they settled into their best-known role as police detective or defense attorney. *Dragnet* and *Perry Mason* are shining jewels which remain in public view whereas *Pat Novak for Hire* is like a tarnished keepsake, lying nearly forgotten in a musty cupboard. But it is still there, somewhere in the night, glowing faintly like the unpolished, rough-cut gem it is.

Edgar Bergen, the man behind Charlie McCarthy and Mortimer Snerd.

The Master's Voice

WHEN THE TOPIC OF VARIETY SHOWS is brought up among fans of old-time radio, the names of Eddie Cantor, Rudy Vallee, Bing Crosby, and other singers who acted as hosts of their programs are presented first. After some deliberation, someone might mention *The Chase and Sanborn Hour* when Edgar Bergen headlined a roster that included, at various times, Nelson Eddy, Don Ameche, W.C. Fields, Dale Evans, Abbott and Costello, Dorothy Lamour, and Ray Noble and his Orchestra. It would be well to remember that even after *The Big Show* seemed to bring down the curtain on full-scale variety shows when it signed off in 1952, Bergen was performing on CBS Sunday evenings in *The New Edgar Bergen Hour*.

The New Edgar Bergen Hour, which ran from October 1955 to July 1956, gave Edgar top billing, although "with Charlie McCarthy" was appended to the introduction before Charlie's famous threat of "I'll clip ya, Bergen, so help me, I'll mow you down" kicked off the proceedings.

Unlike earlier versions of the show, Charlie did not have a major role on *The New Edgar Bergen Hour*, his appearances usually limited to the opening routine and, occasionally, a parody to close the program. Bergen really was the star of this show, but wasn't he always?

McCarthy loved to tease his master about how Bergen sponged off his talent and that without him, Edgar would be nothing, which, in a way, was true. Audiences pictured Edgar Bergen as a well-meaning, amiable fellow, but he purposely made his naturally shy demeanor more humdrum to contrast with Charlie's impudence. We believed Bergen when he told McCarthy that he attended strictly to business and never gave a thought to girls, then added the admonition "You should be ashamed" to which Charlie replied, "You should be embalmed."

When Edgar regaled his pal with a story intended to bring impertinent Charlie back to the straight and narrow, he played the vapid square, unfolding mundane details, leaving him vulnerable to zingers like "Caesar isn't half as dead as this story." McCarthy stated his motto for living more than once: "I just love to heckle." And we loved the way Bergen could be fuddy-duddy and wise guy simultaneously.

Through Charlie, Bergen could get away with sarcastic remarks that would have seemed gauche or cruel coming from his conventional character. Thus, he could play both Dr. Bland and Mr. Snide at the same time as he did on a 1945 show when as Edgar he complimented hefty friend Elsa Maxwell on her gown, waited for Elsa's setup response of "Oh, you like it? Notice the gathering in front?" and as Charlie drove home the sassy insult: "Yes. Quite a crowd in back, too."

When Bergen reached a little deeper into his bag of tricks, he produced Mortimer Snerd who sauntered on chuckling to the accompaniment of his "down on the farm" theme song. Bergen's patience, which had been tested with McCarthy's recalcitrant attitude, was stretched further as he tried to talk sense with his fatuous creation. Even as mentor trying to reason with Mortimer, Edgar played straight man who set up the laughs as in this exchange:

Bergen: What did your father say when he got his first look at you?
Mortimer: He said, "NOOO!"
Bergen: That's not possible.
Mortimer: That's the second thing he said.
Bergen: Is your mother living yet?
Mortimer: No, not yet.

In these routines Bergen slowly increased his level of frustration until he gave up with a declaration of exasperation such as "I don't think you could learn this rhyme in a hundred years," always leaving Snerd the clincher: "Well, if you're going to put a time limit on it, I ain't even going to try."

Midway through *The New Edgar Bergen Hour* when Effie Klinker appeared, Bergen played his part in the "Miss Lonelyhearts" sketches by asking leading questions or by reading letters written to the love-scorned. Edgar treated Effie as a real lady (albeit a dirty old one) by expressing mild surprise at her romantic misadventures but hardly batting an eye when she responded to the written query "Should I try to keep slim?" with a bawdy "Slim who?"

Although Edgar may not have been raising his eyebrows in shock, he could have been moving his lips. Bergen himself poked fun at this habit by making Charlie issue comments like "I can read your lips" and then having McCarthy turn to the audience and say, "That burns him up." As Rudy Vallee stated when he introduced Bergen on his program in 1936, this vocal wizard depended more on cleverness and wit than on the believe-it-or-not nature of the act.

Bergen's unique talent took the form of creating three totally different personas other than his own so that when he spoke as a saucy hellion, a dopey bumpkin, or a spicy spinster we believed that he was conversing with another individual. Nothing in Edgar's natural speaking voice carried over into the three characters. When Charlie said, "It spoils the illusion," he was wrong because even people watching Bergen perform live were captivated by his magical way of creating the illusion of dialogue between himself and an assortment of dummies.

Bergen enhanced the effect by making the exchanges so rapid and seamless that we believed two different people were conversing. Without a breath between speeches, he engaged in give-and-take such as:

Charlie: Well, Bergen, I'll say this for your storytelling. They may not all be great…
Bergen: No, of course not.
Charlie: But they certainly are lousy.
Bergen: I see.

Bergen: Here's the first letter. "Dear Miss Klinker,"
Effie: That's me.
Bergen: Yes. "What should I do if a man gets fresh with me? Signed, Worried."
Effie: If a man gets fresh with me, I tell him a thing or two.
Bergen: What?
Effie: My address and phone number.

Bergen: You see, I'm a numismatist.
Mortimer: If you want to walk around without clothes, that's your business.
Bergen: You don't know what a numismatist is.
Mortimer: I don't even know what an old mismattress is.

Anyone who doubts Bergen's legerdemain should try this exercise: say aloud the following exchange from the June 3, 1956 show, using a normal voice for Edgar's part and a completely different voice for Mortimer's with no pauses between any of the words:

Bergen: You know, the tar pits are one of the most unusual paleontological phenomenon.
Mortimer: NOOO!

Interspersed between the bits with dummies, *The New Edgar Bergen Hour* featured musical numbers performed by Gary Crosby, Carol Richards, and the Mellomen.

Gary's appearance in the lineup may have been a favor to his famous father in an attempt to boast the younger Crosby's singing career. Unsubtle plugs about Gary's latest Decca recording or lame gags about Bing's wealth served as transparent transitions to Gary's songs, usually up-tempo numbers like "Just One of Those Things" and "Pick Yourself Up." That was for the best because when Crosby tried ballads such as "Don't Take Your Love From Me" and "I'm Always Chasing Rainbows" he dragged them out languidly as if sleepsinging. As Gary found out, singing venerable standards in the new era of rock and roll was not the way to success for a young man who had little charisma and no distinctive style of his own.

That the career of Carol Richards did not blossom further is not so easy to explain for she could handle plaintive numbers ("Look at Them," "Little Mistakes") and upbeat songs ("From This Moment On," "Hot Diggity") with equal aplomb. In addition, she proved to be a gifted companion for Charlie in sketches that required her to assume a variety of foreign dialects and delivered her lines credibly, especially in a lampoon of Little Red Riding Hood. It is too bad that her main claim to fame was behind the scenes, providing the singing voice in movie musicals for dancers Vera-Ellen and Cyd Charisse.

Gary and Carol, along with the Mellomen, who frequently backed the leads as well as having one number of their own such as "I've Got My Love to Keep Me Warm," benefited considerably from the arranging skills of Ray Noble. Noble's touch was unobtrusive, yet by adding a cha-cha beat to Carol's rendition of "I Could Have Danced All Night" and a melancholy coda to Crosby's "One for My Baby," he distinguished them from other versions being heard at the time.

Ray also served as show interrupter who appeared occasionally to deliver a gag and some lines of the "I say, old things, and other such quaint British expressions" variety and ask silly questions when confronted with subjects like the River Styx ("Well, I say, if it does, why don't they oil it?") or early plays being done in old Greece ("I say, wasn't that a bit rancid?").

But Noble did not have the corniest lines because they had been reserved for the show's resident reprobate, Jack Kirkwood, who appeared weekly in either the Poet's Corner or the Do-It-Yourself Department. As Poet Laureate of the city dump, he composed doggerel with hokey titles such as "Life—Without it, You're Dead" and a song called "There Are So Many Holes in My Mattress, It Might As Well Be Spring," prompting Bergen to say one night, "You aren't bound by any laws of music or poetry, are you?"

When it came to the handyman department, Kirkwood wasn't bound by any laws, period. He used upholstery taken from an old couch for his toupee kit so his customers got mohair for their money, promoted a bookmaking kit he used on his wife after betting her she wouldn't marry him and she called his bluff and raised him five, and a housebreaking kit he used when burglarizing a women's lingerie shop ("quite an undietaking"). In the how-to-vulcanize-your-girdle skit, Jack leaped on his chance to put a twist on one of his pet sayings from *The Bob Hope Show*, "put something in the pot, boy," by telling Edgar that his host needed one of his kits to "put the pot in something." When Bergen expressed dismay at the scoundrel's gimmicks, denouncing him as "without a doubt the most unscrupulous, conniving, unprincipled, dishonest rogue I have ever met," the unrepentant knave responded with a jovial "Please, no hero worship."

Bergen showed himself to be a good sport in the exchanges with Kirkwood by playing straight man which left him wide open for cutting remarks about his expanding waistline or receding hairline, using old or borrowed jokes, and living off the earnings of others.

In the second half of the program, as a counterbalance to the melodies and mirth, a "Meet the People" segment allowed Bergen a chance to interview interesting people from many different walks of life. While Bergen and cast devoted most of the show to entertaining the audience, this portion provided some edification as Edgar asked experts on, for example, juvenile delinquency or air pollution, their perspectives regarding major social or health issues. Other Sundays he talked with an assemblyman from Nevada about gambling, a woman who had traveled alone around the world about her adventures, and a jockey about his experiences at Santa Anita and other tracks. The advice given by nutritionist Adelle Davis about our eating habits and the cultivation of crops as well as a warning about the greenhouse effect by an oceanographer seem as pertinent now as then. Joe Pasternak's rags-to-riches story is a touching account of determination, humility, and patriotism that Bergen wisely let the producer of numerous MGM musicals tell with little prompting.

But the best-remembered conversations occurred when Edgar purposefully interacted with the interviewees. The dialogue with the president of the Los Angeles Audubon Society contained some instructive information about birding, then turned facetious when Edgar's attempts to do bird calls fell flat and his appeals to the bird expert took the form of waggish invitations ("Could you give us a smattering of that?") that delighted the audience. His discussion with actress Shirley Yamaguchi, which provided some insights into the role of women in American and oriental cultures, served to be just the prelude for a bit in which Edgar played a slightly hammy Romeo while Shirley (as Juliet) spoke in her native tongue. After Shirley released a torrent of words from the balcony scene in Japanese, Bergen nearly brought down the house with a line certainly not in the play: "Well, there is that, too, of course."

After the final musical selection, *The New Edgar Bergen Hour* usually concluded with a segment in which Edgar presided as referee of an unruly panel consisting of Noble, Kirkwood, and Snerd. John Hiestand announced the bit as "Edgar Bergen and his End Table," although a more fitting title would have been "It Pays to be Indifferent." Bergen acted as pompous moderator during discussions of lofty topics such as "Whither politics?" and "Whither etiquette?," but his effort to compliment his colleagues with titles like "most-honored confreres" was met with "What'd he call us?" and his scolding "I'm thoroughly disgusted with my panel tonight. Are you interested?" received a curt "Not a bit."

Professor Kirkwood, ever the lovable rascal, dipped into his depository of wheezes and announced proudly that he had graduated with Dr. Scholl "at the foot of the class." Professor Noble, who had done graduate work at the University of Eagle Rock where he had studied how to rock eagles, proffered his opinion that marriage is one thing every husband and wife should have in common. Mortimer seemed more assertive when sitting among his mental equals than when answering questions alone perched on his master's knee, saucily countering Bergen's query of "Where was I?" with "You were sitting right up there…laying an egg" and responding to Kirkwood's affront of "You've got the brain of an idiot" with "You want it back?"

Bergen continued to dispense leading questions (e.g., "What do you think got Marilyn Monroe all those wonderful parts?") and express dismay over the asinine answers he received ("All those wonderful parts") until, with a sob in his voice, he concluded the session with a list of polysyllabic adjectives intended to shame the pundits like *disputatious, argumentative, equivocal,* and *reprehensible,* but before he could finish his tirade Kirkwood and Noble let the air out of his bombastic balloon by squelching him with "Aw, shut up!"

After the last commercial, rural philosopher Mortimer delivered "Snerd's Words for the Birds," a jocular take on an adage (e.g., "Let sleeping dogs lie. You should tell the truth"), before Edgar bid everyone good night.

It is unfortunate that after *The New Edgar Bergen Hour* left the air, radio essentially bid goodbye to Bergen and that he bid the world goodbye in 1978. To this day the show is a forgotten treasure in need of rediscovery for it provided a smorgasbord of entertainment including hummable tunes, satiric sketches, thought-provoking interviews, and fast-paced routines slathered with good-natured ribbing and none of the stultifying longueurs that hampered *The Big Show*. Even more regrettable is that the star of the program, if he is remembered at all, is known to many people as the father of the woman who played Murphy Brown.

The Edgar Bergen displayed in Candace Bergen's *Knock Wood* comes close to personifying the Latin phrase *vox et praeterea nihil* (a voice, and nothing more), a man quite comfortable with "son" Charlie but ill-at-ease when conversing with his daughter. Such a revelation should not have been totally unexpected for Edgar had been alone for so long both onstage (he started performing as a teenager) and off (he did not marry until the age of forty-two) that McCarthy's usual comeback after one of Bergen's fluffs, "I'm practically doing a single," now seems more an unconscious confession of lifestyle than a putdown.

The man who spent his career talking to himself is still talking to us if we would only listen. Lines spoken over fifty years ago still have the power to amuse. Listen to the words on paper and the voices come alive:

> Bergen: You won't give me away.
> Charlie: No. Who would have you?
>
> Bergen: Have you lost weight?
> Mortimer: No. Did you lose some?
>
> Bergen: What should I do about biting insects?
> Effie: Why, try to cure yourself of the habit.

Four different voices, four separate personalities, one master conjurer who can still cast a spell.

In the midst of a good mood Charlie once told Edgar, "Remember when I used to say you were stingy, cranky, lazy, and untalented? Well, pick one of them and I'll take it back." *I* say that Edgar Bergen, comedian and vocal illusionist, was quick-witted, gracious, creative, talented, and one of the most underrated radio performers in the twentieth century, and I won't take any of that back.

Herb Vigran, bit player so often on radio and TV and in films, got one brief chance to star on *Sad Sack*.

Forgotten Shows to Remember

SINCE THEIR HEYDAY THERE HAS NEVER BEEN any shortage of praise for the first rank of shows which included *Fibber McGee and Molly, The Bob Hope Show, The Jack Benny Program, Vic and Sade,* and *The Fred Allen Show*. Even second-tier favorites like *Duffy's Tavern, The Life of Riley, The Great Gildersleeve,* and *My Favorite Husband* have loyal fans. But there are a number of also-rans, comedies that finished out of the money and are nearly forgotten. So let's blow the dust off a few curiosities buried in radio's attic and shed a little light on five neglected series.

What unites this handful of shows is that each features actors who were primarily supporting players on the air. Even if for only a few months on a program which served as a summer replacement, these veterans finally earned an opportunity to be headliners for a change.

Harry Einstein, who had mangled the King's English as Parkyakarkus on *The Eddie Cantor Show*, continued his assault upon the language in *Meet Me at Parky's* from June 1945 to April 1947 on NBC. Though Parky's restaurant had an urban location, the humor smacked of the country with slow-talking orchestra leader Opie Cates providing many homey gags from the Lum and Abner school of humor. One night, asked if his brother had a sheepskin, Opie replied, "No, his face is wrinkled like that all the time" to which the attorney brother added, "That's good. A sheepskin. Not baaaad" to which Parky said, "Instead of a lawyer, I've got plenty of mutton." After a half hour of these drolleries one begins to wonder if Parky worked in a beanery or a corncrib.

The scripts generally focused on keeping the eatery solvent or Parky out of romantic entanglements. One can quibble about the lukewarm chestnuts being served (the wheeze about following the doctor's advice to take pills and then skip a day and eventually growing tired of skipping constituted one of the nails in vaudeville's coffin), yet the steady stream of patter made the thirty minutes lively for the audience who seemed willing to laugh and overlook the ill-timed interruptions. Songs by David Street and Betty Rhodes were inserted at odd times such as a number by Betty shoehorned into a courtroom scene just before the verdict as if the writers had almost forgotten her that week. However, the commercials for Old Gold cigarettes flowed nicely into the action by commonly having customers at the counter introduce the product.

Another program sponsored by Old Gold provided Herb Vigran, a busy actor known more for his voice than his name because of the bit parts he played on many shows, a chance to march to the forefront as *The Sad Sack*, taking Frank Sinatra's spot on CBS when the singer took his summer break in 1946. Just as Arthur Q. Bryan changed his normal voice when slipping into his Elmer Fudd character so Vigran adopted a squeaky voice to match the meek personality of Sad Sack. He also apparently dressed the part in the studio because the audience exploded with laughter a number of times before he even spoke his first line.

There to take advantage of the chump lurked glib Chester Fenwick (Jim Backus) and not far away stood sympathetic girlfriend Lucy Twitchell (Sandra Gould) with glowering Mr. Twitchell (Ken Christy) perched nearby to monitor the degree of comfort given by his daughter. The predictable situations found Chester or Mr. Twitchell using the malleable Sad Sack to serve their purposes. The jokes are passable if a bit obvious (e.g., Chester says that he gave up steak so the boys in the military could have Spam). Some scenes that showed promise, like the mistaken identity one in which the Sad Sack, thinking he is interviewing for a job as insect exterminator when the position is actually one of playground director, flounder because the idea is woefully underwritten and, instead of hilariously putting his foot in his mouth as Jim Jordan and Phil Harris did in similar situations on their programs, he merely leaves a bad taste in ours because the situation falls flat.

After listening to the shows one longs for more of brash Chester, a vivacious conniver of the Phil Silvers "Glad to see ya" ilk, whereas the Sad Sack is just, well, sad.

Cousin Willie, the titular character of the NBC series that served as a replacement for *Fibber McGee and Molly* during the summer of 1953, could have suffered from the same blandness as the Sad Sack had not his sincerity and innate kindness elevated him above that of a patsy. Bill Idelson brought much of the ingenuousness of Rush Gook, the adolescent he had played on *Vic and Sade*, to this role as semi-permanent guest from

Milwaukee at the home of Californians Marvin (Marvin Miller) Sample and Fran (Patricia Dunlap) Sample.

When the announcer set the stage with "This one is about Cousin Willie," it must have been rewarding for Idelson to know that he had stepped to the head of the class. As with *Vic and Sade*, most of the humor on *Cousin Willie* was low-key with few "nudge in the ribs" gags. Even the broader witticisms leaned more toward cute than corny (e.g., after Marvin learned of Willie's mooning over his girl Freckles, he diagnosed the problem immediately: "He has spots before his eyes").

Arthur Treacher played a key role on *The Smiths of Hollywood*.

Certainly at ease in this part, Idelson expanded his Rush characterization to become a young George Bailey or Jefferson Smith, the type of honest role model portrayed on the screen by James Stewart, a person worth rooting for and caring about. When Freckles joined Willie watching birds after a date with the boss's arrogant son, good had been vindicated and the "square" got the girl after all.

Cousin Willie also rose above other shows built solely on a foundation of gags in that it handled parody and satire deftly. Barney Phillips, who actually played Joe Friday's partner on *Dragnet*, showed up to investigate a possible confidence man as Wash Tuesday, a cop who mocked the terse procedural dialogue favored by Jack Webb with a monosyllabic vocabulary, answering just about any statement with "Right."

An episode about Willie's date with shallow movie star Gloria LaPlunge flung well-aimed arrows at the Hollywood diet of frequent divorces, tawdry possessions, and false publicity. Through the various temptations Willie retained his virtue and returned to his true love, Freckles.

The show biz lifestyle also received a roasting from *The Smiths of Hollywood*, a syndicated series that aired on Mutual in 1947. Harry Von Zell, announcer and sidekick to Eddie Cantor, played attorney Bill Smith, although he could not truly be called the star of the program for he had to share space in the scripts with Arthur Treacher as sponging Uncle Cecil, wife Nancy (Brenda Marshall), and daughter Shirley aka "Bumps" (Jan Ford aka Terry Moore).

Tyler McVey, who announced as well as acted in various roles, introduced the program as "a different half hour of radio." He could have added, "Different, not necessarily better." One difference is that the writers got by with a few racy lines and situations that usually felt the sting of the red pencil. In one episode Uncle Cecil, upon finding himself in Lucille Ball's darkened bedroom, was asked by the redhead, "You are coming to bed, aren't you? Don't people usually go to bed at night?" Cecil's response, "Fantastic place, Hollywood," brought down the house. Another week Bill called his wife on the phone.

> Bill: This is the father of your children.
> Nancy: Bill?
> Bill: Now wait a minute…

Thankfully, the plot veered in another direction quickly before the audience could ponder over the implications of that exchange. The writers probably counted on that for the situations in *The Smiths of Hollywood* were constructed on ground more shaky than the San Andreas Fault. The whole bedroom scene hinged on the assumption that Lucy could mistake the voice of Treacher, as British as fish and chips, for that of her husband, Cuban Desi Arnaz. The contrivance of Nancy becoming a private secretary for William Holden (a red herring who did not appear) led to a futile attempt to hire a pretty maid in order to make Nancy jealous, culminating in a resolution conveniently handled offstage. McVey's closing comment of "Buck up, radio could be worse" was a straight line undoubtedly answered in dozens of ways in hundreds of homes in 1947.

But radio could be better and it was in 1950 when second bananas Gale Gordon and Bea Benaderet starred in *Granby's Green Acres*, half of the summer replacement for *The Lux Radio Theatre* on CBS. Gordon played John Granby, an ex-banker who knew little about farming and proved it every week, much to the chagrin and amusement of wife Martha (Bea), daughter Janice (Louise Erickson), and hired hand Eb (Parley Baer).

Granby displayed more facets of character than despotic Osgood Conklin on *Our Miss Brooks* or hot-tempered Homer LaTrivia on *Fibber McGee and Molly* as Farmer John repeatedly tried to extricate himself from the consequences of imprudent decisions. Louise, cast in boy-infatuated situations on *The Great Gildersleeve* and *A Date with Judy*, took advantage of her chance to be more sarcastic and flippant than usual by offering her lines with sassy relish while Bea adopted a maternal nature that would be expanded further on television's *Petticoat Junction*. Outside of his long run as Chester on *Gunsmoke*, the role of Eb stands as Baer's best continuing role on radio, allowing him some of the funniest lines on the show, including the reason why Eb still attended family gatherings once a decade: "It makes the nine years between reunions worth living."

Chuckles of another sort occurred during the weekly visit with Will Kimble (Howard McNear for the first episode, Horace Murphy thereafter), an absent-minded storekeeper whose befuddlement frustrated Granby to the breaking point where he became apprehensive of using phrases intended to close conversations for fear he would be called Mr. Skipit by the confused Kimble.

Jay Sommers, creator and head writer of the series, played his ace in carefully-constructed set pieces designed to utilize Gordon's slow burn and matchless variety of comedic inflection to maximum effect. One, in which Granby suffered through repeated interruptions while trying to add figures at a table while Martha and Janice came through opposite doors looking for each other, is a brilliantly-paced "waiting for the other shoe to drop" scene that works best in the theater of the mind. Another extended sequence took place at the supper table as an unexpected guest grabbed all the food before it reached John and we got all the laughs as Granby passed on full helpings of muttered comments to us.

Tasty as it was that summer, *Granby's Green Acres* didn't catch on. Gordon went back to his recurring roles on other radio comedies and Benaderet slipped into the part of Blanche Morton on *The Burns and Allen Show* when George and Gracie moved to television that fall. But Sommers knew the idea of a city boy out of his element in the country had legs so he stretched them again fifteen years later with the same network in a different medium. *Green Acres*, a hit from 1965 to 1971 on CBS television, can be found playing perpetually in Rerunland.

Not so with the radio shows that slipped through the cracks of the ether. If not for archivists and collectors, these programs might have been lost forever. If what we hear today does not measure up to the standards set by Benny, Allen, Hope, Red Skelton, Edgar Bergen and others, that doesn't mean that they were poor. B pictures served a purpose by providing worthwhile entertainment and so it was with B radio. What's fair is fair and fair is, if not good, not bad.

Fred Allen with his best radio lineup.

The Best Years of Our Lives

THERE SEEMS TO BE A WIDELY-HELD BELIEF that radio's finest hours occurred during the 1930s and World War II and that after 1945 the quality of programming experienced a steady decline until the early fifties when radio was swept into irrelevancy by the intrusion of televisions into America's living rooms. This opinion, perhaps fostered in part by photographs of Depression-era families gathered around bulky consoles or illustrations of cathedral sets on the covers of books devoted to old-time radio, the numerous salutes to Bob Hope after his death which highlighted the way his program went on the road to entertain the troops months before the attack on Pearl Harbor, and the trumpeting of the Mercury Theater's version of *The War of the Worlds* on the panic-filled evening of October 30, 1938 as the medium's most famous broadcast, may be prevalent, but it is hardly accurate. Anyone who actually listens to the full spectrum of network radio will attest to the fact that its best years were after the end of World War II.

    A case that proves this assertion is a show that remains a favorite of many people, *The Jack Benny Program*. Although some of the earlier Benny broadcasts have historical significance like the episodes in 1937 when Jack meets Rochester or buys his Maxwell or activates his portion of the feud with Fred Allen, far too many of them have the flavor of vaudeville sketches in which Jack, Mary Livingstone, and Phil Harris toss jokes and insults back and forth, and Kenny Baker's inane remarks seem forced when compared with the more natural daffiness of Dennis Day which came later.

    The parodies, like casting Snow White with a gang of crooks in 1939 and spoofs of *Casablanca* and *Algiers* in 1943, plus the first appearances of Mel Blanc and Frank Nelson gave a foretaste of what was to come, but it was not until December of 1945 with the start of the "I Can't Stand Jack Benny" contest and the introduction of the Ronald Colmans that *The Jack Benny Program* picked up comic steam. 1946 marked the first appearance of Artie Auerbach as Mr. Kitzel, the return of Dennis Day from the Navy, and the addition of the Sportsmen, any of whom could drive Jack nuts. Beginning with a December 1946 show, Benny got his chance to return the favor with his holiday torture of the unlucky store clerk (Blanc), who did almost as much unwrapping over the years as Gypsy Rose Lee.

In 1946 and after the running gags took off at a full gallop: visits to railroad stations highlighted by Blanc's call for the perpetual train leaving for Anaheim, Azusa, and Cucamonga; the "Your money or your life" episode in 1948 which precipitated a search for an Oscar that lasted two months, followed later that year by the recurring echo and "Did you hunt bear?" bits; hilarious visits from IRS representatives in 1951; casual meetings with eccentrics "Know Nothing" Benny Rubin, terse tout Sheldon Leonard, and wisecracking waitress Iris Adrian; repetition of lyrics from Jack's pathetic song for which *he* should have begged our pardon; "Dreer Poosen," "grass reek," plus other noteworthy fluffs; and the marvelous lampoons of *The Treasure of the Sierra Madre* and *High Noon* that featured the Benny-Blanc exchanges which made us "*si*" the humor while laughing so hard we had to "Sy."

Even though Bob Crosby could not adequately fill Harris's wobbly shoes when Phil left in 1952, *The Jack Benny Program* remained consistently funny through the last episode three years later. Ask anyone who has listened to the entire range of shows from 1932 to 1955 to select the ten most amusing episodes and, if he or she doesn't choose the majority of them from the last decade of the series when Jack's teammates included not only his usual cast but also the "irregulars" (Blanc, Nelson, Bea Benaderet, et al.), rush that person to the hospital for treatment of a dislocated funny bone.

Just as Benny's early programs seemed stagy, so the banter between George Burns and Gracie Allen sounded like warmed-over routines from their days at The Palace until 1942 when the team abandoned tiresome gimmicks like Gracie's run for the presidency and extended bits about her dotty relatives for domestic comedy emanating from the Burns home. Adding guest stars to the mix brought more variety to *The Burns and Allen Show* so Gracie could hatch her harebrained schemes with other personalities. The episodes from 1949 are particularly outstanding with appearances from baffled James Mason, bewildered Jane Wyman, chagrined Howard Duff as incarcerated Sam Spade, and two visits from Jack Benny.

But the program did not need celebrities to score with audiences, just members of the Beverly Hills Uplift Society, the Mortons next door, or miscellaneous characters to stir the plot. When they left radio for TV in 1950, George and Gracie were right at the top of their form, leaving them laughing with memorable episodes that year like the one in which Gracie literally drives a tax accountant out the window of their home with her wacky deductions.

Unlike the Burnses and Benny, Fred Allen did not become a success on television nor did his radio show reach the 1950s. While it is true that radio was his métier, episodes of *Town Hall Tonight* and *The Texaco Star Theater* have not aged as well as the post-war shows because the sixty-minute broadcasts featured padded interviews with college students, newsreels of weekly events that seem arcane or archaic now, and novelty acts that do not play well on radio. Allen, being the inveterate improviser, tried to keep things lively like ad-libbing freely during the infamous eagle incident, but the strain was showing both on the air and off so that finally hypertension from producing so much material every week pushed Fred off the treadmill to oblivion in 1944.

When he hopped back on in the fall of 1945 as the star of the half-hour *Fred Allen Show*, both he and the program seem fitter. There was no fluff but plenty of fun in this version which moved briskly from badinage between Fred and wife Portland Hoffa to a visit to Allen's Alley featuring fresh, irrepressible Senator Claghorn, laconic Titus Moody, garrulous Ajax Cassidy, and long-suffering Mrs. Nussbaum to a bouncy number by the DeMarco Sisters to a visit from guests such as George Jessel, Bing Crosby, Basil Rathbone, and friendly foe Jack Benny. Fred's ratings may have been in decline by the time the program left the air for good due to stiff competition, but the pacing and the punch remained vibrant right through to the finale on June 26, 1949 when Allen, Benny, and Henry Morgan showed what it meant to go down swinging.

Another program that improved with a change of duration and format was *Amos 'n' Andy*. Accounts of the show's popularity among presidents and with author George Bernard Shaw and of theater owners piping broadcasts to their audiences notwithstanding, the cold fact remains that many of the episodes from the 1930s are not very amusing due to rambling stories and dialogue between characters assumed by Freeman Gosden and Charles Correll which frequently lacked punch lines. A marked improvement occurred in the fall of 1943 when the program shifted from fifteen minutes five times a week to a half hour weekly, and guests like Ginger Rogers and Charles Coburn appeared to enlarge the scope of the narratives. However, the broadcasts from the 1943-1944 season seem stagnant when compared with what was heard during the post-war years. The latter shows featured a wonderful cast of Ernestine Wade, Amanda

Randolph, Lou Lubin, Johnny Lee, Eddie Green, and James Baskett, who, as Gabby Gibson, one of the glibbest talkers ever heard on the air, added "Lovely, lovely" to the catch phrases of the decade.

Episodes of *Amos 'n' Andy* from 1950 through 1952 are as funny as any aired in the entire series, aided not only by some of the regulars listed above but also by the best comic support available. For example, on the April 2, 1950 broadcast Joseph Kearns, Alan Reed, Verna Felton, and Shirley Mitchell added their considerable talents to those of Gosden and Correll.

Fibber McGee and Molly also benefited immensely from a strong supporting cast. Bill Thompson aided Jim and Marian Jordan almost from the beginning of the series, appearing first as Nick Depopolis in 1936, then adding bombastic Horatio K. Boomer, and the more-enduring characters of Old Timer and Wallace Wimple. Both Isabel Randolph as snooty Mrs. Uppington and Harold Peary playing blustery Throckmorton P. Gildersleeve also came on board in the 1930s.

Despite Jim Jordan's claim that the 1939 episode in which Gildersleeve assumed the role of butler for the McGees is the funniest in the series, the pre-war shows are far from the cream of the Wistful Vista crop. Marian was absent from many of those broadcasts and even on the shows on which she appeared her harsh Irish brogue seemed to harangue her husband as much as help him.

The introduction of Gale Gordon as Mayor LaTrivia in October 1941 filled the void left when Peary left to star in his own show but only for a while. After Gordon and Thompson joined branches of the military, Shirley Mitchell as boarder and Marlin Hurt as cook came into the McGee household and Arthur Q. Bryan became the weekly visitor as Doctor Gamble. The war episodes are very patriotic and capture the atmosphere of what domestic life was like during that period as well as any comedy show on the air, but, truth be told, Alice Darling was more cute than funny and Beulah more a curiosity than a panic.

The return of Gordon in October 1945 and Thompson in January 1946 marked the beginning of the best of times for *Fibber McGee and Molly*. The McGees adroitly steered LaTrivia into his best blowups ever, including taking the bull by the horns in December 1948, skating on thin ice in February 1950, and taking a grain of salt in April of 1952. In his kit bag of voices, Thompson brought back from the war an Irish policeman who issued mushy sentiments as if his whistle had lodged in his palate, and, later, a streetcar conductor who called off the names of streets with all the clarity of a yodeler gargling with marbles.

In 1949 Richard LeGrand joined the cast as Ole Swenson, a Swedish janitor whose misinterpretation of colloquial expressions added gentle fun to the show. But *Fibber McGee and Molly* hit the high note of hilarity in 1950 and 1951 when the oddballs assumed by Cliff Arquette entangled the couple in witty name games that are as risible as the best Abbott and Costello routines. The superb timing of the Jordans who, as teasers of LaTrivia and the parties being provoked by Arquette, is wonderfully exhibited on these shows. The McGees could take it and they could also dish it out for us to enjoy.

At the conclusion of the October 14, 1947 broadcast after Molly squelched the effect of one of his puns, Fibber said, "Well, it's hard to hold that terrific pace right to the end," a truism that might apply to other comedy series but not this one. After the main comic force behind the show, Don Quinn, left to oversee *The Halls of Ivy* (itself a shining example of witty radio comedy from the early 1950s), co-writer Phil Leslie kept the dialogue at a high level. Even the fifteen-minute *Fibber McGee and Molly* shows aired from 1953 to 1956 are entertaining.

In the fifties Bryan and LeGrand were still traveling between Wistful Vista and Summerfield to take on the parts of Floyd Munson and Richard Peavey respectively on *The Great Gildersleeve*, radio's top spin-off. They joined the program in 1942 to add variety to the show by providing Gildersleeve more interaction with characters outside of his family and Judge Horace Hooker. Soon wild goose chases in the manner of *The Aldrich Family* gave way to more realistic situations, although the ill-fated engagements between Gildy and Leila Ransom in 1943 and Eve Goodwin in 1944 seem as concocted to fail as Andy's amorous misadventures on *Amos 'n' Andy* which ended up in courts instead of churches, and they do not capture the nostalgia, warmth, and humor of the post-war offerings. The picnic episode of June 9, 1946, for example, is one of radio's best examples of capturing what a summer day in Anytown, U.S.A. sounded like, and the June 4, 1947 broadcast that takes us from Summerfield's movie theater to the theater of the mind is imaginative radio at its best.

As soon as Jack Meakin took charge of the program's music in the fall of 1945 he put a bounce in the theme song, composed a playful bridge that announced visits to Peavey's Pharmacy, and created animated chords to match the show's action such as mimicking Gildy's trips up and down stairs and ladders and his footsteps as he walked along the sidewalk.

Adding Gale Gordon as irascible neighbor Rumson Bullard in 1948 also punched up the show as did focusing more attention on Leroy which allowed him to prod, perplex, and sometimes please his uncle while amusing us. When Willard Waterman took over from Harold Peary as Gildersleeve in 1950, the show scarcely missed a beat because the characters we had grown to love, mercurial Gildy, mossback Peavey, grandiloquent Hooker, and mischievous Leroy, still had the power to amuse.

Red Skelton had been saying amusing things on the air since 1939, but after he returned from the Army in 1945 he brought with him a full arsenal of comic characters including Clem Kiddlehopper, Cauliflower McPugg, Deadeye, Junior, San Fernando Red, and Willie Lump-Lump. *The Red Skelton Show* retained its popularity right into 1952 when Red's long-running television show began.

When Skelton was drafted in 1944, it opened the door at 1847 Rogers Road for his band leader, Ozzie Nelson, and his singer, Harriet Hilliard, to begin having *The Adventures of Ozzie and Harriet*. Like the tubes in a radio, it took a while for the show to warm up, but by 1948 the battle of the sexes was going strong as impulsive Ozzie often found himself out on the shaky limbs of bold challenges and misguided projects. The recurrent themes of a lack of willpower and the folly of indecision kept the Nelson household jumping and audiences chuckling right into 1954, the last year of the radio series.

Other humorous programs started late and finished strong. *Our Miss Brooks*, very likely radio's best comedy show whose debut occurred after the end of World War II, ran from 1948 to 1957 and remains a listening treat due primarily to the peerless delivery of Eve Arden and Gale Gordon. Close runner-up, *The Phil Harris-Alice Faye Show*, brought laughter into millions of homes from 1948 to 1954. Other notable series of the period include *My Favorite Husband* (1948-1951), *Life with Luigi* (1948-1953), *A Day in the Life of Dennis Day* (1946-1951), and *My Friend Irma* (1947-1954). And, oh yes, scowling over in the corner to which the star has been relegated as radio's bad boy, *The Henry Morgan Show* (1946-1950).

But laughs weren't all that radio provided. *Suspense* dispensed chills from 1942 to 1962. While some famous episodes such as "Sorry, Wrong Number" and "The Most Dangerous Game" were broadcast first early in the series and performed again in later years, most of the terrifying and intriguing stories were heard after V-J Day including these thrillers that kept listeners on tenterhooks right to the end: "The Dunwich Horror" and "The House in Cypress Canyon," nightmares par excellence; the pulse-pounding claustrophobia of "On a Country Road" and "The Waxwork"; "3 O'Clock" and "Dead Ernest," masterful races against time; and the eerie "Ghost Hunt" which leaves us wondering "Can such things be?" A number of broadcasts from the late forties and early fifties not only have intriguing plots but also feature performers usually known for comedy like Ozzie and Harriet, Danny Kaye, Benny, Skelton, and the Jordans in serious roles.

The Whistler also began telling his strange tales in 1942. The early stories he unfolded were more peculiar than weird, filled with melodramatic tirades about family insanity, nocturnal masquerades by spectral

The success of *My Friend Irma* on the air carried over to TV and motion pictures.

figures appearing by bedsides trying to scare relatives to death, and unconvincing twists of fate explained by the narrator rather than revealed by the characters. By the late 1940s the fright wigs had been replaced by a well-paced mystery program in which the denouement unveiled in the final vignette may have been unexpected but credible. The program may have reached its apogee in 1948 when it aired "Search for a Woman" and "Tough Guy," expertly-constructed tales told in flashback that conclude with a bang; "Chain Reaction," a noirish maze of double crosses; and the whimsical speculation of "What Makes a Murderer?" As late as 1955 *The Whistler* could still be heard walking by night, deftly hiding the trump card in the shadows until the last moment.

From 1947 to 1954 *Escape*, radio's premier adventure series, allowed listeners to get away from it all. Sometimes the flights of imagination to the land of "She" and "The Country of the Blind" delivered the promised life of romantic adventure. Other times we almost wished we had stayed at home for, after being exposed to the harrowing "Evening Primrose," "Three Skeleton Key," or "Leiningen vs. the Ants," we could never look at a mannequin, lighthouse, or anthill in the same way again.

Similarly, after hearing the dramatized stories of Ray Bradbury, Robert Heinlein, and other experts in the science fiction genre on *Dimension X* (1950-1951) and *X Minus One* (1955-1958), listeners found their imaginations changed forever as they realized that the exploits of Buck Rogers and Flash Gordon heard in the 1930s sounded more like soap opera serials than action geared to those actually living in the space age. Most episodes, such as "Lulungameena" and "A Pail of Air," though set in far from conventional housing, were rooted in the belief that home is where the heart is.

Quiet, Please, which aired from 1947 to 1949, could touch the heart often due to the inventive mind of author Wyllis Cooper and the masterful acting of Ernest Chappell. We never knew what to expect from those crafty craftsmen who one week warmed our spirits with a longing for the past with the poetic "In the House Where I Was Born" and seven days later chilled our bones by bringing us uncomfortably close to a mammoth fly in "Tanglefoot." *Quiet, Please* can lay claim to being one of radio's most provocative series, a show that required imagination both to create and appreciate.

Another program that is a favorite of radio fans is *Night Beat* which starred Frank Lovejoy as journalist Randy Stone from 1950 to 1952. Although a few scripts dealt with criminal acts, the subject of all the episodes was really life's passing parade as Randy encountered the gamut of humanity from frightened children to hardened convicts to that nebulous group of forgotten souls that some might classify as losers. No conventional label fits *Night Beat*; suffice it to say that it remains radio's best human interest dramatic show.

Selecting the best detective show became difficult after 1946. The leading candidates prior to that time, *Boston Blackie*, *The Falcon*, and *Nick Carter*, slipped out of contention with the advent of *The Adventures of Philip Marlowe* (1948-1950, 1951), *The Fat Man* (1946-1951), *Barrie Craig, Confidential Investigator* (1951-1955), *The Adventures of Sam Spade* (1946-1951), *Richard Diamond, Private Detective* (1949-1953), and *The*

Saint (1949-1951). Dick Powell had the sass, Howard Duff the brass, J. Scott Smart the mass, and Vincent Price the class to ride the crest of noir at that time. These actors, along with Gerald Mohr and William Gargan, possessed great radio voices that delivered both dour reflections and snappy rejoinders with panache.

For people who wanted their crimes delivered straight with no sarcastic chaser, *Dragnet* followed procedures to the letter from 1949 to 1957. Larry Thor as Detective Danny Clover claimed *Broadway Is My Beat* from 1949 to 1954. Walking the line between the private and public badges, Johnny Dollar remained ours truly even longer, pursuing false claimants from 1949 to 1962.

The gritty police shows, which evinced a realistic approach to life, were matched by the westerns *Gunsmoke* (1952-1961), *Have Gun, Will Travel* (1958-1960), *Fort Laramie* (1956), *The Six Shooter* (1953-1954), and *Frontier Gentleman* (1958). Unlike *The Lone Ranger, The Cisco Kid, Red Ryder*, and other "shoot-'em-ups" that almost invariably involved overt misdeeds and outlaws, many episodes of these adult westerns dealt with prejudice, intolerance, indifference and other crimes of the heart that continue to strike a responsive chord with home audiences today.

Bob and Ray: the two and only.

Also popular with listeners are three syndicated series which premiered during the Truman era: *Bold Venture* (1951-1952), breathy Caribbean intrigue with Bogie and Bacall; *Box 13* (1948-1949), adventures that were anything but a holiday for Dan Holiday (Alan Ladd); and *The Damon Runyon Theater* (1950-1951), seriocomic tales Runyonesquely narrated with Bronx cheer by John Brown.

Still cheery are the interviews and parodies of Bob Elliott and Ray Goulding, missed by many Americans the first time they aired between 1946 and 1960 and even later, but much-treasured today for how well the clever duo made a little go a long way.

The Big Show, often considered radio's last great counterattack on television, tried from 1950 to 1952 to make a lot go the rest of the way by filling ninety minutes with such an array of celebrities that the public would be dazzled. It did not succeed because there were too many egos and not enough microphones. The enduring variety shows, like those hosted by Eddie Cantor and Bing Crosby, enjoyed long, successful runs because everyone else (guests included) stood in the star's shadow.

If one carefully examines prime-time radio shows from 1935 to about 1955 with ears tuned to the source material rather than eyes influenced by specious notions, the conclusion is inescapable: with few exceptions, the quality of existing programs improved after the end of WWII and many of the shows introduced in 1946 or later significantly enriched the medium. Even dramas like *The Shadow* and *Mr. Keen, Tracer of Lost Persons*, which dispensed weekly doses of hokum in three different decades, and *Inner Sanctum Mysteries*, creaking out horrific hooey from 1941 to 1952, did not regress and kept the hokey from becoming poky.

No one should ever forget that it was not the quality of programming but the quantity of listeners that marked the demise of radio as America's first choice for home entertainment. The cacophony caused by opening Fibber's closet and Benny's vault might have caused just as much laughter in 1960 as they did in 1950 except for the fact that sound does not travel in a vacuum.

There may still be those who associate radio with images of sleek Rudy Vallee gripping a megaphone, somber FDR sitting before a row of microphones delivering his fireside chats, and puckish Joe Penner holding a duck, and they are welcome to retain such memories. But these reminiscences from the medium's early morning hardly reflect the coruscating triumphs achieved during its glorious afternoon.

So the next time someone wistfully declares, "I can remember radio's golden age," the best response is to just smile and say, "It's about time."

THE COLLECTIBLES

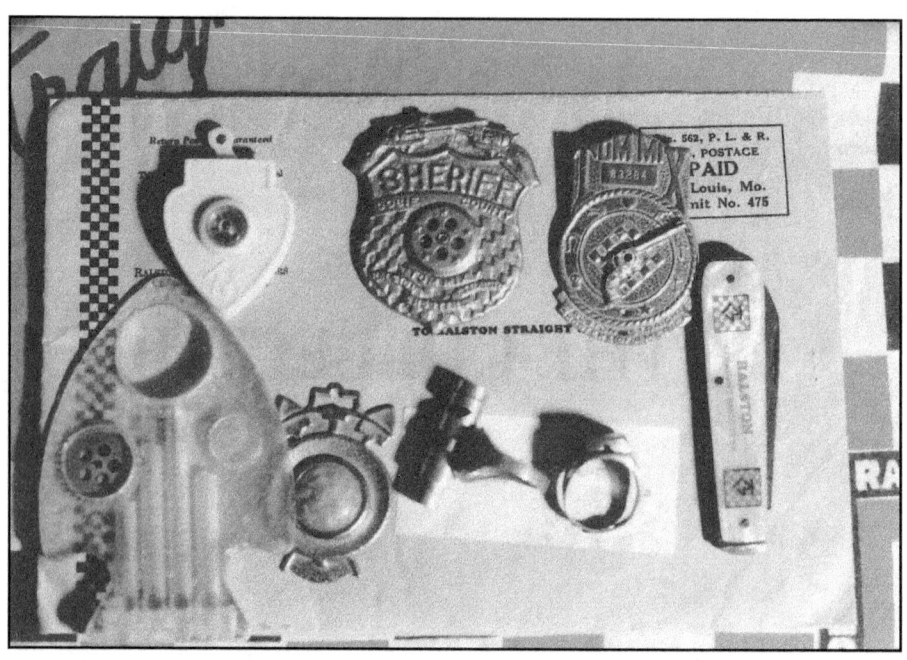
The envelope, please. The winner: any kid, any town U.S.A.

Tom Mix, a Premium Star

OF ALL THE WESTERN HEROES who rode across the silver screen Tom Mix was unique. His life and legend support this claim.

Unlike Roy Rogers and Gene Autry, singing actors playing parts, Tom Mix paid his dues as a bulldogging, hard-riding cowboy on ranches and the rodeo circuit for years before he stepped in front of the cameras.

Without Clarence Mulford and Fran Striker, the creators of Hopalong Cassidy and The Lone Ranger, William Boyd and Clayton Moore would most likely not even be remembered today. But Mix didn't need a writer to shape his character; just like his trademark white Stetson hat, he was larger than life.

A fair number of the sagebrush stalwarts galloped through the radio airwaves into our homes, but Mix's program, which ran from 1933 to 1950, was carried on the strength of his name alone because he never actually appeared on the show (four different actors assumed the starring role).

That name still had selling power even as late as 1947 when Fawcett Publishing started a series of *Tom Mix Western Comics*, seven years after the cowboy died in a car accident in Arizona.

In the 1920s Mix reigned as King of the Cowboys. Later he became the first Prince of Premiums. Before Boyd flooded the market in the early fifties with an avalanche of Hopalong Cassidy merchandise, Tom Mix had been first in the hearts of children who had their ears glued to the radio and eyes fixed on the mailbox.

All it took to get the latest Straight Shooter premium was a small coin and some Ralston Purina box tops. These prizes bear the two most recognizable signposts in Premiumland: the checkerboard pattern and/or the TM "brand."

Over eighteen years Ralston touched every base, sometimes more than once, by dangling anything that might appeal to boys and girls in front of them: knives, rings, badges, decoders, photos, guns, whistles, belts, compasses, bracelets, flashlights, scarves, hats, lariats, marbles, makeup kits, telescopes—even a branded baby turtle.

Children who wanted all of the Tom Mix premiums certainly had to develop a yen for hot or shredded Ralston, especially in the 1930s when ten to fifteen new lures were dangled before them every year.

The most coveted of these premiums is the 1934 Tom Mix Deputy Ring; it probably cannot be found anywhere in collectible condition for less than $1,000. But far more fun for youngsters—and more affordable for today's collectors—are the "Lookaround" ring issued in 1946 that permitted the viewer to "see around corners and over your shoulder without turning your head" and the "Mystery" ring from 1938 with the tiny peephole that allowed Straight Shooters in good standing (and with good eyesight) to see a photo of Tom and his faithful horse, Tony.

It was this sense of mystery residing in youngsters to which the funmakers at Ralston appealed. The white rowels on the aluminum spurs looked ordinary until held up to the light and then hidden under the covers where they glowed, providing more comfort and enchantment than any nightlight ever could.

The plastic belt that came in the mail one day in 1946 didn't look like anything special unless one knew about the secret compartment in the buckle.

Secret seemed to be the key word in merchandizing. Explicit instructions inside the secret manual warned users to "Keep this book in a secret place! Show this book only to friends whom you want to become Straight Shooters. But do not show anybody except your family the sections marked 'confidential.'"

On these sacred pages marked "confidential" Straight Shooters found the secret salute, secret grip, secret password ("Ralston," naturally), secret knock, secret whistle, and secret flashlight signal. Of course, Ralston made sure it was not a closed society by promising rewards like a silver-plated Captain's medal in exchange for the names of two friends plus three seals from cereal packages.

Because they capture a time in our history and a part of childhood so well, it is these premium catalogs and secret manuals that can be more precious to a collector than some of the plastic and metal baubles themselves, particularly if found with the original mailing envelope from Checkerboard Square in St. Louis.

Unlike some of the Captain Midnight manuals which are more expensive than the decoders and other premiums offered during the same year, the Mix booklets are quite reasonably-priced, usually tagged at less than $100.

The most sought-after paper premium is the Tom Mix mask. Locating one that is not bent, torn, or mutilated is a chore and finding one in fine condition for under $400 is even more difficult.

Of sentimental value to people growing up during the FDR and Truman years are the personalized items like the 1936 initial ring and the 1946 identification bracelet. Imagine the ecstasy of a boy named Howard who opened a package in 1938 and discovered a silver frame that contained a photograph of Tom and Tony with the inscription "To my Straight Shooter Pal Howard with best wishes, Tom Mix." That frame may only be worth $75 today, but try telling that to Howard!

One reason why so many Tom Mix premiums are still relatively affordable is that there are so many of them. The pocket knife offered in 1939 is not one in a million but one of over a million produced. The spurs are worth more than the knife (especially with the box), but there were almost 200,000 pair distributed, and more than a few of them are still out there glowing in antique malls and stores.

This is not to suggest that the road to collecting a Tom Mix collection is free from potholes. It is the bits of ephemera that may prove to be the most elusive. In 1934 the National Chicle Company (which also distributed the Deputy Ring) issued a series of twenty-one little booklets with a big stick of their bubble gum. Finding one or two of these eight-page *Tom Mix Adventure Stories* for $25 each is a simple matter, but collecting all of them may require a life span exceeding that of Grandma Moses. It is one of the peculiarities of the collecting world that there seem to be more of the gum wrappers available than there are of certain adventures in the series.

The motion pictures of Tom Mix were very popular in their day so his movie posters and lobby cards are also of great interest to today's collectors. But because Mix rode the range primarily as a silent film star—he last appeared on the screen in the 1935 serial *Miracle Rider*—little from his best work has survived. The one-sheet posters printed for Fox, Selig, and F.B.O. are very colorful with large images of Mix dominating the graphics. Whether linen-backed or not, these posters now sell for $1,000-$5,000. Individual lobby cards are worth $50 and up, with full sets bringing at least $300.

For over seventy years there has been a demand for premiums and other collectibles associated with that miracle rider, the world's greatest cowboy to the first generation of moviegoers. Up until that fateful day in October 1940 when he took the last ride in his sleek Cord Phaeton the good guy in the white hat was a living legend. For collectors, the legend and lure of Tom Mix will never die.

Essential reading for Straight Shooters.

Man vs. Myth

The real Tom Mix was nowhere as perfect as the Tom Mix portrayed in publicity releases and Straight Shooter manuals. Even Pecos Bill would have a hard time living up to the deeds recorded in Mix's press clippings.

"Born in a log cabin not far from El Paso, Texas"? Uh-uh. A prosaic town in Pennsylvania was his birthplace on January 6, 1880.

He did not grow up among "cowboys and bands of roving Indians." Tom was at least ten before he got a hankering for the Wild West after seeing a Buffalo Bill troupe perform.

Tom joined the army during the Spanish-American War but did not see any action and was not "wounded in a daring charge." He could not have been rushing up hills with Teddy Roosevelt's Rough Riders because the closest he got to Cuba during the war was Virginia.

Likewise, Mix could not have been wounded in the Boxer Rebellion; he wasn't even in China. Nor did the British send him "to Africa during the Boer War [to be] in charge of the cavalry mounts." Actually in 1902 he took an "extended furlough" from the army that led to him first being declared AWOL and then a deserter.

He did not head west "because bad men and killers were staging a reign of terror" but for the practical reason that he would be tougher to find in the wide open spaces of Oklahoma and Texas. He served as deputy marshal for a while in Dewey, Oklahoma but never wore the badge of a U.S. Marshal whose "cool courage and daring made him feared by lawbreakers."

However, beginning with the point in his life when he became a headliner for the Selig Polyscope Company during World War I, fiction gives way primarily to fact. At $17,500 a week he was indeed among the highest-paid actors in Hollywood, and it is also true that he performed his own stunts (he had many broken bones to prove the claim).

At the time he "made more pictures than anyone on the screen," completing seventy-eight films for Fox in eleven years. "By now he was a star everywhere," as evidenced by his successful tours both in the United States and Europe.

Left unsaid in these hagiographies were the harsh truths revealed later: five marriages, a wandering eye, near bankruptcy after the Crash of 1929, income-tax problems, the collapse of the circus he bought in 1935, and an affection for the bottle late in life.

But to his credit Tom Mix stood tall in the saddle as a role model before the eyes of his public. The values he espoused in his films (patriotism, courage, kindness to animals, personal heath, cheerfulness, courtesy, and honor) were what people saw when their idol appeared before them as a star of the first magnitude. To his fans, those were the only facts that mattered.

Favorites from comics, radio shows, and movies took on a distinctive shape when they appeared in Big Little Books.

Those Wonderful Big Little Books

WHAT'S BIG AND SMALL AND READ ALL OVER?
To children growing up in the 1930s and 1940s the answer is easy: Big Little Books.

In those days a youngster could carry home a fistful of fun for a dime or fifteen cents. Collectors today may need several fifty-dollar bills for the same privilege.

The format used by Whitman Publishing—the pioneer in the field—and later copied by Saalfield, Lynn, and other publishers, certainly appealed to even reluctant readers: the pictures on the right-hand pages brought to life the words printed on the left. In a way, Big Little Books became the link between comic books and novels. They were the nonclassics illustrated.

Most of the early BLBs transplanted characters from the comic strips, removed the dialogue above their heads, and transferred those conversations over to the left to comprise a significant portion of the narrative.

The Adventures of Dick Tracy started the parade in 1932 and marching right behind came stories featuring Little Orphan Annie, Mickey Mouse, Chester Gump, Tarzan, Moon Mullins, and other denizens of the funny pages.

The stars of radio and motion pictures comprised another principal source of material for BLBs. The exploits of cowboy heroes Buck Jones, Gene Autry, Tom Mix, The Lone Ranger, and Roy Rogers were recorded at least eight times each. Captain Midnight, the Green Hornet, and Gangbusters all proved to be just as formidable in print as on the air.

An interesting feature of a fair number of the screen adaptations is that photographs from key scenes replaced the usual drawings. These stills make Whitman's *Little Women* and *It Happened One Night* of interest not just to collectors of Big Little Books but also to movie buffs and fans of Clark Gable and Katharine Hepburn.

During the Silver Age, which lasted until the end of the 1940s, the quality had slipped a notch, partially because Whitman had no real competition for most of the decade to force them to improve.

Some of Whitman's World War II titles featured "Flip-It" animation—little drawings in the corners of the pages that appeared to move when flipped between thumb and forefinger.

By late 1949 the New Better Little Books didn't even look the same; they had grown tall and lean. In 1958 they shrunk again, this time with color illustrations.

By the 1970s the series came full circle by returning to Mickey Mouse, Popeye, and other characters from cartoons and comics.

But when collectors and dealers talk about Big Little Books, they are usually referring to the pre-1950 volumes, recognizable by their distinctive shape.

The books certainly lived up to their contradictory name. They were thick, often bulging to over 400 pages and an inch-and-half thick, yet their other dimensions were small, measuring 3¾" by 4½"—just the right size for kids to carry.

Learning to read the Big Little Book way.

Unfortunately for today's collectors this portability, making the volumes just perfect for shoving into a pants pocket, has resulted in only a small percentage of these books surviving in fine condition.

The books themselves, made cheaply with glued bindings and pulp paper so they could be sold cheaply, were not designed for permanence. The children who handled the books were concerned with finding out who did what, not with making certain that their hands were clean or that the pages were turned with care.

Couple budget construction with rough treatment and it is no surprise that so many Big Little Books found today bear the scars of torn pages, scuffed covers, and ripped bindings.

It is also common to find Big Little Books with pages missing. For example, if the title page is the first page visible when the front cover is opened, it is likely that someone has excised the front flyleaf.

There seems to be a mindset among some dealers that a Big Little Book has considerable value regardless of condition. At an antique mall I saw a copy of *The Story of Charlie McCarthy and Edgar Bergen* with considerable flaking to the covers and a twisted spine priced at $65. Nearby I spotted a copy of *Jack Armstrong and the Mystery of the Iron Key* with rounded corners and colored-pencil scribbling over some of the illustrations offered at $60.

In another mall four coverless BLBs waited patiently in a shoebox for someone to buy the lot at $12. They may have been overpriced by $12.

It may be hard for some people to accept, but the fact remains that Big Little Books in poor condition have little collector interest—especially when they are priced as if they are pristine copies.

Even though many BLBs vanished into landfills and incinerators decades ago, hundreds of thousands of each title were produced during the vintage years so that today's collectors can afford to be picky because a better copy may be waiting down the road.

Another prevalent misconception is that *any* Big Little Book is worth $50 regardless of subject. The truth is that books about long-forgotten characters such as Ella Cinders, Peggy Brown, Brick Bradford, and Punch Davis, even when found in fine condition, are not in the same league with similar volumes featuring popular and enduring figures like Alley Oop, Donald Duck, Red Ryder, Blondie, and Charlie Chan. Unless it is a rare title, most discerning collectors are not willing to pay the same for BLBs about also-rans as they are for those featuring the legends of comics, film, or radio.

Among those notables are Buck Rogers and Flash Gordon, the masters of time and space who rule the world of Big Little Books as well. Part of their appeal is the artwork of Alex Raymond and Dick Calkins which enthralls the reader from the action covers showing the space gun-toting heroes right up until the last page when the final fiendish invader is vanquished. Also adding to their value is that the Flash Gordon and Buck Rogers titles were released during the first ten years when the most innovative BLBs were published. Bright copies of these volumes with few defects often command over $100.

Who knows who gives the spacemen stiff competition among collectors? The Shadow knows. Also very much in demand are BLBs featuring Dick Tracy, Tarzan, and the Disney characters.

Another ingredient that affects BLB prices is the crossover factor. Many of the people seeking the most popular titles are not just collectors of Big Little Books. The small size of BLBs makes them ideal for display among related collections.

Someone who favors radio premiums, for example, may seek *Orphan Annie and Sandy* to set alongside a display of Ovaltine decoders and manuals. Another buyer may want *Gene Autry and the Gun-Smoke Reckoning* so it can be placed among a display of cap pistols.

A collector who has a wall filled with cups, pins, dolls, mirrors, and other objects associated with America's curly-haired sweetheart might find *The Story of Shirley Temple* just the perfect accent piece for a certain shelf. For these individuals, one Big Little Book may be enough.

But for the hardcore BLB collector there can never be enough. To the newcomer it may seem like there is too much. There were well over 800 different titles published before 1950, many of which can still be found.

For the beginner it is probably best to start with an area of personal interest such as westerns, mysteries, science fiction, Disneyana, motion picture adaptations, or comic-strip characters.

For the collector who is already in knee-deep, there are specialized volumes that make the hunt interesting. Whitman also published scores of "extra added attractions" during the 1930s that vary from larger, Big Big Books (measuring 7¼ by 9½ inches) to tiny stapled booklets (2½ by 3½ inches) which sold for just a penny. Oddities, like those few books which were wider than tall (e.g., *The Big Mother Goose* and *The Big Little Paint Book*), are comparatively scarce and thus highly sought-after by some collectors.

Condensed versions of certain Big Little Books were produced in a soft-cover format during this period and given away as premiums by companies such as Cocomalt and Tarzan Ice Cream that catered to a young clientele. Few children showed disappointment when receiving these gifts because reading Big Little Books and their offshoots was a treat in itself, not a trial like some of the books we were handed at school. Big Little Books truly gave a lot for a little.

Today the riddle may have changed a bit, but the answer is still the same: What's big and small and collected all over? Big Little Books!

Name and Number, Please

It is entirely possible that a disagreement between two collectors of Big Little Books could break out in this fashion:

"But my Whitman book number 1474 is *The Phantom and the Sign of the Skull* and it was published in 1939."

"I don't care," replies the other party. "My Whitman is number 1474 with a date of 1941 and the title very definitely is *Buck Rogers and the Overturned World*."

Who is right?

They both are. Whitman issued six different series of books numbered in the1400s so duplicate numbers were inevitable. Whitman (later Western Publishing) of Racine ruled as major power from beginning to end. The first series of fifty-four titles, published from 1932 to 1936, was numbered in the 700s. From 1934 to 1937 128 more books were released in two series numbered in the 1100s. The six 1400 series yielded almost 400 Big Little Books from 1937 to 1949.

Saalfield of Akron became Whitman's only serious competitor. From 1934 to 1938 they issued seventy Little Big Books priced at fifteen cents in series numbered in the 1000s, 1100s, 1500s, and 1600s. They also produced forty-five Jumbo Books from 1938 to 1940.

Other publishers who entered the field just stuck their toes in the water for a year or two. Engel-van's Five Star Library consisted of twenty-three books with Lynn Books issuing almost as many.

World Syndicate's Highlights of History series contained only five titles and Goldsmith's Radio Stars ended after profiling just four comedians: Eddie Cantor, Jack Pearl, Ed Wynn, and Joe Penner.

After 1936 it became just a two-horse race—between Whitman and Saalfield—for children's nickels and dimes and by the start of World War II Whitman virtually had the field to itself.

Also, from 1938 to 1943 Whitman printed thirty-three soft cover Fast Action Story Books for Dell Publishing which cost the same as the original Big Little Books: ten cents.

Movies kept audiences spellbound in darkness. Photoplay editions brought some of that magic home.

Booking Films: Movie Tie-Ins

"You read the book—Now see the movie" was a hook used for decades by Hollywood PR departments to put people in the seats. Today there are fans of older films who listen to another voice: "You liked the movie—Now collect the photoplay edition."

Movie tie-ins over the last several decades have appeared in paperback form, often with a "soon to be a major motion picture" stripe and/or images of the screen stars on the covers. During filmdom's golden age, however, hardcover books told the story in words and stills.

Reprints is a dreaded word in the collecting world and yet that is what photoplay editions are: cheap books issued to coincide with the release of new movies. (The term *photoplay* came about in the early days of cinema when distributors deemed it more refined than *films, movies,* and *moving pictures*. "Going to the photoplay" sounded positively posh compared with the déclassé "Meet me at the nickelodeon.") The very names of the publishers of these books, Grosset & Dunlap, Triangle, Sun Dial, Books, Inc., A.L. Burt, World, send a "bargain basement" message to the brain, and with a number of tie-ins that line of thinking is correct, particularly if the books are without dust jackets.

A first edition of Raymond Chandler's *Farewell, My Lovely* that lacks a jacket still carries a hefty price tag; a copy of the World/Tower Mystery reprint published to cash in on RKO's adaptation of the novel called *Murder My Sweet* is just another age-toned reading copy without the jacket showing photographs of Dick Powell in scenes from the film.

There were, of course, any number of tie-ins with black-and-white photos inserted on glossy sheets in the text, and it is the stills that rescue these reprints from the unsaleable purgatory inhabited by most book club editions and Reader's Digest Condensed Books. In 1992, after discovering Grosset & Dunlap's *Dracula* and *Frankenstein* which contain photos of Bela Lugosi and Boris Karloff in their signature roles, I bought them immediately for $11 each even though *Dracula* lacked a jacket and *Frankenstein*'s wrapper a color photocopy of the original. Because of the landmark status of those two pictures, decent copies of these G&D novels can be worth $150 and up, and original jacketed copies are now in four-figure territory.

Just as the stars frequently sell the motion picture so the legends of cinema often determine the relative value of the movie tie-ins. Sometimes the literary value of the novel is negligible. The hackneyed novelization of *The Climax*, a tepid effort of Universal to borrow the sets and premise of *The Phantom of the Opera*, has even less going for it than the film, but that photo on the jacket of a ghoulishly green Karloff about to throttle Susanna Foster is probably surpassed only by the "clutching hands" stance on the poster of *The Body Snatcher* as the image that best exemplifies the terrifying power of that master of menace.

The presence of cult figures on jackets does not necessarily make these books expensive. Shots of Humphrey Bogart and Clark Gable in action are going to command more than similar poses of Victor Mature and George Brent, but Bogie on the cover of the World edition of *The Big Sleep* can still be corralled for less than $100. Most photoplays are priced at under $50.

A catchpenny in 1931, a collectible today.

What elevates certain tie-ins above the others is when star power, film significance, and rarity intersect. Copies of Grosset & Dunlap's *The Jazz Singer* and *The General*, two seminal pictures in the history of cinema as well as high water marks in the early careers of Al Jolson and Buster Keaton respectively, are not overpriced at $200 if found in those seldom-seen 1927 jackets.

The old adage "collect what you like" could lead those folks who enjoy certain kinds of films to buy tie-ins related to a genre like mysteries, westerns, horror, adventure, or musicals while others who answer the call to "collect who you like" might concentrate only on those movies featuring James Stewart, Alan Ladd, Shirley Temple or other preferred celebrity.

The movie buff who favors Bette Davis and likes *Now, Voyager* will find it hard to resist Triangle's version of Olive Higgins Prouty's weepie. The romantic pose of Davis and sleepy-eyed Paul Henreid on the front panel makes it seem as if he is about to ask for a kiss, the moon, and the stars.

Gregory Peck had a similar dreamy expression as he gazed into Ingrid Bergman's eyes when he was *Spellbound*. Just so readers didn't think the movie and book were going to be all moonlight and roses, the lettering below the pair spell out "a story of madness and terror" as if appearing in the coming attractions playing on the screen of our neighborhood theater.

Like *Now, Voyager*, *Mrs. Miniver* and *Kitty Foyle* are "women's pictures" which were quite popular during that era of filmmaking. Another reason a movie fan might want *Mrs. Miniver* and *Kitty Foyle* is because Greer Garson and Ginger Rogers won Oscars for playing the titular characters. Such purchases might be the first steps taken in the direction of a sizable collection consisting of books tied to movies which were nominated for or won Academy Awards.

One side street some collectors head down is into the dark alley of film noir. Scenes from *The Woman in the Window* on the front and back panels of the jacket convey the depressing mood created when a professor (Edward G. Robinson) fell into the talons of the predatory femme fatale played by Joan Bennett. *The Postman Always Rings Twice* showcases Lana Turner and John Garfield in their most memorable roles on the wrapper and the book itself which uses the plates from the Knopf edition is well-designed with graphics on the cover repeated to spotlight chapter numbers.

One tie-in from the 1940s that truly ranks (in movie parlance) as a socko blockbuster is World's Tower Motion Picture Edition of *Mildred Pierce*. Not only is Mildred Pierce Joan Crawford's Oscar-winning, best-known role and the movie adapted from the one of James M. Cain's better novels but the dust jacket reveals six scenes from the film, the book

These endpapers alone are worth the price of admission.

is attractively bound in navy cloth with turquoise lettering, stills are also found on the endpapers and both sides of the frontispiece, and a list of the cast appears before the first chapter.

Duel in the Sun, a World offering in its Forum Motion Picture Edition series, earns a spot on the same bill with *Mildred Pierce*. (All the Forum and Tower Motion Picture Editions have extra added attractions.) The intensity between the hot-blooded characters portrayed by Gregory Peck and Jennifer Jones is captured on the jacket and on the endpapers where they are armed and dangerous, a foreshadowing of their violent end.

The jacket of *Duel in the Sun* is often found chipped, but no vintage tie-in is flawless. Regardless of whether these books were published during the war or not, most of them were printed on inferior paper that makes the pages appear browned as if they have fought their own duel in the sun. Because these editions have long been regarded as the poor cousins of those books issued by the major publishers, little care has been taken to protect the wrappers by many booksellers so almost all of them are torn, nicked, or rubbed. The pre-1950 movie tie-in that can truly be described as "fine in like dust jacket" is a rara avis indeed.

When hunting this breed of books, collectors may have to stifle some of their conditioned responses and ignore the danger signals that arise when seeing no dollar signs on the flaps which often suggest products of a book club. Sometimes a sequence of digits such as 049 or 0100 may hint at the retail price, but the absence of any numbers whatsoever signifies nothing with these editions.

Seeing "Fourth Printing" on the copyright page of a tie-in should prompt book-browsers to say "So what?" instead of the usual "Oh-oh." A first printing of a reprint is a prize of sorts, but its value and contents are virtually identical to those copies coming off the press maybe six months earlier. In fact, if that fourth printing has a crisp jacket, it would be worth more than its frayed ancestor. With photoplays, condition supersedes edition.

Inscriptions jotted by owners or presenters, instead of being a liability, can sometimes imbue books with an endearing quality which makes them more precious not in dollars but in quaintness. On a flyleaf of *So Goes My Love* a woman named Rose revealed her affection for both her sibling and the star of the film: "So goes my love to you, dear Sis—As for me I could go for Don Ameche." After writing her name and address on the front pastedown of *Two Years Before the Mast* where it would be hidden by the flap of the dust jacket, a Margaret of Flint, Michigan added this comment under the date of August 12, 1948: "Two years after the movie."

Bookplates, reviews, author photos, and other items affixed to preliminaries are as welcome to collectors as door dings on their new cars, but the lending library sticker of my copy of *Frankenstein* is like a ticket opening the gate to memory lane. This book once belonged to The Smoke Shoppe in some nameless city which, in addition to selling "ice cream, candy, magazines, photo finishing, tobacco, and sundries," allowed customers to borrow books for two weeks at the rate of two cents a day. Such a glimpse into its history makes it seem remarkable that such an oft-used, inexpensively-produced volume has managed to survive, like the monster at the beginning of those Universal sequels, little worse for wear.

The completist who wants to garner all the photoplay editions in jackets is in for a long harvest and will have to tolerate much chaff to get to the wheat. Movie tie-ins have been published since 1912, and books featuring the likes of Sally Eilers, Eric Linden, Arlene Judge, Jetta Goudal, and Leon Janney in bare G&D volumes may appeal only to some film historians. Not so with those novels dressed in bright wrappers which show the well-known grimaces or grins of Barbara Stanwyck, James Cagney, Spencer Tracy, or other luminaries more likely to rate four stars with collectors.

It is these latter books that are a touchstone to the past and their front panels bring back memories of Judy Garland wishing us a merry little Christmas in *Meet Me in St. Louis*, Tyrone Power testing *The Razor's Edge*, Dorothy McGuire scared speechless in *The Spiral Staircase*, Barry Fitzgerald playing deadly games in *And Then There Were None*, Gary Cooper scoring a hit as Lou Gehrig in *Pride of the Yankees*, Bing Crosby crooning as the cleric going out of his way to help ring *The Bells of St. Mary's*, Sydney Greenstreet and Peter Lorre matching wits in *The Mask of Dimitrios*, and John Wayne duking it out with Randolph Scott in *The Spoilers*.

To those who maintain "They don't make 'em like that anymore" one might add "And they don't title 'em like they used to either." Even if the titles leaned toward the grandiose they looked great on the marquee then and on the shelves now. Playing back to back are *Hold Back the Dawn, Tomorrow Is Forever, Till the End of Time, The Ministry of Fear, Our Vines Have Tender Grapes, Reap the Wild Wind, This Above All, Nobody Lives Forever, All This and Heaven Too, From This Day Forward, The Keys of the Kingdom, Nightmare Alley,* and *Keeper of the Flame*. Unlike other jackets that stand mute in such a position, many of these books are always running sneak previews that speak volumes because looking out from the spines are the faces of Ingrid, Clark, Gregory, Humphrey, Bette, Tyrone, Greer et al., and beyond them we know there is surely a cast of thousands.

Those collectors who have photoplay editions lined up in bookcases just as other people stack the video versions of the same titles by their VCRs and DVD players can tell their friends who rave about viewing a revered film like *Rebecca*, "Come over to my house. If you think the movie was good, wait till you see the book."

THE STORIES

The Man Who Knew Too Many

BLAME IT ON FRANK CAPRA AND TRUMAN CAPOTE. That's how I feel about it. It's not my fault that Carl's wife has given him the cold shoulder and his neighbors head for cover when he rolls out the grill. He claims that I ignored his warning when he called to invite me over for supper.

"Come on over and we'll burn some steaks. Jill just got a raise so we thought we'd spend it before we get it."

"Sounds good," I said. "Anything I can bring?"

"No, but there's something you can leave at home. I don't want to hear any stories about William Holden or Rita Hayworth or Buster Brown or—"

"Buster Crabbe."

"Yeah. Whoever. I don't want to hear anything about any movie star you knew way back when. OK?"

I agreed, and I kept my promise. I'm a man of my word. It's like I told Cagney when he was debating whether to return to the screen after twenty years in retirement. "Do the right thing, Jim," I told him. "If you leave it as is, they'll say, 'With Cagney it was one, two, three and out.' But if you do one more, I can hear the raves now: 'Cagney's performance runs through the mind like a ragtime tune you can't forget.'"

But if Carl and Jill wanted to talk about mundane matters of mortgage, weather, and diet, I would wait until my time came. It always did.

Like the last time I stopped by Carl's office two floors above mine. I always rapped on the frame before sticking my head around the corner so I didn't embarrass both of us by catching him checking for signs of age creeping along his temples with the little mirror he kept on his desk. For years Carl has tried to stiff-arm time by using hair color and for months I have been telling him what I told Charlie Rich: "Let it all go to silver and you'll come out looking like a fox."

But this time he seemed more uncomfortable about the disorder on his desk than about his appearance. He pulled some papers together toward his paunch like it was his deal and began shuffling the sheets into one stack.

"Don't mind the mess," he said with a flushed grin. "It's not always like this."

"No problem," I said. "Even Olivier had some rocky stretches. I remember telling him way back in 1978 'Heavens to Betsy, Larry. Getting good roles these days must be like drilling teeth.'"

Carl coughed, then got a steely glint in his eyes.

"You're a gold mine of unfamiliar quotations, aren't you?" he asked as he swung his chair back and forth. "I wonder..." He looked left and right, then added, "If I pointed to any object here, would it remind you of some pearl of wisdom you dropped on a celebrity?"

When I shrugged, he must have accepted that as a gesture of acceptance for he reached over, tapped the phone, and looked up at me expectantly.

"Well," I started, "there was that evening I was sitting on the sofa at Don Ameche's place and said to him, 'Don't keep waiting by the phone as if you invented it. Get out of your cocoon and get into another one. Plunge right in and Oscar will be waiting for you on the other side.'"

"Uh-huh," was all he said. From then on he just pointed.

To an envelope which was the same size as the one I mailed to Melvyn Douglas when I wrote that letter explaining how being here was not as important as being there. To a box of tissues which brought back the day I suggested to Elizabeth Montgomery that she stop wiggling her behind and start twitching her nose. To a stack of CDs which recalled the time I assured Lee Marvin that if he ever did a musical he'd end up talking to the trees. To his chair which reminded me of the advice I gave to Jessica Tandy that to get back into the flow of traffic she needed to take a back seat and let someone else do the driving. Finally, with a thrust of his arm, he pointed to the doorway which meant I should leave. I was tempted to say that was the same gesture I had used when I told Jeremy Brett to move off the street where he lived and get down to cases, but Carl's grim expression made it clear that I had worn out my welcome again. Carl is a man of few words and abrupt action whereas I have, as Martha Raye once told me, "a mouth that mine could get lost in."

When I arrived at the house at 6:30, Carl was already on the deck squeezing the last drops out of a can of fluid over the charcoal. He has the habit of pushing up his glasses with the back of his wrist which always seems to me like he is attempting to imitate a swan with his arm and hand. He tugged on the brim of his baseball cap and said, "We'll be cooking pretty soon."

I volunteered to help Jill set the table and headed toward the kitchen. As I walked across the deck I wondered again why they had used paint instead of stain. They had to repaint the deck every spring and by July the overshadowing maple tree had discarded enough seedlings to make it look as soiled as it was in March. And why they painted it teal is a mystery. It was like the dreadful color in Joan Crawford's guest bedroom. I said to her, "Really, Joan. You must have been in a straitjacket when this was painted. Whoever picked this shade has Bette Davis eyes."

Jill greeted me coolly as usual and handed me bowls and bottles of condiments. I wondered as I carried armfuls to the table how many bottles of her own she was using to keep that jet black mane flowing free of gray. She didn't like it when I said she had hair like Morticia Addams, but, then again, Carolyn Jones didn't think much of my response of "That's right" when she said, "They'll make a movie out of this ghastly series over my dead body."

By the time the meat was sizzling on the grill we were nibbling olives and potato chips and sipping iced tea. As I had predicted, the dreary topics of waistlines, bills, and humidity were dragged out and soon exhausted. It was a waste of time and breath just like when Vincent Price was churning out schlocky films in the mid-sixties and I warned him that if he didn't stop making bombs with girls he would be doing something really abominable someday and find himself in a madhouse.

When the steaks were ready, Carl, who must have noticed that I had been unusually quiet because of his gag order, jiggled a lure in front of me.

"I've been reading Frank Capra's autobiography," he said as he wiped his oily chin. "*The Name Above the Title*. Did you ever read it?"

I could tell by the looks they exchanged that this was a test. I chewed on and just nodded.

"Did you notice how Capra couldn't be topped? We all know what a big bully Harry Cohn was, the way he ruled Columbia Pictures like a dictator. But Capra beat him every single time. And what a memory! It was amazing how in 1971 he could remember detailed conversations he had with Cohn before World War II and how Cohn always came out looking like a jerk. Did Capra have a photographic memory?"

He showed me the beak of the swan as he adjusted his glasses. Jill answered before I could.

"Maybe he had a selective memory." Then, without a glance at me, she added, "Or perhaps a creative one."

I shrugged and said, "When you write your autobiography, you get to make the rules. If Cohn had written his own life story (and with him it probably would have been ghost-written), he would have gotten all the good lines."

"All the good lines," Jill repeated. She paused with her fork in mid-air as if for effect and I think that was its purpose for there was nothing on it and little on her plate except bone and fat. She lowered the fork and watched it all the way down as if threading a needle. Or baiting a trap.

"That reminds me of something I read the other day," she said, leaning forward and folding her hands. "It was in a book by Truman Capote called *Music for Chameleons*. This one part was about a funeral or memorial or mass or something for some actress and who should Capote meet there in the back of the church but Marilyn Monroe! And he goes on for page after page recording word-for-word this conversation they had twenty, twenty-five years before and she comes off sounding like a foul-mouthed, insecure bimbo and he's the Wizard of Oz with all the answers."

Jill laughed and clapped her hands as if applauding her story. She shook the ice in her glass and looked at me with merry green eyes as she swallowed what was left of her tea.

Carl chuckled and said, "Capote was pretty safe. Who was going to dispute him? It was just the two of them there and Marilyn was dead by then. Come to think of it, Cohn had been long buried when Capra wrote his book. Dead men tell no tales. They don't even get a rebuttal."

I wondered, *How did he know it was just the two of them there*? I was beginning to suspect that if I had stopped by at 6:15 I would have interrupted a rehearsal.

"Saaay," he said, stretching the word out with a sly grin on his face. "Now that I think of it, it seems to me that all the celebrities you claim to have met are no longer alive. How is it that you never have any stories to tell about them until after they're dead?"

I wiped my lips with a napkin and leaned back in the wicker chair to look at both of them. Carl looked as smug as George Sanders when I told him he was dying of boredom and Jill was as saucy as Lee Remick the day I said it was time to stop playing sexy young things and experiment in terror.

"I have so many stories to tell," I said calmly. "I sometimes wonder if I will live long enough to tell them all."

Carl slapped the table and pointed a greasy finger at me.

"Now *that's* the truth. Somebody may kill you before you get another one out of your mouth. Right now what friends you have left are probably devising a plot right out of Hitchcock to do you in."

At the sound of that name I could hear my heart pounding in my ears and I knew I couldn't hold it in.

"Speaking of Hitchcock, did I ever tell you about the interview I did with him?"

Carl's smile faded and his shoulders seemed to sag a little. Jill's hands now gripped the tablecloth and her eyes darted between the two of us.

Carl coughed and said, "I thought we agreed not to—"

"Hitchcock, as you know, was a director, *not* a movie star, although he did appear briefly in many of his films. He told me he also had a part in *Bad Day at Black Rock*. He played the black rock."

Jill seemed to be tightening her grip on the cloth as I noticed wrinkles there now while Carl began nervously gnawing on a toothpick.

"He took that part after he made *Dial M for Murder* in 3-D. Hitch didn't like 3-D. I told him he provided his own three Ds: death, deceit, and doubt."

"Sounds like you were interviewing yourself," Carl said glumly. "Didn't he have anything to say?"

"Well, he did say that he would go to his grave regretting that he didn't cast Wally Cox to play Norman Bates in *Psycho*."

The toothpick dropped out of his mouth. "Uh-huh" was all he said.

"He also claimed that it was a mistake not to follow *The Birds* with a sequel called *The Aardvarks*."

Without saying a word Carl took off his cap and flung it over the hedge into the neighbor's yard, but he didn't move an inch away from his chair. Jill's eyes and mouth were now wide open. I knew there was no stopping now.

"And he did have an answer ready when I said that climaxes on sites like the Statue of Liberty and Mount Rushmore seemed a little contrived. He said those high places created more excitement than the prospect of having the villain trying to drown Robert Cummings in Yellowstone Park when Old Faithful came up or having Cary Grant risk lead poisoning from crawling across the Painted Desert."

Before the last word was out, he leaped to his feet, shouted "Enough!" and flung the top of the grill over the hedge like a discus. Jill hustled me by the sliding doors and toward the deck steps.

"You better go," she said hoarsely.

"But you didn't hear the suggestions I gave him that would have improved his pictures. Like he could've done one about a scrubwoman called *The Lady Varnishes* or one about a chubby vixen who disposes of her husbands by sitting on them called *Rear Widow* or—"

Jill pushed me down the steps while a spatula, cooking gloves, and swanless glasses were taking flight. She escorted me around the corner of the garage and nudged me toward my car.

"And what about the one with a dishonest cow called *To Catch a Beef*?"

"You're lucky you didn't catch it" was all she said before hurrying off toward the sound of banging which seemed to indicate that Carl's aim was off and he was now hitting the storage shed with his missiles. I decided it was best to retreat, remembering what I said to Steve McQueen when his career was at a standstill: "Make the great escape and get away or no one will want you, dead or alive."

Needless to say, I haven't been invited back, although I have seen Carl a couple times in the elevator where we have conversed briefly. He seems a little sheepish about his behavior that night and I suspect that he still holds me somehow responsible for what happened. So far I have refrained from trying to cheer him up by saying that everyone has regrets like William Conrad's disappointment after finding out he had been bypassed for the part of Barney Fife and the unfulfilled dream of Orson Welles to direct an animated version of *Citizen Kane* with Andy Devine providing the voice of Kane.

But someday, when I am a safe distance away from him, I am going to tell Carl about the morning I had breakfast at Tiffany's with Audrey Hepburn. *And* Truman Capote. *And* Frank Capra.

One Principal Too Many, One Principal Too Meanie

DURING MY YEARS OF TEACHING ENGLISH at Madison High School I have stood over the wishing well in the nearby park many times tossing in coins and hoping that Mr. Boynton would make his move and that Mr. Conklin would just move. If what happened recently is any indication of how efficacious my wishing efforts have been, the next time I visit that well I am going to keep my purse closed and throw myself in.

If someone had told me that Madison's beloved but autocratic principal, Osgood Conklin, was going to be replaced, I would have been pleasantly surprised. Surprised? I would have helped him move his chair out of his office while he was still in it.

But, as the ancient Greeks said, there's many a slip between the cup and the lip. Or, as they say in my crowd, somebody kiboshed the caboose before it got out of the station.

It all started when Mr. Conklin summoned (or, let's say ordered, because "Be there or be gone" does sound like marching orders) Philip Boynton and myself to his office after lunch last Friday. Technically, the few minutes we have after eating should be our own time and I do so look forward to sharing a table with the bashful biologist, even if it's only to flip a quarter to see who pays for the meal, but Mr. Conklin has always insisted that "For devoted teachers there is no such thing as 'free' time. They should always be vigilant, ready to serve when duty calls." The foreign legion lost a great commandant when Osgood Conklin decided on a career in education.

When I opened the door on that fateful day, Philip was already sitting in the chair next to the walnut desk behind which sat Mr. Conklin with his hands on the arms of the brown leather chair that members of the faculty referred to as "the Throne." Hanging on the wall behind that chair is a faded and cracked oil portrait of Madison's revered founder, Yodar Kritch, in some of his mutton-chopped glory. Whenever I look up at Kritch's stern visage, I imagine him pitching right in and helping the students of his day with some of his jolly pet projects like cutting hickory switches, building pillories and stocks, and doing their stretching exercises on the rack.

Mr. Conklin graciously offered me a seat (i.e., he pointed emphatically to the chair directly in front of his desk that I called the hot seat). Before I could adjust it to medium-well he said, "I'll come right to the point, Miss Brooks. I have asked you and Mr. Boynton here to apprise you of an educational initiative that I believe will be beneficial to all parties involved. As you know, there is an opening on the school district's administrative team and I am being considered for that position. As chief assistant to the superintendent I will be reaching the heights of my ambition and soaring with the big boys. It would be quite a feather in my cap to join that team. You understand what this means, Miss Brooks?"

"Yes," I replied. "It means that you'll not only win your letter but they'll also put a band on one of your legs."

For a moment Mr. Conklin said nothing. He just flicked his salt-and-pepper mustache (he had just finished lunch, too) and stared at me with cold gray eyes. Then, without losing eye contact, he lowered his head like a bull preparing to attack, affording me a view of the receding hairline along his temples and the bald spot on the crown of his head, and calmly noted, "Miss Brooks, there are those who will claim that I am seeking this promotion for financial gain. They are wrong. There are those who will say that I am a status seeker who wants to impress my peers. They also are wrong. But if someone accuses me of trying to find some way to avoid any further contact with you, well, I will have to take the fifth."

"Fine," I said, sliding my foot next to my molars where it usually was. "You pour and I'll get the glasses."

His eyes rolled heavenward and, finding no consolation there, came down to me and my colleague. Still in a prayerful mood, his fingers formed a steeple first under his nose and then under his chin.

"Miss Brooks," he said after his black mood had passed and his ebony one had set in, "I'd like to continue bandying words with you but I don't so I won't. I will be brief. I intend to demonstrate to Mr. Stone, head of the board of education, that I am the best person for this job in the superintendent's office by doing something bold and innovative. I believe Mr. Stone has been somewhat reluctant to promote me because of the shortage of principals. I think he also considers me, shall we say, somewhat of a yes man who kowtows to him and who has no ideas of my own."

"If I may insert a comment here," Mr. Boynton said. "I would like to state unequivocally that you certainly are a fine principal and that you would be difficult to replace."

"All that's missing is *si*, *ja*, and *oui* and he's in the yes man hall of fame," I said sotto voce. Apparently I put too much sotto in my voce for Mr. Conklin shot a very dry gimlet of a glare at me before continuing.

"My plan is to address all of these matters in one sweeping initiative. As you know, Boynton has taken coursework in school administration. My intention is to allow him, as it were, to assume the position of principal for a week under my gentle tutelage. Perhaps, with additional courses this summer, he could acquire the necessary credentials to be hired full-time next fall after I move, shall we say, onward and upward."

Before he started flapping his wings again I tried to form an objection but all that came out was "But—But—But—"

"We can dispense with the imitation of a motorboat, Miss Brooks. Now if—"

"But I don't understand," I continued, steering for the nearest rocks. "Mr. Boynton can't be here acting as principal and in his classroom teaching biology at the same time."

"That is true," he said, nodding his head. "Even you, despite your regular sprints between your room and Mr. Boynton's lab, cannot be in two places at once, although, in some of my more fanciful moments, I have pictured you in another, shall we say, warmer place."

And happy pitchforks to you, I said, this time to myself.

"I, Osgood Conklin," he said, sitting up in his chair and puffing out his chest, "will take charge of the school and assume a role which will prove that I am a multi-faceted, ingenious dynamo who will be a shining beacon on the educational horizon."

That would be a swell movie, I thought: *Osgood Conklin is a Many-Splendored Thing*.

"Mr. Stone has sometimes intimated that I am too removed from the student body and therefore out of touch with today's youth, a baseless claim that I will disprove during the time next week when I temporarily turn the reins of this office over to Boynton for part of the day while I demonstrate my versatility as an educator by taking over some of his biology classes."

"But you—But he—But how—"

"Push down on the throttle, Miss Brooks," he said, leaning forward like a fisherman with gaff in hand. "What are you trying to say?"

I turned to Mr. Boynton, hoping that he would say what I was thinking, but why should he start now? If he said what I was thinking, we would have been married five years ago.

"Mr. Boynton," I pleaded. "You have the certification to teach biology. Mr. Conklin doesn't. Is this fair to the students?"

"It's only for two classes in the morning for just a week, Miss Brooks," he said. "Mr. Conklin wanted you to be here today because you're so popular with the students and teachers he knows you could handle any objections they might have. Besides, this will be a good test to let me know if I'm cut out to be a principal. And who knows," he added with a small laugh, the only kind he ever gave or earned, "maybe Mr. Conklin will like teaching biology so much he'll become the next Luther Burbank."

He's doing a good job as the most recent Simon Legree, I thought before turning back to Mr. Conklin whose smug expression I hoped to erase with my next objection.

"But what does Mr. Stone think of this idea?"

"Mr. Stone is currently on vacation and will return one week from today. At that time I will be able to present to him ample evidence that I can handle any situation, that I am a bold innovator, a highly competent educator, a take-charge administrator, and—"

Mr. Conklin might have added everything from a prince of a fellow to the father of our country had not the bell rung, signaling the end of the lunch period. He dismissed us with a wave of his hand as if to say, "Begone," so we bewent. The last glimpse I had of Conklin before the door closed was of him gazing up at the portrait, chuckling warmly as if he and Yodar were sharing some private joke about Vlad the Impaler.

I didn't see Mr. Boynton again until after school when we met at our usual rendezvous in front of the primate cages at the zoo. You haven't lived until, after getting paid peanuts, you spend a date flipping peanuts to monkeys and their kin with a dreamboat who is more concerned with his feeding than with the woman alongside him who is eating her heart out and, believe me, I haven't lived.

But, even though he's a square who can be obtuse when it comes to things romantic, I still love all four corners of him. There is something about the tender way he proffers a tidbit through the bars that makes me say to myself, "This is the man I'd like to be the father of my chimps, er, children."

The conversation, which had consisted of sweet nothings between Mr. Boynton and his gibbering pals and real nothings between Mr. Boynton and me, turned naturally to Mr. Conklin's plan. Philip had apparently given the matter much thought because he had a ready response to my question as to why Conklin had gone to so much trouble trying to earn his promotion.

"Maybe he doesn't want to be a principal the rest of his life."

"Well, he's been the principal most of my life, or so it seems. Now he just arbitrarily changes schedules solely to suit his own goals so he can move 'onward and upward.' He isn't concerned at all with the fact that by finding a principal right here to take his place it would leave Madison short one very good biology teacher. And he's not qualified to teach biology even for a few days. He hasn't taught a class in at least ten years."

Mr. Boynton raised a forefinger as if testing the wind direction or sending a message to the creatures behind him and said, "You forget, Miss Brooks, that he has a lifetime certificate to teach. He's been grandfathered in."

I waved that objection off with a gesture which may have sent the chimpanzees behind us scurrying in another direction and replied, "I don't care if he's got a notarized letter from his great-aunt. It's not fair to the students. He taught penmanship. What's he going to say when they're dissecting a crawfish? Tell them to put dots over the eyes and ask them to make certain the abdominal incision reads 'Open sesame' in cursive letters?"

He threw a handful of peanuts into the penetralia of the cage and said, "Oh, there won't be anything like that next week. Besides, I'll be right down the hall. That's the nice thing about this arrangement. Mr. Conklin and I have each other to fall back on."

"And while you're both sprawled there on the floor, who's going to pick you up?" I angrily flung a peanut past the nose of a monkey who first looked at the missile and then at me as if asking what he had done wrong before scampering after his treat. "I wonder if it ever occurred to Mr. Conklin that his plan could backfire and he could be demoted instead of promoted."

"I don't think there's much chance of that. You see, the way he explained it to me, the teaching is just part of his grand plan. He wants to prove to Mr. Stone that he's a Renaissance man who can do it all: handle the faculty, communicate to the board, instruct students, write curriculum..."

"Leap tall buildings, climb mountains, do laundry on Saturdays...But even if he can do all those things, what gets me is the sneaky way he usurps authority. He waits until Mr. Stone is on vacation and then sets the rules."

"Well, you know the old saying: 'When the cat's away, the mice will play.'"

"There's another saying I'm making up right now: 'When the rat sets the trap, he better make sure his tail is out of the way.'"

At that Philip's blue eyes sparkled, he flashed a smile, the cleft of his chin seemed to wink, my knees buckled, and, if they had known the tune, my heartstrings would have gone zing.

"I know you're joking," he said, leaning against the railing like me and turning his back to the animals. "But you haven't said anything about me taking over his job for a few mornings. How do you think I'll look behind a principal's desk?"

"Like a dreamboat in dry dock," I muttered. "But it takes a special kind of person to be a principal. Do you think that's the right job for you?"

He turned to me and said, "That's what I want to find out. I've taken some classes, but I need to get in there and see if I've got what it takes."

Since his face was only inches from mine I leaned closer and whispered, "I've got what it takes if you're the one who takes what somebody who's willing to give something for the taking, and if you'll stop this merry-go-round I'll get off at the next funhouse."

He put his left arm behind me on the railing and painted a lovely picture with his right hand. On the painting he pointed to the additional income he would be making as principal, the house he could afford with that money, and the wife and family who would live in that house with him. When I artfully asked him if he would like to sign and date that work, he shyly said that at present he would have to borrow a card from one of the serials titled "To Be Continued" to hang on the piece. I left it at that, though I realized that "To Get Started" would have been a more appropriate sign.

Project Osgood, as I liked to call it, began on Monday and, after three days, all I had to say was that if Thomas Edison's experiments had been as successful his life story would have been called *The Light That Failed*. Word had come to me through the grapevine (Walter Denton being the juiciest grape on that vine) that Mr. Conklin usually deflected questions as if they were pitches to be batted back into the faces of students. During a discussion of trees belonging to the poplar family, for example, Walter asked about the marginal teeth of the quaking aspen, only to be told that anyone whose grades are marginal should be quaking at the prospect of failing and should therefore sink his teeth into his book where the answer quite obviously was if only he had the determination to find it.

Meanwhile, in the principal's office, Mr. Boynton was taking the time to listen to concerns with his usual thoughtfulness and courtesy. The problem was that he had left all his solutions in bottles back in the biology lab. Tuesday morning after I informed him that when I went to the stockroom and discovered that we were nearly out of notebook paper, he proceeded to start a lecture about how paper came from secondary xylem which I stopped with the comment that I didn't care if it came from Upper Sandusky and that if we didn't requisition an order soon all of us would be writing on slate which brought forth a diatribe about metamorphic rock which I never heard the end of because I needed to get to my next class. Trying to get a concise, pertinent answer from Boynton as principal was like working on a book of crossword puzzles and finding the answers in the back had come from an algebra text.

I was discussing the difficulties we had been having at school with my landlady, Mrs. Davis, on Thursday during breakfast. I am reluctant to say *over* breakfast for, considering her penchant for creating exotic combinations like rutabaga muffins and shrimpballs marinated in kumquat wine, I don't want to bring up the inevitable. (I guess I just did that anyway.)

Mrs. Davis sat across from me in her plaid robe, gazing over her spectacles as she attempted to read my fortune in tea leaves. Upon finding a pleasing omen in her cup she exclaimed, "Oh, Connie! I see a handsome man in your future."

"I'd settle for a homely one in my past. But right now I need to get the two men in my present back to where they belong."

"I've always said that Osgood doesn't belong in a classroom. He doesn't have the patience to be a teacher. He's like a fish out of water."

"Especially in biology. Walter told me that yesterday when a student asked Mr. Conklin to explain the difference between the monocots and the dicots, he said he couldn't tell one of those singing groups from another."

Mrs. Davis reached a consoling hand across the table, patted my arm, and said, "Neither can I, dear. I draw the line at Perry Como. He sends me."

I decided to leave unwell enough alone and move on. Mrs. Davis is a dear soul, a sweetheart who rarely asks for the rent money I have owed her since Bette Davis was doing Jezebel, but her mind wanders so often I have to put out an All Points Bulletin daily to bring it back.

"Mr. Boynton is in over his head, too," I said. "He can't give a straight answer. He just cites some analogue from science. Yesterday before school I told him that we needed to get out more publicity about our clean-up-the-parks campaign so our students will be recognized for their citizenship, and instead of taking notes or calling the newspaper, he said, 'Speaking of being recognized, did you know that over 3,000 species of trilobites have been identified?' Imagine that! He wanted to talk about trilobites."

I could tell by her glazed eyes that she had been off somewhere doing the mambo with Perry because her head vacillated between the licorice waffles and the watermelon omelet on the table as she asked, "Try a bite of what?"

"Trilobites, Mrs. Davis. They're fossils from 200 million years ago."

"Well, in that case, I wouldn't want any. I don't even keep hard rolls longer than a week or two."

"Good idea," I said. I threw the switch to prevent another derailment. "But at least by midday when Mr. Boynton is back in the lab and Mr. Conklin is in his office life goes on somewhat normally. If you can call this normal and if you can call this living. Although he's a dictator at times, say between 7:00 a.m. and 6:00 p.m., at least Mr. Conklin can make a decision even if that decision is that he rules the world."

Mrs. Davis punctuated her agreement by raising her cup and declaring, "Once a martinet, always a martinet."

I clinked my cup with hers and offered a toast: "To the only man who would demand to play both leads in *The King and I*."

The horn that sounded then was not that of Triton beckoning me to a frolic in the sea but rather an invitation to put my life in Walter Denton's hands which emanated from under the partial hood of his jalopy. I bid goodbye to Mrs. Davis, who might well have spent the day trying to decide whether to send some of her recipes to Betty Crocker or Robert Ripley, and hurried out to join Walter in a vehicle that looks like it either left the assembly line an hour too soon or thirty years too late.

You could call it a two door except there were no doors and you could call it a hardtop except there was no top. There were no fenders and the license plate in front appeared to be the only thing holding that bumper on. When Walter told me one day that he had been thinking about selling the car for parts I asked, "You mean you haven't been already?"

He gunned the engine which threw a plume of black smoke out of the muffler and into our lungs, then touched the accelerator with all the gentleness of a Mexican hat dancer who had a grudge against sombreros. By the time we were three blocks away and I had peeled the back of my head off the cushion I asked Walter if he was ready for his first period class which just happened to be biology.

"Yes and no," he said, glancing at me with determination in his eyes.

"Well, that makes it clear. At the next corner turn left *and* right."

"What I mean, Miss Brooks, is that I am not ready to answer questions related to today's lesson, but, boy oh boy, am I prepared for what's going to happen in a few minutes."

Without any coaxing he explained that he was tired of being humiliated in class by what he considered to be Mr. Conklin's deliberate attempts to embarrass him. He cited as one example that after Harriet, Mr. Conklin's daughter and Walter's girlfriend, had described a fluke as a parasite noted for its stickers which it attaches to its host, Mr. Conklin told the class it would be a fluke if Walter was ever invited to dinner again so he could stick his host for another meal.

The final blow to his dignity occurred Wednesday morning when Conklin noted that Cro-Magnon man, despite limited intelligence, created admirable wall paintings, and then remarked, "That might explain your passing marks in art, Denton."

"I took umbrage at that, Miss Brooks."

"So would I, Walter. So would Umbrage. That's taking unfair advantage of his position as tyrant, er, teacher."

"Ah, but today the worm will turn. In fact, the worm turned yesterday when I said out loud that the earthworm has five hearts which is five more than someone I know and for that, even though I didn't mention his name, Mr. Conklin made me stay after school to clean up the lab. So while Mr. Boynton and Mr. Conklin were up in the office after school that's when I hatched the plot of all plots."

What emerged next from Walter's throat was a combination snicker, cackle, and giggle that could only be generated by adolescent adenoids. When I convinced him to stop rubbing his hands like John Barrymore's Mr. Hyde and return them to the steering wheel, he revealed his course of action.

After inveigling from Harriet a phone number where Mr. Stone could be reached at an upstate resort, Walter had placed a call to the head of the board after supper and, by using a disguised voice, pretended to be Mr. Conklin with a cold, hinting about an emergency which had arisen that he could not handle and insisting that it was imperative Mr. Stone be at school when classes begin the next morning to deal with "a matter of life and death."

Knowing which one of those two options would be his fate if his plot was discovered, Walter asked me to bring Mr. Stone to the lab as soon as he came to school. Because I do not have a class during first period this term, I told him I would do my best but also expressed displeasure at such a deception.

"It's for the good of the school, Miss Brooks. Old Marblehead, er, Mr. Conklin is a crab who needs to be swimming in his own pool, away from the students most of the time. And, although I know you're fond of Mr. Boynton, I wish he was back in his lab because he's lost in the office. Yesterday when I complained to him about the stale food in the cafeteria and demanded that he do something about it, he spent at least three minutes telling me about the spores of black bread mold which spread with amazing rapidity. Gee, Miss Brooks, as editor of *The Madison Monitor*, I'd hate to have to tell the students in the school paper that if the vegetables in the lunchroom make you sick, Mr. Boynton says you should try the penicillin in the moldy bread."

After we agreed that we better off, to use Walter's ungrammatical but felicitous expression, "when our status was quoed," he unleashed his most fiendish crow before revealing the measures he had taken to assure the success of his stratagem.

"You know the pull-down diagrams above Mr. Boynton's blackboard? Well, when Mr. Conklin pulls them down today, the class will get an anatomy lesson they'll never forget."

Before I could object, Walter explained that he had also borrowed a prop from the school stage to replace the flashlight that Mr. Conklin kept in one of the lab drawers for shining in the eyes of his captives when asking them his version of *Twenty Questions* which the students considered a form of the third degree. Finally, to assure the triumph of his revenge, he had taken liberties with some of the labels in the lab. I refrained from asking him when we could expect the sneezing powder to appear for fear that he might produce a full bag of it from under his seat.

By that time we had reached Madison High School, an austere, three-story red brick building whose architecture can aptly be described as early medieval dungeon. Forbidding gothic archways open into fusty sepulchral hallways harboring bleak classrooms, which, if one spends enough time in them, lead to abject poverty for teachers and severe depression for students. Guests at other high schools seek out trophy cases displaying cups and medals or plaques listing the names of honored scholars; visitors to Madison wonder where is the graffiti that reads "Ygor crept here."

There was no sign of Messrs. Boynton, Conklin, or Stone in the office. In fact, the only creature stirring besides the secretary was McDougall, Mr. Boynton's pet frog, croaking softly (pardon the oxymoron) in his cage just outside Mr. Conklin's door. I suspect that at times during the week, like the sleepy brooder in "The Raven" who had turned to a bird for solace, Mr. Boynton had been consulting McDougall to answer administrative questions, and I am certain that "Glug" shed as much light on educational matters for Philip as "Nevermore" had brightened the nocturnal reader's Plutonian shore.

It was my curiosity and not just my matutinal habit of visiting the lab that drew me to that room. By opening the door a couple inches I could see what was going on inside and still have a commanding view of anyone going into the principal's office down the hall just by leaning my head back.

I heard and saw our beloved leader tap for attention with the mandible of some has-being which happened to be on the black countertop of the long oak desk that served as a demonstration table in the front of the class. *Alas, poor Yorick*, I thought, *I knew you before you became a gavel.*

I could tell that the class had been studying aquatic life by the way Mr. Conklin was talking about the whoppers he had caught at Crystal Lake which were nothing compared with the whoppers he was telling. When Walter, who was sitting near the back of the room under Conklin edict because Harriet had been placed front row center, asked if he had ever caught a coelacanth in Crystal Lake, Mr. Conklin sensed a dodge and, after consulting a reference book, made a comment about one that really got away that only he and Harriet (out of familial devotion and fear of flying jawbones) honored with a laugh.

After a couple minutes of the driest sea discourse since the ancient mariner couldn't swallow a drop of the stuff all around him, Walter glanced back at me and, after I had given him the "no luck" sign, attempted to stall by asking if eating the cartilage of sharks was good for the bones.

The corners of Mr. Conklin's mouth almost formed a smile but instead settled into what might be termed a benign grimace. Then, in carefully measured tones he said, "Denton, as to that I cannot say, but I will state quite emphatically that the sight of a shark nibbling on your bones would be very good for me."

The remark prompted some tittering from a few girls but more significantly spurred Walter into action. After another look back at me, he nudged the boy in front of him who asked if Mr. Conklin could again show them the difference between caudal and dorsal fins.

"Of course," he said, pulling the ring that brought down the charts and diagrams above the blackboard and reaching for his pointer simultaneously. He would have been better off reaching for the pills to control his high blood pressure because the figure displayed behind him was not a slithering fish but a curvaceous Marilyn Monroe in a brief outfit that could stop a bus.

"Notice first the fishnet stockings and shapely legs. Now, if you compare these with—FISHNET STOCKINGS AND SHAPELY LEGS?!!"

With that he snapped the pointer like a matchstick and his head pivoted back and forth like a scarecrow's in a windstorm as if he could not believe what he was seeing. His normal complexion, which could be described as mortician gray, had turned crimson as his lips uttered unintelligible imprecations. He silenced the laughter with a resounding "Quiet!" and moved his left leg up and down like he was pawing for a charge or auditioning for a "Slowly I turned" tryout. With an off-on gesture he adjusted the corners of his mustache as he seemed to be debating between sending the whole class through a sawmill or tying them to the nearest railroad tracks.

"Someone will pay for this act of sabotage," he promised, opening a drawer under the counter and once again leaping before he looked. "I am going to go down each row and shine the light of this stick of dynamite in the eyes of each one of you and when I find the culprit who—THIS STICK OF DYNAMITE?!!"

With that he tossed the stick away from him like it had bitten him, prompting squeals and screams from the girls who either climbed on chairs or sought refuge in the arms of nearby boys.

"Mind if look too, Miss Brooks?"

Like the boy on the burning deck I was on duty but I also got a hot-foot because I had become so preoccupied with the springing of Walter's trap that I had been asleep at the switch and had let down my rear guard. From the upcoming production *How Mixed Was My Metaphor*.

Before I could stammer out an explanation Mr. Stone said, "You know, you don't have to look through a keyhole. Everyone gets in free. Say, what game is going on in there?"

"Ah…Mr. Conklin is teaching biology."

"So I heard. I just came from the principal's office where Boynton seems to be in charge. I mentioned to him that I saw a hot rodder speeding through the parking lot and, when I asked him if anything is being done about that, I was told that the squid also travels quickly by a form of jet propulsion due to stringent contractions. When I left Boynton just a minute ago, he was talking to a frog who, for all I know, is now head of the music department. Shall we go inside?"

He followed me into the classroom where Harriet was applying a damp towel to her father's forehead. When he saw my companion, Mr. Conklin's eyes got even wider than they were when appraising Marilyn's knees.

"Mr. Stone! You're early."

"Mr. Conklin. You're late. Or rather you're about to become the late. Whether it's the late principal or the late Mr. Conklin depends on what I hear from you. And what is the meaning of this disgraceful photograph being displayed here?"

"I can explain everything, Mr. Stone," Conklin asserted. "But first, I need some water." He poured a glass for himself, drained it, looked at the label on the pitcher he had used and said, "Ah, there's nothing like a cool glass of formaldehyde to settle one's nerves. Now, why don't we go back to my office where we can—A COOL GLASS OF FORMALDEHYDE?!! Quick, Harriet. Mr. Stone. I've been poisoned. Call a doctor! Get me back to my office!"

The bell rang and, while the sniggering students filed out, Harriet tried to calm her father whose mouth was opening and closing like a beached flounder gasping for breath. Mr. Stone sniffed the contents of the pitcher with his aquiline nose and said, "I think you'll live." He examined the phony explosive whose fuse appeared to be a piece of clothesline, then nodded as if confirming a suspicion. "But perhaps you're right. We better discuss this in your office. If it still is your office."

Harriet assisted her father down the hall to his office where he pleaded his case. After much groveling from Mr. Conklin, Mr. Stone pronounced his verdict: Conklin needed to learn humility as principal before he would be considered for advancement and he was specifically instructed to leave teaching to those who can; Boynton was advised to gather up his amphibious friend and to take a lesson from the passenger pigeon by flying back to his classroom before his job at Madison became extinct; and I was told to mind my own business by keeping my eyes on my own students and out of drafty places.

Although Walter can secretly gloat that vengeance is his, the scandalous pinup is not because to claim ownership would be to admit he devised the artifice. Mr. Stone said he is going to keep the photograph to remind Conklin if he ever gets too big for his britches again, although I suspect that he has it rolled up somewhere as a reminder to himself of what women look like without britches.

So nothing really has changed. Mr. Conklin is still my nemesis, the man I can't get rid of and Mr. Boynton is my heartache, the man I can't get. If I ever meet that Robert Browning, I am going to ask him just one question: If all's right with the world, what planet am I living on?

The Dummy Up Caper

It all started with a pair of double knocks. (I knew right away it couldn't be that magpie; he flew the coop in "The Salty Tale Caper.") My secretary, Effie Perrine, had developed a code that, in addition to giving me a moment to assume a position of dignity in my chair, also allowed me a chance to close the eighty-proof drawer of my desk with my foot.

Effie stuck the blouse and bracelet part of her anatomy inside the door and said, "Sam, there's a man here to see you. He wants you to find a dummy."

"There are lots of ways to answer that one, but most of them require me to wear a top hat, carry a cane, and have a drummer handy. Does he look like he could end his search with a mirror?"

"Oh, no. He looks normal except, well, except he keeps looking down at his right knee as if he expects it to say something."

"That's nothing. When I'm sitting here, I keep looking down to my right expecting to hear the voice of my Old Grand-Dad calling me. Show him in, but keep your butterfly net handy."

The well-dressed, distinguished man Effie brought in glanced around with the eyes of a wary but not deranged individual so I welcomed him to take a seat in front of the desk. As he did so, he patted down a few wisps of gray on the top of his head and shooed over some of the windblown strings of hair away from his ears.

When I asked him why he had come to see me, he turned his head to his right which initially made me think he was turning the left side of his face to me because that was his good ear. I soon discovered that movement was an occupational quirk.

"Mr. Spade, I would like you to find three dummies for me."

I knew inflation was bad, but I didn't expect it to triple that quickly. He must have noticed my surprised expression for he smiled and continued.

"Let me explain. My name is Edgar Bergen and I am a ventriloquist. I am in San Francisco doing some stage shows. Sometime last night or, I should say, early this morning, when I returned to my hotel room at about 1:30 I discovered that the three dummies I use in my act had been stolen."

After I verified that there was no forced entry and nothing else had been taken, Bergen explained that he had come to me before going to the police because he knew they have many cases to work on while I could give this matter my immediate attention and perhaps recover the stolen items before any performances would have to be cancelled.

"That's asking a lot," I said. "Finding three dummies before tonight with no clues to go on."

"I can pay you…" He stopped to clear his throat as if an unseen figure had just insulted him. "I can pay you an appropriate amount for your time."

There was some more throat-clearing as we settled on a fee after which I asked for detailed descriptions of the missing items. Apparently one of them looks like a little playboy complete with monocle, number two is a freckle-faced hayseed with straw hat, and the third resembles the dreaded card in a game of Old Maid.

After giving me a taste of what each dummy sounds like, Bergen astounded me by, instead of putting words in my mouth, answered the question I was going to ask by providing me with names of people at the hotel he suspected might have committed the theft in order to discredit him or ruin his career in show business.

With the list of names in my hand and Bergen's retainer in my pocket, I wasted no time getting over to the hotel. It seemed like a convention of old vaudevillians because every floor was inhabited by jugglers, dancers, comics, singers, you name it. I wouldn't have been surprised even to see Fink there cleaning up with a twenty-mule team.

Eschewing Effie's way of attacking doors, I found one knock sufficient to get responses. The face behind the first door could have been the one on the barroom floor because it looked like there was a pound of sawdust under each eye. When apprised of the crime, this Mr. Allen said in his nasally way that he already had a braggart, rustic, and sharp-tongued woman in his employ and that he didn't need more kindling to go with the deadwood already stacked up in his alley. His alibi seemed pretty good. When asked where he was at 1:30 that morning, Allen said he was in Portland, although the censor made him take it out.

The next suspect on my list was this blue-eyed character named Benny who came to the door with a violin in his hand. I refused his offer to play for me for a buck, but I did have to fork over a fin before he would sing what little he knew about the case. He claimed that in the room across the hall from Bergen's suite I could find a shady character called Miltie who had been known to steal anything he could lift. When Benny told me he was checking out of the room and moving to a cheaper one in the basement, I asked him the room number down there if I needed to speak to him again. He said that no matter where he goes people will find him at 39.

While walking down the corridor on Bergen's floor I was approached by a stooped-over, shifty-eyed man with a mustache holding a cigar (how that mustache carried that cigar I don't know). He asked me, "What's the secret word?" When I said, "Miltie," he raised his eyebrows mischievously and said, "Fourth door on the left. If a woman answers your knock, that's him."

He scooted his way and I mine. It *was* a woman who opened the door, but she said her name was Gracie. I knew I was in for it when I said, "I'm Spade" and she replied, "I'm no trump. I guess the game is up. I confess." Before I could even form one hard-boiled question, my soft-pated companion was uncovering the tangled strands of her scheme.

As she led me into the bedroom where the lifeless figures were hidden in a closet, she explained how she had switched rooms with this unseen Miltie yesterday so she could be near Bergen's suite. Her husband, George Burns (and, after meeting his wife, I can understand why he's mad), had intimated one night while she was sitting on his lap that she was less than bright so she wanted to show him what three real dummies on his knees looked like.

So before I could even say 137596 the caper was over. Bergen was so grateful to have his dummies back in time for the first show that night that he didn't press charges and gave me free tickets for the performance so I could sit right up front. He even brought George and Gracie up on stage with him for some kidding about stolen dummies being a better stunt than a missing brother. Allen, Benny, and a lot of other entertainers in the audience seemed to be enjoying themselves, too, pointing at me and laughing it up

I can take a joke. I hope Bergen can, too, because that fellow with the shabby tailcoat and cigar I met in the hall and I have sent him a record of us singing "Hooray for Edgar Balding" ending with an off-key chorus of "Good Night, Sweetheart."

EXTRA ADDED ATTRACTIONS

At one time on some road this lone survivor was preceded by signs carrying the sentiments DEAR LOVER BOY, YOUR PHOTO CAME, and BUT YOUR DOGGONE BEARD.

The Passing Parade: Past Times, Passed Signs

AT ONE TIME IN 2004 THE EISNER MUSEUM of Advertising and Design on Water Street in Milwaukee displayed six signs on poles affixed to a plank in an unlit window. People passing by who paused to read the red-and-white signs with the words

>STATISTICS PROVE
>THAT FOLKS
>NEAR AND FAR
>WHO DRIVE LIKE CRAZY
>…ARE
>BURMA-SHAVE

were not just gazing at a window display; they were looking into the past at a bit of Americana.

Motorists driving along roads during the decades from Silent Cal to JFK knew what those signs represented. They meant "Slow down. We're coming to some Burma-Shave signs. They're going to make us smile and think." "And," the folks at Burma-Shave might have added, "Buy the product the next time you go to the store."

That product, a brushless shaving cream pitched to men as a convenient alternative to dealing with mugs and brushes, could be purchased in jars, tubes, or cans (aka "bombs").

Clinton Odell, a Minneapolis attorney and insurance man, has been credited as the person chiefly responsible for the production of Burma-Shave, the proliferation of the sign campaign, and the success of the company which began with a liniment concocted by his father. The company was called Burma (where the oils originated)-Vita (Latin for *vigor*). Clinton, wisely realizing that liniment is only needed when muscles are sore whereas facial hair is always growing, decided to diversify by asking a chemist to create a brushless cream similar to one being made in England. After testing hundreds of formulas, it was determined (as so often happens in the serendipitous world of inventions) that an "unfresh" version of an early formulation received the necessary "Eureka!"

The directions were simple: "Wash face thoroly [*sic*] with soap and water, preferably warm. Spread on Burma-Shave with fingers. After spreading, pat—but do not rub. Allow a minute for Burma-Shave to set. Shave."

During the minute while wiping the sticky residue off his hands and hoping his cheeks would not harden into a rigid mask, the shaver might be reading the insert written by Chairman of the Board Odell himself entitled "The Art of Shaving" which provided specific suggestions including how long to wash the face, how much cream to use, and what shave stokes to use. (He did not indicate what was par for a face.) Never one to waste a chance to promote, Odell made use of every bit of space on the packaging including the flaps of the box which carried the words "For that exhilarating after shave use Burma-Shave Lotion" and "For a perfect shave Burma-Shave blades 10 for 25 cents." A single blade could often be found inside packages with this slogan on the envelope: "No sharper blade ever made." Encircling the tube itself appeared the slogan "No Brush, No Lather" and, above the product name, "New…Improved."

It was Clinton's son Allan who developed a new and improved way of selling Burma-Shave when he observed a series of signs leading to a gas station. Rather than pointing to what was ahead down the road, Allan reasoned, let's lead motorists to our cream with a series of signs containing short messages that stay in the mind.

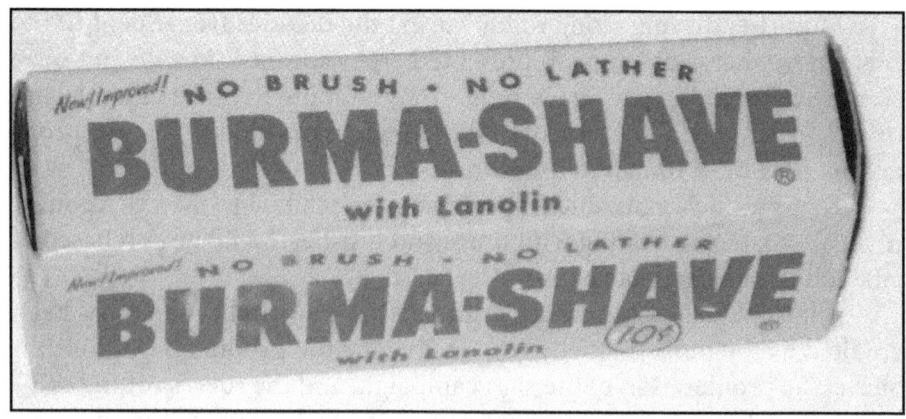

The product behind the sign campaign.

Some of the early sets did just that: used the "no brush, no lather" pitch, pronounced Burma-Shave fine for the skin, gave the price ("half a pound for half a dollar"), and indicated that drugstores carried it.

By 1931 the message was still the same but the rhyming cadence that became the hallmark of Burma-Shave signs was in full force as evidenced by

>HELLO DRUGGIST
>I DON'T MEAN MAYBE
>YES
>SIR
>THAT'S MY BABY
>BURMA-SHAVE

>HALF A POUND
>FOR
>HALF A BUCK
>COME ON SHAVERS
>YOU'RE IN LUCK
>BURMA-SHAVE

In the mid-thirties humor began to appear in jingles like

>SMITH BROTHERS
>WOULD LOOK IMMENSE
>IF THEY COULD JUST
>COUGH UP 50 CENTS
>FOR HALF POUND JAR
>BURMA-SHAVE

>JIMMIE SAID A
>NAUGHTY WORD
>JIMMIE'S MOTHER OVERHEARD
>SOAPSUDS? NO!
>HE PREFERRED
>BURMA-SHAVE

Motorists didn't mind if the galloping rhythm developed a charley horse now and then or if the lines were of uneven length; the fun came just from reading the jingles out loud. In some automobiles the signs became a game in which each passenger read a line. Imagine the groans from the family that recited

> IF HARMONY
> IS WHAT
> YOU CRAVE
> THEN GET
> A TUBA
> BURMA-SHAVE

> YOU KNOW
> YOUR ONIONS
> LETTUCE SUPPOSE
> THIS BEETS 'EM ALL
> DON'T TURNIP YOUR NOSE
> BURMA-SHAVE

That reading the signs had become a family pastime was apparent in this set:

> SLOW DOWN, PA
> SAKES ALIVE
> MA MISSED
> SIGNS FOUR
> AND FIVE
> BURMA-SHAVE

One grouping even encouraged people to join in:

> AS YOU DRIVE
> PLAY THIS GAME
> CONSTRUCT
> A JINGLE
> WITH THIS NAME
> BURMA-SHAVE

It is not a simple task to write a catchy verse in five lines with usually one, two, or three words to a line *and* sell the product so, in effect, the old challenge of "If you think you can do better, you try it" was issued to the public. Thousands of would-be jinglers submitted entries and quite a few of them were rewarded with $100 checks after their rhymes made the cut.

Whether penned by contestants or by copywriters, a number of the jingles possessed sharp teeth that had a satiric bite to them not unlike a remark uttered by Fred Allen. Examples include

> HERE'S SOMETHING
> THAT COULD
> EVEN SOAK
> THE WHISKERS OFF
> A RADIO JOKE
> BURMA-SHAVE
>
> ARE YOUR WHISKERS
> WHEN YOU WAKE
> TOUGHER THAN
> A TWO-BIT STEAK?
> TRY
> BURMA-SHAVE
>
> DRINKING DRIVERS
> ENHANCE THEIR
> CHANCE
> TO HIGHBALL HOME
> IN AN AMBULANCE
> BURMA-SHAVE

By 1939 the Burma-Shave signs had become so popular a roadside attraction that Odell, realizing that drivers slowing down to read them should be aware of traffic safety, increased the number of public service reminders on the signs. Some of these messages still carried a product pitch:

> PAST
> SCHOOHOUSES
> TAKE IT SLOW
> LET THE LITTLE
> SHAVERS GROW
> BURMA-SHAVE
>
> CARELESS DRIVING
> SOON WE HOPE
> WILL GO
> THE WAY
> OF BRUSH AND SOAP
> BURMA-SHAVE

Others were straightforward appeals for caution behind the wheel:

> HARDLY A DRIVER
> IS NOW ALIVE
> WHO PASSED ON HILLS
> AT 75
> BURMA-SHAVE

> AT CROSSROADS
> DON'T JUST
> TRUST TO LUCK
> THE OTHER CAR
> MAY BE A TRUCK
> BURMA-SHAVE

During World II the commitment to public service continued with the fifth sign carrying a plea to buy defense or war bonds preceded by rhymes such as

> LET'S MAKE HITLER
> AND HIROHITO
> LOOK AS SICK AS
> OLD BENITO

> MAYBE YOU CAN'T
> SHOULDER A GUN
> BUT YOU CAN SHOULDER
> THE COST OF ONE

Yet humor remained at the heart of the verses. Everyone admires those who do not take themselves too seriously, and a number of the signs asked us to have a laugh on Burma-Shave:

> THIS IS NOT
> A CLEVER VERSE
> I TRIED
> AND TRIED
> BUT JUST
> GOT WORSE
> BURMA-SHAVE

The Passing Parade: Past Times, Passed Signs • 509

> JUST THIS ONCE
> AND JUST FOR FUN
> WE'LL LET YOU
> FINISH
> WHAT WE'VE BEGUN
> ???

> 'TWOULD BE
> MORE FUN
> TO GO BY AIR
> IF WE COULD PUT
> THESE SIGNS UP THERE
> BURMA-SHAVE

The jingle

> IF YOU DON'T KNOW
> WHOSE SIGNS
> THESE ARE
> YOU CAN'T HAVE
> DRIVEN VERY FAR

suggests that, because of their fame, the folks at Burma-Vita were chuckling with us and also laughing all the way to the bank.

Burma-Vita was, of course, in the business of selling a product, not just a concept of driving diversion so the light touch in the signage never let motorists forget for very long that Burma-Shave was superior to any competitors with jingles which reflected a before and after image such as

> SINCE HUBBY
> TRIED THE SUBSTITUTE
> HE'S 1/3 MAN
> 2/3 BRUTE
> BURMA-SHAVE

> HE ALWAYS USED
> A STEAMING TOWEL
> AND MUG AND BRUSH
> AND LANGUAGE FOUL

'TIL HE TRIED
BURMA-SHAVE

Ultimately, though, it was not competition from other companies that led to the vanishing of the Burma-Shave signs from the countryside. Interstate highways either replaced rural routes or made them the road less traveled by. The motto of drivers became "Let's hurry up and get where we're going" instead of "Let's slow down and read." Also, advertisers were putting more money into television, a medium that can reach millions at any hour of the day with images and sounds more enticing than written messages that only would be seen by those motorists who happened to take their eyes off the road to see some reddish blurs passing at fifty-five miles an hour.

For several years, from 1956 through 1958, no new signs appeared. Some fresh jingles cropped up in 1959 and 1960, but the end was near. By 1963, the last year for the signs, the subject matter of some of them may have seemed irrelevant or irreverent. Two examples:

PEDRO
WALKED
BACK HOME, BY GOLLY
HIS BRISTLY CHIN
WAS HOT-TO-MOLLY
BURMA-SHAVE
[first used in 1952]

IN CUPID'S LITTLE
BAG OF TRIX
HERE'S THE ONE
THAT CLIX
WITH CHIX
BURMA-SHAVE
[a repeat of a 1947 sign]

Also in 1963 Phillip Morris Inc. purchased the Burma-Shave Company. Shortly thereafter it was determined that, rather than spend $200,000 a year to construct and maintain the signs, the signs would be removed and the roadside campaign abolished.

At one time 40,000 individual Burma-Shave signs could be found dotting American byways. Over the years 600 jingles were created. Now one still may be fortunate to find an isolated, weathered sign at an antique mall or perhaps see a complete set exhibited in an institution. The 1943 jingle intended as a jab against competitors rings with a note of ironic prophecy in the 21st century:

>   SHAVING BRUSHES
>   YOU'LL SOON SEE 'EM
>   ON THE SHELF
>   IN SOME
>   MUSEUM
>   BURMA-SHAVE

Certainly some pedestrians who passed the Eisner Museum when the signs were displayed took time to stop and reflect on the significance of those six signs, perhaps remembering a time when they, in flesh or in spirit, traveled a bygone road and put the brake on life's hectic pace. In their hearts they might have been speaking a jingle that was never seen but always felt:

>   TO THIS DAY
>   OUR MESSAGE
>   IS TERSE:
>   THANKS A LOT
>   FOR EVERY VERSE
>   BURMA GAVE

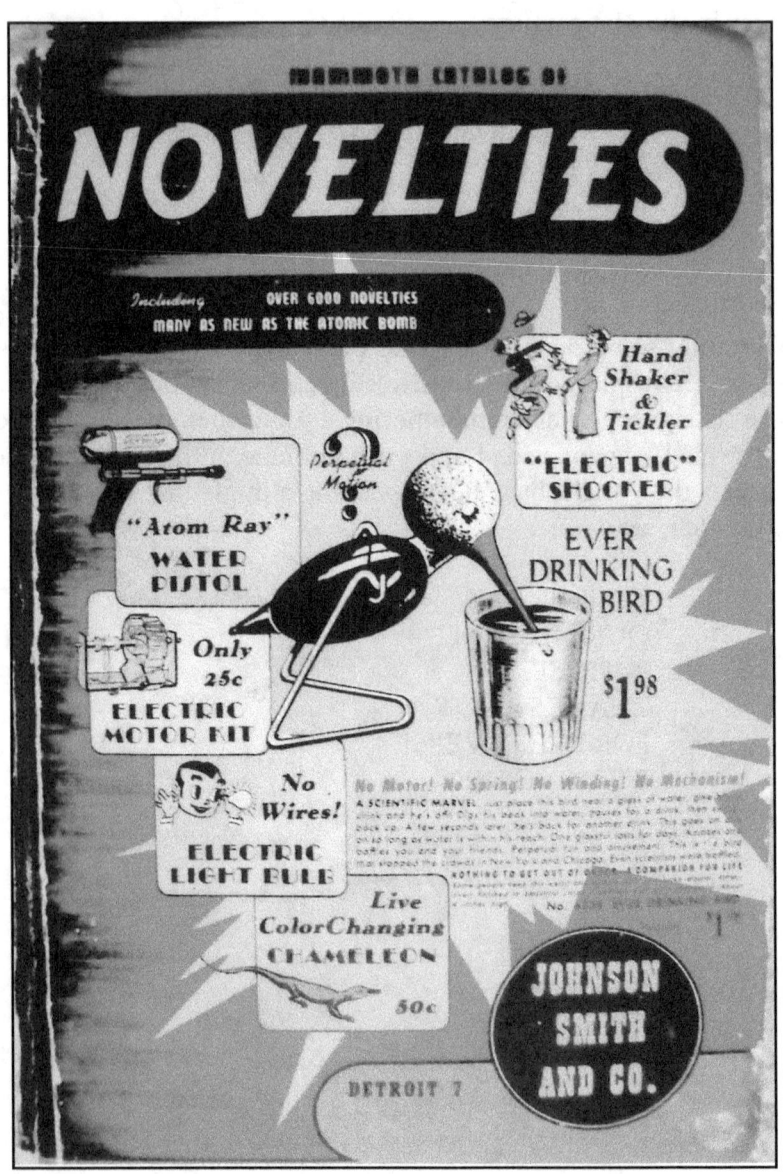

One catalog that really delivered the goods.

Johnson Smith Specialties: Magic Moments

NEARLY EVERYONE CAN RECALL SOME EVENTS of growing up when the sense of excitement and expectation reached its zenith. It may have been those frosty Christmas Eves when the hands of clocks also appeared to be frozen or perhaps an automobile trip to a fair or carnival that never seemed to end. For me the highest point of juvenile anticipation occurred when rushing home from the post office with a package of items I had ordered from Johnson Smith and Company.

Just receiving the catalog alone advanced my pulse rate as I prepared to peruse that printed parade of 6,000 novelties designed to "amaze and amuse." Any company that had adopted as its mottoes "There are tricks in all trades, but our trade is all tricks" and "We are in business for fun" had a live one on the hook the moment it added the address of Master Clair Schulz to its mailing list.

What boy wouldn't have fun with a cornucopia of items at dimestore prices that included shipping? And JS accepted just about any kind of payment: money orders, checks, currency, postage stamps, coins, even refund checks from Sears, Wards, and other companies. Once, when my allowance had not stretched as far as my thirst for gadgets and gewgaws, I briefly considered sending with my partial payment an unused ticket redeemable at our local theater, then realized that it might be a slight imposition to ask Johnson and Smith (I pictured the owners as two jokesters in the mold of Olsen and Johnson who filled orders between pie-throwing contests) to travel from Michigan to Wisconsin just to watch Ma chewing out Pa Kettle or Francis the talking mule munching hay.

Even though my orders were always under $5.00, they were returned with unvarying promptness. I would mail my postal money orders after school on Monday and the following Saturday without fail when I peered with breathless anticipation into Box 368 there would be the little card requesting me to pick up my package of novelties at the counter.

Novelties are "articles of trade whose value is chiefly decorative, comic, or the like and whose appeal is often transitory." Boys want merchandise for the ages—the ages eight to twelve, so Johnson Smith scratched their urge by appealing to their sense of curiosity and adventure with an array of mechanical and mystical items at bargain prices.

Besides quick service and low prices another reason I kept sending my money around Lake Michigan was because I considered the folks at JS trustworthy friends who tried to be straightforward in their descriptions. When they trumpeted the value of the lucky dime ring ("wear one and you'll never go broke"), the wording made it clear that the coin was not included. The copywriters must have been boys at heart for they knew how to tantalize with phrases like "worn by West Indian natives to whom it has a peculiar significance," "appears to be a mystic ring of some sort," and "we do not make any claims for it but merely offer it as an interesting novelty," disclaimers and teasers which disarmed claims of false advertising and yet contained enough mystery to tempt those youngsters experiencing the wonder years.

The dime ring performed like the spare tire we forgot to keep inflated: no problems until we needed it. After I removed Old Mercury the first time for some emergency (probably to satisfy a craving for a handful of nonpareils), the prongs refused to hold its successors in place even when I rubbed my rabbit foot charm and Egyptian lucky pocket coin. After losing two dimes, I realized that my mother had a better plan for never going broke: tie the dime in a corner of a handkerchief, stick it in my pocket, and don't ever spend it.

I did not lose the penny-in-a-bottle marvel, although none of my friends were as intrigued as I was with the mystery of a coin in a tiny glass container barely big enough to hold it with a hole on top the width of a toothpick. They seemed more intent on teasing me by saying that I gave thirty-nine of my pennies to purchase one of Johnson Smith's. To this day I am not certain how the penny got in the jug and I don't want to know for there are some enigmas like why do fools fall in love that are better off unexplained.

Some items, like watches, in the JS catalog had me betwixt and between. I certainly could not afford the seven-jewel Swiss watches priced at $25.00. The only timepiece I could purchase with my meager allowance was the sun dial attached to a leatherette strap, priced at twenty-five cents, which I am certain lived up to its billing of being waterproof and never needing winding but might have proved difficult to read inside, on cloudy days, or at night.

The bottle of invisible ink I did order presented another problem of practicality. In order to read the written message the paper needed to be held close to a source of light like a lamp or a candle and some of the letters never seemed to show through no matter how hard I pressed on the pen or how bright the illumination. Complicating matters was the fact that my handwriting has always been atrocious. One summer day I hid the secret message "Meet me behind our garage at 3:30" for friend Billy who lived next door to read. At the appointed time he was cooling his heels because he thought he was supposed to go down in his basement and cough.

The lures of "Be a movie king!" and "Have a Barrel of Fun!" caught my mind's eye as I pictured myself loading one Castle film after another in one of the illustrated 16mm movie projectors, but I couldn't even afford the cartoons themselves so I settled for a book of hand shadows and ended up wiggling my fingers and saying, "What's up, Doc?," "Sufferin' succotash," and other animated expressions to the north wall from the stage of my bed.

The JS catalog offered merchandise for the artistic like books on drawing and a pantograph as well as microscopes, motors, model airplanes, radios, and chemistry sets for the mechanically-inclined, but I avoided such diversions because those items sounded like school or work. I wanted novelties I could have fun with as soon as I lifted the enchantments out of the box.

The See-o-Scope, a cardboard periscope with crude optics, allowed me to see (not too clearly or too far) without being seen (if I hid in a bush, behind a fence, or stayed in my room).

The Ventrilo consisted of two small curved metal pieces surrounded by a piece of gauze. The accompanying instructions told users to dip the Ventrilo in water, "press it against the roof of the mouth and hiss strongly through it until a sound comes through. Then produce talking and other imitations." Even with an illustrated book and practice I became convinced that I was making as much progress as Mortimer Snerd would have made trying to impersonate Edgar Bergen and that if I ever performed before others the strong hissing noise would not be coming from me.

The Panama puzzle padlock was a trick lock that would not budge when I handed it to friends but which opened magically for me when I held it behind my back. I will reveal the secret of this trick to anyone who sends me thirty-five cents. Money orders, checks, coins, postage stamps, and refund checks accepted.

The spring snake that catapulted out of a metal canister instead of the promised candy proved to be a scream in mores ways than one. Note to potential practical jokers: word spreads quickly about this trick so spring the trap often while the first victim is still recovering from shock. The same dictum applied to the joy buzzer that passed a tingle from donor to recipient. By lunchtime everyone in school had been warned: "Don't shake hands with Schulz."

Hot toothpicks did not go over well because very few of my male classmates used them and the girls would not consider such an unladylike habit, but the pepper candy and gum burned a few tongues.

Sneezing powder left the biter bitten and a little bitter. The directions stated that the user should place the powder on the back of the hand, blow it into the air, and watch other people sneeze which was fine if I stopped breathing (something I have always been averse to doing) or leave the room immediately (which would have prevented me from seeing the effect of the joke). I learned my lesson from that misfire and therefore refrained from ordering the itching powder.

Dirty soap appeared to be white in color but contained a dye that caused it to lather black. I tested this one myself and never used it on anyone else because, although it may have been a riot at boarding houses where blame is difficult to place, I knew that I alone would feel the effects of a filthy lavatory in our only bathroom.

The whizzer sparkler provided my own personal fireworks under the covers as the revolving wheel threw off red, white, and blue sparks, although the display of pyrotechnics left my bedclothes and pajamas smelling distinctly flinty.

A box of comic letterheads that touted spots like the Diaper Towers ("Covers the Water Front") and the Broken Arms Hotel ("Just Another Joint") amused me if no one else. A similar item, the sign "Silence—Genius at work," thumb tacked to the hall side of my bedroom door for years, should have earned me a spot on *You Asked For It* because nearly every pal who saw it taunted me with "Are you renting your room to someone else now?" or similar flippant remark.

The bait for the black eye joke took the form of a promise that a boy would see something dirty if he looked in the kaleidoscope. The dirty part, of course, was the ring around his eye he would see in a mirror after pressing the eyepiece to his face. The trick came with the caveat "it isn't a bad joke if your friend isn't hot-tempered," a wise precaution so the wrong person's eye didn't get blackened.

Likewise common sense led me to find amiable sorts for the dribble glass and to use only water so I could tell the victim, "It will dry up quickly." At least once when pulling this gag I was told to dry up myself.

Books of snappy jokes provided me with patter that I hoped would distract my friends from my fumbling fingers as I clumsily attempted feats of legerdemain. I don't think an appearance by the ghost of Joe Miller whose wheezes I recited could have hidden the fact that the rubber pea seemed to have a will of its own when I manipulated the three plastic walnut shells around or that I had reversed the direction of the sliding portion of the coin-in-a-box trick. It was not in the cards for me either, even with a marked deck, because I could not keep my spiel going and concentrate on deciphering the intricate shapes on the backs at the same time.

Although tattoo transfers never transferred very accurately from sheet to skin, it was still a treat to be a cockney, cockamamie sailor for a day. A celluloid monocle, cardboard mask, or seedy wig could be added for effect. JS asked the question "How would you look with a mustache?" and even though the answer turned out to be "Pretty silly," it only cost me twelve cents to find out.

And it only took a buck to snag a grab bag that promised a dozen novelties which raised my level of expectation on those Saturday mornings even higher. What was that rattle in the box? Could it be a gyroscope that would spin on the point of a pin? Or maybe Hotsy and Totsy, the magnetic Scotty dogs? The five-in-one mystery hidden compass? The mechanical pencil with the magic multiplier on the barrel? A pocket-sized magic wand so I could bedazzle at a moment's notice? Jumping beans? The glow-in-the-dark badge that I could flash in the face of a nocturnal burglar? A magic pocket mirror that distorted faces like those full-sized beauties in fun houses? A lapel squirting flower? A boomerang that comes with the claim "there is no thrill like throwing a boomerang and watching it come back"? No thrill except, of course, for the arrival of an order from Johnson Smith.

People can still order from the Johnson Smith Company which has been located in Bradenton, Florida since 1986. The business was founded in 1914 by Alfred Johnson Smith in Chicago, moved to Racine in 1926 and then to Detroit in 1935 where it remained until the early seventies when it relocated to nearby Mount Clemens. The JS stock continues to lean toward the playful and unusual like a sneezing tissue holder that talks back and plastic pink flamingoes for porch or yard, but a fair share of the offerings now are franchised items like Elvis and Stars Wars collectibles and of well-known products which can be found in stores or in other catalogs.

That was not the case in the JS catalogs I remember. Where else could a boy buy ten pounds of magazines for a mere $1.50 postpaid, then wonder if he should have ordered the Samson gymnasium or a grip-of-steel developer first so he would have the strength to lug the cumbersome box home? Or have live snakes, mice, alligators, turtles, pigeons, and chameleons delivered to his doorstep (and probably delivered a case of the screaming meemies to his mother at the same time)? He could also order charms, cameras, miniature Bibles, gazing balls for telling fortunes, banks, puzzles, kazoos, pennants, copies of the *Hobo News*, books on how to raise chicks and how to do tricks, Ouija boards, plants both innocuous and carnivorous, bottles of snake oil, puppets and marionettes, bicycle horns, billfolds, an ever-drinking, ever-bobbing penguin who never said "when" until its glass was empty, and an automatic fisherman that "will catch fish while you sleep." Who could sleep with visions of exploding dance bombs and wildcat bicycle sirens screeching in our heads?

Readers of these words who open my high school annual will find two points of pertinent interest there. Next to my senior photograph is the quotation "Remember: I'm not always right, but I'm never wrong," a one-liner cribbed from a JS book of snappy jokes. Five pages later I appear again in a photo titled "Wittiest" in which I am grinning like the Cheshire Cat as I pretend to be grabbing for the waist of Susan, my female counterpart, who is standing on a chair and styling my crew cut with an oversized comb. (This caption should appear under the photo: "Comb appears through the courtesy of Clair Schulz who appears through the indulgence of friends and family and the manifold offerings of Johnson Smith and Company.")

Today all that remains from those orders are Ventrilo and an envelope of mummified sneezing powder that wouldn't bring a tear to a gnat's eye. A few years ago while shopping in a store I bought a battery-powered device that could easily be mistaken for a remote control which causes garage doors to open and close. There are buttons marked "laugh," "rim shot," "boing," etc. on the front; pressing each activates the appropriate sound effect from a memory chip. When I take the unit from a desk drawer on certain evenings and touch the magic buttons, for a few moments I am not the balding, arthritic malcontent sitting in a high-backed chair but once again the bright-eyed, smiling youth heading home with legs pumping, lungs congested with an unbearable lust for fun and a heart overflowing with a boundless sense of joy, holding on for dear life with both hands.

What peekaboo meant in 1941.

A Travelogue Down Memory Lane

NOSTALGIA HAS YOU IN ITS POWER

when someone says	and instead of	you think of
pep	energy	pins
cat's eye	feline	Philco
shake-up	change of staff	mug
brownie	chocolate	camera
silver	high yield	hi-yo
bay	Tampa	rum
lead	mineral	Scripto
BO	box office	Lifebuoy
Petty	racecars	pinups
yellow	submarine	kid
premium	gasoline	decoder
Leo	DeCaprio	MGM
hut	shack	sut
bazooka	bubble gum	Bob Burns
alley	garbage cans	Fred Allen
punch	bowl	board
lizards	reptiles	Orphan Annie
Carter	Jimmy	little liver pills
trigger	pistol	Roy Rogers
Vogue	magazine	picture records
Arch	St. Louis	Oboler
bums	hoboes	Brooklyn Dodgers
soapbox	speech	racer

Nostalgia has you in its power

when someone says	and instead of	you think of
sting	bee	Green Hornet
peekaboo	baby	Veronica Lake
Gump	Forrest	Andy
cup	saucer	Dixie
lollipop	candy	Shirley Temple
disc	compact	transcription
notary	public	Sojac
magic	Johnson	Johnson Smith
fearless	brave	Fosdick
viaduct	railroad	Groucho and Chico
sad	gloomy	Sack
mackerel	fishing	Amos and Andy
boys	Backstreet	Bowery
stamps	postage	ration
Bel Air	California	Chevrolet
buck	dollar	Rogers
shave	razor	Burma
splinter	tweezers	Ted Williams
blackjack	cards	chewing gum
cracker	saltine	jack
moon	Neil Armstrong	Mullins
Lincoln	penny	logs
Buffalo	Bills	Bob
cinnamon rolls	bakery	Jack Benny
Richard	Simmons	open the door
gabby	talkative	Hayes
sandwich	peanut butter	Dagwood
eyebrow	pencil	John L. Lewis
whispering	secret	Paul Whiteman
fan	breeze	Sally Rand
weird	strange	tales
bunny	rabbit	Berrigan
Ming	porcelain	the Merciless
old-fashioned	cocktail	Dad's Root Beer
pirates	Pittsburgh	Terry
jingles	slogans	Andy Devine

SELECTED SHORT SUBJECTS

What pleasures moviegoers in Deposit, New York experienced in just one week in 1941: An actor in an Oscar-winning performance, a comedian in his breakthrough role, a western…

And a light romantic comedy. And adventures from the gridiron and hospital ward. *And* a chance to win the jackpot.

Pleasure Palaces

FOR MANY PEOPLE, GOING TO THE MOVIES means being directed into one of four or more chambers that resemble lecture halls, munching on food more expensive and less exotic than what is at home, watching dramas or comedies barely indistinguishable from those found on cable network series or viewing fantasies laden with computer-generated special effects not unlike those seen in video games played countless times, and then exiting into the garish light of shopping mall walkways or nondescript parking lots. The entire experience is as unremarkable as a trip to Target where both the acting and the popcorn are better.

In the thirties, forties, and fifties even small communities could boast of having a theater that was the toast of the town. The marquee shone like a beacon in a lighthouse when glittering and at all times extended a beneficent hand to bless those who passed under it. One look down Main Street told any stranger that this couldn't be a one-horse town with Roy Rogers or John Wayne riding tall in the saddle.

I checked the window cards every week because a film rarely was around for longer than three days. My town was what would be today called a small market so we often got the second-runs or rereleases which didn't bother me. *The Uninvited* could cause as many chills in 1953 as it did in 1944.

When I reached the age of ten or so, my parents allowed me to "go to the show" by myself. Because the theater was scarcely two blocks from my house, I tried to stretch out the adventure because I somehow knew even then that anticipation can be better than realization. I sauntered past the ticket booth a couple times with my hands in my pockets, looking casually at the posters on display like a bon vivant trying to decide between this and a supper club for diversion when my bankroll consisted of a quarter clutched in each fist.

It may seem hard to believe in a time when it takes twenty-five dollars to get a family of four into a theater that two bits would open the magic door, but then a quarter was twenty-five cents. Now tooth fairies who dare leave a measly quarter under a pillow stand a fair chance of having the remaining teeth embedded in them before they reach the door.

I could feel my chest constrict with exhilaration and my mouth go dry as soon as I stepped in the lobby. Though not yet in the sanctum sanctorum, I already felt giddy as I studied the lobby cards and inhaled the aroma of that butter-laden, sodium-loaded, artery-clogging mountain of fluff. But popcorn could be enjoyed at home. I was drawn to the cavity-causing sundries that spoiled appetites and were frowned upon by parents: Necco wafers, Clark bars, spearmint leaves, Boston baked beans, candied almonds, and Black Crows. I liked those Crows, responsible for more lockjaw than rusty nails, and I never felt comfortable doing my Gabby Hayes imitation without a couple of them in my cheeks to garble my words and nauseate those in range of my licorice spray.

With goodies in hand and pocket, I felt my way into the house of no usher. The manager sometimes surreptitiously stepped in to see if anything was amiss, but there was little for him to do except shake a finger at smoochers and point to the screen as if to say, "Pay attention to the movie. There'll be a quiz later."

The seats may have been well-worn and their bottoms encrusted with gum, but in one of them I felt enthroned. When the green velvet curtain parted for Columbia's torch or Leo's roar, I considered it a command performance and very special. And it was. Hollywood's intent then was to entertain, not to stupefy and desensitize.

I always sat in the center section because that seemed the best spot to absorb all the new sights and sounds coming into my life. To this day I have not seen a shade of red that seared my retinas as deeply as that radiating from the tresses of Rhonda Fleming in *A Connecticut Yankee in King Arthur's Court* nor heard any series of notes that moved faster from my ears to my throat than those floating through the opening credits of *The High and the Mighty*.

We were never cheated in one of those pleasure palaces because, in addition to one or two features, we might see a newsreel, a cartoon, previews of coming attractions, sometimes a comedy or musical short subject and, on Saturday, an episode from a serial. Come Monday morning girls caught musing instead of minding their math were probably still Holden William in their arms. If a boy missed school that day, our standard joke was "He isn't sick. He's still chasing bad guys through the balcony with Randolph Scott."

Back then I couldn't think of a better place to be than in that comfortably cool oasis. Now I would give a basketful of quarters to turn the store that sits where legends once lived back into that house of dreams.

I regret not saving those handouts distributed after the shows were over. Even though we had been given a song in our hearts and a smile on our lips to take home, we were also handed something tangible as we left, those folded sheets of paper that heralded a film coming soon to a theater near and dear to us. I now have heralds for *The Paleface* and three Abbott and Costello films that make me smile and bring back fond remembrances, but I wish I had one for *The Best Years of Our Lives* because they certainly were.

Why not "A Smokin' Pipe" or "A Rockin' Chair"?

The Song Is Ended
(But the Malady Lingers On)

LIKE MANY PEOPLE I am fond of listening to music in the car or at home. Over the years I have discovered that my enjoyment is increased if I just listen and don't ask questions about what I am hearing. Trying to figure out the mysteries of pop hits can cause more insomnia than visions of mushroom clouds.

At one time I wondered why one-hit wonders never got to second base, but then I realized it was probably for the best. Maybe Marcie Blane's only object in life was to be Bobby's girl. Depression over being pushed too hard did in the Seeds and the Fendermen never got over the mule skinner blues. The Electric Prunes could not face the light after having too much to dream and the Swingin' Medallions were worn out after taking a double shot of their baby's love.

Likewise it is best just to listen to the lyrics or sing along with them and not expect sense to follow the melody. Most people who have heard "Splish Splash," a hit supposedly written in less than half an hour, will wonder why it took so long to create. Every December radio stations dust off the Beach Boys' holiday album to play "Little Saint Nick" with the memorable line "Christmas comes this time each year," which is a real shock to those of us who expect it in August.

But by far the most perplexing question surrounding popular music is how titles for instrumentals are selected. Some melodies, of course, suggest a name. "Alley Cat" sounds like a cat tiptoeing over the piano keys. "Apache" employs Native American rhythms and "Telstar" effectively incorporates aerospace sounds into the composition. But most of the titles seem to have been created by whim (probably Bud Whim who worked in a cubicle under the Brill Building in New York, sending his suggestions up through cracks in the floor).

"Wipe Out" would have been a hit with the title "Walk, Don't Run" and vice versa. (In fact, either one could have been called "Vice Versa.") A similar trade could have been made between Bill Pursell and Percy Faith with "Our Winter Love" and "A Summer Place." The only drawback might be Pursell's reluctance to have everyone think of Troy Donahue whenever they heard his masterpiece.

Some of the titles lead one to believe they came about after uninspired composers threw darts at a map. "Calcutta" could have become "Midnight in Moscow" or "A Walk in the Black Forest" if someone's aim had been a little higher or lower.

Other writers may have reached for handy refreshments in the recording studio. We can imagine someone saying, "Al, put down that java and tell me what we should call that one. And leave that cotton candy alone." Or maybe "Booker, is your hamburger the one with green onions?"

Still other stumped parties probably took to heart the musical advice "Look through any window. What do you see?" "Hmm. There goes a car with mag wheels. Wheels. We'll call it 'Wheels.'" "Those dudes are strutting right along like they're soulful. They're doing a soulful strut. Hey! That's it!" No need to wonder what had just passed the day "Music to Watch Girls By" was created.

A few titles that made it on labels may have just been a reflection of a recent experience like a wild weekend or a last date. It is probably best not to speculate what kind of a concert or movie brought into being "Classical Gas" and "Love Is Blue."

The unanswered question is still why one title over another. Could it be that Naomi Neville called her composition "Whipped Cream" instead of "Shredded Cabbage" because she presciently knew brunettes do not look very sultry when photographed for album covers sitting in a pile of sauerkraut? When the Champs finished their toe-tapping ditty, instead of "Tequila!" they could have shouted "Papaya!" and been right in rhythm. Rather than selecting "Stranger on the Shore" for his somber piece, Acker Bilk could have called it "Shoebox on the Table" without losing the mood. Dave "Baby" Cortez's happy organ would have been just as pleased if "Rinky Dink" was known as "My Aching Back." The repetitive chords of "On the Rebound" and "Pick Up the Pieces" would sound just as routine but have more label appeal if they were transformed into "Spear the Pickle" and "Take Out the Garbage."

No matter what shape my tummy or mind is in I find it difficult to refrain from thinking about music. I just hope that all this ruminating which has now carried over into the evening hours doesn't disturb my sleep. My worst nightmare might be watching a baby elephant walk over forty miles of bad road to a pipeline by the raunchy part of Washington Square where a lonely bull with sugar lips is dancing a summer samba to cheer up the poor boy in fancy pants doing the wiggle wobble after drinking one mint julep in the quiet village not far from where the horse is grazing in the grass while in the background Porter Wagoner is singing "What is to be will be, what ain't to be just might happen."

A reminder of a time when peeking did not involve prying.

Sweet Mystery of Life, At Last We've Lost You

AMONG THE MOST-PRIZED MEMENTOES of people who grew up listening to old-time radio are the premiums that could be purchased for a box top and a dime. The decoders, badges, and whistles we received entertained us, but none of those trinkets seemed as exciting as the rings that could be worn to school to prove membership in secret organizations like Orphan Annie's Secret Society, Captain Midnight's Secret Squadron, or Tom Mix's Straight Shooters. Among the rings most coveted then were those that suggested a hidden adventure such as the Sky King Mystery Picture Ring, Orphan Annie Silver Star Triple Mystery Secret Compartment Ring, and the Tom Mix Mystery Ring with a tiny hole in the side through which a photograph of Tom and his horse Tony could be seen.

I still cherish the Tom Mix Mystery Ring I have and, although I sometimes think about where some of the other premiums are, I wonder still more about where the mystery has gone in our society. Today nothing seems to be hidden, everything has to be revealed.

At one time people in the public eye were entitled to some privacy. No more. Now if someone remotely related to a member of the British royalty wants to have her feet kissed by an admirer in a secluded spot, it is likely to be caught by a telephoto lens and the lead story on the six o'clock news. A presidential burp or sneeze will be turned into a sound bite before the day is over. It is becoming more difficult for celebrities to write a tell-all autobiography. What can Warren Beatty or Johnny Depp say about their love lives that *People* and *Vanity Fair* have not already told us?

Try to find some mystery or subtlety at theaters. Audiences buying tickets to movies years ago knew they were going to be treated to laughs, songs, dancing, romance, thrills, and something left to the imagination.

Now the warnings following reviews in newspapers tell what to expect: violence, nudity, gore, sexual content, profanity. One hesitates to buy a box of Cracker Jack in a theater lobby these days for fear the prize will be a small trinket of a zombie garroting a topless starlet.

At bookshops mysteries can still be found, but they are usually behind the stacks of true crime and horror titles. Few twelve-year-olds have a complete set of Nancy Drew or the Hardy Boys now; it is more likely he or she has most of the titles in the latest vampire saga. The emphasis on sex and mayhem in literature for adults is so pervasive that readers have come to expect the lurid in best sellers. Ask friends to read Maugham's *Of Human Bondage* and they will probably give up after twenty pages because they do not come across anything involving ropes or handcuffs.

Telephone service providers would like all of us to remove the shadow from a common mystery. When the phone rings, our first thought is usually "I wonder who is calling me?" The sense of wonder is stifled with caller ID which allows one to see the number and name of the person calling. I can get the same information by lifting the receiver and saying, "Hello." It probably won't be long before the electric company tries to promote a device that informs us when the power is off but which requires us to turn on a light to read it.

There used to be some suspense on Election Day. Now the projected victors are announced before the polls close and concession speeches are delivered in prime time. The first question waking spouses ask the next morning is not "Who won?" but "Which network picked the most winners?"

One of life's most intriguing mysteries formerly lasted about nine months. Expectant parents chose a pair of names and then waited until the happy day to find out whether the baby was male or female. Today the result is in before the honeymoon is over. A wife may soon tell her husband "Guess what? I'm pregnant, it's going to be a girl, she'll have braces when she's ten, and she'll get a Ph.D. from Princeton."

Down what digitalized road this trend is taking us I don't know. A glistening highway crowded with information and megapixels is not nearly as appealing to me as a cobweb-covered path hiding nebulous secrets of nature and man. While others search the boundaries of cyberspace I can always retreat to my 1932 Philco radio console whose top is covered with the brass beauties which continue to enchant me with their mystical charm. Ah, here is that Tom Mix Mystery Ring. Now if I hold it up to the light and turn it just a little so I can—Hey! Who put this photo of Sharon Stone holding a bullwhip in here?

Broderick Crawford playing the numbers game on *Highway Patrol*.

Sign Here (and There), Please

A COMMON ATTRACTION AT SPORTS SHOWS now are former athletes who gladly put their names on photographs, cards, jerseys, balls, bats, helmets, and other tools of their trade for money. These signing bonuses have proved to be quite lucrative for retired heroes, some of whom earn more annually at these events than they did when they were playing the game that brought them fame.

Why should the boys (and girls) of summer, winter, and fall reap all the rewards? Why can't other celebrities profit by autographing some items collectors would treasure in their homes?

Imagine the looks of surprise and admiration on the faces of visitors who see that Little Richard has written "Keep a-knockin'" on a doorknocker and that the beret hanging on a hat rack in the front hall bears Mary Tyler Moore's declaration "Life's a tossup." They will be even more impressed in the kitchen when they find Frankie Avalon's name on a gingerbread cookie and Harry Belafonte's "Have a good day-o" on a ceramic banana. In the living room is an ottoman on which Dick Van Dyke has written "You'll flip over this." The tapestry that hangs nearby is, of course, autographed by Carole King.

Unfortunately, as Carole aptly sang, "it's too late" for those luminaries who cashed in their chips before they could cash in on their scripts. Or maybe not. If we could go to the tables down at mori's, to the place where legends dwell, we might find:

Perry Como inscribing "Catch a falling star" on any glove or mitt handed to him.

Red Skelton in Freddie the Freeloader garb and Roger Miller similarly attired, signing old stogies they have found, short but not too big around.

Louise Brooks using a silver marker to authenticate black helmets with "This is a real Lulu!"

James Brown gladly dedicating a message to the father of each fan who presents him with a paper sack but only if it's a brand new bag.

Joe E. Ross putting a 54 on the door of a toy car, then adding "Ooh! Ooh!" on the hood and trunk.

Peggy Lee confessing "You give me fever" on the backs of thermometers.

Art Carney (if he stops flicking his hands in Ed Norton style long enough to pick up a marker) providing the cheerful thought "Things are looking up" on rubberized manhole covers.

Leo Gorcey using the upturned brims of fedoras to state in writing "This is an extinct pleasure."

James Cagney handing out small globes with "Top of the world" lettered across the Arctic Ocean.

Don Adams starting way to the right on the sole of any shoe presented to him so the most that can be written is "Missed it by that muc-."

Edward Everett Horton working between stacks of budget books, putting "What's the fuss?" on the covers.

Richard Boone inking the order "Now get traveling" on barrels of cap pistols.

Joan Crawford distributing small shoulder bags with "Don't pad your part" scrawled on them.

William Bendix thumbing through piles of overexposed glossies, placing the same disconsolate lament on the back of each: "What a revoltin' development this is!"

Steve Allen cackling uncontrollably as he writes "How's your bird?" on a smock.

Glenn Ford chalking "It's a jungle out there" on black boards.

Edgar Kennedy advising "Don't do a slow burn" on bottles of sunblock.

Buffalo Bob Smith signing watchbands with "Say, Kid. What time is it?"

Edmund Gwenn adding the sentiment "You gotta believe" in icing on a crisp kringle.

Eddie Albert, knowing his devotees cannot lug a green acre home with them, affably cutting his name into a square of synthetic turf with a knife.

Gloria Grahame saucily marking "Let's face it—Some like it hot" on coffee mugs.

Nick Adams penning those nine letters in the round so they fit on the label of the hit single "He's a Rebel."

That burly guy with the gruff voice choosing only two playing cards from each suit, jotting *Broderick* on the 10 and *Crawford* on the 4.

Fay Wray asking "Isn't this a scream?" on ape masks.

Phil Harris accepting any indescribable object handed to him and printing on it "You'll never get rid of this [boom boom boom] no matter what you do."

Ken Curtis, after making a hasty self-portrait, adding, "Festus drawer in the West."

Victor Borge using a light touch on inflated balloons to predict "Five-tune will smile on you just this twice."

W.C. Fields disregarding his own advice by passing out lollipops neatly broken in two parts with a scribble on the wrapper signifying "A sucker with an even break."

Jack Benny cursively suggesting "Blow this at midnight" on plastic horns. Jack will stop long enough to answer the question everyone has been asking. "Oh, sure, it's true you can't take it with you. But whatever you make once you get here, you get to keep!"

Everyone listens when Bogart is on the phone.

Casting Calls

THE DAYS OF HAVING A TELEPHONE in the home that provides just speaking and hearing functions appear to be over. Now a phone system isn't complete unless it has thirty-number memory, last number redial, caller ID, call waiting, call forwarding, and call for Philip Morris. There are even speaker phones so people can talk long distance even when chatting with neighbors.

Of all the gadgets produced by inventors with time on their hands, one of the strangest is the cordless voice changer. A caller simply places the changer over the speaker of the handset, makes a selection, and starts talking to the person on the other end of the conversation who hears a disguised voice.

What the ads don't explain clearly is why someone would want to buy this gadget nor do they list the various voices meant to conceal the caller's identity. To satisfy what inquiring minds want to know here are some simple situations where a well-known voice might come in handy.

To the auto repair shop as John Wayne: "Now listen, pilgrim, and listen good. I brought that rig in yesterday and you said it would be done by sundown. I planned to ride on out of here at the first sign of light this morning. Now I don't take kindly to liars. The last jasper who lied to me now has to leave his collar button open to see where he's going. I've had about enough, young feller. Now I wanna saddle up about five o'clock so it better be done or my posse of lawyers will hunt you down."

To a fishing friend as W.C. Fields: "Ah, yes. The love of the outdoors, the aromatic scent of rotting seaweed. It reminds me of the time I was traversing the waves of Lake Rocotogomogo. That was the time I caught a tremendous behemoth, much bigger than anything you've ever seen—

what do you mean? How dare you accuse me of exaggerating? Why, the last bucket of fish you brought home was carried off by two crickets and a ladybug. That I, the man who showed the Maharajah of Malangea how to catch the rare and exotic blue-bellied proloset, should have descended to trolling in a common skiff with the likes of you. Well, come around about one and I will provide the liquid emollients."

To the doctor's office as Humphrey Bogart: "Listen, sweetheart. I'd like an appointment with Dr. Woolsey. My daughter played in some poison ivy and now she has a rash on her arm so we want her to be seen by your dermatologist there. Of all the skin joints in all the cities of the world we want her to show up there. She's been trying to talk her way out of it, but I told her she's going over for what she's done. Look, sister. Here's what I want the doctor to do: I want him to write her a prescription for something she can rub on her arm. How do I know what's in it? The stuff that creams are made of."

To the pizza restaurant as Bob Hope: "This is Bob 'I'm so hungry I just ate my tonsils' Hope. I'd like to order a large pepperoni. Hold the bicarbonate. What's that? Deep dish or crispy crust? Honey, I want it so deep the mozzarella comes smothered with Jacques Cousteau. Speaking of France, I understand things are so tough over there if the franc gets any smaller you won't be able to find them in a bun. Breathe hard once in a while so I know you're still there. Garlic bread? Sure, I won't be going out the rest of the month. But I wanna tell ya…As my old pal Gabby Hayes used to say, 'I'm sure hankerin' to et those vittles.' I may even et two, Brute. Hello? Hello?"

To the in-laws as Johnny Cash: "You ask me why I'm always wearing black? Well, usually I don't wear black except when you're here for a visit. I would rather be pacing in a cage at the zoo than be with you. Because you're mine I walk the lion. You're coming on Friday to stay for a week? I don't like it, but I guess things happen that way."

To a collection agency as Elvis Presley: "I have what I consider a very good reason for being behind on my car payments. You see, I'm in rock and roll heaven so I don't have to do any more of that earthly taking care of business. What's that? Hey, that couldn't have been me at the mall scarfing down that cruller. I'm strictly a doughnut man. But just to show you I'm still a hunk of burning love, I'll send you a check if you give me a couple more days. Don't be cruel. I beg of you. Thank you. Thank you very much."

One danger, of course, in using celebrity voices is that friends may find our true tones so dull they will ask us to put Jimmy Durante or Cary Grant on the phone. I guess that's the time to give them Rich Little's number and hang up.

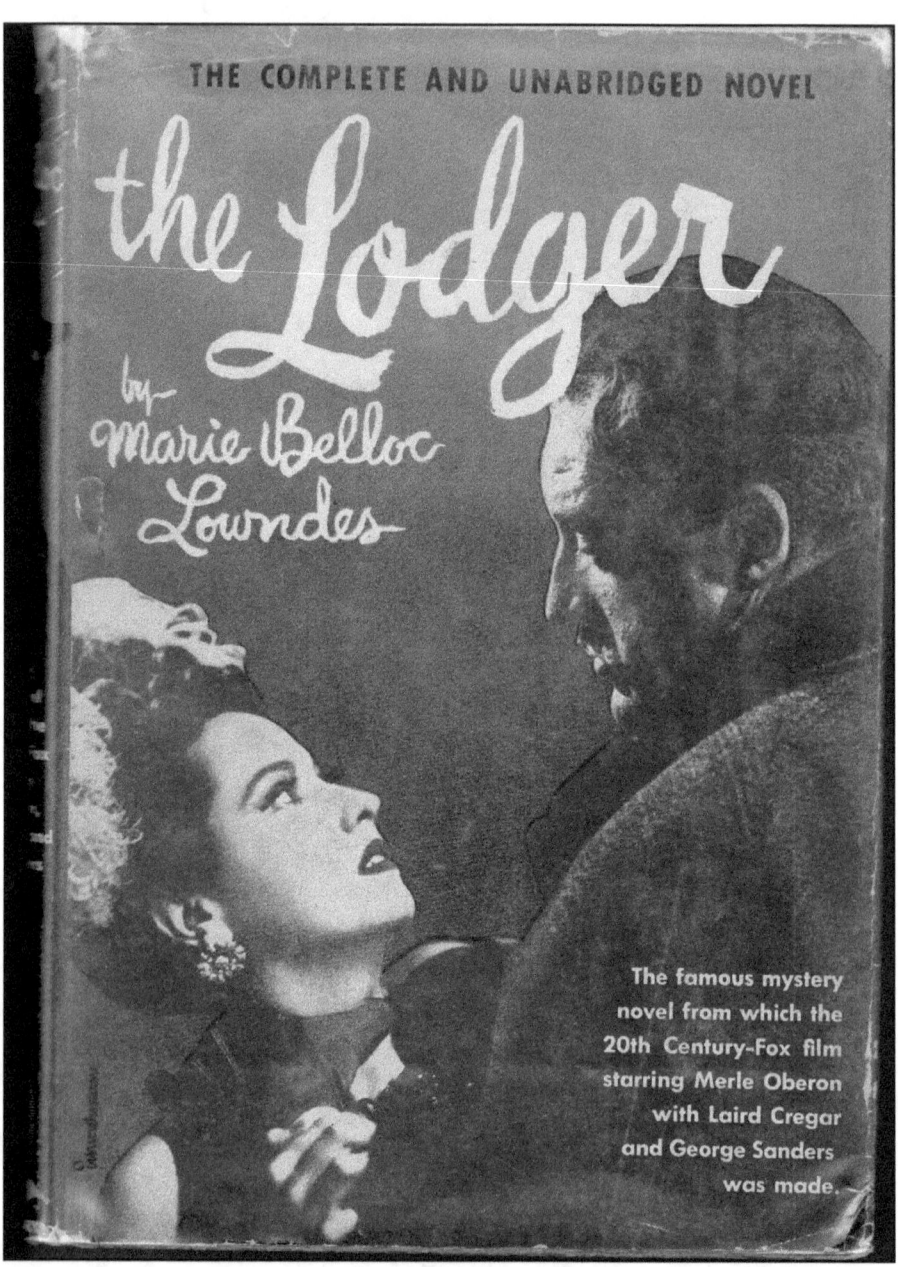

If Laird Cregar had lived to old age, his last film might have been called *The Codger*.

The Best Is Not Yet to Come

AT ONE TIME IN THE LATE 1920S author James Branch Cabell decided to abandon a series of novels because he believed writers cease to develop after their mid-forties. There is some validity to that belief if one examines, for example, the careers of William Faulkner, Ernest Hemingway, and John Steinbeck whose best work was behind them by the end of World War II.

Maybe, then, it is time for the dreamers of what might have been if this poet or that novelist had lived longer to wake up to the reality that an early death before the decline of creative powers set in was for the best. The people who wistfully sigh, "Oh, what might have been" don't consider that what might have been might have been lousy. Thus the world has been spared from reading John Keats's "Ode to a Artichoke," Jack London's *The Sea-Wolf Meets Frankenstein*, Lord Byron's "She Walks in Galoshes," Stephen Crane's *The White Hanky of Cowardice*, F. Scott Fitzgerald's *The Mediocre Son of Gatsby*, Thomas Wolfe's *You Can Go Home Again, But You Have to Sleep in the Attic*, and Edgar Allan Poe's "The Facts in the Strange Case of Lester, aka Lydia."

Many entertainers could not build more stately mansions on the pinnacles they had attained earlier in their careers. Anyone who listens to Dean Martin's "Memories Are Made of This" and compares it to the half-hearted mutterings from the couch on his television show later knows the meaning of decline and fall. Neil Diamond has never reached the heights he attained before Jonathan Livingston Seagull flew into his life shortly after the singer's fortieth birthday. The direction Bruce Springsteen has taken since driving down Thunder Road and through the Badlands in his glory days has been onward but hardly upward.

Here are just a few of the TV and movie stars whose most shining moments were filmed or taped years ago: Jerry Lewis, Goldie Hawn, Jon Voight, Karen Black, Jack Nicholson, Kevin Costner, Jane Fonda, Julie Andrews…The list of survivors that could fill a Beverly Hills phone book are proof that show business life doesn't begin at fifty.

So let us not pity those celebrities who passed on early. Consider what work they might have produced if they had lived past their prime or were still alive.

Elvis might be singing "Black Staid Shoes" and "Good Rocking Chair Tonight" in a girdle and toupee.

Rudolph Valentino's voice, not needed for silent pictures, may have been so bizarre he would have spent his last years putting words in the mouth of Mister Ed.

Patsy Cline could have ended up on the *Saturday Night Fever* soundtrack singing "Jive Talking After Midnight," "She's Got You If I Can't Have You," and "You Should Be Dancing While I Fall to Pieces."

James Dean might have been so down on his luck by 1990 the only part he could have found was that of a derelict who gets to rub his switchblade on Edward's scissorhands.

Buddy Holly might well be squinting at crowds through thick glasses as he tries to remember if it is his love or memory that is not fading away.

Marilyn Monroe would have to insist that any scenes involving her standing over a grating blowing her dress would not reveal any varicose veins or the top of her orthopedic pantyhose.

Errol Flynn, if he could have found employment at all, would likely have ended up in costume dramas playing the dissolute father of a musketeer who is too befuddled to buckle his swash.

Bruce Lee might now be so arthritic that the only kicks he would get are on what's left of Route 66.

George Gershwin might have spent the 1950s composing scores for low-budget films like *Plan 9 from Outer Space* ("Rhapsody for Paper Plate and Flying Saucer") and *The Blob* ("Let's Haul the Whole Thing Off").

In order to earn a living John Garfield might have had to move to Italy in the mid-sixties to appear in spaghetti westerns titled *A Plan Called Dreck* and *For a Few Scruples Less*.

Ernie Kovacs might have found himself teamed with Larry Storch doing a spin-off of *F Troop* called *Take a Good Schnook*.

Bobby Darin might now be heard but not seen on television doing songovers for commercials sponsored by dairy associations with lyrics like "Ice cream lover, where are you?" and "Cheesy mac's back in town."

In 1981 Judy Garland could have been shunned by the networks so her only appearance of the year might have been on the syndicated *Hee Haw* standing up during Roy and Buck's pickin' and grinnin' session to sing "Over the Rainbow in Hillbilly Heaven" and "We're Off to See the Wizard on the Wabash Cannonball."

Consider it a blessing that we and the stars we admired don't have to see what time (and *People*) might have done to them. Fitzgerald was wrong when he suggested there are no second acts in American lives so let us be thankful that some of the greats never came back after intermission.

It was no stretch for W.C. Fields to do a perfect double take.

Double Your Pleasure

IT IS A SHAME THAT the death of Gale Gordon in 1995 passed with little notice for not only did he serve as matchless foil for Lucille Ball on television but he also reigned as unsurpassed master of the double take on radio as described in my article "The Best Second Banana in the Bunch."

Just as Gordon was without peer on the airwaves, W.C Fields and Lou Costello were among the very best on the screen. To me the funniest bit in *The Dentist* is not the tussle with the woman who has the obstinate tooth but rather Bill's brief take when the bushy-bearded man in the bowler hat walks in the door. Fields raises his arms to his chest and leans back in startled revulsion as if has just been accosted by savage curs. When he actually did face a formidable dog after dropping in on Margaret Dumont in *Never Give a Sucker an Even Break*, he recovered from his start to name mutt and mistress Romulus and Remus.

It is a wonder Lou Costello did not suffer whiplash from some of the takes he unleashed. When he discovered dead bodies in closets or laundry carts, his head shot from forward to reverse with no stop in neutral. He got his whole body into the act in one scene of *Africa Screams* when, after bragging to a fellow he has just met about his big-game experiences that outshone those of lion-tamer Clyde Beatty, the man introduced himself as Beatty and that news jolted Costello right out of his chair unto the floor.

On television no one has been able to top Jackie Gleason's show-stopping shtick on *The Honeymooners*. Viewers could see it coming when, for example, Kramden and Norton try to sneak off in the car without Alice and Trixie, who suddenly show up in the back seat and offer a suggestion when the car doesn't start. Gleason could then be counted upon to release a "Whoa!" with eyes like saucers and arms thrust out like an umpire signaling safe. Hammy and hokey? Yes. Funny? Definitely. The Great One did a great double take.

Marlo Thomas once told an interviewer that nobody does double takes in real life. I think if she looked around a bit she might change her mind.

The havoc caused by Jayne Mansfield's walk down the street in *The Girl Can't Help It* didn't emerge from the pipedream of some screenwriter. Many curvy women sashaying along city sidewalks have turned heads and crumpled fenders.

At a major league baseball game keep an eye on that fleet-footed leadoff man when the perfectly-placed bunt he beat out yields an E on the scoreboard from the official scorer.

Study the people glancing through the wanted flyers on the walls of the post office. Observe what happens after they stop flipping and just before they shout "Uncle Louie!"

Watch the woman at the perfume counter who sprays fragrance on her wrists, smells, and then peeks at the price. It isn't the aroma that sends her away from the counter coughing and gagging.

Stand behind the young couple who are unrolling the architect's blueprints for their first home. The two heads that jerk in unison when they see that their dream house resembles a particleboard pup tent is known as the double double take.

The world has been a poorer place since Gordon, Gleason, and other masters of the form passed on, and if double takes ever become extinct, one of life's mirthful pleasures will also be gone. So the next time you look in the mirror and spot new crow's feet by the eyes or wrinkles in the forehead, do a Fields instead of a frown. Before long the only marks on your face that matter will be the laugh lines.

Ordinary turkey is the one without mayo.

A Classic Dilemma

IN 1944 T. S. ELIOT DELIVERED an address before the Virgil Society which was published the following year as a book entitled *What Is a Classic?* Eliot knew what a classic was and so did most of his readers at that time. Now the word has lost most of its meaning because it has virtually supplanted "new and improved" as advertising's favorite come-on.

The soda in the familiar red can that assumed the title for years still does more harm to the body than good and in its most unnatural state contains enough caffeine to keep Morpheus awake. The FDA may soon declare it as addictive as Bing cherries in June and Bing Crosby in December. Yet it was called classic because it has a familiar flavor. So does milk, but I haven't seen any farmers slapping classic labels on udders.

Disc jockeys are quick to pronounce any release a classic. The latest effort by U2 scarcely gets to platinum before it is rubbing elbows with Sgt. Pepper and Maybellene. Some stations pride themselves on playing "lost classics" that more often than not are what might charitably be called one-hit wonders. Lee Michaels knows what I mean, and the people who believe a moment in the sun is worthy of resurrection should have Napoleon XIV come to take them away. People who work at any station that bills itself as the home of classic rock should be reminded that the British Museum has prior claim on the Rosetta Stone.

Motion pictures now do not have to attain any lofty heights to join the ranks of *Casablanca* and *Gone with the Wind*. *Forrest Gump* was called an "instant classic" before the first box of bonbons made it to the bench. Gruesome horror movies shot in two days with a cast of unknowns become cult classics. Older but still awful pictures like *The Creeping Terror* and *The Beast of Yucca Flats* that represent the nadir of filmmaking are "classics of their kind." Better movies of that kind were recorded on grainy film stock by five-thumbed parents while documenting baby's first steps and goo-goos.

The frozen food aisles in supermarkets now are overflowing with dinners bearing the word. If these concoctions, some of which have only been available for a few years, are classics, what are fish and chips and ham and eggs? Chopped liver?

The phrase *classic car* used to mean something. I remember being told by an auto mechanic while on vacation in Ohio during the summer of 1981 that my perfectly ordinary, rusty 1968 Plymouth Satellite qualified as a classic. "They don't make 'em like that any more," he said. They don't make iceboxes and box cameras either, but at least there aren't any frostbitten brownies out there lauding their merits.

There doesn't seem to be any way to stop the trend. *The Flying Nun* has been called a classic and mentioned in the same breath as *The Dick Van Dyke Show* and *All in the Family* which is tantamount to elevating Waller's *The Bridges of Madison County* to the level of Steinbeck's *The Grapes of Wrath*. Now all it takes to qualify for classic status is not to persist but merely to exist.

At this rate it won't be long before new fathers who excitedly ask obstetricians in maternity wards "What is it? What is it?" will be told "Well, at first it was a boy, but now it's a classic."

Norma Desmond on the way to her next close-up.

When You're Called to Play That, Mumble

WALTER PIDGEON CLAIMED that his experiences with John Ford while working on *How Green Was My Valley* forced him to conclude "that he operates by telepathy. He smokes a pipe constantly—I doubt if he removes it from his mouth except to eat. He certainly doesn't remove it merely to talk. Furthermore, when he speaks, he mumbles. There's no kinder expression for it. I listened intently to his instructions and if five words out of seventy-five were intelligible I considered it a good average...You go out on the set and find yourself following orders you haven't heard."

It sets one to thinking. What would have happened if John Ford had directed…

- …*Inherit the Wind* and wanted Fredric March to "look like you mean business and storm up to the bench." March might have buzzed like a bee and asked the judge for a writ of habeas strawberries.

- …*Shane* and said to Jack Palance, "Brandish your pistol, crack a smile, and prance around like you own the place." The lanky actor would have been seen chewing a candle while churning butter with cold cream on his face.

- …*Now, Voyager* and asked Bette Davis to repeat the lines "exactly like I say them." She might have concluded the movie by saying to Paul Henreid, "Don't shoot the baboon. Wear my corset stays."

- …*Sunset Boulevard* and asked Gloria Swanson to "Open your eyes wide, raise your arms, and move past the reporters like you're in your own world." Would she have descended the stairs as Popeye with corncob pipe, flexed a tattooed bicep, and baaed like a sheep while twirling a baton?

...*Kiss of Death* and told Richard Widmark "Toss the lady down the stairs and giggle like a hyena." Widmark might have been seen peeling pears while calling races as if at Hialeah.

...*Sound of Music* and demanded that Julie Andrews "sing it like this." Would some of her favorite things have been "Chilblains and gewgaws and squashed, gooey rivets"?

...*Knute Rockne-All American* and showed Pat O'Brien how to deliver a pep talk. Would Knute have sent his players out with "Let's pin a bun on Flipper"?

...*The Third Man* and told Orson Welles to "Splash through the sewer, climb up the ladder, then turn around and gloat." Picture Harry Lime skulking in the subterranean caverns wearing the tattered uniform of a tour guide, holding a croquet mallet in one hand and a placard that reads "Get out the vote" in the other.

...*Public Enemy* and instructed Cagney to "take that grapefruit and let her have it in the kisser." Would audiences have missed that confrontation and instead seen the gangster baking a gray book in the kitchen?

...*The Road to Rio* and showed Bob Hope how to deliver one of his best lines in the script. Hope would have approached the man in the car and, instead of asking him, "What do you do hear from your embalmer?" probably would have asked, "What drawer has the turnip farmer?"

...*The Treasure of the Sierra Madre* and commanded Bogart to "march over to Huston and shake that bag of gold in his face." Bogie would have done a samba with maracas while wearing old Spanish lace.

...*The Wild One* and Brando would have asked for his motivation. Ford might have said, "Get your hands full of grease, smell some gas, and meditate while gazing at a map," causing Brando to show up wearing a wolf man mask and a stethoscope, yipping like a puppy.

...*Some Like It Hot* and told Jack Lemmon "for this shot let Joe know you don't want to be wooed and tell him you're a man in no uncertain terms." Jack would likely have finished the film in a snood while fishing over the side of the boat with worms.

I don't know if Walter ever regretted his statements about Ford, but they certainly have altered the way I view the actor's final scenes in *Forbidden Planet*. The pain Pidgeon registers as Dr. Morbius and the intensity with which he cries out "I deny you. I give you up" seem all too real to be feigned. But the most remarkable thing is that the last time I studied the writhing and roaring creature produced by the subconscious of the doctor and made visible in the force field, I *thought* I saw, for just a moment during one of the electrified lunges, a grinning set of teeth chomping on a pipe.

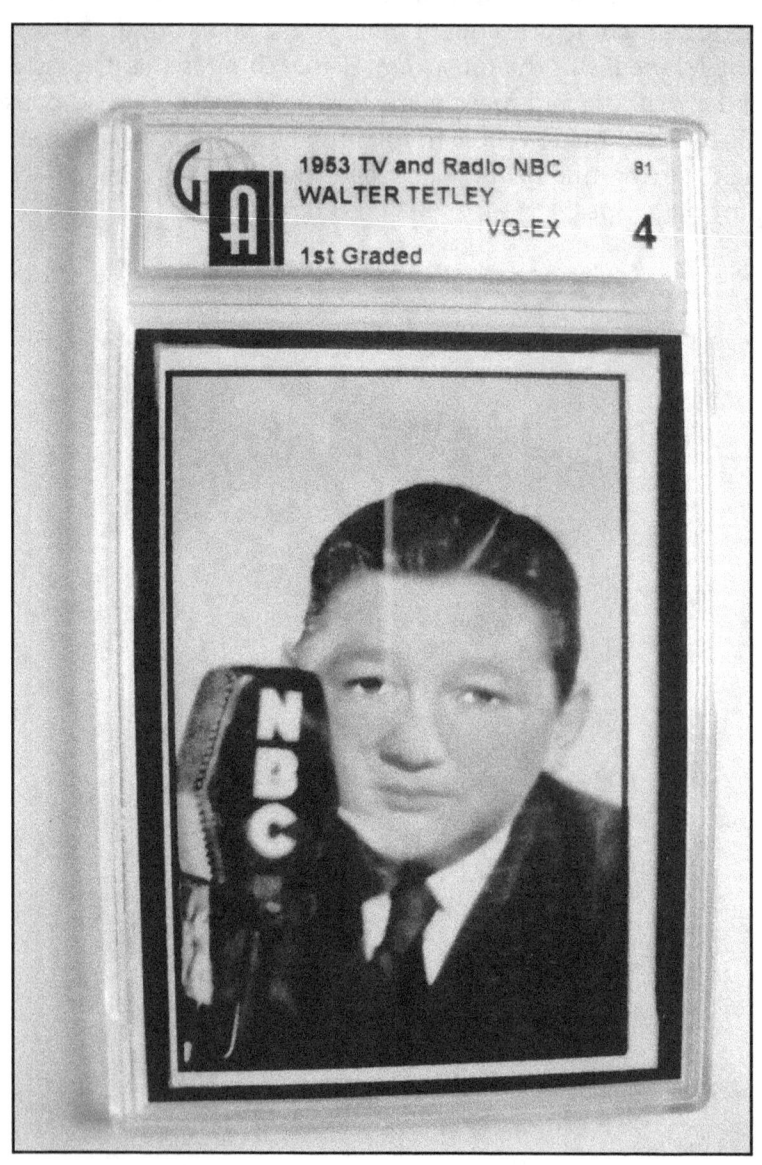

If Walter Tetley could see that his 1953 card has been graded and encapsulated, his response would surely be "Are you kiddin'?"

To Have and Have Lots

AT A MEMORABLE FAMILY GET-TOGETHER when the subject of a grandniece's dolls came up, she proudly announced to those gathered around the dining room table that she has a Barbie worth $175. When asked if she was careful when playing with it she replied, "Oh, I don't play with it. I keep it in its box. It's worth more that way."

After the adults exchanged amused expressions, I used the occasion to suggest that her behavior is just a sign of the times. "Today everything is a collectible," I said. For proof I pointed to objects around us. People collect plates, silverware, salt and pepper shakers, cookie jars, coffee mugs, glasses, and perhaps even soiled napkins. I should have told my sister (the hostess that day) to be careful handling the scraps of food she was tossing in the wastebasket because condition may be important to garbage collectors, too.

When did this passion for collecting everything that isn't nailed down begin? Certainly the value ascribed to baseball and other sports cards fueled the frenzy. Mothers who had been ignored for years started getting calls in the middle of the night from sons who frantically implored them to remember what happened to that 1957 Don Drysdale card. More likely than not, maternal searches do not turn up gold but rather the dross of a pristine Dee Fondy Topps worth $5.00 tops.

The fact that duds lurked among the doozies made collecting cards an adventure in the days of nickel packs. When trading duplicates with friends, we became juvenile general managers, swapping stars, prospects, and even some of the flat (in more ways than one) bubble gum. Now consumers who buy the box which contains a complete set for a year have been dealt the same hand as everyone else and are left with nothing distinctive to exchange except maybe the sales receipt.

Another of the peculiarities of the new age of collecting is the elevated status of the box. What was once regarded as a throwaway is now handled with more care than the prize inside. Even cereal boxes, long considered an obstructive nuisance blocking everything behind them in a cupboard, are revered today, particularly if the front shows a photo of an athlete or a dethroned Miss America. "Mint in box" has supplanted "It's paid for" as the proudest claim in the land.

For me cereal boxes rekindle the memory of comic books. Some boxes contained mini-comics as premiums, though I usually came to the table with my own Walt Disney favorites or copies borrowed from my brother's deep inventory of four-color cowboy comics. I suppose today some fastidious individuals regard the sight of a nine-year-old eating Cheerios or Wheaties over the adventures of Donald Duck and Gene Autry a solecism tantamount to blowing out candles on a birthday cake with a sneeze, but to me comics provided a way of starting my day with a bang and a quack. The prizes inside were meant to be devoured up close, not protected and admired from afar. As my guests they were invited to open up when I gave them a place of honor at the table. Now comics are encapsulated or sealed in plastic bags and given a grade for investment.

It could be that somewhere someone is saving plastic bags by protecting them in comic books. Anything is possible in this mad world where everything is collected: Pez dispensers, credit cards, Bogie stills, bogus bills, pogs, golliwogs, steins, Frankensteins, mugs, jugs, rugs, slugs, puppets, Muppets, posters, toasters, roasters, coasters, marbles, badges, cattle prods, divining rods, telephone cards, chalkware, worn chalk, beer cans, milk cans, canned laughter, Deco flappers, Necco wrappers, guitars, jam jars, pine cones, buttered scones, firecrackers, skates, skis, Skeezix, hubcaps, bottle caps, pour spouts, rich spouts, lures, clocks, crocks, insulators, perambulators, dog tags, combs, catacombs, bookmarks, teeth marks, Groucho Marx, player pianos, piano players, Little Golden Books, Big Little Books, Alley Oop, alley goop, Snow White, snowshoes, snow cones, Bobby Hull's game-used stick, Bob Hope's used-gag shtick, mechanical banks, cranks, pins, tins, cufflinks, sausage links, golf links, tops, pop tops, toothbrush holders, teddy bears, bobbins, bobbin' heads, Bob and Ray, poker chips, potato chips, spark plugs, ear plugs, lobby cards, hobby discards, billboards, and Bill Boyds.

And this is just the tip of the iceberg (someone may be collecting iceberg tips, too). Folks may soon stop taking dirty clothes to the laundry; instead they will head for the antique mall or pawnshop. Teens will fill scrapbooks with their fingernail clippings. Horses will collect flies and clothes dryers will collect lint and books will collect dust. As for me, I will just sit here and collect my thoughts.

The view from where I sit. Bliss, indeed.

Index

Abbott and Costello Go to Mars, 48
Abbott and Costello Meet Frankenstein, 47, 177, 182
Abbott and Costello Show, The, 48-49, 208
Abbott, Bud, 1, 16, 39, **44-50,** 60, 103, 137, 166, 177, 193, 194, 204, 199, 208, 236, 250, 322, 429, 449, 529
Abbott, George, 128
Abie's Irish Rose, 42
Abominable Dr. Phibes, The, 183
Abroad with Two Yanks, 250
Ace, Goodman, 32, 41, 148
Ace, Jane, 39
Across the Wide Missouri, 261
Acuff, Eddie, 296
Adam 12, 170
Adams, Don, 166, 540
Adams, Edie, 91, 93-94
Adams, Nick, 541
Adrian, Iris, 3 **164-167, 170,** 446
Adventures of McGraw, The, 228
Adventures of Ozzie and Harriet, The, **402-409,** 450
Adventures of Philip Marlowe, The, 452
Adventures of Robin Hood, The, 272, 275, 293
Adventures of Sam Spade, The, 266-268, 270, 452
Adventures of Sherlock Homes, The, 275-276
Advise and Consent, 131
Affairs of Annabel, The, 154
Agee, James, 25
Al Jolson Show, 11
Aladdin, 285
Albert, Eddie, 241, 541
Albertson, Jack, 98

Albright, Lola, 245
Alcoa Hour, 261, 269
Alda, Robert, 209
Aldrich Family, The, 121, 409, 449
Alfred Hitchcock Hour, The, 269
Alfred Hitchcock Presents, 245
Africa Screams, 551
All in Favor, 97
All in the Family, 556
All Quiet on the Western Front, 76
All the Young Men, 237
All This and Heaven Too, 474
Allen, Fred, 48, 54, 70-71, 76, 83, 86, 148, 170, 192, 242, 251, 277, 304-311, 314-315, 317-318, 336, 339, 343, 372, 393, 415, 444-445, 447, 506, 521
Allen, Gracie, 11, 39, 113-114, 267, 330, 408, 442, 446-447, 499
Allen, Steve, 48, 94, 540
Allen, Woody, 77, 124
Allman, Elvia, 76, 97
Amazing Mr. Malone, The, 226
Ameche, Don, 129, 309, 429, 473, 478
Americano, The, 229
Amos 'n' Andy, 11, 447-448, 449, 522
Anatomy of a Murder, 122
And the Angels Sing, 25
And Then There Were None, 473
Anderson, Eddie ("Rochester"), 123, 371, 384, 388-389, 411-412, 445
Andrews, Dana, 129
Andrews, Edward, 100
Andrews, Julie, 548, 560
Andrews Sisters, 46
Angels in Disguise, 43
Ankers, Evelyn, 157, 196, 198

567

Anna Karenina, 275
Annabel Takes Over, 154
Annie, 28
Annie Get Your Gun, 22, 27-28, 261, 286
Ann-Margret, 131
Anthony Adverse, 258
Antony and Cleopatra, 145
Ape Man, The, 176
Apple Dumpling Gang, The, 166
Appointment with Danger, 236
Arden, Eve, 2, 21, 24, 32, 76, 116, **118-124**, 135, 154, 245, 359-362, 450
Arnaz, Desi, 123, 155, 158, 160, 176, 441
Arnaz, Desi Jr., 160
Arnaz, Lucie, 160
Around the World, 137
Arquette, Cliff, 449
Arrest and Trial, 269
Arsenic and Old Lace, 189, 192, 208
Arthur, Jean, 236
As the Twig Is Bent, 226
Astaire, Fred, 27, 31, 131, 154, 281, 285
Astor, Mary, 206, 290
Atkinson, Brooks, 145, 229
Atwill, Lionel, 198, 201, 225, 275
Auerbach, Artie, 386, 446
Autopsy for a Ghost, 278
Autry, Gene, 18, 220, 321, 457, 463, 466, 564
Avalon, Frankie, 539
Avalon Time, 60

Babe Ruth Story, The, 249
Bacall, Lauren, 131, 367, 454
Bacharach, Burt, 285
Backus, Jim, 139, 388, 438
Bad Day at Black Rock, 481
Badlanders, The, 237
Badman's Territory, 220
Baer, Parley, 441
Baker, Kenny, 104, 445
Ball, Lucille, 2, 20, 35, 80, 115-116, 119, 135, **152-162**, 374-375, 440-441, 551
Ballard, Kaye, 21, 123
Ballyhoo of 1932, 76
Balzer, George, 383, 411
Bankhead, Tallulah, 3, **142-150**
Banks, Joan, 3, 226, 229, 336
Bar 20 Rides Again, 220
Bara, Theda, 26
Barefoot Executive, The, 166

Bargy, Roy, 19
Barnes, Binnie, 306
Barnes, Clive, 35
Barrie Craig, Confidential Investigator, 452
Barry, Don, 220
Barrymore, John, 93, 181, 273, 275, 294, 491
Barrymore, Lionel, 176, 190
Baskett, James, 448
Bat, The, 182
Bates, Jeanne, 336
Batman, 149-150, 259
Baxley, Barbara, 148
Baxter, Anne, 146
Beach Boys, The, 531
Beast of Yucca Flats, The, 555
Beast with Five Fingers, The, 208-209
Beatty, Clyde, 59, 551
Beatty, Warren, 535
Beau Geste, 259
Beau James, 79
Beaudine, William, 39, 176
Beautiful But Broke, 137
Beauty and the Beast, 285
Begley, Ed, 231, 326
Behind the Rising Sun, 259
Belafonte, Harry, 340, 539
Bellamy, Ralph, 198, 241
Bells, The, 190
Bells of St. Mary's, The, 474
Benaderet, Bea, 97, 113, 157, 167, 330, 336, 351, 385-386, 411, 441-442, 446
Benchley, Robert, 1, 120, 143, 306
Bendix, William, 3, 234-235, **248-255**, 309-310, 315, 540
Benedict, Billy, 38
Bennett, Constance, 154
Bennett, Joan, 314, 471
Benny, Jack, 11, 70, 76, 99, 113, 114, 167, 170, 192, 242, 307, 308, 315, 317, 331, 339, 343, 366, 368, 371-372, 374, **382-391**, 408, 410-413, 415, 417, 442, 445-447, 450, 454, 499-450, 522, 541
Benoff, Mac, 260
Bergen, Candace, 435
Bergen, Edgar, 7, 11, 76, 155, 214, 374, **428-435**, 442, 497-499, 515
Bergman, Ingrid, 471, 474
Berle, Milton, 92, 98, 100, 121, 162, 277, 366, 418

Index • 569

Berlin, Irving, 9, 281, 284
Berman, Albert, 393, 396
Bernds, Edward, 39
Berner, Sara, 167
Berns, Larry, 169
Best Foot Forward, 156
Best Man, The, 229-230
Best Years of Our Lives, The, 529
Betty Hutton Show, The, 28
Beverly Hillbillies, The, 162
Bewitched, 169-190
Big Boy, 8, 9
Big Broadcast of 1938, The, 76, 281
Big Circus, The, 209
Big Land, The, 237
Big Show, The, 148-149, 429, 435, 454
Big Street, The, 155
Big Town, The, 314
Bilk, Acker, 532
Bird, Billie, 28
Birds, The, 481
Bishop Murder Case, The, 274
Black Bart, 228
Black Castle, The, 194
Black Cat, The, 174, 191
Black Hand, 261
Black, Karen, 548
Black Room, The, 192
Black Sleep, The, 277
Blackjack Ketchum, Desperado, 269
Blanc, Mel, 54, 113, 384-385, 410-412, 445-446
Blane, Marcie, 531
Blind Bargain, A, 214
Blondie, 409
Blondie Goes to College, 323
Blood and Sand, 259
Blue Beetle, The, 226
Blue Dahlia, The, 234-235, 252
Blue Ribbon Town, 103-104
Blue Steel, 220
Blues Busters, 41, 323
Bob Hope Show, The, 62, 77-78, 86, 308, 433, 437
Body Snatcher, The, 193, 470
Bogart, Humphrey, 131, 206-207, 229, 257, 266, 273, 307, 367, 454, 470, 474, 542, 544, 560
Bold Venture, 454
Bombo, 8

Bonanza, 245, 261, 269
Boogie Man Will Get You, The, 208
Boone, Pat, 284
Boone, Richard, 540
Booth, Shirley, 168
Borge, Victor, 541
Boston Blackie, 452
Botany Bay, 236
Bottom of the Bottle, The, 246
Bow, Clara, 26, 144
Bowery Boys, 1, **38-43**, 100, 321, 323
Bowery Buckeroos, 41
Bowery to Bagdad, 43
Bowman, Lee, 156
Box 13, 236, 454
Boyd, William, 220-221, 324, 457, 564
Bracken, Eddie, 24-25
Bradbury, Ray, 452
Brady, Pat, 219
Branded, 236
Brando, Marlon, 147, 560
Brecher, Irving, 252
Breen, Richard, 424-426
Brennan, Walter, 258
Brent, George, 470
Brett, Jeremy, 275, 478
Brice, Fanny, 76, 98, 120, 135, 140
Bride Came C.O.D., The, 242
Bride of Frankenstein, 192
Bride of the Monster, 177
Brigham Young, 181
Bright Horizon, 167, 226
British Agent, 258
Broadside, 100
Broadway Is My Beat, 453
Brooks, Louise, 540
Brown, James, 540
Brown, Joe E., 258
Brown, John, 113, 253-254, 309, 311, 405-406, 454
Browning, Tod, 176, 214-215
Bruce, Nigel, 128, 275-276, 324
Brute Force, 268
Bryan, Arthur Q., 113, 330, 352-353, 377, 438, 448-449
Bryan, Jane, 297
Buck, Frank, 18
Buck Privates, 46
Bulldog Drummond Comes Back, 259
Burke, Johnny, 281

Burke's Law, 255, 269
Burnett, Carol, 119
Burnette, Smiley, 219
Burns, Bob, 242, 521
Burns and Allen Show, The, 267, 314, 442, 446
Burns, George, 9, 11, 113-114, 236, 406, 408, 442, 446-447, 499
Burr, Raymond, 422, 425-426
Burrows, Abe, 32, 315
Butler, Daws, 55, 341
Buttram, Pat, 219
Byrne, George, 75

Cabell, James Branch, 547
Caesar, Sid, 277
Café Trocadero, 11
Cagney, James, 242, 257, 473, 477, 540, 560
Cahn, Sammy, 284-285
Cain, James M., 471
Caine Mutiny, The, 315
Calamity Jane, 284
Calamity Jane and Sam Bass, 269
Calcutta, 252
Calkins, Dick, 465
Calling All Detectives, 226
Calling Dr. Death, 201, 259
Calvert, John, 324
Camel Comedy Caravan, 415
Canby, Vincent, 316
Candido, Candy, 48
Canova, Judy, 135, 322
Cantor, Charlie, 168, 315, 317, 358
Cantor, Eddie, 2, 8, 11, 15-16, 83, 84, 103, 138, 154, 258, 429, 440, 454, 467
Capote, Truman, 145, 477, 480, 482
Capra, Frank, 50, 69, 477, 479-480, 482
Captain Blood, 258, 275, 293
Carbone, Antony, 183
Carefree, 242
Carey, Macdonald, 28
Cariboo Trail, The, 220
Carmichael, Hoagy, 284
Carney and Brown, 176
Carney, Art, 70, 367, 540
Carnival in Costa Rica, 259-260
Carol, Sue, 234-235
Carpetbaggers, The, 237
Carradine, John, 176, 201, 267, 306
Carroll, Bob Jr., 156, 158
Carroll, Madeleine, 77, 206

Carson, Jack, 3, **240-246**
Carson, Johnny, 77
Caruso, Enrico, 8
Casablanca, 207, 286, 445, 555
Casanova's Big Night, 277
Case of the Black Cat, The, 297-300, 302
Case of the Caretaker's Cat, The, 297
Case of the Curious Bride, The, 291-295, 297, 303
Case of the Dangerous Dowager, The, 302
Case of the Howling Dog, The, 288-291
Case of the Lucky Legs, The, 293-295, 302
Case of the Stuttering Bishop, The, 300-302
Case of the Velvet Claws, The, 295-297, 302
Casebook of Gregory Hood, The, 115
Cash, Johnny, 544
Cassini, Oleg, 128, 131
Castle, William, 182
Cat and the Canary, The, 77
Cat on a Hot Tin Roof, 246
Cates, Opie, 437
Caught in the Draft, 77
Caulfield, Joan, 78
CBS Radio Mystery Theater, The, 101
Champagne for Caesar, 182
Champion, 314
Champs, The, 532
Chandler, George, 138
Chandler, Jeff, 121, 225, 359
Chandler, Raymond, 235, 355, 424, 469
Chaney, Lon, 190, 197, **212-216**
Chaney, Lon Jr., 47, 78, 192, **196-202**, 262
Channing, Carol, 64
Chaplin, Charlie, 45, 75, 153
Chappell, Ernest, 393, 396-397, 399, 452
Charge at Feather River, The, 229
Charge of the Light Brigade, 258
Charisse, Cyd, 28, 432
Charlie Chan at the Circus, 259
Charlie Chan in Egypt, 320
Chase and Sanborn Hour, The, 48, 429
Cheer Up and Smile, 258
Chevillat, Dick, 343, 346, 348
Chicago Deadline, 236
Children of the Ghetto, 7
China, 252
Christy, Ken, 353, 438
Cimarron City, 261
Cinderella, 384
Cisco Kid, The, 453

Citizen Kane, 234, 482
Clash by Night, 146, 286
Clayton, Lou, 16
Clemens, William, 297, 301
Clements, Stanley, 43
Clift, Montgomery, 230
Climax, 269
Climax, The, 193, 470
Cline, Patsy, 548
Clive, Colin, 190, 206
Clooney, Rosemary, 245
Close to My Heart, 131
Clown, The, 170
Clyde, Andy, 219
Cobb, Lee J., 146
Coburn, Charles, 447
Cochran, Steve, 269
Cockeyed Miracle, The, 322
Cocteau, Jean, 147
Cohan, George M., 17
Cohan, Phil, 19
Cohn, Harry, 479-480
Cole Younger, Gunfighter, 228
Colgate Comedy Hour, The, 49
College Swing, 76
Colman, Benita, 387
Colman, Ronald, 242, 387, 412, 446
Colonna, Jerry, 76, **82-86,** 295, 308-309, 417
Columbia Workshop, 227
Combat, 269
Comden, Betty, 284
Comedy of Terrors, The, 183, 194, 209, 277-278
Comin' Round the Mountain, 48
Como, Perry, 489, 539
Connecticut Yankee in King Arthur's Court, A, 253, 528
Conquerer Worm, The, 183
Corman, Roger, 182, 186, 209
Conrad, William, 97, 334, 336, 482
Conreid, Hans, 94, 113, 261, 311
Conway, Tom, 324
Cook, Donald, 148
Cooper, Gary, 144, 201, 231, 236, 273, 284, 473
Cooper, Wyllis, 393-400, 452
Corby, Ellen, 138
Correll, Charles, 447-448
Cortez, Dave, 532
Cortez, Ricardo, 297-298, 302

Costello, Lou, 1, 16. **44-50,** 60, 103, 114, 137, 166, 167, 177, 193, 194, 199, 208, 236, 250, 322, 365, 429, 449, 529, 551
Costner, Kevin, 548
Court Jester, The, 33, 277
Cousin Willie, 438-440
Cover Girl, 120
Cowan, Jerome, 312
Cox, Wally, 481
Crabbe, Buster, 477
Crashing Las Vegas, 43
Crawford, Broderick, 538, 541
Crawford, Joan, 130, 240, 243, 471, 479, 540
Creeping Terror, The, 555
Cregar, Laird, 234, 546
Crehan, Joseph, 301
Crenna, Richard, 121, 336, 358
Crime and Punishment, 205
Crimson Cult, The, 194
Critic's Choice, 80, 160, 246
Croft, Mary Jane, 361
Crosby, Bing, 2, 11, 25, 31, 34, 76-79, 83, 104, 282-284, 286, 415, 429, 432, 447, 454, 473, 555
Crosby, Bob, 446
Crosby, Gary, 432
Crosland, Alan, 290, 298
Cross My Heart, 26, 28
Crowther, Bosley, 315
Cuban Love Song, The, 17
Cugat, Xavier, 417
Cullen, Bill, 66
Cummings, Robert, 481
Curtain Call at Cactus Creek, 118, 182
Curtis, Ken, 541
Curtiz, Michael, 292-293
Czarina, The, 274

Dailey, Dan, 322
Daley, Cass, 135
Dallas, 270
Damon Runyon Theater, The, 453
Dance, Girl, Dance, 155
Dance with Me, Henry, 48
Dancers, The, 144
D'Andrea, Tom, 254, 269
Danny Kaye Show, The, 32, 35
Dante, 269
Darin, Bobby, 548

Dark Corner, The, 254
Dark Fantasy, 398
Dark Passage, 285
Dark Victory, 145
Darnell, Linda, 130
Darwell, Jane, 136
Date with Judy, A, 168, 366, 441
Davenport, Harry, 297
David Copperfield, 275
David, Hal, 285
Davis, Adele, 433
Davis, Bette, 123, 130, 181, 242, 258, 471, 479, 489, 559
Davis, Joan, 2, 47, **134-140**, 169, 267, 322
Dawn Patrol, The, 275
Day, Dennis, 123, 383, 386, 389-390, 411-412, 445-446
Day, Doris, 245, 282, 284
Day in the Life of Dennis Day, A, 450
Day-Time Wife, 137
de Corsia, Ted, 336
de Havilland, Olivia, 242-243
De Niro, Robert, 3
De Vol, Frank, 245
De Wilde, Brandon, 236
Dead End, 42
Dean, James, 237, 548
Deep Six, The, 237
Defense Rests, The, 258
DeFore, Don, 28
Delmar, Kenny, 76
DeMille, Cecil B., 149
DeMarco Sisters, 447
Denning, Richard, 156-157
Dentist, The, 551
Depp, Johnny, 535
Desilu Playhouse, 254, 261
Destry Rides Again, 242
DeSylva, B.G., 24
Detective in the House, 270
Detective Story, 254
Detour, 321
Devil and the Deep, The, 144
Devil Bat, The, 176
Devil in Love, The, 258
Devine, Andy, 219, 482, 522
Dial M for Murder, 481
Diamond, Neil, 547
Diamond, Selma, 148
Dick Van Dyke Show, The, 556

Die! Die! My Darling!, 149
Dietrich, Marlene, 144
Dietz, Howard, 147
Dimension X, 452
Dingle, Charles, 143
Dirty Dancing, 285
Dobkin, Larry, 336
Dr. IQ, 393
Dr. Phibes Rises Again, 183
Dr. Renault's Secret, 260
Dodd, Claire, 292, 295-296
Donahue, Troy, 532
Donovan's Brain, 198
Doud, Gil, 267
Doughgirls, The, 243
Douglas, Jack, 349
Douglas, Melvyn, 220, 230, 470
Doyle, Sir Arthur Conan, 276
Dracula, 174, 176-177, 190, 214
Dragnet, 421, 427, 440, 453
Dragonwyck, 182
Drake, Alfred, 24
Drake, Dona, 311, 316
Drake, Frances, 206
Dratner, Jay, 314
Dream Girl, 26, 28, 156
Drumbeat, 237
Du Barry Was a Lady, 61, 155
Duchess of Idaho, The, 61
Duel in the Sun, 472
Duel of Champions, 237
Duff, Howard, 169, **264-270**, 446, 453
Duffy's Tavern, 39, 148, 165, 266, 358, 437
Dumont, Margaret, 110, 551
Dunlap, Patricia, 439
Dunne, Irene, 154
Durante, Jimmy, 3, 11, **14-21**, 39, 76, 103, 148, 165, 192, 245, 544
Durbin, Deanna, 314
Duryea, Dan, 241
Dvorak, Ann, 301

Eagle Has Two Heads, The, 147
Easy to Wed, 156
Eddy, Nelson, 429
Edward Scissorhands, 185
Egyptian, The, 131
Eilers, Sally, 473
Einstein, Harry, 11, 437
Electric Prunes, The, 531

Eliot, T.S., 555
Elliott, Bob, 339, 353-354
Elliott, Gordon (Bill), 220-221, 295, 297
Elliotte, John, 377
Ellis, Georgia, 336
Ellis, Patricia, 293
Elmer the Great, 258
Emery, John, 145-146
Enter Arsene Lupin, 259
Erickson, Louise, 441
Ernie Kovacs Show, The, 93-94
Errand Boy, The, 166
Errol, Leon, 322
Erwin, Stu, 242
Escape, 185-186, 226, 452
Evans, Dale, 245, 429
Evans, Ray, 283
Eve Arden Show, The, 122
Ever Since Venus, 322

Face Behind the Mask, The, 207-208
Facts of Life, The, 80, 160
Fairbanks, Douglas, 216
Fairbanks, Douglas Jr., 234
Faith, Percy, 532
Falcon, The, 452
Fallen Angel, 345
Fanatic, 149
Fantastic Voyage, 315
Farewell, My Lovely, 469
Fat Man, The, 452
Father Knows Best, 409
Faulkner, William, 547
Faye, Alice, 10, 116, 136, 282, 284, 342-349
Feld, Fritz, 138
Felony Squad, 269
Felton, Verna, 63, 113, 138, 448
Fendermen, The, 531
Fenneman, George, 105, 110-111
Feuding Fools, 323
Fibber McGee and Molly, 1, 62, 114, 116, 155, **329-331**, 372-374, 437-438, 441, 448-449
Fields, W.C., 7, 46, 90, 114, 176, 295, 346, 429, 541, 543, 550-552
Fighting Fools, 323
Fine, Sylvia, 31-32
Finger Man, 229
Fireside Theater, 254
Fitzgerald, Barry, 473

Fitzgerald, F. Scott, 547, 549
Five Pennies, The, 33
Five Weeks in a Balloon, 209
Flamingo Road, 270
Flash Gordon, 115
Fleet's In, The, 24
Fleischer, Richard, 315
Fleming, Rhonda, 528
Fly, The, 182
Flying Down to Rio, 281
Flying Nun, The, 556
Flying Wild, 39
Flynn, Errol, 77, 181, 225, 243, 272, 275, 292, 384, 548
Foley, Red, 60
Fonda, Henry, 128, 131, 155, 231, 241, 243, 273
Fonda, Jane, 548
Fontaine, Frank, 16
For Love or Money, 255
Foray, June, 341
Forbidden Planet, 561
Ford, Glenn, 322, 540
Ford, Jan, 440
Ford, John, 559-561
Ford Theatre, 245, 269
Foreman, Carl, 314
Forester, C.S., 106
Forrest Gump, 555
Forsaking All Others, 144
Fort Laramie, 453
Forte, Joe, 261
42nd Street, 9
Foster, Louis, 314
Foster, Preston, 241, 250
Foster, Susanna, 470
Four Star Playhouse, 228
Four Star Revue, 20, 245
Frankenstein, 174, 190-191
Frankenstein Meets the Wolf Man, 177, 199
Frankenstein 1970, 194
Frawley, William, 158
Freaky Friday, 166
Freberg, Stan, 2, **52-57**, 69, 338-341
Fred Allen Show, The, 70, 148, 305, 318, 437, 447
Frees, Paul, 208
Frisco Jenny, 258
From This Day Forward, 474
Front Row Center, 269

Frontier Gentleman, 453
Frosty the Snowman, 21
Fugitive Kind, The, 149
Fuller, Barbara, 336
Fuller Brush Girl, The, 158
Fuller Brush Man, The, 61, 245

Gable, Clark, 120, 234, 273, 464, 470, 474
Gallop, Frank, 98
Gamet, Kenneth, 301
Gangbusters, 226, 249, 334
Garbo, Greta, 144, 150, 176, 275
Gardner, Ed, 168, 236
Gardner, Erle Stanley, 289, 297, 302
Garfield, John, 259, 471, 548
Gargan, William, 139, 453
Garland, Judy, 27, 76, 120, 282, 473, 549
Garrett, Betty, 61-62
Garson, Greer, 471, 474
Gaxton, William, 156
Gay Divorcee, The, 281
General, The, 471
General Electric Theatre, 48
Gentleman at Heart, 260
Gentleman Jim, 243
Gentlemen Prefer Blondes, 28
Gershwin, George, 11, 17, 277, 281, 548
Gershwin, Ira, 281
Gerson, Betty Lou, 424
Get Rich Quick, 393
Get Smart, 166, 261
Ghost and Mrs. Muir, The, 131
Ghost Breakers, The, 77
Ghost Chasers, 323
Ghost in the Invisible Bikini, 194, 278
Ghost of Frankenstein, 176, 199
Giant, 237
Gibbs, Georgia, 19
Gielgud, John, 206
Gilbert, Jody, 261
Girl Can't Help It, The, 552
Girl in Every Port, A, 253
Glass, George, 316
Glass Key, The, 234, 252
Gleason, Jackie, 71, 94, 100, 114, 254, 551-552
Gleason, James, 257
Glen or Glenda?, 177
Go Chase Yourself, 154, 242

Go Into Your Dance, 6, 9, 10
Goddard, Paulette, 77
Godfrey, Arthur, 93, 311
Goff, Norris, 324
Going My Way, 282-283
Gold Diggers of 1935, 297
Gold Diggers of 1937, 165
Goldbergs, The, 98
Goldman, Hal, 383
Goldwyn, Samuel, 32
Gone with the Wind, 145, 155, 275, 555
Good Humor Man, The, 245
Good Morning, Judge, 322
Good Sam, 318
Goodson, Mark, 71
Goodwin, Bill, 314
Gorcey, Bernard, 38, 42, 43
Gorcey, David, 38
Gorcey, Leo, 1-2, **38-43**, 100, 103, 313, 316, 323, 540
Gordon, Al, 383
Gordon, Bert, 84
Gordon, Gale, 2, **112-116**, 121-122, 157, 160, 162, 330, 346, 353, 359-360, 441-442, 448-450, 551-552
Goren, Charles, 106
Gorme, Eydie, 284
Gosden, Freeman, 447-448
Gosfield, Maurice, 100
Gottlieb, Alex, 250
Goudal, Jetta, 473
Gould, Sandra, 165. **167-170**, 361, 438
Goulding, Ray, 339, 353-354
Grahame, Gloria, 541
Granby's Green Acres, 115, 441-442
Granny Get Your Gun, 302
Grant, Cary, 481, 544
Grant, John, 46
Gray, Coleen, 269
Grease, 124
Grease II, 124
Great Gatsby, The, 235
Great Gildersleeve, The, 115, 155, **350-354**, 372, **376-380**, 437, 441, 449
Great Hospital Mystery, The, 136
Great Lover, The, 79
Great Mouse Detective, The, 185
Greatest Show on Earth, The, 27
Green Acres, 162
Green, Adolph, 285

Green, Bernie, 367
Green, Eddie, 448
Green Hornet, The, 226, 336, 522
Greenstreet, Sydney, 76, 206-207, 474
Gregg, Virginia, 336
Grey, Virginia, 311-312, 316
Groom Wore Spurs, The, 244-245
Guadalcanal Diary, 250
Guedel, John, 104-105
Guess Who's Coming to Dinner, 315
Guestward Ho!, 261
Guinan, Texas, 25
Guns of the Timberland, 237
Gunsmoke, 340, 441, 453
Gus, 166
Gwenn, Edmund, 541
Gypsy, 28

Hagen, Jean, 28
Hairy Ape, The, 251
Haley, Jack, 156
Hall, Huntz, 1, 38, 40-41, 43, 100, 323
Hall, Porter, 293
Hallelujah, I'm a Bum, 9
Halliwell, Leslie, 317
Halls of Ivy, The, 449
Halop, Florence, 99, 168
Hammerstein, Oscar, 282
Hammett, Dashiell, 145, 266-267
Hans Christian Andersen, 33
Happy Go Lucky, 24
Hard Way, The, 243
Harem Girl, 138
Harrigan, Nelda, 298
Harris, Phil, 39, 123, 284, 342-349, 372, 383, 388-390, 408, 411, 438, 445-446, 541
Hart, Moss, 32
Hatchet Man, 258
Haunted Palace, The, 182, 201
Haunted Strangler, The, 194
Have Gun, Will Travel, 453
Having Wonderful Time, 60, 242
Hawn, Goldie, 548
Hayes, Gabby, 3, **218-222**, 522, 528, 544
Hayes, Helen, 181
Hayward, Susan, 322
Hayworth, Rita, 120, 242, 320, 320, 477
Heaven Can Wait, 126, 129
Heflin, Van, 236, 241

Heinlein, Robert, 452
Heinreid, Paul, 471, 559
Heiress, The, 277
Heist, The, 270
Hellman, Lillian, 145, 267
Hello Down There, 101
Hello, Frisco, Hello, 282
Hemingway, Ernest, 547
Henry Morgan Show, The, 68-69, 98-100, 305, **365-368**, 450
Hepburn, Audrey, 582
Hepburn, Katharine, 131, 154, 250, 464
Her Husband's Affairs, 156
Her Jungle Love, 259
Herbert, F. Hugh, 298
Herbert, Hugh, 313, 322
Here Come the Waves, 25
Here Comes the Groom, 284
Here Today, 148
Here's Lucy, 116, 160-161
Hicks, Russell, 289
High and the Mighty, The, 528
High Noon, 201, 284, 314, 446
Highway Patrol, 538
Hill, Benny, 95
Hillbillys in a Haunted House, 201, 278
Hilliard, Harriet, 63, 402-409, 450
Hitchcock, Alfred, 146, 206, 284, 480-481
Hitch-Hiker, The, 229
Hodiak, John, 147
Hoffa, Portland, 447
Hold Back the Dawn, 474
Hold That Baby, 42
Hold That Co-ed, 137
Hold That Ghost, 46, 47, 137, 322
Hold That Line, 42
Holden, William, 24, 159, 441, 477, 528
Hole in the Head, A, 284
Holliday, Judy, 123, 225
Holloway, Sterling, 254
Holly, Buddy, 548
Hollywood Canteen, 243
Hollywood Palace, The, 21
Hollywood Preview, 266
Holmes, Brown, 292, 295
Holy Terror, The, 136
Home of the Brave, 228, 314
Homicide Squad, 258
Honeymoon Express, The, 8
Hopalong Cassidy, 220

Hope, Bob, 3, 11, 18, 24, 31, 61, 64, **74-80**, 83-86, 97, 100, 104, 113, 120, 134, 148-149, 160, 162, 166, 235, 277, 281, 283, 286, 317, 331, **414-418**, 424, 442, 445, 544, 560, 564
Horn Blows at Midnight, The, 70
Horne, Lena, 61
Horton, Edward Everett, 540
Hound of the Baskervilles, The, 275
House of Dracula, 199
House of Frankenstein, 193, 199, 260
House of Usher, 182
House of Wax, 182, 229
House on Haunted Hill, 182
How Green Was My Valley, 559
Howland, Olin, 291, 294
Huckleberry Finn, 277
Hudson's Bay, 128, 181
Hughes, Russell, 335
Hull, Henry, 202
Humoresque, 259
Hunchback of Notre Dame, The, 197-198, 214-215
Hurt, Marlin, 448
Husky, Ferlin, 201
Huston, John, 206
Hutton, Betty, 3, **22-28**, 135
Hutton, Marion, 23-24

I Dood It, 61
I Dream of Jeannie, 169, 261
I Dream Too Much, 154
I Love Lucy, 153, 155, 157, 159, 169
I Married Joan, 139-140, 169
I Spy, 269
I Was a Communist for the FBI, 228
Idelson, Bill, 438, 440
If I Were King, 275
If You Knew Susie, 138
I'll See You in My Dreams, 229
Illegal Entry, 268
I'm Nobody's Sweetheart Now, 322
In a Lonely Place, 229
In the Money, 43
In the Navy, 46, 49
Incendiary Blonde, 25
Indestructible Man, The, 198
Inherit the Wind, 559
Inner Sanctum, 192, 201, 396, 454
Inspector General, The, 33

Invisible Man Returns, The, 181
Invisible Menace, The, 192
Invisible Ray, The, 191-192
Island of Doomed Men, 206
It Happened to Jane, 94
It's a Great Feeling, 244
It's a Mad, Mad, Mad, Mad World, 21, 101, 315
It's in the Bag, 70, 86, 251, **304-311**, **314-318**
I've Got a Secret, 66, 71-72

Jack and the Beanstalk, 48
Jack Benny Program, The, 97, 113, 165, 167-168, 317, **382-391**, **411-413**, 445-446
Jackson, Eddie, 16, 20
Jail Busters, 41, 323
Jalopy, 41
James, Ed, 349
James, Harry, 32
James, Henry, 277
Jameson, Joyce, 209
Janney, Leon, 473
Jazz Singer, The, 7-9, 471
J.B., 277
Jenkins, Allen, 100, 290, 292-294
Jesse James at Bay, 220
Jessel, George, 8, 447
Jimmy Durante Show, The, 18-20
Joan Davis Time, 138
Joanie's Tea Room, 138
Johnny Holiday, 254
Johnny Stool Pigeon, 268
Johnson, Bess, 397
Johnson, Van, 18
Johnstone, Bill, 336
Joker is Wild, The, 284
Jolson, Al, 2, 3, **6-12**, 75, 98, 208, 471
Jolson Sings Again, 12
Jolson Story, The, 11
Jonathan Trimble, 115
Jones, Buck, 220, 463
Jones, Carolyn, 479
Jones, Jennifer, 130, 472
Jones, Spike, 68, 208, 367
Jordan, Bobby, 38
Jordan, Jim, 116, **328-331**, 368, 372-374, 438, 448-450
Jordan, Marian, 116, **328-331**, 368, 373-374, 448-450
Josefsberg, Milt, 383, 411

Joy, Dick, 270
Judd for the Defense, 269
Judge, Arlene, 473
Judgment Day, 225
Judy Canova Show, The, 115
Jumbo, 18, 21
Junior Miss, 115

Kael, Pauline, 317
Kansas City Kitty, 137
Kaplan, Marvin, 100
Karloff, Boris, 47, 174-175, 183-184, **188-195**, 199, 201-202, 206-210, 278, 394, 470
Kate Smith Show, The, 46
Kaufman, George S., 55, 166
Kaye, Danny, 2, **30-35**, 104, 120, 277, 317, 450
Kazan, Elia, 146
Kearns, Joseph, 208, 267, 448
Keating, Fred, 147
Keaton, Buster, 17, 61, 94, 153, 253, 471
Keel, Howard, 27, 61
Keeler, Ruby, 6, 9, 10, 17
Keep 'Em Flying, 46
Keep Off the Grass, 18
Keeper of the Flame, 474
Keith, Robert, 28
Kellaway, Cecil, 78
Kelly, Al, 93
Kelly, Gene, 28, 61, 120
Kelly, Grace, 284
Kennedy, Edgar, 114, 540
Kennedy, Tom, 301
Kern, Jerome, 282
Keyes, Evelyn, 241
Keys of the Kingdom, The, 474
Kid from Brooklyn, The, 32, 121
Kid from Spain, The, 258
Kill the Umpire, 253
King and I, The, 286
King, Andrea, 209
King, Carole, 539
King, Joseph, 295
King of Alcatraz, 259
King of Chinatown, 259
King of the Roaring 20s, 246
Kirkpatrick, Jess, 170
Kirkwood, Jack, 408, 432-434
Kiss Me Kate, 286

Kiss of Death, 560
Kissing Bandit, The, 260
Kitty Foyle, 471
Knight, Fuzzy, 219
Knock on Wood, 33
Knot's Landing, 270
Knute Rockne-All American, 560
Korman, Harvey, 35
Kovacs, Ernie, 2, **88-95**, 106, 548
Kraft Music Hall, 11-12
Kramer, Stanley, 315-317
Kramer vs. Kramer, 270
Kruschen, Jack, 336
Kyser, Kay, 206

La Belle Paree, 8
La Cava, Gregory, 120
Ladd, Alan, 1, 131, 230, **232-238**, 251, 252, 454, 471
Ladies of the Big House, 258
Lady in the Dark, 32
Lady of Burlesque, 166
Lake, Arthur, 323
Lake, Veronica, 131, 234, 235, 522
Lamas, Fernando, 160
Lamour, Dorothy, 18, 24, 74, 77, 197, 259, 429
Lancaster, Burt, 237, 273
Lane, Allan, 220
Lang, Fritz, 128, 182, 205
Langford, Frances, 417
Lansing, Joi, 201
Larceny, Inc., 243
Lardner, Ring, 314
Lark, The, 194
Last Hurrah, The, 277
Last of Mrs. Cheyney, The, 274
Late Show, The, 270
Latimer, Ed, 397
Latitude Zero, 266
Lauck, Chester, 324
Laughton, Charles, 131, 144, 176, 181
Laura, 129-130, 132, 182
Laurel and Hardy, 49, 166-167, 295
Law of the Lawless, 255
Law of the Underworld, 242
Lawrence, Steve, 284
Leave Her to Heaven, 130
Leave It to Joan, 138
Lee, Bruce, 548

Lee, Johnny, 448
Lee, Peggy, 540
Leeds, Peter, 336, 340
Left Hand of God, The, 131
LeGrand, Richard, 330, 352-354, 448-449
Leigh, Vivien, 145
Lemmon, Jack, 560
Lemon Drop Kid, The, 79
LeMond, Bob, 138
Leno, Jay, 3
Leonard, Shelton, 310, 336, 372, 386-387, 412, 446
Lerner and Loewe, 284
Lescoulie, Jack, 398
Leslie, Phil, 330-331, 343, 449
Let's Dance, 27
Let's Face It, 24, 32, 120
Let's Pretend, 97, 167, 170
Letterman, David, 3, 95
Levant, Oscar, 11, 315
Lewis, Al, 121, 359
Lewis, Cathy, 170, 351
Lewis, Elliott, 170, 265, 345-348, 372, 406
Lewis, Jerry, 253, 548
Lewis, Joe E., 18
Lewis, John L., 522
Lewis, Warren, 335
Lewton, Val, 193
Life of Riley, The, 168, 252-254, 406, 409, 437
Life with Lucy, 116, 162
Life with Luigi, 260-262, 450
Lifeboat, 146-147, 251
Lights Out, 192, 254
Linden, Eric, 473
Lindsay, Margaret, 291
Linkletter, Art, 406
Lion King, The, 285
Little Foxes, The, 142, 145
Little Game, A, 270
Little Giant, 47
Little Mermaid, The, 285
Little, Rich, 544
Little Richard, 539
Litvak, Anatole
Live Wires, 42
Lives of a Bengal Lancer, The, 258
Livingston, Bob, 220
Livingston, Jay, 283
Livingstone, Mary, 113, 307, 371-372, 384, 388, 390, 408, 411-412, 417, 445
Loden, Barbara, 93
Loesser, Frank, 27
Lombard, Carole, 297
London After Midnight, 215
Lone Ranger, The, 453
Longstreet, Stephen, 11
Look Who's Laughing, 155
Lopez, Vincent, 23-24
Lorre, Peter, 78, 83, **204-210**, 278, 324, 474
Lost City, The, 219
Lost in a Harem, 49
Lost in Alaska, 48
Lost Jungle, The, 219
Love Bug, The, 166
Love Crazy, 242
Love Thy Neighbor, 242, 315
Lovejoy, Frank, 3, **224-231**, 333, 336, 452
Lover Come Back, 158
Loy, Myrna, 131, 242, 297
Lubin, Lou, 170, 448
Lubitsch, Ernst, 121, 129, 146-147, 176
Lucky Jordan, 234
Lucky Partners, 242
Lucky Texan, The, 220
Lucy Show, The, 116, 160-161
Lugosi, Bela, 2, 47, **172-178**, 190-193, 198-202, 206-207, 214, 275, 470
Lund, John, 28
Lupino, Ida, 225, 264, 269, 276
Lured, 156, 193
Lux Radio Theatre, 12, 55, 79, 156, 168, 227, 234, 393, 441
Lux Video Theatre, 228, 245, 261
Lydon, Jimmy, 323
Lynley, Carol, 131
Lynn, Dianna, 25, 241

M, 205
McClintock, Bill, 395
McConnell Story, The, 237
McCoy, Tim, 220
McGann, William, 298
McGuerins from Brooklyn, The, 252
McGuire, Dorothy, 473
McHale's Navy, 169
MacKeller, Helen, 300
McKenzie, Fay, 104
McKinney, Mira, 300

MacLeish, Archibald, 277
McNally, Stephen, 264
McNear, Howard, 97, 441
McQueen, Steve, 482
McVey, Tyler, 440-441
McWade, Edward, 300
Mad Doctor, The, 275
Mad Game, The, 258
Mad House, 184
Mad Love, 204-206
Magic Sword, The, 277
Magnum, P.I., 270
Maher, Wally, 170
Make Your Own Bed, 243
Male Animal, The, 128, 243
Maltese Falcon, The, 206, 266-267, 307
Mame, 162
Mammy, 9
Man Against Crime, 228
Man Made Monster, 198
Man of Conquest, 220
Man with the Golden Arm, The, 100
Man They Could Not Hang, The, 192
Man Who Came to Dinner, The, 71
Man Who Knew Too Much, The, 206, 284
Man Who Lived Again, The, 192
Mancini, Henry, 285
Mannix, 269
Mansfield, Jayne, 552
March, Fredric, 275, 559
Marcus, Larry, 335
Marcus Welby, M.D., 170
Mark of the Vampire, 214
Mark of Zorro, The, 275
Markson, Ben, 295
Marshall, Brenda, 440
Martin and Lewis, 49, 177
Martin, Dean, 547
Martin, Mary, 24
Marvin, Lee, 478
Marx Brothers, 49, 103, 120, 124, 155, 166, 252, 314, 331, 367, 412
Marx, Chico, 103, 295, 377, 522
Marx, Groucho, 3, **102-111**, 148, 176, 295, 346, 377, 522, 564
Marx, Harpo, 159
Mask of Dimitrios, The, 207, 474
Masque of the Red Death, The, 182
Mason, James, 446
Master Minds, 41

Matheson, Richard, 185, 209
Mating Season, The, 131
Mature, Victor, 28, 97, 234, 470
Maverick, 170
Maxwell, Elsa, 430
Maxwell, Marilyn, 79, 414
Mayehoff, Eddie, 100
Mayer, Louis B., 61
Maynard, Ken, 220
Mayo, Archie, 295
Mayo, Virginia, 77, 229
Me and the Colonel, 33
Meadows, Jayne, 71
Meakin, Jack, 449
Medal for Benny, A, 259
Meeker, Ralph, 28
Meet McGraw, 228, 333
Meet Me at Parky's, 437-438
Meet Me in St. Louis, 473
Meet the People, 156
Mellomen, The, 432
Melody Ranch, 18
Menuhin, Yehudi, 84
Mercer, Johnny, 132, 284-285
Merkel, Una, 351
Merman, Ethel, 18, 24, 27, 76, 148
Merrick, David, 56
Merry Andrew, 33
Merton of the Movies, 61
Merv Griffin Show, The, 150
Methot, Mayo, 292
Michaels, Lee, 555
Mildred Pierce, 121, 130, 241, 243, 471-472
Milk Train Doesn't Stop Here Anymore, The, 149
Milland, Ray, 166
Miller, Glenn, 24
Miller, Marvin, 377, 439
Miller, Roger, 539
Milton Berle Show, The, 98, 100
Ministry of Fear, The, 474
Miracle Man, The, 214
Miracle of Morgan's Creek, The, 25
Miracle Rider, 459
Miss Grant Takes Richmond, 158
Mrs. Miniver, 471
Mrs. O'Brien Entertains, 128
Mr. Adams and Eve, 269
Mr. and Mrs. North, 92, 226-227

Mr. Deeds Goes to Town, 219
Mr. District Attorney, 226
Mr. Doodle Kicks Off, 242
Mister Ed, 169-170, 255, 548
Mr. Keen, Tracer of Lost Persons, 454
Mr. Novak, 269
Mitchell, Grant, 290
Mitchell, Shirley, 138, 330, 351, 448
Mitchum, Robert, 273, 322
Mix, Tom, **457-461**, 463, 535-536
Models, Inc., 269
Mohr, Gerald, 336, 453
Monroe, Marilyn, 28, 434, 480, 493, 548
Monsieur Beaucaire, 61, 78-79
Monster, The, 214
Monsters, Inc., 285
Montalban, Ricardo, 61
Montgomery, Elizabeth, 478
Montgomery, George, 130
Moore, Carlyle Jr., 297
Moore, Clayton, 457
Moore, Garry, 18-19, 66
Moore, Mary Tyler, 539
Moore, Sam, 377
Moore, Victor, 20, 206, 309
Moorehead, Agnes, 208, 225
Moran, Betty, 336
Moreno, Rita, 28
Morgan, Claudia, 392, 397
Morgan, Dennis, 243-244
Morgan, Frank, 9, 322
Morgan, Henry, 2, 3, **66-72**, 98-100, 305, 311-318, 340, 364-368, 447
Morgan, Jane, 121, 245, 357
Morgan, Wesley, 248
Morison, Patricia, 259
Morris, Chester, 242, 324
Morrow, Bill, 315
Morton, Gary, 160
Mothers-in-Law, The, 21, 123
Mowbray, Alan, 257, 269
Mulford, Clarence, 457
Mummy, The, 190-191
Mummy's Curse, The, 199
Mummy's Ghost, The, 199
Mummy's Tomb, The, 199
Murder in Trinidad, 258
Murder, Inc., 71, 315
Murder My Sweet, 469
Murder, She Wrote, 270

Murders in the Rue Morgue, 174
Murphy, Horace, 441
Music for Chameleons, 480
My Dream Is Yours, 245
My Fair Lady, 286
My Favorite Blonde, 77
My Favorite Brunette, 78, 80
My Favorite Husband, 115-116, 156-158, 374-375, 437, 450
My Favorite Spy, 166
My Friend Irma, 450-451
My Man Godfrey, 314
My Sin, 144
My Sister Eileen, 97
Myerson, Bess, 66, 71
Mystery in the Air, 208
Mystery Squadron, 258

Nagel, Anne, 300
Naish, J. Carrol, 3, **252-262**
Naked City, 268
Name Above the Title, The, 479
Name of the Game, The, 194
Nash, Ogden, 1
Naughty Nineties, The, 166
Navy Blue, 242
Nelson, David, 403, 405-408
Nelson, Frank, 113, 170, 252, 311, 347, 371, 383-384, 411-412, 445, 446
Nelson, Harriet. See Hilliard, Harriet.
Nelson, Ozzie, 63, 402-409, 450
Nelson, Ricky, 403, 406-408
Neptune's Daughter, 61-62, 283
Never Give a Sucker an Even Break, 551
Neville, Naomi, 532
New Adventures of Charlie Chan, 261
New Adventures of Get Rich Wallingford, 17
New Centurions, The, 315
New Edgar Bergen Hour, The, 2, **429-435**
New Yorkers, The, 17, 165
Newman, Paul, 3, 237
Nicholson, Jack, 548
Nick Carter, 452
Night and the City, 131
Night Beat, 227-228, **333-337**, 452
Nightmare Alley, 474
No Holds Barred, 42
No Other Woman, 258
Noble, Ray, 429, 432, 434
Nobody Lives Forever, 474

Nolan, Jeanette, 336
Nolan, Lloyd, 250
Normand, Mabel, 26
North, Robert, 345
Nothing But the Truth, 77
Now, Voyager, 471, 559

O. Henry's Full House, 315
Oakie, Jack, 154, 242
Oboler, Arch, 265-266, 521
O'Brien, Pat, 560
O'Connor, Donald, 28
O'Curran, Charles, 27
Odd Couple, The, 71
Odell, Allan, 504, 507
Odell, Clinton, 503-504
Of Human Bondage, 536
Of Mice and Men, 198
Oh Doctor!, 120
O'Hara, Maureen, 155
O'Keefe, Dennis, 231, 250, 322
Oklahoma!, 286
Oland, Warner, 320, 324
Old Dark House, The, 192
Oliver, Edna May, 97
Oliver Twist, 214
Olivier, Laurence, 478
Olsen and Johnson, 513
Olson, Maud Jeanne, 16, 18
O'Malley, J. Pat, 397
On Again–Off Again, 242
On the Avenue, 136
On the Beach, 315
On the Corner, 70
On the Riviera, 131
One is Guilty, 258
One More Tomorrow, 243
One Night in the Tropics, 46
$1,000 a Minute, 219
One Touch of Venus, 121
Operation Mad Ball, 94
Oppenheimer, Jess, 156
Othello, 274
Our Man in Havana, 94
Our Miss Brooks, 113-116, 121-122, **356-362**, 441, 450
Our Relations, 166
Our Vines Have Tender Grapes, 474
Ouspenskaya, Maria, 198
Out of the Past, 393

Outside the Law, 214
Overland Trail, The, 255
Owen, Garry, 299
Owen, Tudor, 336, 423

Pacino, Al, 3
Palance, Jack, 559
Paleface, The, 78-79, 166, 283, 529
Paley, William, 121, 411-412
Palmer, Betsy, 66, 71
Palooka, 17
Panama Hattie, 24
Pangborn, Franklin, 257
Pardon My Sarong, 46
Paris Playboys, 42
Parker, Dorothy, 143, 145
Parks, Larry, 11-12
Passage to Versailles, 207
Pasternak, Joe, 433
Pat Novak for Hire, 2, 341, **421-427**
Pearl, Jack, 467
Pearson, GeGe, 63
Peary, Harold (Hal), 245, 323, 330, 350, 352-354, 372, 448-449
Peattie, Yvonne, 424
Peck, Gregory, 237, 471-472, 474
Penalty, The, 214
Penner, Joe, 154, 242, 454, 467
Penny Singleton Show, The, 115
Perils of Pauline, The, 26, 28
Perrin, Sam, 383, 411
Perry, Linda, 300
Perry Mason, 427
Persons in Hiding, 259
Peter Ibbetson, 274
Peter Pan, 194
Peters, Ken, 261
Petrie, Howard, 18-19
Petticoat Junction, 162
Phantom Creeps, The, 176
Phantom of the Opera, The, 197, 199, 212-213, 470
Phantom Pilot, 265
Phantom President, The, 17
Phil Harris-Alice Faye Show, The, 114, **343-349**, 450
Philbin, Mary, 212
Philco Radio Time, 11
Philco Television Playhouse, 255
Phillips, Barney, 440

Pidgeon, Walter, 131, 559, 561
Pierce, Jack, 190-191, 199
Pillow of Death, 201
Pinocchio, 282
Pious, Minerva, 307, 367
Pit and the Pendulum, 182-183
Plan 9 from Outer Space, 177-178
Playhouse 90, 245, 254
Pleasure Seekers, The, 131
Plummer, Christopher, 277
Plymouth Adventure, 131
Pocahontas, 285
Police Squad, 269
Porter, Cole, 2, 17, 18, 24, 32, 61, 120, 281, 284
Postman Always Rings Twice, The, 471
Powell, Dick, 24, 453, 469
Powell, Eleanor, 61
Powell, William, 131, 242, 273, 289, 297
Power, Tyrone, 10, 77, 130, 225, 259, 275, 473, 474
Preminger, Otto, 122, 129, 131, 147
Presenting Al Jolson, 11
Presley, Elvis, 544, 548
Preston, Robert, 234
Price, Vincent, 64, 97, 118, 129, **180-187**, 193, 209, 278, 453, 479
Pride of the Yankees, 473
Prince of Egypt, The, 285
Princess and the Pirate, The, 77
Prisoners, 174
Private Eyes, 41, 42
Private Hell 36, 269
Private Lives, 148
Private Lives of Elizabeth and Essex, The, 181
Proud Rebel, 237
Prouty, Jed, 242
Prouty, Olive Higgins, 471
Psycho, 481
Public Enemy, 560
Pugh, Madelyn, 156, 158
Pursell Bill, 532

Queen of the Mob, 259
Quick as a Flash, 393
Quiet, Please, 3, **392-400**, 452
Quinn, Anthony, 322
Quinn, Don, 330-331, 343, 449

Raft, George, 165
Rainbow Man, 219
Rains, Claude, 181-182, 198-199
Raksin, David, 129
Rally Round the Flag, Boys!, 246
Rand, Sally, 522
Randolph, Amanda, 447-448
Randolph, Isabel, 138, 448
Randolph, Lillian, 350, 354
Rathbone, Basil, 33, 176, 201, 209, **272-278**, 289, 318, 324, 447
Raven, The (1935), 174, 191
Raven, The (1963), 182, 194, 209
Raye, Martha, 11, 135, 255, 478
Raymond, Alex, 465
Razor's Edge, The, 130, 473
Reagan, Ronald, 35, 121, 224
Reap the Wild Wind, 474
Rebecca, 474
Red Canyon, 269
Red Garters, 245
Red, Hot and Blue, 18, 26, 28, 76
Red Ryder, 453
Red Skelton Show, The, 63-64, 450
Redford, Robert, 3
Reed, Alan, 2, 252, 260-261, 311, 448
Reed, Donna, 322
Reed, Tom, 292, 297
Reiner, Carl, 94
Remarkable Miss Tuttle, The, 97
Remick, Lee, 480
Renaldo, Duncan, 325
Restless Gun, The, 261
Retreat, Hell!, 228
Return of Jesse James, The, 128
Return of the Badmen, 220
Return of the Fly, The, 182
Return of the Terror, 258
Return of the Vampire, The, 177
Reville, Alma, 314
Reynolds, Craig, 293, 297
Reynolds, Debbie, 28
Reynolds, Marjorie, 78, 241, 248, 254
Rhodes, Betty, 438
Rhymer, Paul, 54, 343
Rice, Edgar, 156, 225
Rich, Charlie, 478
Richard Diamond, Private Detective, 168, 452-453
Richards, Carol, 432

Ride 'Em Cowboy, 46
Riders in the Desert, 219
Rio Rita, 46
Rippling Rhythm Revue, 76
Ritter, Tex, 284
Roach, Hal, 250
Road to Hong Kong, The, 80
Road to Morocco, The, 197
Road to Rio, The, 77, 86, 560
Road to Singapore, The, 77
Road to Zanzibar, The, 166
Robert Montgomery Presents, 254
Roberta, 76, 154
Roberts, Beverly, 9
Robertson, Cliff, 229
Robinson, Edward G., 242-243, 257, 397, 471
Robson, May, 302
Rockford Files, The, 269
Rockwell, Robert, 359
Rocky, 282
Rodgers and Hart, 9
Rodgers, Richard, 282
Rogers, Ginger, 60, 154, 166, 242, 244-245, 258, 281, 285, 315, 447, 471
Rogers, Roy, 79, 220, 321, 457, 463, 521, 527
Roland, Gilbert, 325
Roman Scandals, 154
Romance on the High Seas, 282
Romeo and Juliet, 275
Romero, Cesar, 94, 325
Room Service, 155
Rooney, Mickey, 64
Roose, Jeanine, 345
Rorick, Isabel Scott, 156
Rose, Billy, 18, 146-147
Rose of Washington Square, 9-10
Rosenbloom, Maxie, 208
Rosener, George, 297
Ross, Earle, 352-353
Ross, Joe E., 540
Ross, Shirley, 76, 281
Roxie Hart, 166
Roy, Cecil, 392, 398
Royal Scandal, A, 146
Rubin, Benny, 386, 446
Rudy Vallee Show, The, 137
Ruman, Sig, 138, 261
Rumba, 165
Runyon, Damon, 16, 79, 155, 454

Russell, Jane, 79, 166
Ruth, Babe, 249
Ryan, Don, 301
Ryskind, Morrie, 314

Sad Sack, The, 168, 436, 438
Sahara, 259
Saigon, 234
Sail a Crooked Ship, 94
St. Germain, Kay, 243
Saint in New York, The, 242
Saint, The, 185, 289, 324, 452-453
Sally, Irene and Mary, 137
Sanders, George, 324, 480
Sanders, Lugene, 248
Sands, Billy, 98
Saroyan, William, 250
Saskatchewan, 256
Say It with Songs, 9
Scarecrow and Mrs. King, 270
Schildkraut, Joseph, 78
Schlitz Playhouse of Stars, 254, 261, 269
Scott, George C., 122
Scott, Randolph, 220, 474, 529
Scott, Zachary, 240
Screen Director's Playhouse, 79, 245, 254, 310
Sealtest Village Store, The, 121, 137, 245
Sears Radio Theater, The, 270
Second Fiddle to a Steel Guitar, 100
Secret Agent, 206
Secret Life of Walter Mitty, The, 33
Secret of Convict Lake, The, 131
Seeds, The, 531
Selznick, David, 155
Sennett, Mack, 136
Serling, Rod, 254
Seven Days' Leave, 97
Seven Little Foys, The, 79
Seymour, Anne, 392, 397
Shadow, The, 454
Shaft, 269
Shaggy D.A., The, 166
Shakedown, 268
Shall We Dance, 281
Shane, 232, 236-238, 559
Shanghai Gesture, The, 258
Shannon, Peggy, 293
Shaw, George Bernard, 447
Shaw, Winifred, 292, 295-297

She Gets Her Man, 138-139, 322
She Wrote the Book, 138
Shearer, Norma, 274
Shell Chateau, 11
Sherdeman, Ted, 266
Sheridan, Ann, 71, 242-243
Sheridan, Nancy, 397
She's Back on Broadway, 229
Shine On Harvest Moon, 243
Ship Ahoy, 61
Shipp, Mary, 261
Shock, 182
Show Boat, 286
Show Business, 138
Show Girl, 17
Show-Off, The, 61
Shubert, Lee, 120
Sidewalks of New York, The, 75
Signal Caravan, The, 245
Silent Command, The, 174
Silents Please, 94
Silvers, Phil, 438
Sinatra, Frank, 18, 99, 260, 284-285, 307, 438
Sinbad, 8
Singer, Ray, 343, 346, 348
Singing Fool, The, 9
Singing Kid, The, 9
Singleton, Penny, 323
Siodmak, Curt, 198
Sis Hopkins, 86, 322
Sitting Bull, 261
Six Shooter, The, 453
Skelton, Red, 3, 31, **58-64**, 100, 155, 160, 170, 192, 245, 365, 366, 370, 375, 442, 450, 539
Skidoo, 101
Skin of Our Teeth, The, 146
Skirball, Jack, 305, 317
Skokie, 35
Skyblazers, 249
Smart, J. Scott, 453
Smiling Irish Eyes, 219
Smith, Alfred Johnson, 517
Smith, Bob, 540
Smith, Leonard, 358
Smith, Verne, 408-409
Smiths of Hollywood, The, 444-441
Smugglers' Cove, 40
Snatched, 270
Snow White and the Seven Dwarfs, 285

So This Is New York, 70, **305, 311-318**
Some Like It Hot, 560
Somebody Loves Me, 27-28
Sommers, Jay, 441-442
Son of Dracula, 199-200
Son of Frankenstein, 176, 192, 275
Son of Paleface, The, 79
Son of Sinbad, 182
Sorrowful Jones, 79
Sorry, Wrong Number, 393
Sound of Music, The, 286, 560
South Pacific, 286
Southern Yankee, A, 61
Speak Easy, 17
Spellbound, 468, 471
Spider Baby, 201
Spier, William, 266
Spiral Staircase, The, 473
Spoilers, The, 474
Spook Busters, 42, 323
Sportsmen, The, 383-384, 446
Springsteen, Bruce, 547
Spy Chasers, 42, 43, 323
Stage Door, 120, 154, 314
Stage 7, 228
Stagecoach, 275
Stan Freberg Show, The, 55-56, **338-341**
Stander, Lionel, 32
Stang, Arnold, 2, 69-70, **96-101**, 313, 318, 367
Stanwyck, Barbara, 130, 166, 473
Star Is Born, A, 246
Star Spangled Rhythm, 24, 282
Stars in Your Eyes, 18
State Fair, 282
Steele, Barbara, 183
Steele, Bob, 220
Steinbeck, John, 198, 547, 556
Stella Dallas, 226
Steve Allen Show, The, 48
Stevens, George, 237
Stevens, Warren, 397
Stewart, Blanche, 76
Stewart, James, 71, 122, 397, 440, 471
Stillwell, Edna, 59, 63
Stolen Harmony, 165
Stone, Ezra, 323
Stone, Sharon, 536
Stop the Music, 311
Stork Club, The, 25, 28, 92
Story of Mankind, The, 209

Story of Molly X, The, 170
Strange Dr. Weird, 398
Strange Door, The, 194
Strange, Glenn, 47, 193
Strawberry Blonde, The, 242
Street, David, 438
Streetcar Named Desire, A, 149
Streets of Laredo, The, 253
Streets of Paris, The, 46
Streets of San Francisco, The, 269
Strike It Rich, 393
Strike Me Pink, 18
Striker, Fran, 457
Studio One, 245
Study in Scarlet, A, 276
Sturges, Preston, 25
Such Men Are Dangerous, 174
Sullivan, Barry, 122
Sullivan, Ed, 100
Sunset Boulevard, 559
Super Circus, 86
Suspense, 185-186, 208, 226, 259, 266-267, 450
Swanee River, 10
Swanson, Gloria, 559
Swing Time, 282
Swingin' Medallions, The, 531

Tackaberry, John, 383, 411
Take a Good Look, 94
Take Her, She's Mine, 255
Talbot, Lyle, 293
Tale of Two Cities, A, 275
Tales from the Darkside, 101
Tales of Terror, 182, 209, 277
Tallman, Bob, 267
Tandy, Jessica, 478
Targets, 184, 294
Tarnished Angels, The, 246
Tarnished Lady, 144
Tarzan, 285
Tattered Dress, The, 246
Taylor, Elizabeth, 322
Taylor, Robert, 225
Teahouse of the August Moon, 71
Ted Knight Show, The, 166
Tell It Again, 54
Temple, Shirley, 136, 149, 314, 466, 471, 522
Tetley, Walter, 97, 309, 345-346, 351, 354, 372, 379, 562

Texaco Star Theater, The, 447
Texan, The, 261
Texas Carnival, 61
Thank Your Lucky Stars, 243
That Darn Cat!, 166
That Girl from Paris, 154
That Uncertain Feeling, 121
That Wonderful Urge, 130
Theater Guild of the Air, 277
Theatre of Blood, 183-184
There's One Born Every Minute, 322
They Got Me Covered, 77, 97
Thin Ice, 137
Think Fast, Mr. Moto, 259
Third Man, The, 560
Thirteenth Chair, The, 174
Thirty Foot Bride of Candy Rock, The, 48
This Above All, 474
This Day Is Yours, 226
This Gun for Hire, 234
This Is Your FBI, 226, 334
Thomas, Danny, 100, 245
Thomas, Marlo, 552
Thompson, Bill, 330, 370, 373, 448
Thor, Larry, 453
Those We Love, 116
Three Stooges, The, 49
Three Strangers, 207
Thriller, 194, 245
Thunder in the East, 236
Thurber, James, 1, 104, 243, 424
Tierney, Gene, 2, 103, **126-132**, 182
Tiffin, Pamela, 131
Tight as a Drum, 270
Till the End of Time, 474
Time for Beany, 55
Time of Their Lives, The, 47
Time of Your Life, The, 250, 254
Time Out for Romance, 136
Time, the Place, and the Girl, The, 244
Tingler, The, 182
Tiomkin, Dimitri, 284, 316
Titantic, 285
To Have and Have Not, 286
Tobacco Road, 128
Tobin, Genevieve, 294
Todman, Bill, 71
Toler, Sidney, 307, 324
Tomack, Sid, 28
Tomb of Ligeia, The, 182

Tomorrow Is Forever, 474
Tonight Show, 94
Too Busy to Work, 137
Too Many Blondes, 166
Too Many Girls, 155
Top Cat, 100
Top Hat, 154, 281
Tower of London, 275
Town Hall Tonight, 447
Tracy, Lee, 230
Tracy, Spencer, 79, 131, 250, 277, 473
Traveling Saleswoman, 138
Travis, June, 297
Treacher, Arthur, 20, 245, 439-441
Treasure Island, 214
Treasure of the Sierra Madre, The, 446, 560
Treasurer's Report, The, 306
Tree, Dorothy, 289
Treen, Mary, 294-295
Trenholme, Helen, 291
Trevor, Claire, 241
Trouble Makers, 41
Trouble with Women, The, 166
Truman, Margaret, 76, 311
Try and Get Me, 229
Tucker, Forrest, 231
Tucker, Sophie, 26
Tufts, Sonny, 26, 28
Turner, Lana, 120, 471
Tuttle, Lurene, 63, 168, 266, 346
Twelve Chairs, The, 314
20,000 Leagues Under the Sea, 209, 315
Two by Two, 35
Two for the Show, 24
Two Guys from Milwaukee, 243
Two Guys from Texas, 244
Two Latins from Manhattan, 137
Two Senoritas from Chicago, 137
Two Smart People, 156
Two Years Before the Mast, 235, 252, 473
Tyler, Dickie, 306
Typhoon, 259

Unconquered, 194
Unholy Three, The, 214-215
Uninvited, The, 527
Unknown, The, 214
Untouchables, The, 255
Up in Arms, 32
Upper World, 258

U.S. Steel Hour, 245
Usher, Guy, 299

Vague, Vera, 76, 103, 417
Valentino, Rudolph, 216, 548
Valiant Lady, 226
Vallee, Rudy, 60, 167, 309, 313, 316-317, 415, 429, 431, 454
Valley of the Sun, 155
Van Dyke, Dick, 539
Van Heusen, Jimmy, 282, 284-285
Vance, Vivian, 158, 160
Vera-Ellen, 34, 260, 432
Vera Violette, 8
Verdict, The, 207
Vic and Sade, 54, 351, 437-439
Victory, 214
View from the Bridge, A, 261
Vigran, Herb, 168, 436, 438
Vivacious Lady, 242
Voice of the Turtle, The, 121
Voight, Jon, 548
Von Zell, Harry, 138, 309, 371, 440
Vonn, Veola, 406
Voodoo Island, 194
Voodoo Man, The, 176

Wade, Ernestine, 447
Wagon Train, 48, 170, 261
Wagoner, Porter, 533
Wake Island, 250
Wake Me When It's Over, 94
Wake Up and Live, 136
Waldo, Janet, 405-406
Walking Dead, The, 192
Wallace, Richard, 311, 314
Wallington, Jimmy, 415
Wanted: Dead or Alive, 261
War of the Worlds, The, 445
Watch the Birdie, 61
Waterfront, 259
Waterman, Willard, 138, 354, 449
Way Up Thar, 136
Wayne, John, 159, 220, 231, 474, 527, 543
We Live and Learn, 226
Webb, Clifton, 129
Webb, Jack, 97, 420, 422, 424, 426-427, 440
Weird Woman, 201
Weissmuller, Johnny, 324
Welcome to Hard Times, 201

Weldon, Ben, 306
Welles, Orson, 97, 482, 560
Wellman, William, 258
We're Not Married, 315
Werewolf of London, 202
West, Adam, 150
West, Brooks, 122, 124
Westcott, Gordon, 289
Weston, Paul, 138
Whale, James, 190
What Is a Classic?, 555
What's My Line?, 71, 92
What's Your Racket?, 258
Whedon, John, 377
Wheeler and Woolsey, 49, 242
When Radio Was, 57
Where the Sidewalk Ends, 131
While the City Sleeps, 182, 269
Whirl of Society, 8
Whispering Smith, 236
Whistler, The, 259, 324-325, 450-452
Whistling in Brooklyn, 60
Whistling in Dixie, 60
Whistling in the Dark, 60, 524
White, Andy, 377
White Christmas, 33
White Zombie, 175-176
Whiteman, Paul, 522
Whitfield, Anne, 345
Who Done It?, 46, 250
Widmark, Richard, 560
Wilcox, Harlow, 330
Wild One, The, 560
Wildcat, 154, 160
Wilde, Cornel, 130
Wilder, Thornton, 146, 354
William, Warren, 288-289, 291-299, 302
Williams, Esther, 61
Williams, Ted, 522
Williams, Tennessee, 149
Willock, Dave, 241, 243, 245, 309, 311
Wills, Serenus, 136
Wilson, Don, 85, 167, 371, 383, 411
Wilson, Marie, 243, 253
Winning Team, The, 224, 229
Winslowe, Paula, 253
Winters, Jonathan, 192
Winters, Roland, 324
Winters, Shelley, 268
Winwood, Estelle, 148

Wistful Widow of Wagon Gap, The, 166
Withers, Jane, 266
Wizard of Oz, The, 275
Wlaschin, Ken, 28
Wolf Man, The, 177, 196, 198-199, 202
Woman in Hiding, 264, 269
Woman in the Window, The, 471
Woman of the Year, 250
Women's Prison, 269
Wonder Man, 30, 32
Wood, Douglas, 300
Wood, Ed Jr., 177-178
Woods, Donald, 291, 300-302
Woollcott, Alexander, 143
World of Disney, The, 245
Wray, Fay, 541
Wright, Ben, 336
Wright, Will, 314
Wyman, Jane, 243, 322, 446
Wynn, Ed, 245, 345, 467
Wynn, Keenan, 24, 156, 322
Wyoming, 221

X Minus One, 452

Yamaguchi, Shirley, 434
Yellow Cab Man, The, 61
Yokel Boy, 137
You Bet Your Life, 104-111
You Gotta Stay Happy, 318
You Only Live Once, 241-242
You'll Find Out, 206-207
Young Bill Hickock, 220
Young, Loretta, 176, 258
Young Widder Brown, 226
Youngman, Henny, 77
Yours Truly, Johnny Dollar, 453

Zane Grey Theatre, 245
Zanuck, Darryl, 128, 130, 137
Zero Hour, 270
Ziegfeld, Flo, 17,
Ziegfeld Follies, 76, 120, 165

www.ingramcontent.com/pod-product-compliance
Lightning Source LLC
Chambersburg PA
CBHW071430300426
44114CB00013B/1374